JAVA™ MESSAGING

JAVA™ MESSAGING

ERIC BRUNO

CHARLES RIVER MEDIA, INC.
Hingham, Massachusetts

Cover Design: The Printed Image

CHARLES RIVER MEDIA, INC.
10 Downer Avenue
Hingham, Massachusetts 02043
781-740-0400
781-740-8816 (FAX)
info@charlesriver.com
www.charlesriver.com

This book is printed on acid-free paper.

Eric Bruno. *Java Messaging.*
ISBN: 1-58450-418-8

Library of Congress Cataloging-in-Publication Data

Bruno, Eric J., 1969-
  Java messaging / Eric Bruno.
     p. cm.
  Includes bibliographical references and index.
  ISBN 1-58450-418-8 (alk. paper)
  1. Instant messaging. 2. Java (Computer program language) I. Title.
  TK5105.74.J32B78 2005
  005.2'762--dc22
                              2005022084

Printed in the United States of America
05 7 6 5 4 3 2 First Edition

*To my wife Christine and our children,
Brandon and Ashley.*

Contents

Preface

*J*ava Messaging is a book that explores the various methods of intraprocess and interprocess messaging for Java™ software, such as JavaBean™ events, JMS, JAX-RPC, JAXM, SOAP, and Web Services. This book not only covers the basics of the APIs, but includes architectural discussions on when and how to use them, design patterns that can be applied to them, and helper classes to help you more easily use the APIs. By the end of the book, you will have practical knowledge of when and how to use each API alone, as well as together, with a working example of a distributed Java application that uses all of them.

As software becomes more complex, and the Web is leveraged further, the need for messaging software will likely continue to grow for many years. For this reason, and because of the wide variety of messaging APIs offered for Java, this book focuses on JMS and the APIs in the Java Web Service Developer Pack. It's my opinion that Java messaging, Web Services, and grid computing will gradually merge as products from vendors such as Sun™ and IBM® evolve. This book will prepare you for this today, providing you with the knowledge to make the right choices in the future.

THE BOOK'S SOFTWARE

Throughout the book, the practical side of each technology discussed will be explored through the development of an in-depth sample application. The application, an online stock trading system, will be built using the topics discussed in the book, along with a software toolkit that is extended and described within each chapter. The application will integrate a simulated order-execution system, a stock quote service, a stock broker system, and a fundamental data service.

Throughout the book, design patterns and helper classes related to enterprise messaging and distributed software design will be constructed. These classes ultimately combine into a generic messaging framework that will help the reader avoid the common pitfalls of using messaging software. The framework, explained throughout the book, can be used by anyone building distributed applications based on Java, JMS, and SOAP.

ON THE CD   *The entire sample application discussed within each chapter, along with the messaging framework, can be found on the CD-ROM included with this book.*

THE BOOK'S STRUCTURE

Java Messaging is structured as follows:

Chapter 1—Introduction: Messaging is Everywhere: This chapter provides an overview of the various intercomponent communication APIs available to Java developers. JavaBean events, RMI, CORBA®, JMS, and Web Services are introduced and contrasted.

Chapter 2—JavaBean Events: This chapter describes JavaBean events and how they form the basis of intraprocess communication. Some of the problems related to events are addressed and solved with the Java event agent—the first component in the messaging toolkit described in this book.

Chapter 3—Basic Java Messaging: This chapter begins with a basic discussion on messaging software concepts and continues with an in-depth look at the Java Message Service. The topics covered include publish-and-subscribe, request-and-reply, and point-to-point messaging.

Chapter 4—Advanced Java Messaging: The messaging theory and concepts discussed in the previous chapter are expanded with in-depth discussions of selectors, reliable messaging, message-based transactions, and message-driven beans. A unique discussion on queue theory—including strategies for developing reliable queue-based enterprise software—is included in this chapter.

Chapter 5—JMS Development, Deployment, and Support: In this chapter, the messaging toolkit is extended, and messaging-specific design patterns are discussed, and applied, using the sample trading system sample application. Topics such as JMS software deployment and support are discussed, revealing the practical side of messaging systems.

Chapter 6—Web Services and Messaging: Web Services define the standard in distributed component connectivity. This chapter discusses the basics of Web Services, the specifications, and their practical application.

Chapter 7—Web Services Specifications: New Web Service specifications are introduced each year. This chapter discusses the specifications related to messaging, reliability, security, and management.

Chapter 8—The Java Web Service Developer Pack (JWSDP):   Sun opened the world of Web Services to Java developers with the introduction of the JWSDP years ago. This chapter discusses the plethora of APIs and specifications that the JWSDP introduced to the Java world.

Chapter 9—Distributed Application Architecture: How does JMS operate over the Internet? What role does XML play in distributed software? Can JMS be combined with Web Services, or is it solely a choice to make? This chapter helps answer these questions and provides patterns for building robust, distributed software.

Chapter 10—Grid Computing: Grid software can be considered the extreme in distributed software architecture. Multiple vendors are jockeying for position in the grid-software race. This chapter discusses grids as the logical extension of messaging and distribution while looking at the set of technologies available to developers today.

Appendix A—UML Overview: Since UML is used extensively in the book, this appendix provides a quick overview of UML diagrams and how to interpret them.

ABOUT THE PHOTOS

The photographs included on the first page of each chapter were taken by the author at various locations in Long Island, New York. Each picture, although of nature, has some connection to a Java programming concept used in the book. See if you can figure out the connections as you read each chapter.

1

Introduction: Messaging is Everywhere

In This Chapter

- Component Software
- Distributed Software Systems
- Events
- Java RMI
- CORBA
- Enterprise Messaging
- Web Services

COMPONENT SOFTWARE

Virtually all software written today requires at least one form of internal, and even external, communication. The days of building monolithic, standalone software are mostly behind us. As software requirements grow in complexity, so do the software systems that are built to meet those requirements. There is a need to break complex systems down into smaller, simpler pieces. Designing component-based software is one way to achieve this breakdown. The need for communication within, and between, the components of these software systems forms the basis for a concept called *messaging*. In its most abstract form, messaging is the exchange of data between one piece of software and another. Figure 1.1 illustrates this using email as the example. At a high level, email software is composed of a component that runs on the client, a component that runs on the server, and messages that are sent between.

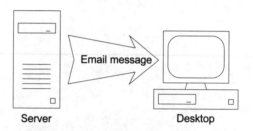

FIGURE 1.1   Email is the classic example of interprocess software messaging.

Software component development is not new; it's been a natural way to develop software for decades. The C programming language provides a simple means for software component development through procedure-based software modules and software libraries. C++ refines this concept by introducing classes that encapsulate behavior and help hide implementation details. Java has taken this one step further by abstracting the physical location of software components.

Regardless of platform or language, a software component is a standalone entity that encapsulates some behavior and is accessible to other components via a well-defined contract, called an interface. While this concept helps solve some of the complexity of large-scale software development, it introduces a new one: component interaction and communication.

Mobility

In the world of computers, mobility is defined as the ability to take processing power with you, where and when you need it. It allows you to securely and reliably receive information (such as breaking news or price quotes) as well as to enter information (such as inventory levels or customer orders) at the point of service. Java is a language that was designed with mobility in mind right from the very start, when it was called Oak, as part of Sun's Green project. A glance at some of the application programming interfaces (APIs) available for Java shows you how it is designed for mobility and communication:

- Java I/O and New I/O (NIO)
- Java Remote Method Invocation (RMI)
- The Java Naming and Directory Interface™ (JNDI)
- JavaMail™
- The Java Message Service (JMS)
- Java's Jini™, JavaSpaces™ and JXTA™ efforts
- The Java API for XML-based Remote Procedure Calls (JAX-RPC)
- The SOAP with Attachments API for Java (SAAJ)
- The Java 2 Mobile Edition (J2ME™)

THE GREEN PROJECT

In late 1990, a small team of Sun engineers began what was called the Green project. The team was tasked with defining what they felt would be the future of computers, and had envisioned that handheld, mobile devices would become popular. With this vision, the team set out to create a hardware and software platform as a prototype. The result was a handheld computer based on the Sun SPARC® CPU with a small color screen and wireless communication. The software for it was written using a new language designed for small, mobile devices, called Oak [Byous98].

Oak was designed as a fast, secure, multithreaded language, with all of the features that modern Java has today—which is exactly what it became. Although the Green project was a success in that it delivered a truly mobile handheld computer, there are only two artifacts that remain to this day: the Java programming language, and Duke™, the Java mascot (*http://java.sun.com/features/2001/06/goslingduke.html*).

DISTRIBUTED SOFTWARE SYSTEMS

A *distributed* software system is one where the software is broken down into multiple components that have the ability to run in parallel. When designed correctly, these software systems typically work better when deployed across many smaller computers than on one larger, more powerful computer. The best example of a distributed processing system is the human brain. While the brain is relatively slow at crunching numbers, it has enormous capacity and ability because it is massively parallel. The goal of distributed software architecture is similar: utilize parallel processing to achieve overall better performance on small, relatively inexpensive hardware.

In most cases, breaking down a single computer process into multiple processes not only improves performance but also makes it easier to build and manage—hence the growing popularity of service-oriented architectures. Distributed computing systems seem obvious and widespread today, but at one time they were prohibitive. In the days of mainframe computers, and even mini-computers, distributing an application across multiple machines was not feasible for most organizations. However, over the years computer prices have dropped, sizes have shrunk, and power has increased. Because of this, organizations around the world own sophisticated networks of powerful workstations, running the applications they need to do business.

Today it makes perfect sense to design a modern complex application to run on multiple computers distributed within an organization or around the globe. In many cases, it's not a luxury; it's the only way to solve a business problem affordably. For example, the original implementation of eBay's software systems revolved around a single database server (with a standby server in case of failure) [Gibson04]. This server became a system bottleneck, and the software kept hitting the performance wall that exists when one cannot distribute an application's processing across multiple servers. Eventually, eBay was able to distribute the database across multiple servers (50 of them) and spread application processing across multiple sites—dispersed geographically—to remove system bottlenecks and performance delays.

The advent of the World Wide Web thrust distributed application architecture to the forefront. Issues regarding software component communication are constantly being addressed, and their solutions repeatedly refined. Here are some examples of the evolution in distributed software technologies:

- Systems based on electronic data interchange (EDI) are moving to eXtensible Markup Language (XML).
- Software component architecture is moving toward service-oriented architecture.
- Interapplication communication is moving from remote procedure calls to Web Services.

- Queue-based processing software is moving to an enterprise service bus, which is a communication infrastructure that spans an entire organization's IT system.
- Dedicated farms of Web and application servers are moving toward grid computing.

Forgetting for a moment the distributed technologies in this list, distributed software architecture begins within an application—even within a computer itself. For example, the distributed application architecture in Figure 1.2 contains some of the components that make up a sample online stock-trading system. Notice how the concept of distributed components has been applied to software running within a computer (Enterprise JavaBeans™ (EJB) and JavaServerPages™ (JSP)), components running in separate computers (Web server, application server, and quote server), and even across the data centers. At this level, the architecture treats the bank's data center the same way it does a single EJB: as a component.

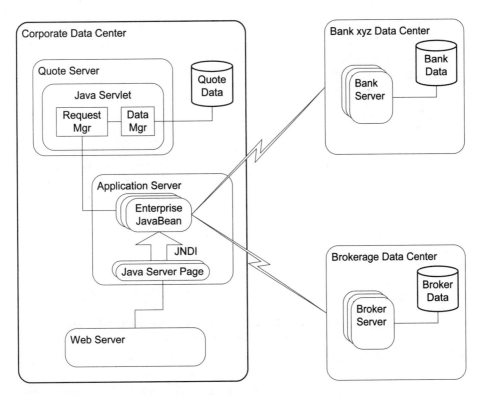

FIGURE 1.2 Distributed software architectural concepts are echoed within and across software running on the servers.

A software system meant to run on just one computer can exhibit a design that resembles that of a massively distributed system. Object-oriented development methodologies and design patterns have evolved to teach us how to break an application down into loosely coupled components that run well together, though their physical locations are abstracted. The journey to understanding messaging within a distributed Java application begins within the application itself at the component interface level.

EVENTS

A component request can be encapsulated using the *command* design pattern [Gamma95]. This design pattern defines how requests can be made of components, without knowing the details of the requests or the details required to fulfill the requests. The basic premise is that neither the command source nor the command target need to know very much about one another. They only have a contract for communication, usually defined as one or more methods on an interface. The Unified Modeling Language™ (UML) class diagram in Figure 1.3 shows the classes and relationships involved in the command pattern for a stock quote notification system.

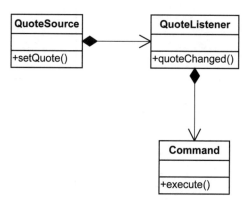

FIGURE 1.3 The command pattern's UML class diagram for a stock quote system.

In the implementation of the pattern, the source component triggers a command when it calls a method on a well-known interface implemented by otherwise anonymous target components. The target components know nothing about the source component; they simply adhere to the communication contract by implementing the methods defined by the interface. The end result is an event model that is supported by Java in the JavaBeans specification.

Events are a basic form of component communication, where the source and target implementations behind the events are well abstracted from one another. The one drawback of the JavaBeans event specification is that it works only within a Java virtual machine™ (JVM). You must turn to more complex means to communicate with remote Java components.

JAVA RMI

Java components running in remote JVMs can communicate with one another via network sockets. However, developing the code for this requires a working knowledge of Java I/O, Java networking, and networking concepts in general—not a trivial task. Using this approach for each application will most likely result in the tedious rewriting of a lot of network-related code. Thankfully, there is an alternative that is much simpler: Java RMI.

Java RMI allows a Java component in one virtual machine to make method calls on a Java component running within a different virtual machine. RMI is Java's version of a remote procedure call that uses Java's object model end-to-end. Method calls are made as though the components are running within the same JVM, even though they are not. RMI does all of the work required to transfer the elements of the call (the method, the parameters, and the return value) over the network transparently. This makes RMI very appealing and nearly effortless to use.

As an example of how to use RMI, assume we have a class (see Figure 1.4) that implements the functions of a simple trading system. This class provides an interface, `TradingSystemInterface`, through which components call and access the implementation class, `TradingSystemImpl`.

To support RMI, the `TradingSystemInterface` definition must be modified to extend the `java.rmi.Remote` interface, and each method must throw `java.rmi.RemoteException`. Additionally, the implementation class, `TradingSystemImpl`, must extend `java.rmi.UnicastRemoteObject`. These simple source-code changes make the trading system functionality accessible to remote clients and can be seen in Listing 1.1.

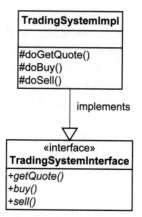

FIGURE 1.4   The trading system implementation is hidden, and accessed, with the interface `TradingSystemInterface`.

LISTING 1.1   Code for the Remote Trading System Interface and Implementation Class

```
import java.rmi.*;
import java.rmi.server.*;
public interface TradingSystemInterface extends Remote
{
public String getQuote(String stock)
throws RemoteException;
public String buy(String stock, int shares)
throws RemoteException;
public String sell(String stock, int shares)
throws RemoteException;
}

import java.rmi.*;
import java.rmi.server.*;
public class TradingSystemImpl extends UnicastRemoteObject
implements TradingSystemInterface
{
public TradingSystemImpl()
throws RemoteException {
}
public String getQuote(String stock)
throws RemoteException {
```

```
    return doGetQuote(stock);
    }
    public String buy(String stock, int shares)
    throws RemoteException {
    return doBuy(stock, shares);
    }
    public String sell(String stock, int shares)
    throws RemoteException {
    return doSell(stock, shares);
    }
    // private implementation here...
    }
```

As stated previously, with Java RMI, method calls are made on remote objects as though the objects were local. In order to achieve this illusion, a *proxy object* that mirrors the remote object is instantiated in the caller's JVM. Conversely, a proxy object representing the caller is instantiated in the remote object's JVM. These proxy objects are called a *stub* and a *skeleton,* respectively. Figure 1.5 illustrates how this concept relates to the trading system application and a remote caller, `Buyer.java`.

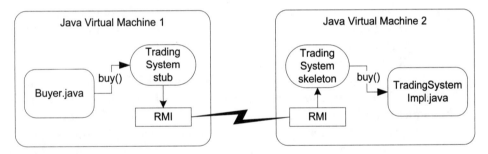

FIGURE 1.5   Java RMI uses proxy components to abstract remote object communication.

In the trading system example, the `TradingSystemImpl` class is used to generate a client stub and a server skeleton for RMI. Java's stub/skeleton compiler, `rmic`, is called with the class name for which it is to generate the stub and skeleton classes. After running successfully, the results are two new class files: `TradingSystemImpl_Stub.class` and `TradingSystemImpl_Skel.class`. The stub class is loaded by Java for each client process that requests a reference to the `TradingSystemImpl` remote class. The skeleton class is loaded by Java when the RMI server process (which creates the `TradingSystemImpl` object) is started. The `TradingSystemImpl` object is only available to clients when the RMI server process is running.

In this example, the `TradingSystemImpl` RMI server is defined as a Java application that instantiates the `TradingSystemImpl` class, and then registers the resulting object with the RMI registry running on the host machine. The registry is started by launching the application, `rmiregistry`, which is located in the Java Development Kit (JDK™) `bin` directory. Once the registry is running, the trading system RMI server process can be started.

The semantics involving parameters and return values are different for remote methods calls when compared to local method calls. For instance, parameters and return values must be one of the following:

- A Java primitive type, such as `int`
- A nonremote object; one that implements the `java.io.Serializable` interface
- A remote object; one that extends the `java.rmi.server.RemoteObject` class

When a Java primitive type or a nonremote object is passed in a remote method call, the object is passed *by-copy*, also known as *by-value*. This means that, before the call is made, the state of the object is serialized, sent over the network as a stream of bytes, and reassembled into a copy of the original object on the other side. Hence, modifications made to nonremote objects will not be reflected in the real object. Remote objects, however, are treated much differently in RMI. If a parameter or return result is a remote object, a stub for the real object will be passed to the server. Modifications to the parameter or return object's stub *will* be reflected in the original object.

RMI is an elegant solution that uses Java end-to-end, and, for the most part, object location is abstracted and hidden. To work over the Internet, and through firewalls, RMI will alternatively use HTTP as its transport, using a POST request for a method call, and a POST response for the return result. By adding an extra step during the compilation process to create the stub and skeleton classes and configuring a server to run the RMI registry tool, you can avoid writing low-level network code for your distributed Java software. Despite the advantages of RMI, some shortcomings are worth noting:

- The remote method calls are only synchronous. That means that when a client process calls a method on a remote object, the calling process's thread will block until that call returns. If there are network latencies, the calling process is exposed to potentially long delays.
- RMI is serial by nature. Regardless of the number of client threads making remote calls or the number of server threads to service those calls, the amount of parallelism RMI can achieve is nondeterministic at best.

- The remote calling component is exposed to remote object failures—software and hardware related. This is another case where the calling process is exposed to potentially long delays before the RMI service detects a failure.
- RMI does not natively support redundant RMI servers for the remote objects. Although it is possible to configure multiple RMI registries, with multiple copies of the remote objects running in separate servers—each bound to a different RMI registry—this solution is tedious, error-prone, and does not scale well.
- RMI does not support atomic transactions.
- With RMI, there is no way to guarantee that data arrives or that it's completely processed when it does.
- RMI is a Java-only solution that does not directly support calling distributed objects written in other languages.

With this last point made, it is fair to mention that by combining Java RMI with Java's Native Interface (JNI) API, it is possible to create a layer of Java code that interfaces with a C++ component or library of components. The JNI code can then be exposed using RMI, making it accessible to local and remote Java code. However, most would consider this solution to be a kludge, and it may not be possible if the C++ code is part of a legacy system running on a platform that does not support Java, such as an older mainframe.

CORBA

The *Common Object Request Broker Architecture* (CORBA) is one potential solution to accessing non-Java objects in a distributed software system. CORBA is a standard, well-known, distributed software architecture created and supported by the Object Management Group® (OMG™). CORBA supports software written in C/C++, Java, COBOL, Smalltalk, Ada, Lisp, and Python, allowing them to communicate with one another transparently. Component interfaces are defined using the language-neutral *Interface Definition Language* (IDL™), from which stubs and skeletons are generated in any of the supported programming languages.

Listing 1.2 contains the IDL for the trading system interface that we explored in Listing 1.1. IDL mostly follows C++ syntax, such as requiring a semicolon after the closing brace of interface definitions and its use of :: when referencing interfaces within the IDL (i.e., `TradingSystem::TradingSystemInterface`). However, by running the Java IDL compiler, which comes with the JDK, `idlj`, the result is 100% pure Java code: a stub, a skeleton, a Java interface, and an empty Java class (for the implementation).

LISTING 1.2   IDL for a Trading System Interface

```
module TradingSystem {
interface TradingSystemInterface {
string getQuote(in string name);
string buy(in string name, in short qty);
string sell(in string name, in short qty);
};
};
```

The CORBA components that implement the defined interfaces register with an object request broker (ORB) through which client components locate them. After a client locates an object, all method invocations are made through the ORB, achieving true separation of interface from object implementation. ORBs running on different servers can communicate, facilitating remote object lookups and method calls. A commonly used inter-ORB network communication protocol is the Internet Inter-ORB Protocol (IIOP), based on TCP/IP. Figure 1.6 illustrates CORBA's location, platform, and language-independent architecture, where diverse client and server components interoperate equally.

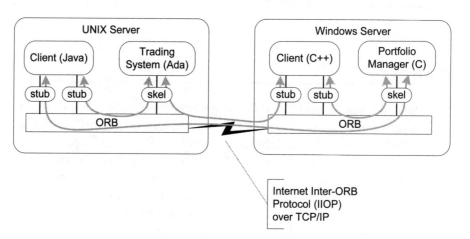

FIGURE 1.6   CORBA is a location, platform, and language-independent distributed software architecture.

On paper, CORBA appears to be a strong candidate for distributed enterprise architecture. When CORBA was first introduced, it was met with enthusiasm from developers hoping to eliminate language and platform lock-in. In practice, however, it didn't work out that way. Historically, the very independence that makes

CORBA powerful has also led to its greatest downfall: the lack of a reference ORB implementation. Lacking this, software vendors proceeded to build ORB software; each one was implemented according to the vendor's interpretation of the CORBA specification. This resulted in the difficulty, and sometimes inability, of an ORB from vendor A to communicate with an ORB from vendor B. This was not the intent of the CORBA designers, and it led to the problem that CORBA was intended to free developers from: vendor lock-in.

Because of the inability to seamlessly integrate distributed CORBA systems, the cost associated with purchasing an ORB, and the associated performance overhead, CORBA's adoption has been very limited. Microsoft experienced similar problems with its Distributed Component Object Model (DCOM) technology. In general, component frameworks, platform lock-in, and proprietary technology are not reasonable solutions for distributed software architecture. What's required is a platform- and language-independent method of distributed object *communication*, not construction. The concept of enterprise messaging software is designed to meet this requirement.

ENTERPRISE MESSAGING

Messaging software is more than email or chat. It's a reliable exchange of data between software entities—one that requires a framework of tools and design patterns to help overcome the complexities involved. In practice, messaging software provides an infrastructure that allows data to be passed between software systems via messages instead of direct method calls. Computer systems distributed around the globe rely upon messaging infrastructures to provide mission critical services to users. When someone uses a credit card, deposits money in a bank, checks inventory, ships a package, or performs a search on Google, data is quickly and reliably exchanged between multiple disparate software systems. Messaging software forms the infrastructure for modern, component-based, object-oriented software development.

Messaging software systems are often referred to as *message-oriented middleware* (MOM). *Middleware* is the software that other software systems are built upon. In particular, MOM provides the services that message-based software requires, including:

- Queue-based messaging
- Reply-based messaging
- Anonymous, subscription-based messaging
- Asynchronous message processing
- Guaranteed message delivery
- Transaction-based messaging

These are the types of services that a remote procedure call (RPC) alone will not provide. An enterprise-level messaging system is required to build robust, distributed software systems. To build this type of software reliably and efficiently, a thorough understanding of the nuances of messaging, at all levels within a software system, is also required. The goal of this book is to provide this understanding, along with a toolkit of design patterns and classes that can be used to build robust Java software around a messaging system. Further, this book will illustrate how messaging concepts can be used within small projects, as well as large projects, and how they can be combined with other technologies such as Web Services.

Message Paradigms

Enterprise messaging software provides the infrastructure needed for reliable, robust, inter-process communication. However, messaging software is just a means to an end. The real goal is to move data from one software system to another. Whether the data is simply a notification of an event or part of a critical business transaction, the successful sending and receiving of the data is the goal of the message itself. Not all messages are created equal, though. Some messages are meant to be received by many listeners, while others are to be received by only one. This difference is represented by two popular messaging paradigms: *publish-and-subscribe* and *point-to-point* (a.k.a. *message queues*).

With publish-and-subscribe messaging, components publish messages to, or subscribe to receive messages from, a *topic*. In this paradigm, messaging is generally anonymous, meaning the publisher and subscriber components do not need to know of each other's existence. This level of abstraction allows the developer to build loosely coupled code. Each topic in the publish-and-subscribe paradigm may have zero or more publishers and zero or more subscribers. Every message that a publisher component sends is received by all components that have subscribed (and are currently listening) to the applicable topic, sort of like a multicast. Figure 1.7 illustrates this.

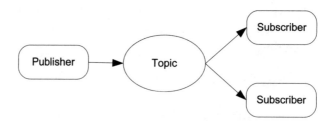

FIGURE 1.7 Publisher components publish messages to a topic, and all subscriber components receive the messages.

The point-to-point paradigm defines messaging in terms of queues. A *queue* is similar to a topic in that it has a name and it forms the basis for which messages are sent and received. In this paradigm, message producers put messages on a queue, and message consumers take messages off a queue. So far, this may sound similar to the publish-and-subscribe message paradigm. However, the differences lie in the semantics of the message delivery. Queues follow the store-and-forward model, where messages are held for later delivery even if there are no current queue consumers. If there happen to be multiple consumers available, each message is received by only one consumer (see Figure 1.8). This is very different than publish-and-subscribe messaging, where every subscriber receives a copy of every message.

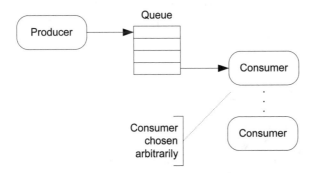

FIGURE 1.8 Queue producers place messages on a queue, while consumers listen for, and remove, messages from a queue.

Take, for example, a stock quote change notification sent to computers globally on the trading floors of brokerage houses. This is a system event that should be made available to all software entities that have expressed interest in it. Furthermore, the event should be received by all entities equally, regardless of the quantity or the physical location of the entities. All else being equal, it would create an unfair advantage for a set of computers to have received this notification, while others have not—disregarding for a moment the failure of an individual computer or network connection. For this example, the publish-and-subscribe messaging paradigm is ideal. The quote change notifications are multicast to all of the distributed subscriber components.

Alternatively, take the example of a notification of a new order for 100 shares of stock being entered into a trading system. If this event were multicast to more than one receiving computer, the order would be executed multiple times, resulting in the purchase of more than 100 shares of stock, which is clearly not the intent.

Instead, this message should be received by exactly one software entity to execute the order, regardless of the number of computers deployed to run the order execution software. The point-to-point message paradigm is ideal for this case. With a message queue, buy or sell requests are safely stored and then forwarded to only one consumer for processing.

The Java Message Service

The *JMS* specification describes an enterprise messaging system for Java that supports the publish-and-subscribe and point-to-point message paradigms. JMS also specifies many types of message objects with the goal of interoperating with other, non-Java/JMS messaging systems. With enterprise messaging—and in particular, JMS—one can build distributed software systems that are truly platform and language independent. Several chapters in this book deal with the details and complexities of JMS.

WEB SERVICES

A *service-oriented architecture (SOA)* involves building independent software systems that provide a well-defined set of functionality and thereby offer that functionality to other software systems. The set of functionality is the "service" that the software provides, which is analogous to that of a bank, travel agency, or restaurant. Building an enterprise, and hence its software applications, around a core set of service-based software systems involves the transfer of data, the coordination of transactions, and the orchestration of entire business processes.

You cannot speak about modern software architecture and design without mentioning the term Web Services. At the very least, a Web Service can be defined as a software system that is accessible over HTTP, where the message itself is based on XML. Throw in the Simple Object Access Protocol (SOAP) for data transport, the Web Service Description Language (WSDL) for the service description, and the Universal Description, Discovery, and Integration (UDDI) standard for service discovery, and you have a complete set of rules for finding and using Web Services in a service-oriented architecture.

SOAP is a topic that has gotten a lot attention over the past few years. It's also a simple concept that involves abstracting the details of a remote procedure call using XML. Every detail of a method call is represented in XML according to a defined schema. Listing 1.3 is a sample SOAP message representing a call to purchase 100 shares of IBM stock.

LISTING 1.3 A sample SOAP request message.

```
<SOAP-ENV:Envelope xmlns:SOAP
ENV="http://schemas.xmlsoap.org/soap/envelope/">
    <SOAP-ENV:Header />
    <SOAP-ENV:Body>
        <Buy>
            <symbol>IBM</symbol>
            <quantity>100</ quantity >
        </Buy>
    </SOAP-ENV:Body>
</SOAP-ENV:Envelope>
```

The Web Service standards are all about connecting SOA-based software services within an enterprise and throughout the world. Enterprise messaging is all about communication, with its many paradigms, between software entities. Combining messaging with Web Services opens the world to secure, guaranteed, and robust communication for distributed application development that is completely platform, language, and location independent (see Figure 1.9). This is precisely what this book is about.

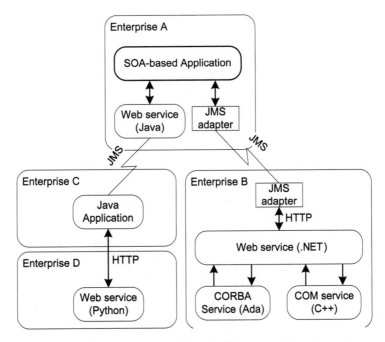

FIGURE 1.9 Web Services combined with messaging software is an example of advanced distributed SOA-based software development.

SUMMARY

This chapter explored the idea that messaging encompasses more than process-to-process or server-to-server communication. It can also be used efficiently within software systems to improve their design. From simple events within an application, to remote procedure call mechanisms such as Java RMI and CORBA, and finally with enterprise technologies such as message queues and Web Services, the concept of messaging is everywhere in modern software development.

2 JavaBean Events

In This Chapter

- The JavaBean Event Model
- Component Dependencies
- The Java Event Agent
- The Modified Stock Quote Example

This chapter is made up of two main sections. The first provides an overview of the basics of JavaBeans events. The second section provides a unique design pattern, with implementation, that improves upon the JavaBeans event model and should prove interesting to even the most experienced JavaBeans developer. If you are comfortable with the JavaBeans event model, jump right to the section "The Java Event Agent."

THE JAVABEAN EVENT MODEL

The JavaBean specification defines a software component model for Java. The goal of JavaBeans is to provide a set of standards for implementing Java building block components that can be used in constructing entire applications. The specification defines component data access (properties) and component actions and notifications (events), using standard Java method calls that can be made from other Java classes or script code. Building JavaBeans components doesn't require the use of a different framework, compiler, or Java runtime. It's mostly a set of guidelines and interfaces, leaving all of the features of Java intact. This means that all Java has to offer is available to JavaBeans components, such as threading, reflection, serialization, internationalization, Java Database Connectivity (JDBC™), Remote Method Invocation (RMI), Interface Definition Language™ (IDL), Java Message Service (JMS), and so on.

The first chapter introduced the command design pattern and the related concept of component events. Events are a simple form of component messaging and are a big part of the JavaBean component architecture. The JavaBean event model provides a standard implementation of the command pattern for Java. A source Bean sends an event to anonymous listener Beans via a method call on an interface. The source does not need to know anything about the components that are listening to the events—or what happens when the events are received—and the listeners don't need to know the implementation behind these events. The JavaBean event model is powerful in its simplicity. An event can be a button click within an application's user interface or some other application-specific change in behavior implemented within a non-GUI component.

The event model is made up of an event source, an event interface, an event object, and an event listener that implements the event interface. An event interface extends `java.util.EventListener` and defines additional methods that make up a related set of events. Each method defined represents a unique event notification. The parameter for each method on the event interface is typically a subclass of `java.util.EventObject`. This object should be used to encapsulate the details of the event, but it is not mandatory to use it; an arbitrary list of parameters is acceptable.

The event source component fires an event by invoking a method on the event interface of the event listener.

An event source is identified by its implementation of a registration method that accepts instances of a particular event interface. A component can be a source to multiple event interfaces by implementing a registration method for each one it supports. Conversely, a component can listen to more than one event set by implementing each event interface.

Figure 2.1 is an updated view of the command processing Unified Modeling Language (UML) diagram specific to the JavaBean event model. The diagram appears more involved now than in the previous chapter (see Figure 1.3), but this is due only to the addition of the standard interfaces; the basic model is still the same. The QuoteSource and QuoteListener components exist as they did in Figure 1.3. However, the listener component is shown specifically implementing QuoteListenerInterface, a custom interface that extends the standard java.util.EventListener interface. Additionally, the event data is encapsulated using an object that implements the EventObject interface—the QuoteEvent object in this example. The source component, QuoteSource, triggers a command on the target component, QuoteListener, when it calls the quoteChanged method. In this example, when the event is fired, QuoteListener extracts the data from the event object and executes the command, showQuote, on the associated Display object.

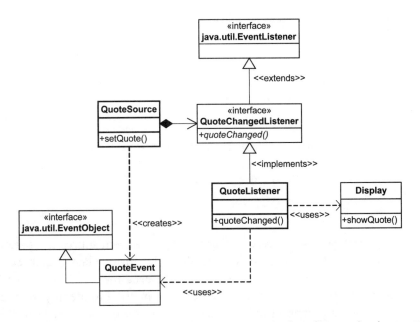

FIGURE 2.1   The updated command pattern UML class diagram for the JavaBean event model.

To further illustrate, let's begin to implement the quote system shown in Figure 2.1. The QuoteChangedListener interface defines an event that fires when a stock quote changes. This interface is defined as a JavaBean listener interface because it extends java.util.EventListener.

```
public interface QuoteChangedListener
    extends java.util.EventListener
{
    // called when the stock quote changes
    public void quoteChanged(QuoteEvent qe);
}
```

The event is defined as the method, quoteChanged, with a parameter that is the event object, QuoteEvent, shown in Listing 2.1.

LISTING 2.1   Code for the JavaBean Event Object Quote

```
public class QuoteEvent extends java.util.EventObject
{
    protected double quote; // the quote value
    public QuoteEvent(Object source, double quote)
    {
        super(source);
        setQuote(quote);
    }

    public double getQuote()
    {
        return quote;
    }

    Protected void setQuote(double newQuote)
    {
        this.quote = newQuote;
    }
}
```

The QuoteEvent class constructor takes the event source as a parameter, which is stored by the base class with a call to the super-class constructor. The java.util.EventObject interface defines a getSource method that returns a reference to the source object. A listener can call this method to identify the source component when an event is fired. See Listing 2.2 for the QuoteSource Java class definition. The specification suggests that event source components implement a method to add event listeners that follows the pattern add<*EventInterfaceName*>, which is addQuoteChangedListener in this case.

LISTING 2.2   Code for the Event Source Java Class QuoteSource

```java
public class QuoteSource
{
    protected Vector listeners = new Vector();
    public QuoteSource()
    {
    }

    public void addQuoteChangedListener(
        QuoteChangedListener listener)
    {
        listeners.add( listener );
    }

    public void fire_quoteChanged( double newQuote )
    {
        QuoteEvent quote =
            new QuoteEvent( this, newQuote );

        // Give each listener in the Vector
        // this QuoteEvent object

        Vector listenersCopy;
        synchronized ( this )
        {
            listenersCopy = (Vector)listeners.clone();
        }

        int cnt = listenersCopy.size();
        for (int i = 0; i < cnt; i++)
        {
            Object obj = listenersCopy.elementAt(i);

            QuoteChangedListener client =
                (QuoteChangedListener)obj;

            client.quoteChanged( quote );
        }
    }
}
```

An event listener component must define an implementation for the methods on each event listener interface it implements. In this example, the QuoteListener class (see Listing 2.3) provides an implementation of the quoteChanged event method.

LISTING 2.3　Code for the Event Listener QuoteListener

```
public class QuoteListener
    implements QuoteChangedListener
{
    protected QuoteSource quoteSource;
    public QuoteListener()
    {
        quoteSource = new QuoteSource();
        quoteSource.addQuoteChangedListener( this );
    }

    public void quoteChanged(QuoteEvent qe)
    {
        // do something with the new quote
        ...
    }
}
```

Figure 2.2 provides an overview of the JavaBean event model, and all of the individual components involved, as outlined in the JavaBean specification. You can see from this diagram that although a source does not need to know the details of its listeners, each listener needs to know a lot about the source. Specifically, the listener needs to know the name of the source component's implementation class and where to get a reference to it.

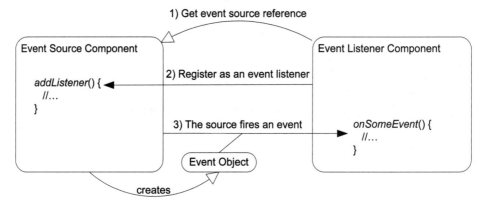

FIGURE 2.2　The ordering of method calls in the JavaBean event model.

Threading Issues

It's important to remember that there are no threading models defined for JavaBean event processing, as there are in other component models. This means that a listener's event methods may be called on a different thread than the one the listener used when it registered with the source. This also means that a listener component may, in response to an event, call a source component back on a different thread than the event was fired on. This can result in a deadlock of both the listener and the source components.

CAUTION

To avoid deadlock, a source component should take care not to call a listener event method from a synchronized block of code. Therefore, you should avoid using synchronized methods to fire events, such as

```
// BAD!
public void synchronized fire_quoteChanged {
    // fire the event
}
```

You should also avoid using synchronized lock objects around the code that fire events, such as

```
// BAD!
synchronized ( someLock) {
    for (int i = 0; i < cnt; i++) {
        // fire the event
    }
}
```

A developer can, however, choose to safely synchronize a listener component's event methods to avoid concurrency issues. With the event model, as defined, there is no risk of deadlock in this situation.

Note that the implementation of the method `fire_quoteChanged` in Listing 2.2 makes a copy of the list of listeners before firing the event. This is done to avoid an exception that might occur if a listener deregistered for an event while the original list was used in a loop to fire the event. A copy of the list is made using the `clone` method, within a synchronized block of code that does not extend further, ensuring that a thread-safe copy of the list is used in the nonsynchronized loop that fires the event.

Be aware that this means a listener may receive an event even after it has deregistered with the event source. This is a scenario that every listener component must be prepared for. Event source components may be coded to avoid this, but they are not required to do so.

Unicast and Multicast Events

So far our discussion has centered on multicast events—those for which one or more listeners may be registered. Typically, this is how most event interfaces are implemented. However, the JavaBean specification allows a source component to declare itself as a unicast event source, meaning only one listener may register for (and receive) a particular set of events. An event source component specifies this by adding the clause throws TooManyListenersException to its event registration method:

```
public void addQuoteChangedListener(
    QuoteChangedListener listener)
        throws java.util.TooManyListenersException
{
    //...
}
```

Although the meaning of the TooManyListenersException exception is nebulous (how many is too many?) it indicates that an event source supports *at most* one listener. Keep in mind that even a multicast event source is not required to send an event to all registered listeners. A multicast source may limit event recipients to a subset based on certain conditions or limit recipients because it caught an exception from a listener while firing the event.

Event Adapters

Sometimes your code may need to handle the same events from multiple event source components. Since a Java class can only provide one implementation for an event interface, this may appear to be a problem. Take, for example, a window with three buttons in it: an OK button, a Cancel button, and an Apply button. Let's say each button is implemented by a class named Button and fires an event, onClicked. Your code implements the event interface, including onClicked, and then registers with each of the three Button objects. Certainly, your code needs to handle each button differently; but when it receives the onClicked event, how will it know which button the event came from?

The correct solution is to use a JavaBean *event adapter*, which implements a design pattern whereby events from similar event sources are de-multiplexed to individual method calls in your code. The first approach is to create an event adapter as an inner class that implements the event interface and forwards the event on to the containing class via a unique method call. An inner class per event source will need to be created and instantiated in order to handle and forward the events properly. As you can imagine, this strategy can get unwieldy as the number of inner classes grows. It's impractical to maintain all of the inner classes, especially when most of their code is duplicated.

A second approach to implementing event adapters is designed to solve this problem. Called a *generic adapter*, this design pattern uses Java Reflection to call the proper method on the event target object. As seen in Figure 2.3, the onClicked event is handled in the button event adapter. As per the JavaBean specification, the event's parameter is an event object that provides access to the event source object. The object's name, which is the button's name in this case, is used to invoke the correct target class method using the invoke call on the java.lang.reflect.Method class. To set this up, the target class simply provides the event adapter with the method name as a String, along with the button it corresponds to, when the adapter is created.

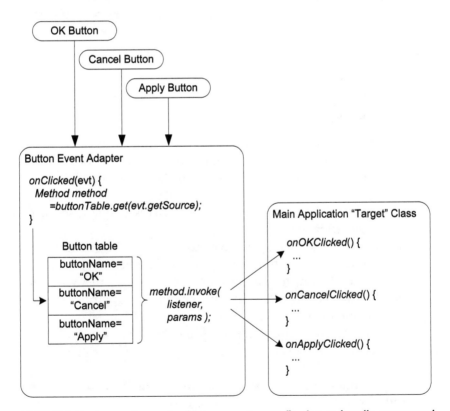

FIGURE 2.3 A generic event adapter uses Java Reflection to handle events and forward them to the target class.

THE ADAPTER DESIGN PATTERN

An adapter allows components to work together even when they were not originally designed to do so. In some cases, the interfaces implemented by these components may be outdated or incompatible. In other cases, the components may be completely unrelated or the integration of these components may have been unforeseen at the time they were implemented. In either case, an adapter can be designed to allow for the integration of these components.

An example of an adapter class is one that implements an interface that the adaptee (the using component) is expecting, yet calls the interface of the target component that actually implements the functionality. Another example is an adapter interface that is designed to generalize a set of functionality, where the intent is that a target component will implement specific behavior related to the interface. An example of this type of implementation may be in the area of communication. The adapter in this case defines methods of generic communication. The target component chooses the specific communication protocol. The adaptee simply calls the adapter interface to send data; the communication protocol details are completely abstracted from it.

The Pros and Cons of Events

A JavaBean event is a relatively simple form of messaging implemented at the component interface level. Using the event model has some advantages over making direct component-to-component method calls, such as:

- The model is object oriented. Interfaces define associated behavior, not implementation.
- The events are *mostly* anonymous. Event source and listener components do not need to know too much about one another, but listeners do need to know specifically which components source the events they are interested in.
- The model supports zero, one, or multiple event listeners per event source without modification.
- The implementation details of firing the events, as well as handling the events, are encapsulated and hidden.

JavaBean event processing is based on a design pattern that has been used in software development for years—since well before Java's widespread use.

However, basic JavaBean event processing does have some drawbacks that limit its usefulness:

■ *The events are only synchronous. The source must wait for each method call to complete before continuing with its processing.*

■ *As defined, JavaBean events work only within a Java virtual machine (JVM).*

■ *An event listener implementation can potentially impact the event source (i.e., by throwing an exception or entering an infinite loop).*

■ *JavaBean events are not completely anonymous; listeners need to know specifically which components source their events.*

■ *Transactions are not supported.*

■ *There are no built-in guarantees that every listener will get every event; an exception may preempt the firing of events to all listeners.*

■ *The event model introduces complexities related to component dependencies.*

Despite the drawbacks, the JavaBean event model provides a simple, powerful, and consistent form of intraprocess communication. Additionally, there are ways to address some of the drawbacks, such as the lack of complete anonymity, component dependency issues, and the restriction of working only within a JVM. The rest of this chapter deals with the first two issues. Extending JavaBean events beyond one JVM is explored in Chapter 5, "JMS Development, Deployment, and Support."

COMPONENT DEPENDENCIES

A component dependency is defined as one component's use of another component, typically via method calls. This is obviously something that cannot be avoided in component software development but can nevertheless lead to unwanted complexity. With JavaBean events, the complexity begins when a component implements multiple event interfaces. This situation gets more complex when a source component is also a listener of another source component. The example in Figure 2.4 illustrates this complex web of components.

In this example, the quotes system contains a component that manages system state. The StateChangeSource component fires system state change events. The QuoteDisplay component listens to these events and will "gray out" the display if the state changes to "unavailable." The QuoteChangedSource component has a requirement to maintain a history of quote changes and thus needs to retrieve quote history data when the state changes back to "available." The PortfolioValueChangedSource component tracks all changes to quotes in the user's portfolio, and all changes to this value are reflected by the QuoteDisplay component.

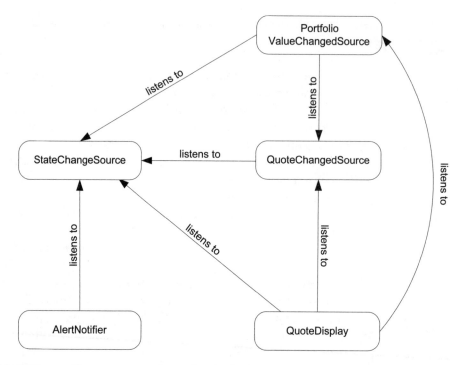

FIGURE 2.4 The component dependencies in this sample stock quote system, although necessary, lead to unwanted complexity.

On the surface this seems like a reasonable quote system design: a component-based software system that uses events for abstraction. However, the end result of this design is a set of components that are interdependent with many other components. The component dependency matrix this creates can become a huge maintenance problem, mainly because the JavaBean event specification does not adequately hide the event source from listeners.

A developer should not need to know which component is the source to a particular set of events. If another developer decides to combine two source components into one component that now sources the combined events, this will affect the listener component's code. Of course the opposite could occur, where one source component is broken out into multiple source components. These are implementation details that you as an event listener developer shouldn't need to know about. At the least, you should not need to modify your code as a result of such changes.

Circular Dependencies

A more complex component relationship arises when two source components are also listeners to one another's events, as illustrated in Figure 2.5. This is known as a *circular dependency*, also called a *circular reference.*

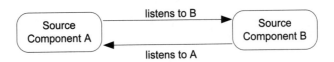

FIGURE 2.5 A component circular dependency usually leads to problems.

A circular dependency indicates a design problem because it creates a very tight coupling between the two components. A change in one component directly affects the other component. It can also lead to other, more serious, problems:

Memory leaks: The objects may never release their references to one another.

Source code compilation issues: If component A calls a method on component B, it requires access to it in compiled form. However, component B has the same issue and requires access to component A in compiled form. This is a chicken-and-egg scenario.

To solve this problem, you may examine component A and component B and decide to combine them into one component. However, combining components does not usually make design sense, and it may be impossible if you do not have the source code to one of the components. Properly abstracting event source components from the events themselves (and hence the listeners) would help the situation.

Event Source Abstraction

Placing a component in between that abstracts all source and listener components one more level is a solution to this problem. This component, or agent, could be implemented as a singleton and exist on behalf of *all* source components. At first glance, this may sound like the job of an event adapter, but this would not be correct. An event adapter is meant to de-multiplex multiple event source interface implementations, where the event source components are known and exposed. The agent described so far will hide the event source components from listener components, including their event adapters.

THE SINGLETON DESIGN PATTERN

Many real-world scenarios require certain components in your software to be instantiated once and only once. Perhaps you have a component that manages bids on an item in an auction or a component that manages system state. Both of these are examples of singleton components. One option is to create a global variable of some sort, and build application logic around it to ensure that only this one instance is used—but this is not foolproof. Besides, the fact that a component is to have only one instance is part of the behavior of the component itself; therefore, it should be enforced by the component's code, not the application using it.

The singleton design pattern describes a method of designing classes that enforce the singleton requirement. Figure 2.6 shows the UML class diagram for the singleton pattern implemented in Java. There are three requirements for a singleton Java object:

1. The component must create its own, single, instance.
2. The component must ensure that no more instances can be created. For Java, this means that only one instance exists per JVM.
3. Access to the single instance must be provided through the component's interface.

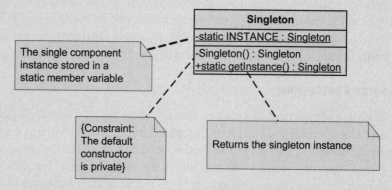

FIGURE 2.6 This is the UML class diagram for the singleton design pattern implemented in Java.

THE JAVA EVENT AGENT

The event agent described here is a Java component that provides this level of abstraction, and it's the first component in the messaging toolkit described in this book. The sole purpose of the event agent is to match up listener components to event source components, independent of one another. It does not act as a router of the events themselves, as this would make the event agent a bottleneck. A source component can register itself with the agent as the source for a particular event interface. Other components can register themselves as listeners, thereby removing the need to know which specific components source each event interface. The event agent notifies the source components when listeners arrive. Once a source and a listener component are matched together, the event agent is out of the picture.

In the implementation described here, the event agent uses the singleton design pattern to ensure that only one instance of it exists. To achieve this, the constructor is made private, and the class contains a private, static, final instance of itself, accessible via a static method named getInstance. The code in Listing 2.4 implements this design pattern and can be used to make any Java class a singleton. The full source code for the Java event agent can be found on the CD-ROM in the folder labeled Chapter2, in the directory that matches the package, com\toolkit\messaging.

ON THE CD

LISTING 2.4 Code for the Java Event Agent Singleton Class

```
package com.toolkit.messaging;

import java.util.*;
import java.beans.*;

public class EventAgent
{
    // private constructor ensures no other instances
    // making this object a singleton
    private EventAgent() { }

    // static member variable and method enables callers
    // to get to the one-and-only object instance
    private static final EventAgent SINGLE_INSTANCE
        = new EventAgent();

    public static EventAgent getInstance()
    {
        return SINGLE_INSTANCE;
    }
```

```
private HashMap sourceObjects = new HashMap();
private Vector listenerObjects = new Vector();

// ...
}
```

The UML class diagram in Figure 2.7 shows all of the member variables and methods within the EventAgent class. The only publicly accessible methods of this class are:

getInstance: A static method that provides access to the event agent's singleton instance (see Listing 2.4)

regSource: Allows a component to register itself as an event source for the supplied event interface

regListener: Allows a component to register itself as a listener of the supplied event interface

deRegSource: Allows a component to deregister as a source for the supplied event interface, hence making it unavailable to listeners through the event agent

deRegListener: Allows a component to deregister as a listener of the supplied event interface and deregisters it with the source component (if previously registered)

The event agent allows source and listener components to register independently of one another, meaning a source can register before any listener components do, and vice versa. As soon as an event source component registers itself as a source for an event interface, the source component is notified of the existence of all listeners for that event interface. The event agent notifies the source component when each new listener registers thereafter.

Registering a Source Component

This implementation of the event agent allows only one source component for each event interface. If multiple source components were allowed per event interface, the choice of which source component to notify when a listener registers would be ambiguous. Additionally, giving the listener the ability to choose its event source defeats the purpose of the event agent. However, for cases such as the example of multiple buttons in a window, your code specifically needs to know which button fired its onClicked event. This is a valid scenario (one that arises mainly in user interface development) for which the event agent is not a good fit. In the author's opinion, user interface development is the only time where this is

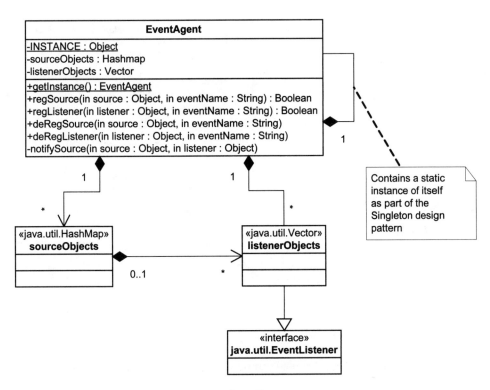

FIGURE 2.7 The Java Event Agent UML class diagram.

acceptable. In most other cases, if there is reason to listen to events from one source compared to the same events from a different source, then the events are truly unique and should be implemented as unique event interfaces.

A source component registers with the event agent by calling the regSource method (see Listing 2.5), providing a reference to itself and the name of the event interface as a String. The following steps occur when regSource is called, as illustrated in Figure 2.8:

1. A check is made to ensure that the source component implements SourceInterface by using the Java instanceof keyword.
2. A reference to the source component is stored in a HashMap, with the key being the event interface name. A check is made to ensure that no other source has registered for the given event interface.
3. A check is made to see if any listener components have already registered for this event set. If so, the source component is notified by calling its addListener method for each listener component. A Vector of objects is

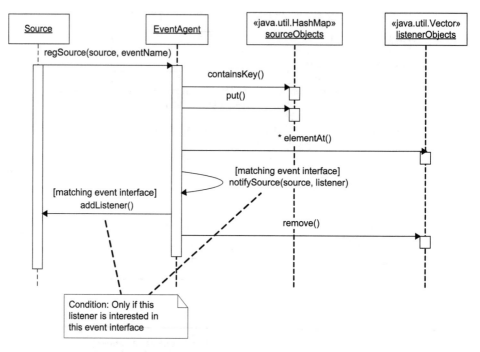

FIGURE 2.8 An event source component registers with the Java event agent.

used to encapsulate each listener component and the event interface it has registered for. The event interface name for each listener is compared to that of the source component. For each matching listener, the following steps are taken:

- The source is notified by calling its addListener method, passing a reference to the listener.
- The listener is removed from the Vector. All other listener components remain in this Vector until a matching source component registers with the event agent, whereby this process is repeated.

LISTING 2.5 Code to Register an Event Source Component with the Java Event Agent

```
public synchronized boolean regSource(
    Object sourceObj,
    String eventName)
{
    try {
        // sourceObj must implement SourceInterface
```

```
   if ( ! ( sourceObj instanceof SourceInterface ) )
      return false;

   // Add this source object to our HashMap once only
   if ( sourceObjects.containsKey(eventName) == true )
      return false;

   sourceObjects.put( eventName, sourceObj );

   // Since listener and source objects can register
   // at any time, check if there are matching
   // listener objects in the Vector
   int i = 0;
   int count = listenerObjects.size();
   while ( i < count )
   {
      EventComponent listener =
         (EventComponent)listenerObjects.elementAt(i);

      // Check the listener's event interface name
      if ( eventName.equals(listener.getEventName()) )
      {
         notifySource(sourceObj, listener.getObject());

         // Remove the listener. All remaining
         // elements will shift left so don't
         // increment vector index i
         listenerObjects.remove( i );

         count--; // one less item in the list now
      }
      else
      {
         i++; // Check the next listener
      }
   }
   return true;
}
catch ( Exception e ) {
    e.printStackTrace();
}

return false;
}
```

Registering a Listener Component

It is completely acceptable, and likely, that your software will have multiple listener components that are interested in the same event interface. The event agent entirely supports this.

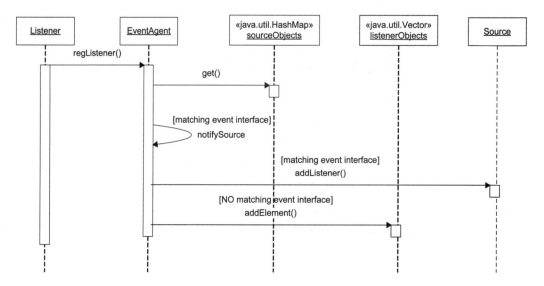

FIGURE 2.9 This UML diagram is the listener's event agent registration sequence.

The registration process for an event listener (illustrated in Figure 2.9) is similar to that of an event source. A listener component registers with the event agent by a calling the regListener method (see Listing 2.6). It provides a reference to itself and the name of the event interface as a String. If a listener implements multiple event interfaces, it will need to register itself for each interface individually, by making multiple calls to regListener. The following steps occur when regListener is called:

1. The HashMap of source components is checked for a source that implements the given event interface. If a matching source component is found, the source component is notified by calling its addListener method.
2. If a matching source component is not found, this listener component is added to a Vector of listeners in anticipation that a source component will register at some future time.

LISTING 2.6   Code to Register an Event Listener with the Java Event Agent

```
public synchronized boolean regListener(
    Object listenerObj,
    String eventName)
{
    try {
        if ( listenerObj == null || eventName == null)
            return false;

        // Search for the Matching Source in the HashMap
        Object source = sourceObjects.get( eventName );

        if ( source != null )
        {
            notifySource( source, listenerObj );
        }
        else
        {
            // Didn't find the matching Source. Add the
            // listener to the list in anticipation that
            // the source will register later
            EventComponent listener =
                new EventComponent( listenerObj, eventName );

            listenerObjects.addElement( listener );
        }
        return true;
    }
    catch ( Exception e ) {
        e.printStackTrace();
    }

    return false;
}
```

Source and Listener Deregistration

Under some conditions a source component may need to stop accepting listeners. Similarly, a listener component may no longer be able to wait for a matching source component. For these reasons the event agent supports deregistration for both source and listener components. A source or listener component can deregister itself by calling deRegSource or deRegListener, respectively. Both methods take the component's object reference and the name of the event interface as parameters. If the component is in the list of source or listener components with the given event interface name, it will be removed from the list.

There is still an issue regarding the extra step required to deregister the listener with the source component, if the source has previously registered. To ensure that the event source remains hidden from the listener, the event agent takes care of this step for you internally when deRegListener is called. The code in Listing 2.7 shows the implementation of this method.

LISTING 2.7   Code to Deregister a Listener

```
public synchronized boolean deRegListener(
    Object listenerObj, String eventName )
{
    try {
        if ( listenerObj == null || eventName == null)
            return false;

        // Search for the listener for this event type
        int cnt = listenerObjects.size();
        for ( int i = 0; i < cnt; i++ )
        {
          EventComponent listener = (EventComponent)
              listenerObjects.elementAt(i);

          String name = listener.getEventName();
          if (eventName.equals(type) )
          {
            // Found a listener for this event type
            // Make sure it is the same listener
            if ( listener.getObject() == listenerObj )
            {
              listenerObjects.removeElementAt( i );

              // deregister the listener from the source
              SourceInterface source =
                  (SourceInterface)sourceObjects.get(eventName);
              if ( source != null )
                  source.removeListener( listenerObj );

              return true;
            }
          }
        }
    }
    catch ( Exception e ) {
```

```
            e.printStackTrace();
        }

        return false;
    }
```

Listener and Source Component Collections

The event agent stores all source components in a HashMap, with the key being the event interface name. This helps enforce the rule that only one event source component is allowed per event interface. Since this constraint does not apply to event listeners—there can be more than one listener per event interface—the event agent stores all listener components in a Vector of EventComponent class objects (see Listing 2.8). This class is implemented as a nested class within the event agent main class and simply wraps the listener component and the String representing the event interface it implements.

LISTING 2.8   Code for the EventComponent Class

```
class EventComponent
{
    protected Object theObject = null;
    protected String eventName = null;

    public EventComponent(Object obj, String s)
    {
        theObject = obj;
        eventName = s;
    }
    public Object getObject()
    {
        return theObject;
    }
    public String getEventName()
    {
        return eventName;
    }
}
```

THE MODIFIED STOCK QUOTE EXAMPLE

Using the stock quote example from the beginning of this chapter, the modifications required to use the event agent are minor and otherwise quite helpful. The event agent requires that all source components implement the interface named SourceInterface.

This interface contains the methods addListener and removeListener. Since all source components need similar methods to allow clients to register and deregister, the requirement that this interface be implemented is not unreasonable. As a result, the event agent will be able to call the respective method when a listener registers or deregisters for any source component's event interface.

For event listener components and event objects, there are no additional interface requirements. Your code should, however, follow a simple design pattern that includes the interface name as part of the listener interface, implemented as a static String. This is used by the source and listener components as the second parameter when they call regSource or regListener, respectively, and helps avoid errors due to typos.

```java
public interface QuoteChangedListener
    extends java.util.EventListener
{

    public static final String eventName
        = "QuoteChangedListener";

    // called when the stock quote changes
    public void quoteChanged(QuoteEvent qe);
}
```

The final modification needed is for the source and listener components to register themselves with the event agent. Starting with the QuoteSource class (see Listing 2.9), the following changes need to be made:

- Add the clause implements SourceInferface to the class declaration.
- Obtain a reference to the event agent instance by calling EventAgent.getInstance.
- Call the regSource method to register the source component with the given interface name. This needs to be done for each event interface the component sources.

LISTING 2.9 The QuoteSource Component Modified to Use the Event Agent

```java
public class QuoteSource
    implements SourceInterface
{

    protected Vector listeners;

    protected EventAgent eventAgent
        = EventAgent.getInstance();
```

```
public QuoteSource()
{
    eventAgent.regSource(
        this, QuoteChangedListener.eventName);
}

public void addListener(Object listenerObj)
{
    listeners.add( listenerObj );
}

public void removeListener(Object listenerObj)
{
    listeners.remove(listenerObj);
}

public void fire_quoteChange(double newQuote)
{
    // ...
}
}
```

The `QuoteListener` component also needs to be modified to use the event agent, although the changes are minor. The changes (see Listing 2.10) are listed here:

■ Some of the code is obsolete and can be removed, such as creating the event source component, and the explicit registration with it.

■ Obtain a reference to the event agent instance by calling `EventAgent.getInstance`.

■ Call the `regListener` method to register the listener component with the given interface name. This needs to be done for each event interface the component implements.

LISTING 2.10 The `QuoteListener` Component Modified to Use the Event Agent

```
public class QuoteListener
    implements QuoteChangedListener
{
    protected EventAgent eventAgent
        = EventAgent.getInstance();
```

```
         // NOTE: no longer need to know the source:
         // OBSOLETE: protected QuoteSource quoteSource;

         public QuoteListener()
         {
             eventAgent.regListener(
                 this, QuoteChangedListener.eventName );

             // OBSOLETE: quoteSource = new QuoteSource();
             // OBSOLETE: quoteSource.addListener( this );
         }

         public void quoteChanged(QuoteEvent qe)
         {
             // ...
         }
     }
```

Overall, the event agent creates a virtual wall of abstraction between the source and listener, as seen in Figure 2.10. The only direct communication that occurs between the source and listener components are event notifications.

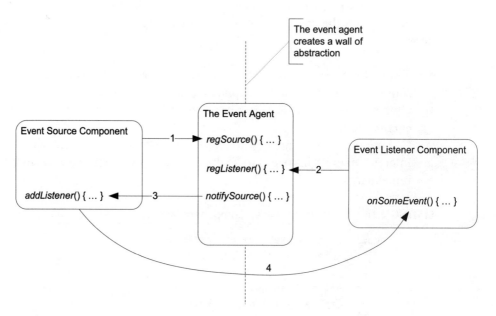

FIGURE 2.10   The event agent completely hides event source and listener components from one another.

ON THE CD

The complete source code for the quote ticker example can be found on the CD-ROM included with this book in the folder labeled Chapter3. The sample application consists of the following components:

QuoteSource.java: The stock-quote source component

QuoteListener.java: The stock-quote source component

QuoteEvent.java: The quote event object

QuoteChangedListener.java: The quote event listener interface (to be implemented by components interested in receiving stock quote events)

QuoteSystemTester.java: A test class that creates a quote source object and two quote event listener objects and then triggers the source object to fire quote events.

The test application is started by executing the Windows® batch file runquotetest.bat, or UNIX® command script runquotetest.sh. Both startup files execute the following Java command:

```
java —cp (classpath details here)
com.TradingSystem.StockTicker.QuoteSystemTester
```

When you run the application, you should see output similar to that shown in Figure 2.11:

```
Z:\Chapter2>java -cp ./; com.TradingSystem.StockTicker.QuoteSystemTester
QuoteSystemTester - creating two QuoteListeners
QuoteSystemTester - creating QuoteSource
QuoteSystemTester - triggering QuoteSource to fire an event
QuoteListener: quote changed to: 10.01
QuoteListener: quote changed to: 10.01
QuoteSystemTester - triggering QuoteSource to fire another event
QuoteListener: quote changed to: 11.01
QuoteListener: quote changed to: 11.01
Z:\Chapter2>_
```

FIGURE 2.11   This screen capture shows the output of the sample stock quote application from this chapter.

SUMMARY

This chapter explored the JavaBean event model, along with the positive and negative aspects that come along with it. Events represent a simple form of intraprocess messaging that follows a well-known design pattern. The Java event agent was introduced to help eliminate some of the negative aspects of the event model.

Reducing component coupling and dependencies within your code goes a long way toward reducing bugs. The event agent accomplishes this by properly abstracting event interfaces and hiding event source and listener components from one another. The improvements this yields include anonymous events, the reduction of component dependencies, and the avoidance of circular references. As an added bonus, programming events becomes more consistent through the use of the common `SourceInterface` and the unified method of event registration for both source and listener components. Overall, the event agent should help simplify your event-handling code as well as further insolate components from implementation changes.

3

Basic Java Messaging

In This Chapter

- Messaging Concepts
- Message-Oriented Middleware
- The Java Message Service (JMS)
- Synchronous and Asynchronous Delivery
- JMS Message Objects
- JMS Publish-and-Subscribe
- JMS Request-and-Reply
- JMS Point-to-Point (Queues)

MESSAGING CONCEPTS

The concept of messaging, introduced in Chapter 1, begins with the goal of delivering data. Enterprise messaging forms the basis for an infrastructure dedicated to communication between disparate components in a distributed software system. Consisting of more than a method call, or an event, enterprise messaging defines a model of data delivery that follows many object-oriented principals [Booch94]. The first principle is that of *abstraction*. The important components in a messaging system—producers, consumers, and the messages themselves—are abstracted through the use of interfaces. The result is a set of *loosely coupled* components that are part of a cohesive, efficient, and reliable software system. Components that are loosely coupled have as few direct interactions with one another as possible. This isolation leads to more robust software, as changes to one part of the system do not ripple through to other parts. A good messaging system achieves this goal by abstracting the components from one another in the system.

The next principal is that of *information hiding*, also called encapsulation, which is the next logical step after abstraction. With abstraction, interfaces are defined to achieve component abstraction, but now the implementation of message delivery, and the messages, are encapsulated so as to remain hidden from all components within the system. This means that the messaging software does not need to know the purpose or content of a message in order to deliver it. Conversely, the implementation behind the delivery of messages is not exposed to producer components that send them. Furthermore, the receiver components can remain blissfully ignorant of the origin of their received messages and the effort involved in their ultimate delivery. Questions such as which components sent the messages, why they were sent, how they arrived, and which components will receive them can remain secret.

The next principle is that of *polymorphism*, which allows a single body of code to work with objects of differing types. For example, a single messaging system can send stock price change messages just as it would send chat messages. This is achieved through the implementation of parametric polymorphism, where a message's type is transparent to the messaging system. Polymorphism is also used at the function level, overriding a producer component's send method to either publish a message or place it on a queue. Both examples of polymorphism rely on object inheritance to achieve their respective goals.

The last principle, building on the concept of inheritance, is that of *hierarchy*. The components of a messaging system are carefully ordered to form a class–object structure with strict relationships. Later in this chapter, we will explore all the details of the JMS class hierarchy. For now, here are some general examples of hierarchy and relationship in a messaging system:

- Both publish-and-subscribe topics and point-to-point queues are types of destination objects (an "is a" relationship).
- A queue contains message objects (a "has a" relationship).
- Publisher and subscriber objects use topic objects (a "uses" relationship).
- Factory objects (see the sidebar on the factory design pattern) are typically used to create message producers, message consumers, and message destination objects (a "creates" relationship).

Message systems such as those based on JMS 1.1 go one step further and combine the object-oriented principles described above. For example, a single body of code can publish messages to a topic, or place messages on a queue, without being written to specifically know that the destination is a topic or a queue. The same principle is true for a message receiver component. This is a powerful example of how polymorphism is used to abstract the destination type, which, when combined, encapsulates the message domain (publish-and-subscribe or queue). The result is that the sender's (and receiver's) code is not written for a specific message domain or destination type. To change the message domain, only the destination type needs to change via an administrative interface—the sender and receiver component code remains the same.

THE FACTORY DESIGN PATTERN

Most object-oriented development languages contain the `class` construct, which is a structure that contains both data and methods that act on that data. Writing code to use classes is common and is considered good practice, but the code within these classes may change over time even as the code that uses those classes changes. The class developer may even offer multiple versions of the same class in order to maintain compatibility with older software systems. How does the application developer know which class to instantiate without hard-coding this choice? One potential answer is to use a *factory* class.

A factory is a class that creates other, often related, classes. The factory will usually accept one or more parameters that are used to describe the type of object your code wishes to instantiate, such as the use of transactions, for example. The resulting object may be one of two completely different classes, neither of which was known specifically at the time the code was written. The factory design pattern therefore abstracts the notion of specific class type from the application developer.

→

This pattern is particularly useful in user interface development, where various forms of the same type of component are created based upon characteristics provided to a factory object. It allows the class developer to control when and how certain classes (and versions of those classes) are used by applications. This, in turn, leads to consistent and predictable behavior across software systems and may also make them easier to test.

Asynchronous Component Communication

Regardless of the message paradigm, enterprise messaging offers the ability to provide *asynchronous component communication*. This makes the process of sending a message truly independent of the process of receiving a message. There's no synchronization between the producer and receiver components' processing. The message producer sends a message and is immediately free to continue with whatever other tasks it needs to perform. Some time later—hopefully not much later—a message consumer will receive the message and process it without affecting the producer in any way. This type of communication has many advantages:

Loose component coupling: The message producer and consumer components are not dependant on one another. Neither component is tied to, or affected by, the processing of the other.

Parallel processing: Since neither one waits on the other, producer and consumer components are capable of doing their processing in parallel, offering higher system throughput, especially on systems with multiple CPUs.

Deferred (disjoint) processing: In some software systems, the components that consume and act on messages are not always available when the messages are produced. Take, for example, a remote salesperson entering orders into a laptop at a site without network connectivity. The resulting new order messages are placed on a queue for later processing by the order processing system once the laptop is placed back on the network. With asynchronous messaging, the order-entry software on the laptop does not "freeze" because the server isn't available to process the orders. Instead, it's free to continue taking orders independently of them being filled. Without asynchronous message processing, this type of system behavior would not be possible.

Request-and-Reply Messaging

The most well-known form of messaging is one that is familiar to anyone who uses the Internet: *request-and-reply*. This straightforward form of messaging, illustrated in Figure 3.1, involves a client application that sends a request to a server, followed by a reply from the server to the client.

FIGURE 3.1   Request-and-reply messaging consists of a client that makes a request to a server, which in turn sends a reply back to the client.

Distributed applications that are based on request-and-reply messaging are typically called *client/server* applications. In a client/server-based architecture, it's important for the client and the server to be up and running simultaneously, or the application will not work properly. For example, one widespread application of request-and-reply messaging is the World Wide Web, where Web browsers make requests to Web servers, and receive Web pages in response. If either the browser or the Web server fails in the middle of the request-and-reply cycle, the end result is an error—such as the dreaded "404–page not found" error.

Anyone familiar with Web site development knows that, although straightforward theoretically, request-and-reply messaging can get complex in reality. First, this type of messaging is not necessarily synchronous; the browser is not "frozen" waiting for a reply, and the Web server is free to queue up requests. Second, the Web site most likely consists of many physical servers, where a server is chosen to send the actual reply based on availability.

Figure 3.2 illustrates how complex a request-and-reply messaging cycle can become when applied to the Web browser/Web server example. First, in this diagram, a client request is handled by a load-balancing component. Second, the load-balancer chooses a server to handle the request based on some load criteria. Third, the server that gets the request most likely will need to queue it, as it may still be processing earlier requests. Finally, the server sends a reply back to the original client, satisfying the request.

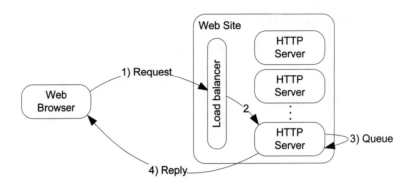

FIGURE 3.2   Request-and-reply messaging can involve many components and complex interactions.

Request-and-reply messaging may be a straightforward and obvious form of communication, but it's not the only one. The fact that both the client and server components of the system must be operational during the entire messaging lifecycle may be considered a drawback in some systems. Additionally, there is a relative lack of anonymity in this paradigm (the client is aware of the server, and the server must remain aware of each client), which is also a drawback in some systems. Furthermore, there are times when sending a message to a system component (server or otherwise) does not necessitate a reply. One-way messaging, one-to-many messaging, and anonymous messaging, are each better served through other messaging paradigms.

Multicast Messaging

With the *multicast messaging* paradigm, there is a one-to-many relationship: one message is sent to (potentially) many consumers. However, the term *multicast messaging* is not meant to imply the underlying network transport; IP multicast is not necessarily used to implement the multicast nature of this form of messaging. It simply indicates that a message, which is sent once by a producer, will be received by all consumers that have expressed prior interest in receiving it. It's also the first step toward truly *anonymous messaging*, where the producer is not made aware of the details of its listeners, or even that they exist.

Logically, this form of messaging is not a broadcast, although it might be physically implemented using User Datagram Protocol (UDP) broadcast network messages. Not all message consumers will receive all messages, as a broadcast implies. Instead, consumers must register interest in a specific subject in order to receive messages produced for that subject. This is sometimes referred to as subject-based messaging [Chappell01], but it's much more widely known as *publish-and-subscribe messaging,* or simply *pub/sub,* as illustrated in Figure 3.3. With publish-and-subscribe messaging, once a consumer has subscribed to the applicable subject, each message is simply handed to the consumer when they arrive. Nothing has to be done to get, or pull, the message.

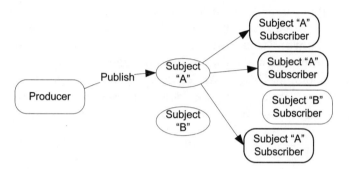

FIGURE 3.3 With publish-and-subscribe messaging, listener components subscribe to a subject to receive published messages.

In this paradigm, the subject is the basis for the message multicast. Messages are published by a producer to a subject, and consumers that have subscribed to that subject receive those messages. By combining the concepts of abstraction and anonymity, this powerful form of messaging is useful in a wide range of applications. Although it may seem contradictory, multicast messaging *can* be combined with request-and-reply messaging, allowing each consumer to reply to a message's publisher. This is usually implemented by adding a special reply subject to the message, allowing a consumer to itself publish a message back to the original producer. We'll explore the details of how this is implemented using JMS later in this chapter.

The multicast messaging concept, although elegant, suffers a drawback similar to request-and-reply messaging: message producer and consumer components must be operational during the entire messaging lifecycle for messages to be processed. The anonymity of this paradigm, which is an advantage, also means that the publisher is unaware if any consumers exist at all. What happens to published messages when there are no subscribers? An entirely new message paradigm needs to be defined to handle *off-line* messaging, where messages are not lost even if a consumer is not available when they are sent.

Queue-Based Messaging

Off-line message processing is typically implemented with *queue-based messaging*. In this paradigm, message producers define queues to send messages to, and consumers take messages off the queues they are interested in. If a consumer exists at the time a message is added to a queue, it is processed almost immediately. If not, the message will persist in the queue until a consumer is available. If multiple consumers exist, messages that are in the queue, or added to the queue, may be processed in parallel by each consumer.

Queue-based messaging offers all of the benefits of multicast messaging, including anonymity and abstraction (through the queue itself). It also adds a further level of abstraction and reliability by remaining functional even when message consumers go offline. This message paradigm typically supports either a one-to-one or a many-to-one relationship for message processing. Either way, the intent is for each message in a queue to get processed exactly once, as shown in Figure 3.4.

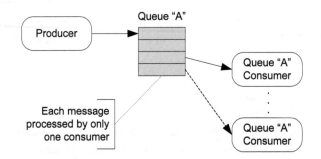

FIGURE 3.4 With queue-based messaging, messages are persisted in order and are each processed by only one consumer.

Regardless of the apparent advantages and disadvantages, each message paradigm has its own uniqueness that makes it useful in very specific messaging scenarios; no one is better than the others. For this reason, most enterprise messaging systems provide support for all three messaging paradigms, giving you the freedom to implement the right one on a case-by-case basis.

MESSAGE-ORIENTED MIDDLEWARE

The family of enterprise software systems that support the various forms of inter-component messaging just described is called *message-oriented middleware* (MOM). Most MOM software packages offer more than just queue-based, or publish-and-subscribe-based, messaging; they may include features such as:

- A specialized database for persistent message storage
- A built-in message communication protocol that includes algorithms for the best routing of messages in a WAN environment
- Transactional support for atomic messaging
- Message compression techniques to more efficiently transfer message data
- A robust distributed architecture to ensure reliable message delivery

Various MOM implementations (many proprietary) have been offered through the years, including TIBCO® Rendezvous®, IBM MQSeries® (now Websphere® MQ), Microsoft® Message Queue, Oracle® Advanced Queue, CORBA ORBs such as Iona® ORBIX®, transaction processing monitor packages such as BEA® Tuxedo™, and application servers such as IBM WebSphere. Although some of these packages began as proprietary, supporting only mainframes or single operating systems, most now include support for Sun's Enterprise Java standard of message, JMS. The only package mentioned that does not support JMS is Microsoft Message Queue, although it is being usurped by various Web Service communication protocols.

The Information Pipe

Overall, you can think of a MOM implementation as a huge pipe that spans networks, into which information is sent. We'll call this the *information pipe* (see Figure 3.5). Client applications tap this pipeline of information to receive the messages intended for them. Figure 3.5 conveys the important concept that the information pipe exists independent of the clients. Even if no messages are flowing, or no clients exist at that time, the pipe is still there. This often means that MOM software is implemented as a service or daemon that runs continuously on the computers that make up the pipeline.

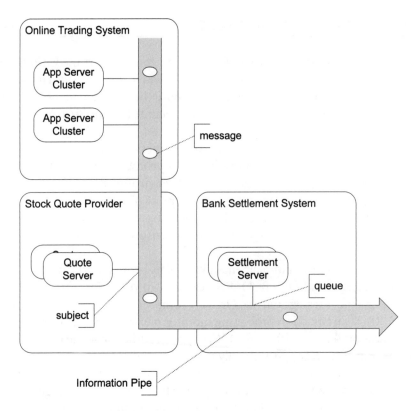

FIGURE 3.5 Messaging software forms the concept of a pipeline of information, within which messages flow around a network.

THE JAVA MESSAGE SERVICE (JMS)

JMS is a specification [Hapner02] that describes the properties and behavior of an information pipe for Java software. It also describes how Java client applications interact with the information pipe. These are two very important distinctions that must be understood before implementing JMS software. They are named a *JMS provider*, and a *JMS application*:

JMS Provider: This is a MOM implementation that adheres to the JMS specification for message definition, delivery, storage, processing, and error handling. It is the implementation of the message pipe itself, not the software that uses it. The specification suggests, but does not require, that JMS providers be written as 100% pure Java applications. The intent is to allow the provider to be as platform independent as the Java software that uses it.

JMS Application: Sometimes called a JMS client, this is the Java software that uses a JMS provider to send and receive messages over an information pipe. This software can be any application, small or large, that generates or processes messages. The JMS application generally has no knowledge of the implementation behind the information pipe itself (the JMS provider); it's developed using the JMS interfaces as defined in the JMS specification.

All communication with the specific JMS provider is abstracted by the *JMS API*, as shown in Figure 3.6. This means that a JMS application's code is not customized for a specific JMS provider and should work with any provider without modification. Because of the thoroughness of the JMS specification, you should experience a great deal of consistency in the behavior of the various JMS providers on the market. Some providers will be faster than others, or a vendor may use message routing algorithms that make the use of their product more efficient than others.

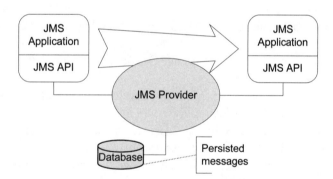

FIGURE 3.6   In JMS, applications communicate through a JMS provider, using the JMS API as an abstraction layer.

JMS supports the message paradigms described earlier in this chapter—request-and-reply, publish-and-subscribe, and queues—although JMS refers to them as *domains*. The remainder of this chapter will focus on JMS and how to apply the concepts that were just described to your Java software. You can download the latest JMS specification, currently at version 1.1, from Sun at *http://java.sun.com/ products/jms/*.

JMS Providers

Many JMS providers are implemented as part of a J2EE™-compliant application server. The current list of Sun licensed JMS-compliant application servers includes:

- BEA WebLogic (*www.bea.com*)
- IBM WebSphere (*www.ibm.com/software/integration/wmq*)
- Oracle Application Server 10g™ (*www.oracle.com/appserver*)
- JBoss™ Application Server (*www.jboss.org*)
- Macromedia® JRun™ (*www.macromedia.com/software/jrun*)

The JMS specification includes a section dedicated to application server facilities for messaging support. This includes issues such as concurrency, resource pooling, and distributed transaction support. Another item specific to application server messaging is that of message-driven beans, which are special enterprise JavaBean objects that are activated when JMS messages arrive for them. Message-driven beans are covered in detail in Chapter 4, "Advanced Java Messaging."

Standalone JMS providers exist as well, making JMS accessible to non-EJB software such as Java Servlets and standalone Java applications. JMS providers may also be integrated with application servers using the J2EE Connector Architecture (JCA; see sidebar). The current list of Sun licensed JMS providers includes:

- The Sun Java System Message Queue (*www.sun.com/software/products/message_queue*)
- TIBCO Enterprise Message Service™ (*www.tibco.com/software/enterprise_backbone/enterprisemessageservice.jsp*)
- Sonic Software® SonicMQ® (*www.sonicsoftware.com/products/sonicmq*)
- Pramati® Server (*www.pramati.com*)
- SeeBeyond™ eGate™ Integrator (*www.seebeyond.com/software/egate.asp*)
- Novel® exteNd® (formerly SilverStream) (*www.novell.com/products/extend*)

There also exist some notable JMS providers that are not official Sun JMS licensees. These providers support the JMS specification (in whole or in part) nonetheless, and they include:

- FioranoMQ™ (*www.fiorano.com/products/fmq*)
- Softwired™ iBus™ product family (*www.softwired-inc.com*)
- SwiftMQ™ (*www.swiftmq.com*)

Finally, there are also some open-source JMS providers that are worth noting, although they are also not official Sun JMS licensees:

- SourceForge™ OpenJMS (*openjms.sourceforge.net*)
- Codehaus® ActiveMQ (*activemq.codehaus.org*)
- ObjectWeb® JORAM (*joram.objectweb.org*)

THE J2EE CONNECTOR ARCHITECTURE

The *J2EE Connector Architecture* (JCA) specification defines a standard pattern for building resource adapters that allow J2EE application servers to connect to external information systems. A resource adapter is analogous to a hardware device driver that allows a computer's operating system to communicate to the hardware device it is connected to, except in this case, we have external software systems and data providers that we want to connect to a J2EE application server. By defining a standard resource adapter architecture, application server vendors do not need to rewrite their data access layer code; they simply write to the standard once, and it will work with all data providers that adhere to the same standard.

Version 1.5 of the JCA specification (*http://java.sun.com/j2ee/connector*) defines the following set of contracts for integration between a data provider and an application server:

Connection management: The contract defined by the resource adapter standard

Security: Provides authorization and authentication information for the data provider

Lifecycle management: Defines the creation/destruction envelope for a data provider

Work management: An optional contract whereby the data provider can defer processing of a submitted "job" to the application server, which provides the resources (such as thread pools) to get the job done

Transaction management: The contract that defines the distribution and coordination of transactions from the data provider to the application server and with other data providers

Transaction inflow: A standard way of allowing the data provider to serve its own started transactions back into the application server

Message inflow: The contract that defines the distribution of messages to destinations using the application server's messaging facilities

$\rightarrow$

> In short, the JCA provides a standard interface—the Common Client Interface—into which the application server can call data providers it was never built to specifically know about. Thus, it provides a plug-in-based extension model for third-party database vendors, legacy system maintainers, and proprietary software systems to be able to access the world of enterprise Java software.

Codehaus ActiveMQ Message Broker

The samples in this book were written and tested with the open source JMS provider from Codehaus, called ActiveMQ. You can download the latest provider at *http://activemq.codehaus.org/download*; the latest release as of this writing is version 2.1. Once downloaded, you install ActiveMQ simply by extracting the contents of the zip file to a directory of your choice. The scripts to run the sample applications from this book assume the directory is /java/activemq, for both Windows and UNIX.

Codehaus calls their JMS provider the ActiveMQ Message Broker. To run the message broker on Windows, launch the following file:

```
/java/activemq/bin/activemq.bat
```

For UNIX, launch the following file (make sure the execute bit is set):

```
./java/activemq/bin/activemq &
```

In both cases, let the broker run in the background while you try the samples from the book. To stop the message broker on Windows, simply type ctrl-c in the command prompt window that it's running in. For UNIX, you'll need to use the kill command with the message broker's process ID. Before we get into any more details of ActiveMQ and the sample JMS applications, let's discuss the JMS interfaces and classes.

JMS Interfaces

The JMS API is composed of many Java interfaces with a hierarchy of relationships. The hierarchy in particular is extensive and may seem confusing at first glance (Figure 3.7 illustrates the relationships among the interfaces within JMS). However, this complexity is necessary for JMS to:

- Abstract the implementation details of the underlying messaging software
- Interface with existing messaging systems using familiar JavaBean patterns
- Provide and enforce thread-safe code practices
- Support integration with other platforms and non-JMS messaging systems

As a JMS application developer, you should use the domain-independent, common interfaces, as shown in Figure 3.7. However, JMS does provide domain-specific interfaces. If your code is meant to work only with one message domain, you may choose to use the interfaces specific to that domain—but again, this is not encouraged. The following sections describe the domain-specific interfaces and their relationships with the common interfaces.

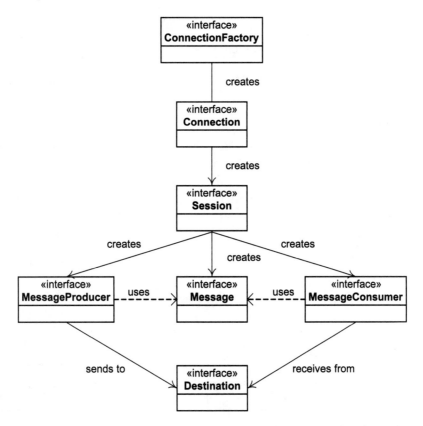

FIGURE 3.7   This UML class diagram represents the JMS interface hierarchy.

javax.jms.ConnectionFactory

To use JMS, you first must get an active connection to your JMS provider. Through JNDI (see sidebar), retrieve the `javax.jms.ConnectionFactory` object, which you'll use to get this connection in the form of a `javax.jms.Connection` object. Figure 3.8 shows the `ConnetionFactory` interface, which contains two methods to create a `Connection` object. One method takes a user name and password to create a `Connection` object using the specified user's identity. The other uses the default user identity. The affects of (and potential restrictions to) using the default user identity depend upon the JMS provider you are using, as well as settings applied by your JMS system administrator.

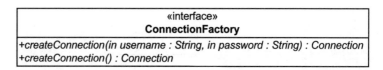

FIGURE 3.8 The JMS `ConnectionFactory` interface with its available methods.

Your JMS application code should be written to use the `ConnectionFactory` interface, regardless of whether it will use a topic or a queue. However, as stated in the previous sections, if your code is meant to work only with one message domain, you may choose to use the interfaces specific to that domain. For this reason, JMS provides the `TopicConnectionFactory` and `QueueConnectionFactory` subinterfaces, as shown in Figure 3.9.

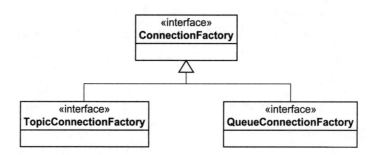

FIGURE 3.9 This UML diagram shows the `ConnectionFactory` interface and its subinterfaces.

`ConnectionFactory` objects are administered objects. This gives application designers control over connection configuration parameters, such as which servers manage client connections, in addition to message routing information. These parameters are typically defined by an administrator using an administration console provided by the JMS provider.

JAVA NAMING AND DIRECTORY INTERFACE (JNDI)

Directory services provide a naming facility designed to give human-readable labels to computer resources. In general, these resources can be users, applications, computers, networks, and other services. In the case of JNDI, the resources are Java components. JNDI allows developers to attach their own Java objects to a namespace. It also allows applications to find implementations of particular services based on a standard naming convention.

JMS uses the facilities of JNDI to allow client applications to access a provider's implementation of JMS without knowing the details of the provider. For instance, a JMS application can be coded to use JNDI to instantiate an instance of the `javax.jms.TopicConnectionFactory` class. The application does not need to be coded to use a particular vendor's JMS provider. Later, if the user of the JMS application decides to use a different JMS provider, the application will work seamlessly with no code changes. However, this does assume that both JMS providers adhere to the JNDI specification.

How Does JNDI Work?

JNDI provides a mechanism to map names to Java objects. The code in Listing 3.1 is a simple example of how JNDI can be used to get an instance of a JMS `ConnectionFactory` object specifically.

LISTING 3.1   Sample JNDI Code

```
// props contains JMS provider information
Hashtable props = new Hashtable();
props.put(
  Context.PROVIDER_URL,
  "rmi://localhost:1099/JndiServer");

props.put(
  Context.INITIAL_CONTEXT_FACTORY,
  "org.codehaus.activemq.jndi.ActiveMQInitialContextFactory");
Context jndiContext = new InitialContext(props);
```

→

```
ConnectionFactory connFactory =
            (ConnectionFactory)jndiContext.lookup(
                "ConnectionFactory");
```

The first step is to retrieve a JNDI Context object reference. To do this you must provide the URL to the JNDI provider's server and the name of the provider's initial context factory. The next step is to instantiate a new InitialContext object with the JNDI provider's properties. Then, you can use the JNDI Context reference to obtain references to objects in the provider's object tree via the lookup method. In the case of a JMS provider, some of the objects in this tree are TopicConnectionFactory, QueueConnectionFactory, Destination, Topic, and Queue.

javax.jms.Connection

A JMS javax.jms.Connection object encapsulates an open, working, connection with the JMS provider's server software. The Connection object is used to create javax.jms.Session objects, each of which represents a single-threaded conversation with a JMS provider that allows you to send or receive messages. When a Session object is created, your application can specify whether or not it is a transacted session, as well as specifying the *acknowledge mode*. The acknowledge mode can be either automatic, where message producers are automatically notified of message receipt, or client-based, where the message consumer code must explicitly acknowledge receipt of messages based on its own criteria.

Your application should only require one Connection object—regardless of the number of threads in your application that need to use it—as it is thread-safe, and it's a relatively resource-intense object. Creating multiple Connection objects in your application is usually considered wasteful, unless you have a good reason to do so.

The Connection interface allows your code to do more than just create Session objects. Other important methods on the interface (see Figure 3.10) include start and stop, which start and stop message delivery for all clients of the connection, and setExceptionListener. This method allows you to provide an ExceptionListener object that is notified if any problems occur with the connection to the JMS provider.

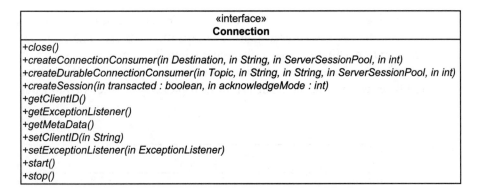

«interface»
Connection

+*close()*
+*createConnectionConsumer(in Destination, in String, in ServerSessionPool, in int)*
+*createDurableConnectionConsumer(in Topic, in String, in String, in ServerSessionPool, in int)*
+*createSession(in transacted : boolean, in acknowledgeMode : int)*
+*getClientID()*
+*getExceptionListener()*
+*getMetaData()*
+*setClientID(in String)*
+*setExceptionListener(in ExceptionListener)*
+*start()*
+*stop()*

FIGURE 3.10   The JMS Connection interface with its available methods.

Figure 3.11 shows the publish-and-subscribe and queue-specific Connection interfaces offered by JMS. These interfaces inherit all of their behavior from the common Connection interface and provide no additional benefits if used.

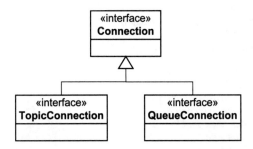

FIGURE 3.11   This UML diagram shows the Connection interface and its subinterfaces.

javax.jms.Session

Only one thread at a time may use a javax.jms.Session object; therefore, you will want to create one per thread in your application. Typically this amounts to creating one Session object for each message producer and consumer thread in your application per domain. The Session object also acts as an object factory. Use it to create javax.jms.MessageProducer objects to send messages, javax.jms.MessageConsumer objects to receive messages, and the javax.jms.Message objects themselves.

Besides the numerous methods used to create messages, producers, and consumers, the `Session` interface also contains methods (see Figure 3.12) that create temporary destinations (described later), handle transactions, set up durable subscriptions, and create queue browsers (components that read, but do not remove, messages within a `Queue`). The last three topics will be discussed in Chapter 4.

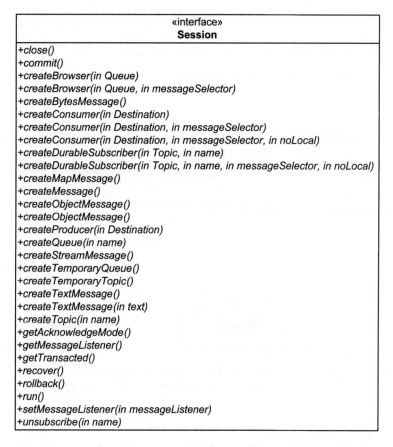

«interface»
Session
+close()
+commit()
+createBrowser(in Queue)
+createBrowser(in Queue, in messageSelector)
+createBytesMessage()
+createConsumer(in Destination)
+createConsumer(in Destination, in messageSelector)
+createConsumer(in Destination, in messageSelector, in noLocal)
+createDurableSubscriber(in Topic, in name)
+createDurableSubscriber(in Topic, in name, in messageSelector, in noLocal)
+createMapMessage()
+createMessage()
+createObjectMessage()
+createObjectMessage()
+createProducer(in Destination)
+createQueue(in name)
+createStreamMessage()
+createTemporaryQueue()
+createTemporaryTopic()
+createTextMessage()
+createTextMessage(in text)
+createTopic(in name)
+getAcknowledgeMode()
+getMessageListener()
+getTransacted()
+recover()
+rollback()
+run()
+setMessageListener(in messageListener)
+unsubscribe(in name)

FIGURE 3.12 The JMS `Session` interface with its available methods.

Figure 3.13 shows the publish-and-subscribe and queue-specific `Session` interfaces offered by JMS. These interfaces inherit all of their behavior from the common `Session` interface, and provide no additional benefits if used.

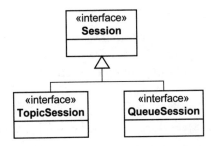

FIGURE 3.13 This UML diagram shows the `Session` interface and its subinterfaces.

javax.jms.Destination

A `javax.jms.Destination` object is an administered object that represents the message pipe destination itself, such as a publish-and-subscribe topic or a point-to-point queue. Typically, these objects are defined and created from an administrative tool before the applications that use them are executed—hence the term *administered object*. This gives application designers control over the existence and locations of topics and queues in an application that are distributed across many machines over a network, possibly even the Internet. It also allows for the creation of `Destination` hierarchies, with specialized destination address rules, such as the use of wildcards to send and receive messages for sets of `Destinations`.

Although it may seem logical to create domain-specific `Destination` objects in your client code (see Figure 3.14), you should still use the common interface, `Destination`. Since it is an administered object, a `Destination`'s message domain is defined by an administrator, not by whether a producer or consumer accesses it through a `Topic` or `Queue` interface.

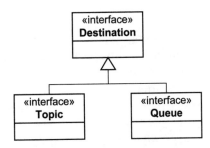

FIGURE 3.14 This UML diagram shows the Destination interface and its subinterfaces.

javax.jms.Message

There are no domain-specific messages, but there are, instead, content-specific messages (see Figure 3.15). There are `javax.jms.Message`-derived interfaces for sending messages of different types, such as:

`javax.jms.TextMessage`:   Used to send plain-text messages.

`javax.jms.ObjectMessage`:   Used to send opaque, `serializable` object messages.

`javax.jms.MapMessage`:   Used to send messages that contain collections of key-based data, also known as name-value pairs.

`javax.jms.StreamMessage`:   Used to send messages whose data is filled and re-read sequentially, in a certain order.

`javax.jms.BytesMessage`:   A special message type that allows you to embed your data as a stream of uninterpreted bytes. This is typically used when interfacing with other message systems, or legacy software systems, that do not directly support JMS.

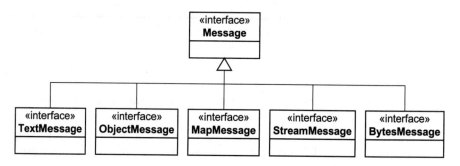

FIGURE 3.15   This UML diagram shows the hierarchy of Message interfaces.

With the array of message types supported by JMS, you can write JMS applications that equally support sending Java objects as data, XML data, or even raw data. One message type in particular (`BytesMessage`) allows your application to communicate with software written in other languages, on a variety of operating systems. Regardless of message type, all messages are composed of the following parts:

Message header: All messages contain the *same* set of message header fields, which can be assigned or read using JavaBean-style setter and getter methods. These fields contain information useful to the JMS provider and client application in the routing and identification of a message.

Message properties: A message can contain application-specific property fields (implemented as name–value pairs) that serve as custom message header fields. Properties may be used for message filtering, specialized message routing within a JMS application, or any other reason an application may have for defining them.

Message body: This is the message payload, or simply the message data, to be delivered. The form of the body itself (text, object, etc.) is what varies among the various `Message` interface types.

The use and structure of JMS messages are discussed in detail later in this chapter.

javax.jms.MessageProducer

A JMS application creates a `javax.jms.MessageProducer` by calling the method `createProducer` on the `Session` interface, where a `Destination` object is provided as a parameter. The returned `MessageProducer` object is used to send messages to the `Destination` provided. An application can create a producer without specifying any `Destination` object at all. In this case, a `Destination` will need to be specified each time the producer sends a message. This functionality allows you to create generic, stateless message producer components.

Figure 3.16 shows all of the methods on the `MessageProducer` interface. The JMS client application has many options when sending a message. The destination, delivery mode (persistent or nonpersistent), message priority, and message time-to-live values can be specified as each message is sent. However, if these values are

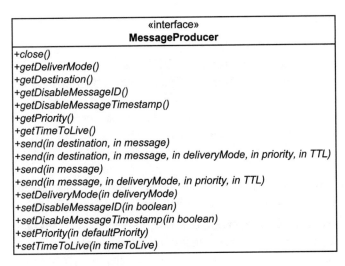

FIGURE 3.16   This is the JMS MessageProducer interface with its available methods.

to remain the same for each message—which will most likely be the case—the client application can set the default values for these properties by calling the methods setDeliveryMode, setPriority, and setTimeToLive at any point. These default values will be used unless specifically overridden in the send method call.

The methods setDisableMessageID and setDisableMessageTimestamp suggest to the JMS provider that it can stop generating message IDs and timestamps with each message that is sent by this message producer. This can be done to increase performance if the application does not use these message header fields.

Figure 3.17 shows the message domain-specific MessageProducer interfaces TopicPublisher and QueueSender. These can be used when your application wants to enforce (and hence hard-code) the use of a Topic or Queue as a Destination.

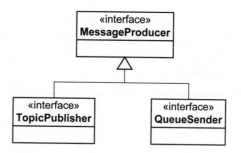

FIGURE 3.17   This UML diagram shows the MessageProducer interface and its subinterfaces.

javax.jms.MessageConsumer

A JMS application creates a javax.jms.MessageConsumer by calling the method createConsumer on the Session object, where a Destination object is provided as a parameter. The returned MessageConsumer object is used to receive messages from the Destination provided. Unlike with a MessageProducer, you must specify a valid Destination object when creating a MessageConsumer object.

The Session interface defines three methods to create a MessageConsumer:

createConsumer(Destination dest):   This method creates a MessageConsumer that is to receive messages for the supplied Destination.

createConsumer(Destination dest, String messageSelector):   This method creates a MessageConsumer that is to receive messages for the supplied Destination, using the given String as a message selector. Only messages that match the message selector's filter criteria will be delivered.

`createConsumer(Destination dest, String, Boolean noLocal):` This method is the same as the previous, with one additional restriction. If the `noLocal` parameter is set to `true`, this consumer will not receive messages sent by producers created from the same `Connection`. This basically means that consumers created with `noLocal` equal to `true` will not receive messages from producers in the same process, if the process uses only one `Connection`.

The `MessageConsumer` interface (see Figure 3.18) contains about half as many methods as the `MessageProducer` interface. A consumer can receive messages two ways: synchronously and asynchronously. For synchronous message delivery, a call is made to one of the `receive` methods. For asynchronous delivery, the consumer can either poll for messages by calling `receiveNoWait` or provide a callback object that implements the `javax.jms.MessageLisentener` interface by calling `setMessageListener`. This interface, along with asynchronous message delivery, will be discussed in more detail later in this chapter.

As with the rest of the JMS hierarchy, Figure 3.19 shows the domain-specific `MessageConsumer` interfaces `TopicSubscriber` and `QueueReceiver`. Again, the common interfaces should always be used, but the domain-specific interfaces can be used when your application wants to enforce (and hence hard-code) the use of a `Topic` or `Queue` as a `Destination`.

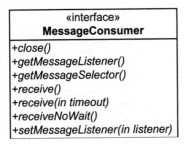

FIGURE 3.18 This is the JMS `MessageConsumer` interface with its available methods.

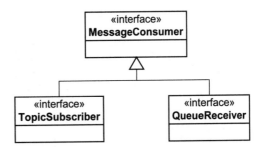

FIGURE 3.19 This UML diagram shows the `MessageConsumer` interface and its subinterfaces.

SYNCHRONOUS AND ASYNCHRONOUS DELIVERY

If a message consumer wishes to receive messages synchronously, it must call the `MessageConsumer.receive` method with or without a timeout value (specified in milliseconds). This method will block indefinitely if a timeout value is not provided, otherwise the call will block until a message is received or the wait time surpasses the timeout value. Figure 3.20 shows the sequence of method calls between a client application and a JMS provider for synchronous message delivery. In this sequence, the following steps occur:

1. The client application calls receive on the MessageConsumer object. This call blocks until a message is received.
2. A message producer calls the MessageProducer.send method to send a message to the same destination that the MessageConsumer from the first step is listening to. This method call returns without blocking.
3. The JMS provider sends a message notification (with the message itself) to the MessageConsumer object.
4. The receive method from step 1 finally returns, returning a JMS Message object.

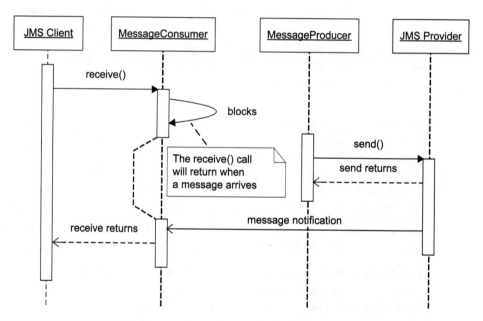

FIGURE 3.20 This UML diagram shows the method call sequence for a synchronous message consumer.

Asynchronous message delivery in JMS is achieved when the JMS provider calls a method on a callback reference provided by a message consumer. The callback reference must be an object that implements the javax.jms.MessageListener interface. The only method defined by this interface is onMessage, which provides the message through a parameter defined as `javax.jms.Message`. The `MessageConsumer` object will call the `MessageListener` object's implementation of this method when a message arrives. Figure 3.21 shows the sequence of method calls between a client application and a JMS provider for asynchronous message delivery. In this sequence, the following steps occur:

1. The JMS client provides a `MessageListener` object reference in the method call `MessageConsumer.setMessageListener`. This method returns without blocking.
2. A message producer calls the `MessageProducer.send` method to send a message to the same destination that the `MessageConsumer` from the first step is listening to. This method call returns without blocking.
3. The JMS provider sends a message notification (with the message) to the `MessageConsumer` object.
4. The `MessageConsumer` object calls the `onMessage` method on the `MessageListener` object provided in step 1. The JMS `Message` is delivered as a parameter to the call.

The sample application described later in this chapter contains code examples that implement both synchronous and asynchronous message consumers.

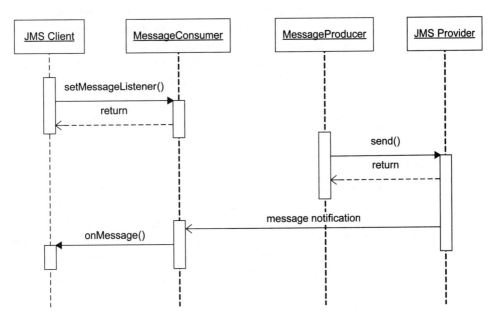

FIGURE 3.21 This UML diagram shows the method call sequence for an asynchronous message consumer.

JMS MESSAGE OBJECTS

The sole purpose of enterprise message-oriented middleware systems is to deliver data in the form of messages. As we've already seen, JMS defines many types of messages to ensure that your data will be transported efficiently to almost any messaging system running on virtually any computer in the world. Since we've already covered the types of messages that can be sent, let's dive into the Message object structure in more detail now.

Message Body

The message body contains the payload of the message: the data. For the JMS client application, this is the most important part of the message, but it is left untouched by the JMS provider. All messages, when they are received, are in a read-only state. Any attempt to modify a message that has been delivered will result in a MessageNotWritableException. However, a message's entire body can be cleared by calling Message.clearBody. This method does not affect a message's properties; to clear those, you must call Message.clearProperties. You may choose to call these methods to clear a message once it has been received and processed if its contents are large or resource-intense in some way.

JMS purposely does not specify how the message body is to be implemented by the JMS provider. This flexibility allows the provider to choose the most efficient implementation to store and deliver the data within the messages. However, JMS does specify the structure of a message by offering various forms of message interfaces: TextMessage, ObjectMessage, MapMessage, StreamMessage, or BytesMessage.

Each message interface derives from the common base, Message. Although this base interface does not define a payload, it still can be sent to a destination like any other message. It's typically used as a distributed event notification, where just the arrival of the message is meaningful. Let's look at each message subtype and examine how they are used within a JMS application.

TextMessage

The payload of this message type is a java.lang.String object. Although this message is useful in sending text-based description messages to listeners (such as "The system will be shutting down"), its real strength is in its ability to transport XML data. XML-based messages have an advantage in that they are self-describing, flexible, and platform agnostic. Figure 3.22 is a class diagram showing the methods available on the TextMessage interface.

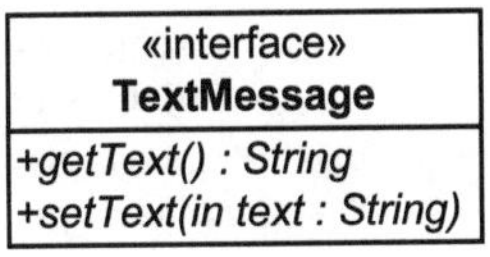

```
            «interface»
            TextMessage
+getText() : String
+setText(in text : String)
```

FIGURE 3.22 The UML class diagram for the `TextMessage` interface.

Creating and sending a `TextMessage` is very straightforward. Listing 3.2 shows code that assembles a text message to send XML data.

LISTING 3.2 Sending a JMS `TextMessage` Object

```
String xmlStr = "<LastTradePrice><Stock>";
xmlStr += "<Name>SUNW</Name>";
xmlStr += "<Quote>4.13</Quote>";
xmlStr += "</Stock></LastTradePrice>";
// Send the text message
TextMessage txtMsg = session.createTextMessage();
txtMsg.setText( xmlStr );
producer.send( txtMsg );
```

The text in this example is a simple XML structure that contains the last-trade price for the stock ticker representing Sun Microsystems. A new `TextMessage` object is created using a `Session` object. The XML string is set as the message payload via the call to `setText`, and the producer's `send` method is called to deliver the message. When received, the message consumer simply calls `getText` to retrieve the text content of the message.

ObjectMessage

The payload of an `ObjectMessage` is a serializable Java object. This can be a single object that implements the `java.io.serializable` interface or a set of serializable objects contained within one of the Java collection classes, such as `java.util.Vector`. Figure 3.23 is a class diagram showing the methods available on the `ObjectMessage` interface.

Being able to send entire Java objects as messages enables you to build applications with a true, distributed object model. It's nice that you aren't *required* to convert your application's Java objects into streams of BYTEs to communicate using

```
              «interface»
            ObjectMessage
+getObject() : java.io.Serializable
+setObject(in object : java.io.Serializable)
```

FIGURE 3.23   UML class diagram for the ObjectMessage interface.

JMS. This allows you to maintain a pure object-oriented design, without compromise, for your distributed application. Listing 3.3 shows just how easy it is to send and receive an object using JMS' ObjectMessage interface.

LISTING 3.3   Sending and Receiving a JMS ObjectMessage

```
// ObjectMessage producer code
StockQuote quote = getLastTradePrice("SUNW");
ObjectMessage objMsg = session.createObjectMessage();
objMsg.setObject( quote );
producer.send( objMsg );
...
// ObjectMessage consumer code
ObjectMessage objMsg = (ObjectMessage)message;
StockQuote quote = (StockQuote)objMsg.getObject();
```

The object in this example represents a stock quote for Sun Microsystems. The ObjectMessage that is transported via JMS acts as a container for the original object. The JMS application does not need to perform any serialization or Java IO in any form to send and receive the original object.

MapMessage

A JMS MapMessage allows a JMS application to send data as name-value pairs, where a String is used as the key and a Java primitive is used as the data for each pair. Figure 3.24 is a class diagram showing the methods available on the MapMessage interface.

A MapMessage can store as many name–value pairs as the application requires, with no particular ordering of the data. This means the message sender can set the data items in the MapMessage in one order, yet the receiver can read all *or part* of the data in a different order. Often, the message receiver has some idea of the keys used for the data in the message and can therefore pull out the values using the known keys. Table 3.1 shows the result if, for some reason, a call is made to retrieve a data value using a key that is not in the MapMessage object for each get method.

```
                    «interface»
                    MapMessage
+getBoolean(in name : String) : boolean
+getByte(in name : String) : byte
+getBytes(in name : String) : bytes[]
+getChar(in name : String) : char
+getDouble(in name : String) : double
+getFloat(in name : String) : float
+getInt(in name : String) : int
+getLong(in name : String) : long
+getObject(in name : String) : Object
+getShort(in name : String) : short
+getString(in name : String) : String
+setBoolean(in name : String, in value : boolean)
+setByte(in name : String, in value : byte)
+setBytes(in name : String, in value : bytes[])
+setBytes(in name : String, in value : bytes[], in offset : int, in length : int)
+setChar(in name : String, in value : char)
+setDouble(in name : String, in value : double)
+setFloat(in name : String, in value : float)
+setInt(in name : String, in value : int)
+setLong(in name : String, in value : long)
+setObject(in name : String, in value : Object)
+setShort(in name : String, in value : short)
+setString(in name : String, in value : String)
+getMapNames() : Enumeration
+itemExists(in name : String) : boolean
```

FIGURE 3.24 UML class diagram for the `MapMessage` interface.

TABLE 3.1 The Result of Getting Data for a Nonexistent Key

Method	Result
getString	`null` is returned
getObject	`null` is returned
getBoolean	`false` is returned
getChar	A `NullPointerException` is thrown
getBytes	The value of 0 is returned
getShort	The value of 0 is returned
getLong	The value of 0 is returned
getByte	The value of 0 is returned
getFloat	The value of 0 is returned
getDouble	The value of 0 is returned

Listing 3.4 shows sample code to populate and send a `MapMessage` via JMS. Although it's not as convenient as sending a Java object, populating a `MapMessage` object is still easy. The receiver is then free to retrieve and store the data contained within the message as it sees fit.

LISTING 3.4   Code to Populate and Send a JMS `MapMessage`

```
MapMessage mapMsg = session.createMapMessage();
mapMsg.setString("stock", "MSFT");
mapMsg.setDouble("quote", 25.67);
mapMsg.setLong("volume", 67595725);
mapMsg.setBoolean("active", true);
producer.send( mapMsg );
```

Listing 3.5 shows sample code for a receiver of a `MapMessage`. Calls are made to get the data from the `MapMessage` object using known keys. Take a moment to examine the two statements in bold. In the first bold statement, a call is made to get the name of company using the key "companyname" which was never set by the message producer. The result is not an error, but it will be as though a null value were set for the nonexistent key. If the receiver has any doubt that a name–value pair exists in the message, a call to `MapMessage.itemExists`, passing the key as the parameter, can be used to verify.

LISTING 3.5   A `MapMessage` Consumer

```
MapMessage mapMsg = (MapMessage)message;
String stock = mapMsg.getString("stock");
String company = mapMsg.getString("companyname");
String quote = mapMsg.getString("quote");
long volume = mapMsg.getLong("volume");
boolean active = mapMsg.getBoolean("active");
```

In the second bold statement, the data for the key "quote" is retrieved as a `String`, yet the producer set it as a `double`. This is not an error; JMS allows data that is set as one Java type to be retrieved as a different Java type for convenience. In this example, the developer felt it was easier to deal with the quote as a `String`, as opposed to a `double`. Table 3.2 illustrates all of the valid `MapMessage` data conversions. In this table, a data item written as a row type can be read as a column type. For example, if a data item is added to a message as type `short`, it can be read as type `short`, `int`, `long`, or `String`. These conversions also apply to the JMS `StreamMessage` interface, described in the next section.

If a conversion is attempted that is not supported, the JMS provider will throw a `MessageFormatException`. For the cases where a `String` is converted to a numeric value, the `String` must be formatted correctly for the conversion, or a `NumberFormatException` will be thrown.

TABLE 3.2 Valid `MapMessage` and `StreamMessage` Data Conversions

Written as	Read as
boolean	String, boolean
byte	byte, short, int, long, String
short	short, int, long, String
char	char, String
int	int, long, String
long	long, String
float	float, double, String
double	double, String
String	boolean, byte, short, int, long, flat, double, String
byte[]	byte[]

Listing 3.6 shows sample code for a receiver that is coded to discover the name–value data pairs dynamically when a `MapMessage` is received.

LISTING 3.6 Code to Retrieve Unknown Name–Value Pairs from a JMS `MapMessage`

```
MapMessage mapMsg = (MapMessage)message;
java.util.Enumeration keys = mapMsg.getMapNames();
while (keys.hasMoreElements() ) {
    String key = (String)keys.nextElement();
    String data = mapMsg.getString(key);
    // do something useful with the data...
}
```

The `MapMessage.getMapNames` method returns a `java.util.Enumeration` object containing the keys for all of the name–value pairs contained within the `MapMessage`. Each key is pulled from the enumeration in a loop and used to retrieve the associated data value. In a real application, the data could be used to populate a list, create an HTML table, and so on.

StreamMessage

A JMS `StreamMessage` allows a client application to store data sequentially, requiring that the data be read from the message in the same order that it was written.

With this message type, data is *not* stored using name–value pairs. Instead, calls are made to the various `write` methods. The particular `write` method that is called must match the Java type of the data being written to the message. Figure 3.25 is a class diagram showing the methods available on the `StreamMessage` interface.

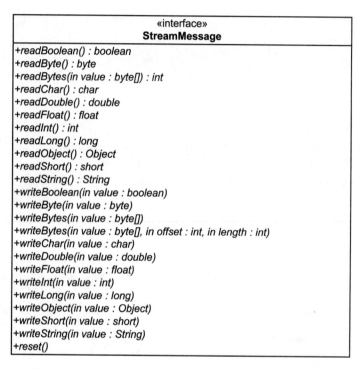

«interface»
StreamMessage
+readBoolean() : boolean
+readByte() : byte
+readBytes(in value : byte[]) : int
+readChar() : char
+readDouble() : double
+readFloat() : float
+readInt() : int
+readLong() : long
+readObject() : Object
+readShort() : short
+readString() : String
+writeBoolean(in value : boolean)
+writeByte(in value : byte)
+writeBytes(in value : byte[])
+writeBytes(in value : byte[], in offset : int, in length : int)
+writeChar(in value : char)
+writeDouble(in value : double)
+writeFloat(in value : float)
+writeInt(in value : int)
+writeLong(in value : long)
+writeObject(in value : Object)
+writeShort(in value : short)
+writeString(in value : String)
+reset()

FIGURE 3.25   UML class diagram for the `StreamMessage` interface.

When a message producer has created a `StreamMessage`, it is in a write-only state; any attempt to read from the message will result in a `MessageNotReadableException`. Conversely, when a message consumer receives the message, it is in a read-only state; any attempt to write to the message will result in a `MessageNotWriteableException`. The same conversion rules for reading data from a `MapMessage` object also apply to a `StreamMessage` object, as shown in Table 3.1 and Table 3.2.

Listing 3.7 shows sample code for a message producer that adds quote data to a `StreamMessage`. Again, the data is stored within the message object in the order that the `write` calls are made. Therefore, not only does the message consumer need to know the data types stored within the message (to call the correct `read` methods), it must also know the order in which the data was written.

LISTING 3.7   Code to Populate and Send a JMS `StreamMessage`

```
StreamMessage streamMsg = session.createStreamMessage();
streamMsg.writeString("IBM"); // ticker
streamMsg.writeDouble(91.79); // quote
streamMsg.writeLong(4749200); // volume
streamMsg.writeBoolean(true); // active
producer.send( streamMsg );
```

The sample code for a message consumer to read the `StreamMessage` from the previous example is shown in Listing 3.8.

LISTING 3.8   Code for a `StreamMessage` Consumer

```
StreamMessage streamMsg = (StreamMessage)message;
String ticker = streamMsg.readString();
double quote = streamMsg.readDouble();
long volume = streamMsg.readLong();
boolean active = streamMsg.readBoolean();
```

For convenience, the `StreamMessage` interface allows Java primitive types other than `char` and `byte[]` to be read as a `String`. Also, data written as properly formatted `String` values can be read as Java primitive types, as shown below:

```
// Message producer
streamMsg.writeString("91.79");
...
// Message Consumer
double quote = streamMsg.readDouble();
```

A call to the method `reset` repositions the data stream to the beginning and places the message in the read-only state, even if the message was in a write-only state prior to the call. Afterwards, data can be read from the message as though it were just delivered, starting from the first data item that was written to the message. This may need to be done, for example, if an exception occurred within the `MessageConsumer` and it's uncertain which data item was last read. Another, more common scenario is when a message is redelivered by the JMS provider because of a possible lack of message acknowledgment on a previous delivery attempt. In this case, the client code is responsible for resetting the message.

A call to the method `clearBody` clears all data from the message and places it in the write-only state, regardless of the state prior to the call. Data can then be added to the message as though it were just created.

BytesMessage

A JMS provider is responsible for converting a message from either a non-Java client, or a non-JMS messaging system, into the appropriate JMS message type before it is delivered to a JMS client application. At the very least, the message will be delivered as a BytesMessage, which contains the raw BYTE stream of the original, non-JMS message. A JMS client application can then read the BYTE stream as Java primitive types using the read methods on the BytesMessage interface (see Figure 3.26). Of course, this assumes that the message consumer understands the layout and structure of the BYTEs within the message.

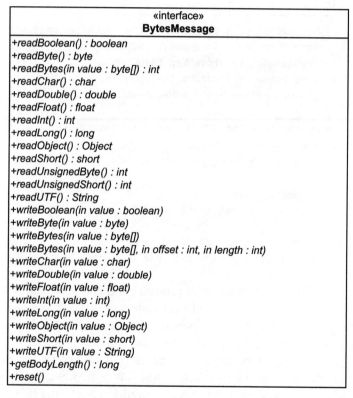

«interface»
BytesMessage
+readBoolean() : boolean
+readByte() : byte
+readBytes(in value : byte[]) : int
+readChar() : char
+readDouble() : double
+readFloat() : float
+readInt() : int
+readLong() : long
+readObject() : Object
+readShort() : short
+readUnsignedByte() : int
+readUnsignedShort() : int
+readUTF() : String
+writeBoolean(in value : boolean)
+writeByte(in value : byte)
+writeBytes(in value : byte[])
+writeBytes(in value : byte[], in offset : int, in length : int)
+writeChar(in value : char)
+writeDouble(in value : double)
+writeFloat(in value : float)
+writeInt(in value : int)
+writeLong(in value : long)
+writeObject(in value : Object)
+writeShort(in value : short)
+writeUTF(in value : String)
+getBodyLength() : long
+reset()

FIGURE 3.26   UML class diagram for the BytesMessage interface.

The same data conversion rules that apply for the StreamMessage and MapMessage message types also apply to the BytesMessage message type. The methods reset and clearBody work the same way.

There are some additional methods in the BytesMessage interface not seen in the other message types. For instance, there is a new method, getBodyLength, which returns the total number of BYTEs contained within the payload of the message object. This value can be used, for example, to allocate a byte array of the correct size to hold the data. The read and write methods of the BytesMessage interface match very closely to the StreamMessage and MapMessage interfaces. However, two additional read methods, readUnsignedByte and readUnsignedShort, have been added. Both methods return int values because the Java primitive types, byte and short, are signed. Therefore, they can not express the full value range of an unsigned byte and an unsigned short, respectively. Returning the values as the type int solves this problem.

Character strings are handled as UTF-compliant strings to support the platforms and string types of non-JMS messaging systems. Therefore, the methods readString and writeString are renamed readUTF and writeUTF, respectively.

The code to fill and read a BytesMessage is almost identical to that which uses the StreamMessage message type. Because of this, Listing 3.9 shows an abbreviated code sample to both send and receive quote data via a BytesMessage object.

LISTING 3.9   Sending and Receiving a BytesMessage Object

```
// Message producer code...
BytesMessage bytesMsg = session.createBytesMessage();
bytesMsg.writeUTF("IBM"); // ticker
bytesMsg.writeDouble(91.79); // quote
...
// Message consumer code...
BytesMessage bytesMsg = (BytesMessage)message;
String ticker = bytesMsg.readUTF();
double quote = bytesMsg.readDouble();
```

Message Header Fields

All JMS messages contain a standard set of headers. Most are set automatically by the JMS provider, while others can optionally be set by the JMS application. For the JMS-provider–set header fields, the setter methods yield no results if called by a JMS application. They are meant to be set by the JMS provider exclusively and are then read-only. JMS applications gain access to the data through the getter methods. The read-only message header fields that the provider sets are:

JMSDestination: The Destination to which this message was sent. Its intent is to allow a Message object to identify which Destination it was sent to. This comes in handy when a message consumer uses one implementation of the onMessage method to receive messages from multiple Destinations. Without it, it would be difficult to identify a message's destination.

JMSDeliveryMode: The delivery mode of the message: persistent or nonpersistent. This gives the message consumer some indication of what would happen if it failed while processing this message, allowing it to take steps to preserve the message if it deems it important to do so.

JMSMessageID: A value that uniquely identifies the message. Each message is assigned a unique message ID as it is sent, serving as a key for message identification in a historical repository or transaction log. Although the details of message ID value are provider specific, JMS does require that all IDs begin with the text "ID:" followed by a unique value or identifier. Example: "ID:200501201." Message producers can suggest that the provider turn ID generation off, hence saving the provider the processing time required to generate them.

JMSTimestamp: A timestamp, measured in milliseconds, representing the time that the message was handed off to the JMS provider—not the time it was delivered. Message producers can suggest that the provider turn timestamp generation off, hence saving the provider the processing time required to generate them.

JMSRedelivered: This value is set by the provider if the message is being redelivered because of the possible lack of a message acknowledgement on previous delivery. It is meant as an indicator to an application that the message may have already been delivered and it should take steps to avoid duplicate message processing

JMSExpiration: The expiration time (GMT) of the message. Although client applications should not receive expired messages, there are no guarantees it will not happen. Therefore, if this value is not zero (indicating no expiration), a client should compare it to the current GMT time to see if it has expired.

JMSPriority: A value from 0 to 9, indicating the priority of the message. In general, values of 0 through 4 are considered in the normal range, while values of 5 through 9 are considered high priority. JMS providers may use this value to support priority ordering of messages, but they are not required to.

In addition to the provider-set fields, some header fields can be optionally set by the JMS application (the message producer component specifically). Keep in mind that setting these header fields is optional and they are not required to be set by an application. However, these fields do allow an application to define some potentially useful information, including:

JMSType: An arbitrary value that is meant to identify the message data type. It may identify the message according to a provider's message repository, a database table name, or an application's arbitrary message type numbering scheme. Its main purpose is to provide compatibility with JMS providers and other message systems that require that message type identification be included with each message.

`JMSCorrelationID:`   An arbitrary value that allows an application to link one message to another. Typically, an application will set this value to the message ID of a previous message to associate the two messages. Some uses for this field include tagging a message as a reply—or an acknowledgement—to a previous message and coordinating communication among many producer/consumer components.

`JMSReplyTo:`   A `Destination` object that the message recipient is meant to send a reply message to. Although the presence of a `Destination` in this field indicates that the sender is expecting a message in reply, it is optional—the consumer does not *have* to send a reply.

Message Properties (Optional Header Fields)

The JMS `Message` interface provides support for message properties that serve as additional, optional message header values. Message properties are not meant to store data that would otherwise go into the message payload. JMS providers are typically built to handle data in the payload section of a message more efficiently than in the properties section. Instead, properties are mainly used in defining message selectors, which is discussed in detail in Chapter 4, "Advanced Java Messaging." There are three types of JMS message properties:

> **Custom properties:**   Application-defined properties that serve as custom header fields
>
> **JMS-defined properties:**   Optional properties defined in the JMS specification for all JMS messages
>
> **Provider-defined properties:**   Properties that a JMS provider sets and uses

Properties are added to a JMS message as name–value pairs, similar to the payload of a `MapMessage` object. Appropriately, message properties follow the same conversion rules outlined in Table 3.2. The only difference is that message properties are limited to the following types: `boolean`, `byte`, `short`, `int`, `long`, `float`, `double`, `String`, and `Object` (the conversion rules do not apply to `Object` properties). The types `char` and `byte[]` are *not* supported for message properties. The existence of a property can be verified by calling the `Message.propertyExists` method. The entire set of properties for a message can be iterated through by calling the method `Message.getPropertyNames`, which returns a `java.util.Enumeration` object.

JMS defines a set of properties, each beginning with the text *JMSX*, whose support by JMS providers is optional. The only mandatory properties are `JMSGroupID`, and JMSGroupSeq, which a JMS application can use to optionally group messages. The full set of JMS-defined properties includes:

JMSXUserID: The sending user identity; type String.

JMSXAppID: The sending application identity; type String.

JMSXDeliveryCount: The number of delivery attempts; type int.

JMSXGroupID: The message's group identifier; type String.

JMSXGroupSeq: The message's sequence number within its message group; type int.

JMSXProducerTXID: The transaction identifier within which this message was produced (sent); type String.

JMSXConsumerTXID: The transaction identifier within which this message was consumed (received); type String.

JMSXRcvTimestamp: The time the consumer received the message; type long.

JMSXState: Message state (for use within an optional message store) of type int, where the value of 1 indicates *waiting*, 2 indicates *ready*, 3 indicates *expired*, and 4 indicates *retained*. This property is not available to a message producer or consumer.

Message Selection

Although the details of JMS message selection are discussed in Chapter 4, this discussion of message properties warrants an introduction to the topic. *Message selection* is the term used to describe the ability of a message consumer to filter incoming messages based on some criteria. The criteria are defined in the message itself using message properties and are used by the JMS provider to filter out messages based on a MessageSelector object provided by the message consumer. The message selection is processed using a String that adheres to a rule-set based on a subset of the SQL92 expression syntax. It's important to remember that JMS message selection is performed using a MessageSelector object and a message object's properties only—the message body cannot be used in the filtering process.

JMS PUBLISH-AND-SUBSCRIBE

The publish-and-subscribe message domain is the JMS version of the multicast message paradigm discussed earlier in this chapter. With the JMS publish-and-subscribe (or pub/sub) domain, message producer components publish messages to a topic, and message consumer components subscribe to a topic to receive messages. These components are generally anonymous, meaning the publisher and subscriber components do not need to know of each other's existence. This level of abstraction allows the developer to build loosely coupled code.

Topics

JMS defines the Destination interface used to represent subjects to which messages are produced and by which messages are consumed. JMS destinations allow the client application to categorize messages, with some examples being "orders," "quotes," and "business news." The concept is simple, but it gets interesting when you consider how destinations are defined for message delivery. For instance, there are two types of destinations in JMS: a Topic and a Queue. Depending upon which one your application uses, the semantics of message delivery change.

A JMS Topic is a Java interface that extends the Destination base interface. Topics are administered objects, retrieved by name via JNDI code in a JMS client application and abstract the producer and consumer components from one another. For each topic in the publish-and-subscribe domain, there may be zero or more publishers and zero or more subscribers. Every message sent by each publisher component is received by all components that have subscribed to the applicable topic. You can write JMS application code to use the common interfaces, or the publish-and-subscribe specific interfaces, and still expect the same message delivery behavior. Table 3.3 shows the common interfaces and their equivalent publish-and-subscribe domain-specific interfaces.

TABLE 3.3 JMS Common and Point-to-Point Interface Comparison

JMS Common Interfaces	JMS Publish-and-Subscribe Domain Interfaces
ConnectionFactory	TopicConnectionFactory
Connection	TopicConnection
Destination	Topic
Session	TopicSession
MessageProducer	TopicPublisher
MessageConsumer	TopicSubscriber

The Stock Quote Ticker Example

The best way to describe the details of JMS publish-and-subscribe messaging is to start with a code example. The application we'll build is a simple stock quote ticker, where each last-trade price of company stocks we are interested in are published in real time. Of course, in this example, the trade prices are only simulated, but it serves as an interesting use of publish-and-subscribe messaging and it's also the first component in this book's sample online stock-trading system.

The complete source code for the stock quote ticker example can be found on the CD-ROM included with this book in the folder labeled Chapter3. The application consists of two main components: a stock quote listener and a stock quote publisher. The listener is started by executing the Windows batch file runquotelistener.bat or UNIX command script runquotelistener.sh. Both startup files execute the following Java command:

```
> java -cp (classpath details here) com.TradingSystem.StockTicker.Listener
```

The stock quote publisher can be started by executing the Windows batch file runquotesender.bat, or UNIX command script runquotesender.sh. Both startup files execute the following Java command:

```
> java -cp (classpath details here) com.TradingSystem.StockTicker.Sender
```

It is recommended that you run these components now by first starting the ActiveMQ message broker, then the stock quote listener, and finally the stock quote sender, in that order. If all goes well, you should see output similar to that shown in Figure 3.27.

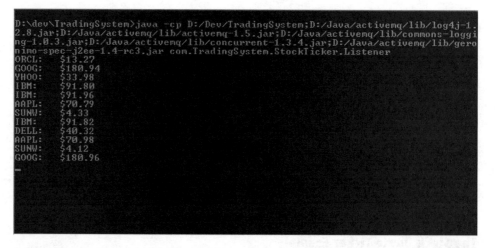

FIGURE 3.27   Screen capture showing the output of the sample stock quote listener JMS application.

The simulated last-traded prices for 10 company stocks (all of which happen to be in the technology sector) are displayed by the listener as they are received. The sender continuously publishes last-trade price updates for random stocks. The fact that this is just a simulation is not important; what is important is that it serves as an interesting use of JMS publish-and-subscribe messaging. Let's look at the code behind sender and listener JMS applications.

The `com.TradingSystem.StockTicker.Sender` JMS Application

Listing 3.10 shows the complete source code for the JMS client application that uses publish-and-subscribe messaging to broadcast last-traded stock price notifications.

LISTING 3.10   The JMS Stock Ticker Publisher

```
package com.TradingSystem.StockTicker;

import java.util.*;
import java.text.*;
import javax.jms.*;
import javax.naming.*;

public class Sender
{
    // Use the common JMS interfaces!
    private Connection connection;
    private Session session;
    private MessageProducer producer;

    private Random random;

    private String[] stocks = {
        "IBM", "MSFT", "SUNW", "ORCL", "SBL",
        "BEAS", "AAPL", "DELL", "GOOG", "YHOO" };

    private double[] prices = {
        91.79, 25.67, 4.09, 13.24, 17.41,
        8.50, 70.76, 40.12, 180.72, 33.93 };

    public Sender()
    {
        try {
            // Stock and price changes are chosen randomly
            random = new Random(System.currentTimeMillis());
```

```java
            InitialContext jndi = new InitialContext();
            ConnectionFactory conFactory =
                (ConnectionFactory)jndi.lookup("ConnectionFactory");

            connection = conFactory.createConnection("","");

            session = connection.createSession(
                    false, // no transactions
                    Session.AUTO_ACKNOWLEDGE);

            Topic tickerTopic = (Topic)jndi.lookup("StockTrades");
            if ( tickerTopic == null )
                tickerTopic = session.createTopic("StockTrades");

            producer = session.createProducer(tickerTopic);

            connection.start();
        }
        catch ( Exception e ) {
            e.printStackTrace();
        }
    }

    public void sendLastTradeLoop()
    {
        while ( true ) {
            try {
                // Pick a stock at random
                int stock = random.nextInt(10);

                String newPrice = getLastTradePrice( stock );

                TextMessage message = session.createTextMessage();
                message.setText(stocks[stock] + ":\t" + newPrice);

                producer.send(message);

                Thread.sleep(2000);
            }
            catch ( Exception e ) {
                e.printStackTrace();
            }
        }
    }
```

```
private String getLastTradePrice(int stockIndex)
{
    // Modify the last-trade price by a random amount
    // within a 25-cent range
    double price = prices[stockIndex];
    double change =
        (double)random.nextInt(25) / (double)100;
    price += change;
    return NumberFormat.getCurrencyInstance().format(price);
}

public static void main(String[] args)
{
    Sender sender = new Sender();
    sender.sendLastTradeLoop();
}
}
```

For purposes of simulation, two matching arrays are defined at the top of the Sender class: one for stock ticker names and another for the starting prices. Since this is a standalone Java application, execution starts in main, where an object of the Sender class is instantiated. The following steps occur in the constructor for the Sender class:

ON THE CD

1. JNDI is used to obtain a ConnectionFactory object reference for our JMS provider. Notice that no provider-specific JNDI properties exist within the code; they are defined in a file named jndi.properties (also included with the code on the CD-ROM) that exists within the classpath for the application. The advantage of doing this is that the code will not change if we change JMS providers. Simply modify the settings in the jndi.properties file and restart the application to take effect.

2. The application creates a connection to the JMS provider using the ConnectionFactory object. If the security settings for the JMS provider were set up by an administrator, you would need to specify a valid username and password in the createConnection method call. For the sake of simplicity, the sample skips this and uses empty strings.

3. The Connection object is used to create a Session object. The value of false for the first parameter indicates that this is a nontransacted Session. The second parameter specifies that message delivery will be automatically acknowledged to the message producer by the JMS provider.

4. JNDI is again used to look up a `Destination` object using the name "StockTrades." If this destination was not preconfigured administratively, the sample code uses the `Session` object to dynamically create it. Either way the end result should be the same—a valid `Destination` object to send messages to.

5. The `Session` is used to create a `MessageProducer` for the supplied `Destination`.

6. In order for the messages from this `MessageProducer` to be sent, a call is made to `Connection.start`. Messages sent by producers created from this `Connection` object will not be delivered unless `start` is called.

After the constructor for the `Sender` class completes, the JMS application is ready to publish last-trade price messages to the "StockTrades" destination. This action is started when `main` calls the method `Sender.sendLastTradeLoop`, where the following steps occur:

1. The code enters an infinite `while` loop (remember, this is just a simulation).

2. A stock array index between 0 and 9 is chosen at random. The stock array contains the stock name, while the prices array contains starting prices.

3. A new last-trade price for the chosen stock is generated.

4. The Session object is used to create a new `TextMessage` object that will contain the last-trade price update data.

5. The text of the `TextMessage` is set, containing the stock ticker name and the new last-trade price.

6. The `send` method of the `MessageProducer` is called, with the new `TextMessage` object as a parameter. The result is that the content of the message is published to the destination to be received by all listeners of the destination.

7. The simulation then sleeps for two seconds before repeating this entire process again.

In this sample scenario, let's assume multiple listeners are deployed across our network. Using publish-and-subscribe messaging is ideal because all listeners will receive the last-trade price notifications at more or less the same time. Let's examine the listener application now.

The `com.TradingSystem.StockTicker.Listener` JMS Application

Listing 3.11 shows the complete source code for the JMS client application that uses publish-and-subscribe messaging to *receive* last-traded stock price notifications.

LISTING 3.11   The JMS Stock Ticker Subscriber

```java
package com.TradingSystem.StockTicker;

import javax.jms.*;
import javax.naming.*;

public class Listener implements javax.jms.MessageListener
{
    private Connection connection;
    private Session session;
    private MessageConsumer consumer;

    public Listener()
    {
        try {
            InitialContext jndi = new InitialContext();
            ConnectionFactory conFactory =
                (ConnectionFactory)jndi.lookup("ConnectionFactory");

            connection = conFactory.createConnection("","");

            session = connection.createSession(
                            false, // no transactions
                            Session.AUTO_ACKNOWLEDGE);

            Topic tickerTopic = (Topic)jndi.lookup("StockTrades");
            if ( tickerTopic == null )
                tickerTopic = session.createTopic("StockTrades");

            consumer = session.createConsumer( tickerTopic );
            consumer.setMessageListener( this );

            // The Connection must be started for messages to fly
            connection.start();
        }
        catch ( Exception e ) {
            e.printStackTrace();
        }
    }

    public void onMessage(Message message)
    {
        try {
```

```
              TextMessage textMessage = (TextMessage)message;
              String text = textMessage.getText();
              System.out.println(text);
          }
          catch ( JMSException e ) {
              e.printStackTrace();
          }
      }


      public static void main(String[] args)
      {
          Listener listener = new Listener();
      }
  }
```

As with the Sender application, the Listener class is also a standalone Java application. Execution starts in main, where an object of the Listener class is instantiated. The following steps occur in the constructor for the Listener class:

1. The ConnectionFactory, Connection, Session, and Destination objects are created in exactly the same way as they were in the Sender class. Since we discussed these steps in the previous example, we'll skip over them here, as they are the same.
2. The Session is used to create a MessageConsumer for the supplied Destination.
3. Asynchronous message delivery is desired, so the Listener class is declared to implement the javax.jms.MessageListener interface. A reference to the Listener object (the this pointer) is provided via a call to the method MessageConsumer.setMessageListener.

The last-trade-price notification messages will be sent asynchronously to the Listener object's method onMessage, defined by the javax.jms.MessageListener interface. When messages arrive, the following steps occur:

1. The received Message object is casted to a TextMessage object.
2. The text of the message is extracted via a call to getText.
3. For illustrative purposes, the text is simply output to the console.

JMS REQUEST-AND-REPLY

Earlier in this chapter, request-and-reply messaging was discussed conceptually, with a Web server being used as an example. Request-and-reply messaging can be achieved in JMS with publish-and-subscribe messaging by setting the JMSReplyTo property of the JMS message header. JMS even offers a utility class, TopicRequestor, as a facade to using request-and-reply messaging in your code. Let's explore this by reexamining the stock quote application built earlier.

The stock quote sender application allows listeners to receive updates to stock quotes as each stock is traded. Imagine that one of the listener applications contains a stock quote user-interface display component. What would happen if the listener application were started before or after trading hours? Even during trading hours, a particular stock may be experiencing a low-volume trade day, resulting in a great deal of time between updates. If the listener application is forced to wait for an update in order to display a valid last-traded quote, this field in the display might appear empty for a long period of time. What is needed is a way for the listener application to explicitly request the current last-traded quote for a particular stock and get the reply right away. This is a good candidate for request-and-reply messaging.

Temporary Topics

The JMS Session interface contains the methods createTemporaryTopic and createTemporaryQueue, which prove quite useful in JMS request-and-reply messaging. These methods allow you to dynamically create a topic or queue quickly and easily, which is ideal for one-time use. The sample code in Listing 3.12 illustrates the use of a temporary topic, with the JMSReplyTo header property, to send a request to a listener.

LISTING 3.12   Code to Send A JMS Request Message

```
// Create a producer for the quote request
MessageProducer requestor = session.createProducer(quoteDest);

// Create a temporary topic for the reply, and a subscriber
// to listen for the reply. A different Session is used
Topic tempTopic = requestSession.createTemporaryTopic();
MessageConsumer subscriber =
requestSession.createConsumer(tempTopic);

// Create the request message
MapMessage mapMsg = requestSession.createMapMessage();
mapMsg.setJMSReplyTo(tempTopic);
mapMsg.setString("ticker", "SUNW");
requestor.send(mapMsg);
```

```
// Listen synchronously for a reply
Message replyMsg = subscriber.receive();
onMessage(replyMsg);
```

Assume the `Destination` object for the quote request has already been retrieved using JNDI. In the first step, a message producer is created that is used to send the quote request message. Second, a temporary topic is created using a new `Session` object named `requestSession`. The quote reply will be sent to this topic and handled by the message consumer (`subscriber`) that is created to listen for the reply. Third, the quote request message is created. The temporary topic (for the reply) is set in the message header property `JMSReplyTo`, and the message payload is the ticker symbol for the stock quote we are requesting. Now that the quote-request message is set up properly, it's sent to the quote-request destination. As soon as the `send` method returns, the code *synchronously* listens for the reply via a call to the temporary topic subscriber's `receive` method. This call blocks (with no timeout) until a reply message is received, at which point it's handled by the method `onMessage`—the same code that handles a quote update from Listing 3.11.

The `TopicRequestor` Utility Class

The JMS utility class `TopicRequestor` is a helper class provided to make request-and-reply messaging using a JMS `Topic` a little easier. The quote-request code in the previous example is a perfect candidate for simplification using this class. Listing 3.13 illustrates how much the request code gets cleaned up by using the `TopicRequestor` class.

LISTING 3.13   Code to Send a Request Message Using the JMS `TopicRequestor` Class

```
TopicRequestor requestor =
    new TopicRequestor(requestSession, quoteDest);

// Don't set the JMSReplyTo property-TopicRequestor does it
MapMessage mapMsg = requestSession.createMapMessage();
mapMsg.setString("ticker", stocks[i]);

// The TopicRequestor handles sending the message
Message reply = requestor.request(mapMsg);
onMessage(reply);
```

Even though there are fewer lines of code in this example, the process outlined in the previous example still occurs; it's just done in the `TopicRequestor` class. This class performs the following steps so your code does not have to:

1. The `TopicRequestor` constructor creates a temporary topic to handle the reply for this request-and-reply sequence only. (The constructor also creates both a `Publisher` and `Subscriber` object for the supplied request topic.)
2. When `TopicRequestor.request` is called, the temporary topic is set as the message object's `JMSReplyTo` property.
3. The message is published to the destination topic provided in the `TopicRequestor` constructor. In this example, the destination is the `quoteTopic` object.
4. A call is made to the temporary topic subscriber object's `receive` method, which blocks indefinitely until a reply is received.

Although the `TopicRequestor` class saves you from writing some tedious code, it's only useful in simple scenarios such as this example. This class does have some limitations, such as the fact that it does not support more than one reply for each request; all other reply messages received on the temporary topic are ignored. It also restricts you to using a publish-and-subscribe `Topic` to receive the reply; there is no support for a point-to-point `Queue`. There is also no built-in support for persistent messaging or transactions. Finally, the request method makes a blocking `receive` call; there is no way to specify a timeout value. Therefore, your code can potentially block forever if no reply is received. However, the class is provided as both a convenience, and as a model for building your own, enhanced version of a `TopicRequestor` class. There's no reason you cannot modify the code to support these missing features, which is exactly what we will do later in this chapter.

Sending a Reply

To make the request-and-reply example complete, let's explore the code required to send a reply message. Listing 3.14 contains the code for a message consumer that handles quote requests.

LISTING 3.14   Code that Sends a Reply Message to Satisfy a Request

```
class QuoteRequestListener implements MessageListener
{
    MessageConsumer quoteListener;
    MessageProducer quoteResponder;

    public QuoteRequestListener()
    {
        try {
            // quoteTopic retrieved using JNDI
            ...
```

```
            quoteListener = session.createConsumer(quoteTopic);
            quoteListener.setMessageListener(this);

            quoteResponder = session.createProducer(null);
        }
        catch ( Exception e ) {
            e.printStackTrace();
        }
    }

    public void onMessage(Message message)
    {
        try {
            MapMessage mapMsg = (MapMessage)message;
            String ticker = mapMsg.getString("ticker");

            int stock = getStockIndexFromName(ticker);
            Destination reply = mapMsg.getJMSReplyTo();

            TextMessage textMsg = session.createTextMessage();
            if ( stock != -1 ) {
                String newPrice = getLastTradePrice( stock );
                textMsg.setText(stocks[stock] + ": \t" + newPrice);
            }
            else {
                textMsg.setText("Stock ticker not supported");
            }

            quoteResponder.send(reply, textMsg);
        }
        catch ( Exception e ) {
            e.printStackTrace();
        }
    }
}
```

The class QuoteRequestListener implements the MessageListener interface, making it an asynchronous message consumer for the quote-request topic. The code to create the Session object and retrieve the quote-request topic from JNDI has been omitted from Listing 3.14 for the constructor since it is not the focus of the example. The remaining constructor code creates the quote-request MessageConsumer, provides a this pointer reference as the MessageListener object, and creates the message producer, `quoteResponder`, without specifying a `Destination` object. This is because, at this point, we don't know what destination we will need to send the reply to. Ultimately this is the topic that will be pulled from the request message's `JMSReplyTo` property.

When a quote-request message is received, it's handled in `onMessage`. Here, the message is cast to a `MapMessage`, the stock name (`ticker`) is pulled from the message as a `String`, and the index within the array of stock quotes is deduced using the stock name. Next, the reply destination—a `Topic` object in this case—is pulled from the message header. After a `TextMessage` reply message is created and its data is set, the generic message producer, `quoteResponder`, is used to send the reply message to the temporary destination. Notice that the `onMessage` code is written using the common JMS interfaces; the destination is not assumed to be a `Topic` object. Therefore, this code should also work if the reply destination is a `Queue` as well.

Because a `TemporaryTopic` is used for the request-and-reply messages in this example, it's important that the quote-sender application be started before the quote-listener application. Otherwise, if the listener were started first, it would publish a request message, only to be lost forever since there were no subscriber components listening on the same `Topic`.

This completes the entire request-and-reply cycle for the sample stock quote application. Armed with your knowledge of JMS messaging so far, some new questions should arise. How are requests handled when there are no components listening for them at the exact time they are made? What are the best ways to handle multiple replies to a single request? How can the request-and-reply cycle be made into a transaction? The answers to some of these questions lie mainly in our discussion of durable subscribers, persistent messaging, and message transactions in Chapter 4, "Advanced Java Messaging." However, to truly understand how to answer these questions, an understanding of the JMS point-to-point message domain (a.k.a. message queues) is required.

JMS POINT-TO-POINT (QUEUES)

The JMS point-to-point domain is Java's version of the message queue paradigm discussed earlier in the chapter. While publish-and-subscribe messaging is typically a one-to-many relationship, queue-based messaging is many-to-one, or one-to-one. The following are the unique characteristics of the point-to-point message domain:

Store-and-forward: The point-to-point domain follows a store-and-forward paradigm where messages are stored (and not lost) if there are no message consumers available—hence the use of a queue.

One-time delivery: For each queue there may be zero or more producers and zero or more consumers. However, each message sent by a producer component is received by at *most* one consumer component that is listening to the applicable queue, even if multiple consumers are listening to the same queue. It's up to the JMS provider to choose which consumer receives each queued message. Some providers may balance the load across consumers; others might continue sending each message to the same consumer until it stops listening, at which point the provider should deliver the remaining messages to another consumer.

FIFO: Messages are stored in the queue in the same order they are placed in the queue. This is sometimes referred to as a first-in-first-out (FIFO) queue.

Reliable: Point-to-point messaging is chosen when reliable messaging is desired because the messages are stored to live beyond the lifetime of the applications that send and receive them. A JMS administrator will sometimes specify the database properties for message storage if the JMS provider supplies the facility to do so.

Connection independent: Queue-based messaging is ideal for a situation where network connectivity is not guaranteed or is otherwise unreliable. For the scenario of a traveling salesperson using a disconnected laptop to enter sales at remote customer sites, queue-based messaging is necessary.

From this point on, the terms *queue* and *point-to-point* will be used interchangeably. We'll discuss guaranteed messaging, persisted messages, and transactions for the point-to-point domain in Chapter 4. For now, let's examine the basics of using queues.

Queues

A JMS Queue is a Java interface that extends the Destination base interface. Queues are administered objects, retrieved by name via JNDI code in a JMS client application, and they abstract the producer and consumer components from one another. You can write JMS application code to use the common interfaces, or the point-to-point specific interfaces, and still expect the same message delivery behavior. Table 3.4 shows the common interfaces and their equivalent point-to-point domain-specific interfaces.

TABLE 3.4 JMS Common and Point-to-Point Interface Comparison

JMS Common Interfaces	JMS Point-to-Point Domain Interfaces
ConnectionFactory	QueueConnectionFactory
Connection	QueueConnection
Destination	Queue
Session	QueueSession
MessageProducer	QueueSender
MessageConsumer	QueueReceiver

The Enhanced Stock Quote Example

When we discussed request-and-reply messaging, the stock quote sample application was modified to support requests for stock quotes. This was done so that the listener application would have the quote data needed to create its quote display without waiting an undetermined amount of time for quote updates to arrive. In the real world, a similar stock quote application might have client applications distributed around the world—potentially thousands of them. Consider how many potential publish-and-subscribe requests the stock quote application might receive from its clients in this case. Serializing all requests through a single quote request subscriber would probably not scale well. This situation calls for a design change.

The first alternative to consider is the addition of multiple quote-request subscribers. However, since the underlying message domain is publish-and-subscribe, *every* subscriber would receive *every* quote request. Since each subscriber is independent of the others—they are unaware of each other—each one would send a reply. This would add inefficiency and increase network traffic as single requests are multicast to multiple consumers and result in multiple (identical) replies to each requestor. While the required solution needs multiple listeners for system throughput and scalability, it requires that an individual listener be chosen (from a pool) to handle a single request. The use of a JMS queue should help to meet the criteria.

The class com.TradingSystem.StockTicker.Listener needs to be modified to send quote requests to a queue instead of a topic. Since this class was written to use the JMS common interfaces, not much code needs to change. The immediate difference is that the TopicRequestor utility class can no longer be used because it works only with publish-and-subscribe topics. The JMS developers also thought of this scenario, and they have provided a `QueueRequestor` utility class that supports request-and-reply messaging using a point-to-point queue. However, it not only assumes you want to send a request to a queue; it creates a temporary queue from which to receive the response. This is fine for most cases, but in some cases (like this example) the response does not need to be received from a queue.

Queues tend to require more overhead than publish-and-subscribe topics with nonpersistent messaging. Because of its store-and-forward behavior, the JMS provider must set up the persistent storage for each queue. The creation of a temporary queue for each quote request the code makes, multiplied by each client application running, may lead to a lot of extra processing that is not needed in this scenario. Our situation calls for a utility class that will send a request message to a named queue and will accept the reply on a temporary publish-and-subscribe topic. JMS doesn't supply a class that meets these criteria, so we need to create it ourselves.

The `GenericRequestor` Toolkit Class

Listing 3.15 contains the code for a generic requestor class, `com.toolkit.messaging.GenericRequestor`, which allows a JMS application to provide either a `Topic` or a `Queue` destination for the request and to specify the destination type (`Queue` or `Topic`) for the reply message. The complete source code for this class, which is part of the book's messaging toolkit, can be found on the CD-ROM in the folder `\Chapter3\com\toolkit\messaging`.

ON THE CD

LISTING 3.15   The `com.toolkit.messaging.GenericRequestor` Class

```
package com.toolkit.messaging;
import javax.jms.*;

public class GenericRequestor
{
    Destination requestDest; // The request destination
    Destination replyDest; // The reply destination
    Session session; // The request destination session
    MessageProducer producer;
    MessageConsumer consumer;

    public GenericRequestor(Session session,
                            Destination dest)
        throws JMSException
    {
        // Defaults to TemporaryTopic reply destination
        this(session,dest,TemporaryTopic.class);
    }
```

```java
public GenericRequestor(Session session,
                        Destination dest,
                        Class reply)
    throws JMSException
{
    this.session = session;
    this.requestDest = dest;

    String replyStr = reply.getName();
    if ( replyStr.equals("javax.jms.TemporaryQueue"))
        replyDest = session.createTemporaryQueue();
    else
        replyDest = session.createTemporaryTopic();

    producer = session.createProducer(requestDest);
    consumer = session.createConsumer(replyDest);
}

public Message request(Message message)
    throws JMSException
{
    message.setJMSReplyTo(replyDest);
    producer.send(message);
    return (consumer.receive());
}

public Message request(Message message, int timeout)
    throws JMSException
{
    message.setJMSReplyTo(replyDest);
    producer.send(message);
    return (consumer.receive(timeout));
}

public void close()
    throws JMSException
{
    session.close();
    if ( replyDest instanceof TemporaryTopic )
        ((TemporaryTopic)replyDest).delete();
    else
        ((TemporaryQueue)replyDest).delete();
}
}
```

There are two GenericRequestor constructors: one that takes just a Session and a Destination object and one that takes a Class object as a third parameter. The Class object is used to specify the destination type for the reply. You can pass either a javax.jms.TemporaryTopic or a javax.jms.TemporaryQueue Class object. If the first constructor is called, where the reply type is not specified at all, the class will default to use a TemporaryTopic object for the reply. If an invalid reply type is provided (something other than a TemporaryTopic or a TemporaryQueue), the class will also default to use a TemporaryTopic object for the reply.

The constructor creates the appropriate temporary destination and then uses the common JMS interfaces to create a message producer (for the request) and a message consumer (for the reply). Both of these classes will work with either a Topic or a Queue. When a client application wants to send the request message, it has to call one of the two request methods. The first request method, without a time-out parameter, works like the TopicRequestor and QueueRequestor classes; it sends the request and then calls consumer.receive to wait synchronously for the reply with no timeout. The second request method is more flexible; it allows you to spec-ify a timeout value, which is passed along to the consumer.receive method. This method will return if a reply is not received within the time specified (in millisec-onds). You should notice that regardless of the request destination type, Topic or Queue, the message producer code is the same. The destination type simply affects the *behavior* of message delivery, not the client code that uses it.

The code in Listing 3.16 shows how the quote-listener application uses the GenericRequestor class to send the quote requests. The section of code that creates the GenericRequestor object provides a TemporaryTopic.class object to specify a topic as the reply destination type. This can be replaced with a TemporaryQueue.class object to otherwise specify a queue. The sample code then calls the request method with a timeout of 10 seconds (10,000 milliseconds). In the case of a timeout, the message object returned will be null; therefore, it is checked before calling the mes-sage handler method, onMessage.

LISTING 3.16 Code to Send A Request Message Using the JMS GenericRequestor Class

```
InitialContext jndi = new InitialContext();
Destination quoteDest =
    (Destination)jndi.lookup("RequestQuote");

for ( int i = 0; i < stocks.length; i++ ) {
    Session requestSession =
        (Session)connection.createSession(
                false,
                Session.AUTO_ACKNOWLEDGE);
```

```
GenericRequestor requestor =
    new GenericRequestor(
            requestSession,
            quoteDest,
            TemporaryTopic.class);

MapMessage mapMsg = requestSession.createMapMessage();
mapMsg.setString("ticker", stocks[i]);

Message response = requestor.request(mapMsg, 10000);
if ( response != null )
    onMessage(response);

requestor.close();
}
```

The quote Sender class also contains only slight modification. In particular, the nested QuoteRequestListener class checks the "RequestQuote" destination type and throws an Exception if it is not a Queue:

```
Destination quoteDest =
    (Destination)jndi.lookup("RequestQuote");
if ( quoteDest == null || ! (quoteDest instanceof Queue) )
    throw new Exception("RequestQuote destination must be a Queue");
```

The code to create the quote request consumer does not change, regardless of the destination type. As for the final modification to the Sender class, the code creates a pool of quote request listener components. In order for the pool to work as we intend, each MessageConsumer object must be for a Queue, and not a Topic. If the quote request destination were a Topic, we would end up with the problem scenario described earlier where every component in the pool would receive every request, and each would send a reply. The check for a Queue ensures this will not occur. The code below declares and creates a pool of five quote-request message consumer objects:

```
private QuoteRequestListener[] quoteListeners;
// ...
quoteListeners = new QuoteRequestListener[5];
for ( int i = 0; i < 5; i++ )
    quoteListeners[i] = new QuoteRequestListener();
```

Because the quote requests are now sent to a Queue (as opposed to being previously published to a Topic) it doesn't matter which component–Listener or Sender–you start first. Because of the nature of using a Queue, if the quote listener is started first, the requests will persisted. When the quote-sender application is started, it will read the requests off of the queue. The next chapter will explore the more advanced queue-related topics, such as transactions, and how the different message acknowledgment modes affect message delivery. Figure 3.28 shows an illustration that provides an overview of the quote-request message model.

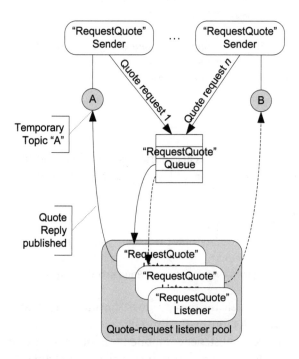

FIGURE 3.28 A pool of listeners service quote requests from the queue.

SUMMARY

This chapter explored the concept of messaging and the typical message paradigms used in distributed application architecture. The fundamental concepts and the understanding needed to develop systems using enterprise messaging were discussed before delving into the details of JMS messaging and application code. Fully understanding the message paradigms—publish-and-subscribe, request-and-reply, and queues—independent of a message server's implementation of them is important because it allows you to make an apples-to-apples comparison of any software vendor's product. It also allows you to develop messaging application code that works consistently regardless of the message server used for message delivery.

This chapter presented a list of choices of JMS providers that you can deploy with your applications. Of these, this book has chosen the open source JMS provider ActiveMQ. To illustrate the JMS message domains (publish-and-subscribe, request-and-reply, and point-to-point), a sample stock quote system was developed. This code, along with the ActiveMQ libraries and binaries, can be found on the book's CD-ROM in the directories Chapter3, and java/activemq, respectively.

ON THE CD

Now that a foundation of messaging knowledge has been built, the next chapter will explore the more advanced topics related to the Java message service.

4 Advanced Java Messaging

In This Chapter

HIERARCHICAL TOPICS

The previous chapter covered the basics of Destination objects such as Topics and Queues. Both destination types are named entities that use a String for easy identification. With some Java Message Service (JMS) providers, a Topic can be named using a hierarchy of names that form a tree structure, where an individual Topic is a leaf on the tree. Figure 4.1 contains a visual example of a Topic hierarchy.

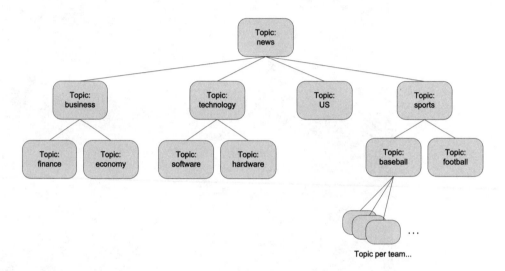

FIGURE 4.1   A sample JMS destination hierarchy for a news-related system.

In Figure 4.1, the root of the tree is the topic named news. There are subtopics under news named business, technology, US, and sports. Some of those subtopics have subtopics of their own, and so on. This topic hierarchy can be expressed in a JMS Topic name using the subtopic names divided by some sort of separator character, such as a period. For example, the full topic name for finance in this hierarchy would be news.business.finance. This implies that it is possible to subscribe to a topic at any level within the hierarchy, such as news.business.

Of course, the exact behavior of subscribing to subtopics arranged in a tree structure is left up to the individual JMS provider. JMS does not require that a provider support it at all. However, many providers support topic hierarchies and define the behavior as an aggregation of topics as you move to the root of the tree. In other words, by subscribing to the topic named new.business, a MessageConsumer would receive all messages sent to the subtopics of new.business, including those sent to news.business.finance and news.business.topics. Furthermore, by subscribing to the root topic news, a consumer would receive all the aggregate news messages for every subtopic in the tree.

JMS providers that support hierarchies include:

- TIBCO Enterprise Message Service
- Codehaus ActiveMQ
- WebSphere MQ
- Pragmati Server
- SonicMQ

Composite Destinations

ActiveMQ implements a twist on the destination hierarchy concept with a feature they call *composite destinations*. A composite destination is defined as the use of one *virtual destination* name used to send messages to multiple JMS Destinations in one send method call. In other words, a virtual destination is a collection that can consist of two or more destinations. A single collection can contain a mixture of both Topic and Queue destinations. For example, to send a message to three Queue destinations, QueueA, QueueB, and QueueC, the following destination name would be used:

```
"QueueA,QueueB,QueueC"
```

However, to send a message to a Topic and a Queue, the text topic:// and queue:// must be used before each name, respectively. For example, to send a message to a Topic named TopicA and a Queue named QueueA, the following destination name would be used:

```
"topic://TopicA,queue://QueueA"
```

This is a feature specific to ActiveMQ that is not required, or even mentioned in the JMS specification. Don't assume that you will find it in other JMS providers.

MESSAGE SELECTORS

Message selection was defined in the previous chapter as the ability of a message consumer to filter incoming messages based on some criteria. The message consumer defines the selection criteria in a String object, and the JMS provider uses the combination of the message's properties and the message selector to filter messages. The message selector String is provided in the Session.createConsumer call. Only messages that match the message selector's filter criteria will be delivered, and these are defined using message selector expressions. Of course, the client application can do its own message filtering as each message arrives, but it's far more efficient for the provider to filter out a message since it doesn't need to deliver the message to the client.

A message selector contains a `String` expression, such as `Ticker = 'IBM'`, that is evaluated using the message's properties. In this case, the `Message` object must have had a property named `Ticker` with a value of `IBM` to evaluate to `TRUE` and to be delivered to the client. If the expression evaluates to `FALSE`, or something other than `TRUE`, the message will not be delivered, as shown in Figure 4.2. All message selectors are case insensitive and follow a set of rules similar to Standard Query Language (SQL) query:

- The expression can contain an identifier.
- An identifier can be a series of any number of characters that follow the same rules as valid Java identifiers.
- An identifier should match a message header property name (including case); otherwise it will evaluate to `NULL`.
- Identifiers cannot be any reserved names such as `NULL`, `TRUE`, `FALSE`, `NOT`, `AND`, `OR`, `BETWEEN`, `LIKE`, `IN`, `IS`, or `ESCAPE`.
- To compare an identifier to a `String` literal, single quotes should be used to enclose the literal, such as `'IBM'`.
- A numeric literal has the same range as the Java primitive `long`.
- Boolean `TRUE` and `FALSE` are valid literals. For example, `ActiveStock = 'TRUE'` is a valid expression that uses a Boolean literal.
- An expression can contain logical operators such as `=, <>, <=, >=, <, >, NOT, AND`, and `OR`.
- An expression can contain mathematical operators such as `*, /, +`, and `-`, listed in order of evaluation.
- The `BETWEEN` operator can be used to test ranges of values. For example, `TradeQty BETWEEN 1000 and 10000`.
- Sets can be used in evaluations using the `IN` operator, such as `StockTicker IN ('IBM', 'MSFT', 'YHOO')`.
- Wildcard text string comparisons can be performed using the `LIKE` operator and `%` for any sequence of characters, and `_` for any single character. For example, for `StockPrice LIKE '100.%'`, the values 100.23, 100.00, and 100.99 each evaluate to `TRUE`, but 101.23 and 99.87 do not. However, the expression `StockPrice LIKE '100._3'` would only be `TRUE` for 100.23.
- White space (which includes spaces, tabs, new lines, and linefeeds) can be used within an expression.
- The order of evaluation of the parts of the message selector follows the normal mathematical rules: expressions are evaluated from left to right; parentheses can be used to change the order of evaluation.

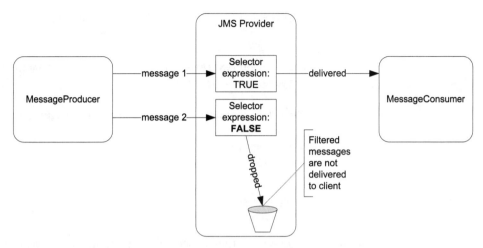

FIGURE 4.2 The JMS provider evaluates message selectors internally and does not deliver messages whose properties cause the selector to evaluate to FALSE.

Stock Quote Filtering Example

Let's watch message selection in action with a modified stock quote sample application. In this example, the listener is only interested in updates for the subset of stocks of IBM, Microsoft, and Yahoo® (perhaps that's all the user has in his portfolio). The first requirement is for the message sender to set the applicable message property value on the Message object. In this example let's use the Sender class from Chapter 3, and add a property called StockTicker to the message, which will contain the stock ticker name for which the quote update applies. Listing 4.1 shows the Sender.sendLastTradeLoop method modified to support this property; the changes are in bold type.

LISTING 4.1 Code to Add a Message Property for Message Selection

```
public void sendLastTradeLoop()
{
    while ( true )
    {
        try {
            int stock = random.nextInt(10);

            String newPrice = getLastTradePrice( stock );

            TextMessage message = session.createTextMessage();
```

```
                    message.setStringProperty( "StockTicker",
                                             stocks[stock]);

                    message.setText(stocks[stock] + ": \t" + newPrice);
                    producer.send(message);

                    Thread.sleep(500); // This change not required
                }
                catch ( Exception e ) {
                    e.printStackTrace();
                }
            }
        }
    }
```

This one minor change is all that is needed to make message selection work. The change to the value passed in the Thread.sleep call is made to cause more updates to be generated and is not required for message selection. This is done for illustrative purposes so you don't need to wait too long for a quote update for one of the three tickers in the message selector.

The changes to the Listener class are also minor and are limited to the class constructor as shown in see Listing 4.2. (The code that is unimportant to this discussion has been omitted from this listing.) The message selector is defined as a String that uses the IN operator with the set of company stock ticker names we are interested in. In this case, the selector text is StockTicker IN ('IBM', 'MSFT', 'YHOO'). The selector String is then provided in the createConsumer call, and the JMS provider will now handle the process of filtering out all update messages unless they pertain to one of the stocks in the selector.

LISTING 4.2   Code to Add a Message Selector to a Message Consumer

```
public Listener()
{
    try {
        // ...

        String messageSelector =
                "StockTicker IN ('IBM', 'MSFT', 'YHOO')";

        consumer = session.createConsumer( tickerTopic,
                                            messageSelector );

        consumer.setMessageListener( this );
```

```
         // ...
      }
      catch ( Exception e ) {
         e.printStackTrace();
      }
   }
}
```

Go ahead and make these changes to the `Sender` and `Listener` classes in the stock quote sample applications from Chapter 3. The initial stock quote requests will still be made for all stocks, but you should notice that updates for only Microsoft, Yahoo, and IBM are displayed thereafter; be sure to give it extra time as the messages for other stocks will be filtered out.

DURABLE SUBSCRIPTIONS

A *durable subscriber* is one that will receive all published messages for a given `Topic`, even if that subscriber is not listening when the messages are sent. To be precise, a durable subscriber is a normal `TopicSubscriber` object that has registered a unique *durable subscription* with the JMS provider. You register a durable subscription via the `Session` object's `createDurableSubscriber` method, which returns a `TopicSubscriber` object. Only one durable subscriber may be active at one time. In addition, a unique client identifier must be provided to the `Connection` object used to create the `Session`. If the durable subscriber is running at the time, and at least one message is sent to it, it will receive the message(s) as any other subscriber would (see Figure 4.3).

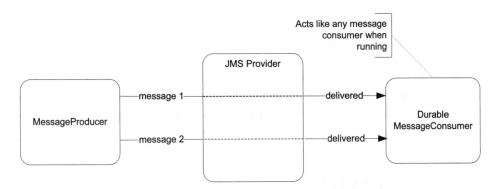

FIGURE 4.3   A subscriber with a durable subscription receives messages like any message consumer while running.

However, if the durable subscriber stops executing for any reason, the messages that are sent to it while it's not running are stored until either the durable subscriber starts executing again or the messages timeout. As soon as the durable subscriber starts running, the stored messages that haven't timed out will be delivered immediately (see Figure 4.4).

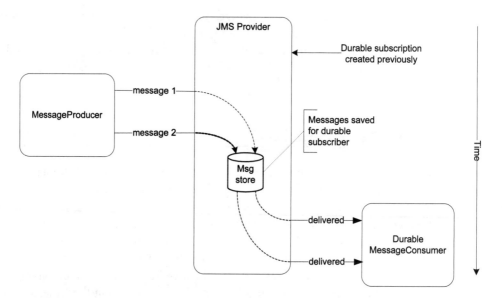

FIGURE 4.4 A durable subscription causes all sent messages to be saved until the subscriber for that subscription is restarted.

Message storage starts when the durable subscriber terminates, at which point the subscription still exists but is deemed to be *inactive*. The JMS provider will stop storing messages when the durable subscriber begins executing (becomes active again) or a call is made to the Session object's unsubscribe method. The unsubscribe method requires, as a parameter, the same client identifier provided to the JMS Connection object when the subscription was created. The Session object's createDurableSubscriber and unsubscribe methods work as a pair for a valid client identifier.

A Simple Stock-Order System

To demonstrate durable subscriptions, let's examine a very simple stock-order system that is made up of two components: an order client application that places orders, and an order manager application that accepts orders. In this example, client applications send stock buy or sell order messages to a JMS Topic to be executed by a remote system. It is not desirable to lose a client order; therefore, the remote order execution system creates a durable subscription to ensure that all orders are processed, even if the subscriber or the entire application stops working. To implement this system, the OrderClient class has been created to simulate a client that wants to place orders for stock. The OrderManager class is a sample implementation of the remote order system that uses a durable subscription to avoid losing orders.

The OrderClient Application

The OrderClient application is like any other client that sends messages and uses the JMS common interfaces. No changes need to be made to a component that sends messages to a topic for which there exists a durable subscription. Listing 4.3 contains the code for the OrderClient class. The orders are sent as MapMessage objects that contain three pieces of data:

Ticker: The company's stock ticker

OrderType: A buy or sell order

Quantity: The number of shares to buy or sell

LISTING 4.3   Code for the OrderClient Application

```
package com.TradingSystem;
import javax.jms.*;
import javax.naming.InitialContext;

public class OrderClient
{
    private Connection connection;
    private Session session;
    private MessageProducer producer;

    private String[] stocks = {
            "IBM", "MSFT", "SUNW", "ORCL", "SBL",
            "BEAS", "AAPL", "DELL", "GOOG", "YHOO" };

    public OrderClient()
    {
        try {
            InitialContext jndi = new InitialContext();
            ConnectionFactory conFactory =
                (ConnectionFactory)jndi.lookup("ConnectionFactory");
```

```
                        connection = conFactory.createConnection("","");
                        session = connection.createSession(
                                            false,
                                            Session.AUTO_ACKNOWLEDGE);

                        Destination orderDest =
                          (Destination)jndi.lookup("Orders");
                        producer = session.createProducer(orderDest);
                        connection.start();

                        sendOrders();
                }
                catch ( Exception e ) {
                    e.printStackTrace();
                }
            }

            private void sendOrders() throws Exception
            {
                // Place a buy order for 100 shares of each stock
                for ( int i = 0; i < stocks.length; i++ ) {
                    MapMessage msg = session.createMapMessage();
                    msg.setString("Ticker", stocks[i]);
                    msg.setString("OrderType", "BUY");
                    msg.setInt("Quantity", 100);
                    producer.send(msg);
                }
            }

            public static void main(String[] args) throws Exception {
                OrderClient client = new OrderClient();
                client.connection.close();
            }
        }
```

The OrderManager Application

The OrderManager class (see Listing 4.4) implements a durable subscription to receive order requests. The only lines of code that separate the durable subscriber from a normal Topic subscriber are shown in bold type. First, when the Connection object is created, a call is made to the method setClientID, where the class name is provided as the unique client identifier. The class name is certain to be unique to the application, and will reactivate the durable subscription each time an instance of this class is created. Next, the durable subscriber is created by a call to the Session object's `createDurableSubscriber` method, providing the same unique client identifier given to the `Connection` object.

LISTING 4.4 Code for the `OrderManager` Class

```
package com.TradingSystem;
import javax.jms.*;
import javax.naming.*;

public class OrderManager implements MessageListener
{
    private Connection connection;
    private Session session;
    private MessageConsumer consumer;

    public OrderManager()
    {
        try {
            InitialContext jndi = new InitialContext();
            ConnectionFactory conFactory =
                (ConnectionFactory)jndi.lookup("ConnectionFactory");

            connection = conFactory.createConnection("","");

            connection.setClientID( this.getClass().getName() );

            session = connection.createSession(
                                    false,
                                    Session.AUTO_ACKNOWLEDGE);

            Topic orderTopic = (Topic)jndi.lookup("Orders");

            consumer = session.createDurableSubscriber(
                                    orderTopic,
                                    this.getClass().getName());

            consumer.setMessageListener(this);

            connection.start();
        }
        catch ( Exception e ) {
            e.printStackTrace();
        }
    }
```

```
public void onMessage(Message message)
{
    try {
        MapMessage mapMsg = (MapMessage)message;

        String ticker = mapMsg.getString("Ticker");
        String type = mapMsg.getString("OrderType");
        int qty = mapMsg.getInt("Quantity");
        System.out.println( "Received a "
                            + type + " order for "
                            + qty + " shares of "
                            + ticker);

        // Place the order here...
    }
    catch ( Exception e ) {
        e.printStackTrace();
    }
}

public static void main(String[] args) throws Exception
{
    OrderManager orderMgr = new OrderManager();
}
}
```

Make sure your JMS provider is running before trying the sample application.

The code for both the OrderManager and OrderClient applications can be found on the CD-ROM included with this book, in the folder labeled Chapter4. The OrderClient application sends a buy-order message for each of the 10 stocks and then exits. To experience the durable subscription in action, start the listener first (without the OrderManager application running) via the Windows batch file runorderclient.bat (or runorderclient.sh on UNIX). Both startup scripts execute the following Java command:

```
> java -cp (classpath here) com.TradingSystem.OrderClient
```

When the client application exists, you can start the OrderManager application via the Windows batch file runordermanager.bat (or runordermanager.sh on UNIX). Both startup scripts execute the following Java command:

```
> java -cp (classpath here) com.TradingSystem.OrderManager
```

As soon as the application starts, the saved messages will be delivered to it. You should see the following 10 messages indicating that the order messages were received and processed:

```
Received a BUY order for 100 shares of IBM
Received a BUY order for 100 shares of MSFT
Received a BUY order for 100 shares of SUNW
Received a BUY order for 100 shares of ORCL
Received a BUY order for 100 shares of SBL
Received a BUY order for 100 shares of BEAS
Received a BUY order for 100 shares of AAPL
Received a BUY order for 100 shares of DELL
Received a BUY order for 100 shares of GOOG
Received a BUY order for 100 shares of YHOO
```

Now, while the OrderManager application is still running, start the OrderClient application in a separate command prompt window. You should see messages appear in the OrderManager window indicating that it has received 10 more order requests.

As a final experiment, once again stop the OrderManager application from running. Next, execute the OrderClient application multiple times sequentially. Finally, restart the OrderManager application and you should notice that all of the order messages are displayed (precisely 10 times the number of times you ran the client).

RELIABLE MESSAGING

The concept of *reliable messaging* can be defined as the consistent, error-free, and guaranteed delivery of messages to end-point receivers with predictable performance, and without unreasonable delay. In JMS, a durable subscription as defined in the previous section is one example of reliable messaging. However, the common messaging paradigm associated with reliable messaging in JMS is the point-to-point (or queue-based) message domain. Queues typically offer the best facilities to ensure that a message is delivered once and only once. The ideal qualities of reliable messaging are:

■ Every message is delivered once and only once.
■ Every message is delivered in the same state it was sent.
■ Every message is autonomous; the failure of the JMS provider does not equate to the loss of the message. The entire message is always preserved.
■ Failed message delivery is made known to the sender and/or the receiver.

We live in an imperfect world—one in which there are many imperfect software systems. Living up to the expectations of reliable messaging means adding a level of complexity to the software systems we build, but it shouldn't be confusing. Unfortunately, because JMS offers different choices and options, and it tries to integrate with existing messaging systems, achieving reliable messaging can seem tricky. Let's discuss message delivery conceptually before we get into the mechanics of JMS reliable messaging.

At-Most Once Delivery

In some situations, it's reasonable and acceptable to lose some messages, even if it's not desirable. Perhaps the goal is to get as many messages as possible sent without being concerned about the overhead involved with guaranteed messaging. Take for example a noncritical chat system or a news ticker that flashes potentially hundreds of headlines continuously around the world on teletype displays such as those found in Times Square, New York. If an occasional line in a chat is lost (see Figure 4.5) or a headline is skipped, it may be inconvenient but not critical.

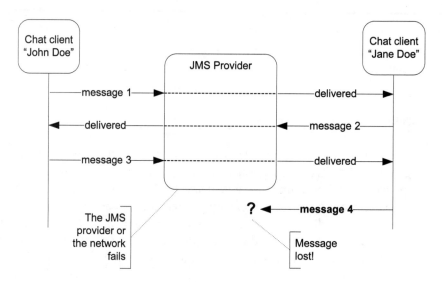

FIGURE 4.5 With at-most message delivery, a failure with the JMS provider, or the network, may result in lost messages.

These scenarios are examples of *at-most once* message delivery. With this delivery mode, the messaging software does its best to deliver each message, and under normal circumstances it will continue to do so. The developer that chooses this message delivery mode puts his faith in the reliability of the underlying hardware, operating systems, network protocols, messaging software, and his own software, to ensure that messages arrive most of the time. With the state of hardware and network technology today, this is not an unreasonable risk to take, but it is still a gamble. Furthermore, determining the criticality of a software system is ambiguous. The moment a user complains that his chat conversations are being misunderstood by clients because your software drops an occasional sentence—or a business makes a poor decision because they missed an important news headline—you may feel the need to reconsider your messaging strategy.

At-Least Once Delivery

Let's assume that the developers from the previous section have decided that losing even one message is no longer acceptable. A better choice is a delivery mode where each message is guaranteed to be delivered, but every once in a while a message may be delivered more than once. Under normal circumstances, this shouldn't happen, but it can if there is a failure with the provider, the network, or the client application. In certain cases, the provider may determine that a message needs to be redelivered because there was a chance it was not delivered with the first attempt. However, in the cases where it was originally delivered, the result is that the receiving client will receive the message more than once (see Figure 4.6).

It's important to note here that messaging systems do not intentionally duplicate messages. There are scenarios where a message consumer may process a message entirely just prior to a system failure. If the messaging software does not get a clear indication that the message was processed, it will redeliver the message when the system recovers. In this case, the message will appear to be a duplicate to the consumer. This is a scenario that every message consumer should be prepared for.

In the chat example, this situation might present itself as two chat sentences being displayed twice, or in the news example, as two of the same headlines being displayed in a row. Although this is still an undesired outcome, at least no data is lost, and the application's users should be happy. Also, there may be some way that your application can detect the redelivery and maybe even take steps to avoid processing messages twice. However, none of these scenarios is ideal; a duplicated chat sentence at the wrong time can inadvertently change the meaning of what a person was trying to say, and building logic into your application to work around duplicate messages defeats the purpose of using reliable messaging. In many cases, your applications will require 100% guaranteed delivery of each message, once each.

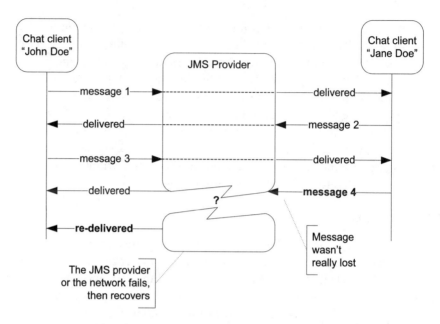

FIGURE 4.6   With at-least once message delivery, a JMS provider or network failure can result in the redelivery of an already-received message.

Once-and-Only-Once Delivery

In certain applications, such as an order processing system, or a trading system, you must be guaranteed that each message sent is delivered to a recipient exactly once. For example, a redelivery of a customer order may result in a duplicate customer order. Depending upon what is being sold, this may result in manufacturing double the merchandise, or shipping excess merchandise to the customer. Whatever the case may be, it will most likely end up costing the company money. A lost order, or buy notification, can also result in lost revenue, and it may even tarnish a company's reputation.

For the requirements of mission-critical messaging applications such as these, each message must be guaranteed to be delivered once and only once. This is known as once-and-only-once message delivery (see Figure 4.7). Licensed JMS providers are required to support once-and-only-once message delivery, but its implementation usually requires more resources and processing time to achieve. Therefore, your applications should invoke this delivery mode only when absolutely required. In addition, the burden of achieving reliable message delivery lies not only with the provider, but with the client application as well. The first responsibility you have as a JMS application developer is to understand the concept of message acknowledgment.

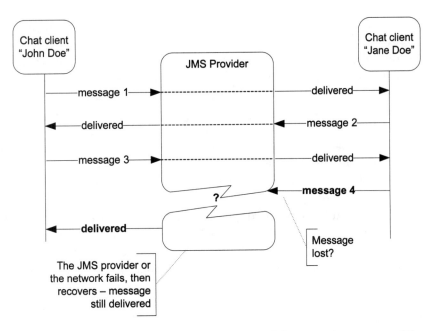

FIGURE 4.7 With once-and-only-once message delivery, each message will be delivered exactly one time regardless of failures.

Message Persistence

JMS defines two models of message delivery that directly indicate their level of reliability. The client application that produces messages indicates the delivery mode with each message it sends:

NON_PERSISTENT: This mode indicates that the message is not saved to non-volatile storage, leaving the risk that the message may be lost if a failure occurs before the message is delivered. Because the provider does not incur the over-head of storing the message (to a relatively slow medium such as a disk) prior to delivery, it is free to deliver the message as quickly as possible.

PERSISTENT: This mode indicates that the message is to be saved to non-volatile storage before sending it, ensuring that the message will not be lost in the event of a failure of the provider or otherwise. There is a cost associated with storing the message, and this may directly impact the provider's message delivery performance.

Choosing a message delivery mode means trading off performance for reliability or vice versa. The nonpersistent message mode directly maps to the at-most once delivery we discussed in the previous section. Conversely, persistent messaging directly maps to once-and-only-once message delivery. You need to make a choice as to which is more important on a case-by-case basis: getting the message there as quickly as possible or making sure it just gets there no matter what. Fortunately, JMS allows you to make this choice with each message that is sent. Therefore, one Destination can support both persistent and nonpersistent messages. No special administration is required.

However, message delivery mode alone does not guarantee reliable messaging. Persistent messaging must be coupled with either a durable subscription (for a publish-and-subscribe Topic) or a point-to-point Queue to guarantee delivery to all consumers. Additionally, you should recall from our definition of reliable messaging that message delivery should also be predictable. To achieve true reliability (by coupling guaranteed delivery with predictability), the client application must get involved with individual message acknowledgment and transactions.

Message Acknowledgment

The JMS provider's ability to reliably deliver every message to a client application is also related to how that application acknowledges received messages. There are message acknowledgment choices, and with each choice come certain characteristics you must be aware of. The following message acknowledgment choices are available, which must be specified when a Session is created:

AUTO_ACKNOWLEDGE: This acknowledgment mode indicates that the Session object itself will automatically acknowledge each message as it is delivered to the message consumer. The acknowledgment is sent when the call to receive returns (for synchronous message consumers) or the given MessageListener's onMessage method returns (for asynchronous message consumers).

DUPS_OK_ACKNOWLEDGE: This mode is fundamentally the same as AUTO_ ACKNOWLEDGE. It implies, however, that the Session can invoke some built-in optimization to minimize the overhead involved with message acknowledgment at the expense of the potential duplication of messages. In reality, the benefit received from this acknowledgment mode is questionable, and many JMS providers don't even support it; they simply default to AUTO_ACKNOWLEDGE mode.

CLIENT_ACKNOWLEGDGE: This mode indicates that the client will acknowledge message delivery on its own via a call to the acknowledge method of each Message object received. This can be misleading, as one acknowledge method call acknowledges all messages received for the client's Session.

Transacted Session: When a `Session` is created with the *transacted session* indicator set to `true`, message acknowledgment and recovery are handled automatically when transactions are committed or rolled back, respectively, by the client application.

The acknowledgment mode is specified as the second parameter of the `Connection` class' `createSession` method. The acknowledgment modes are defined as static members of the `Session` class; therefore, you must use class-level scope when providing the value to the call:

```
connection.createSession( false, Session.AUTO_ACKNOWLEDGE );
```

or:

```
connection.createSession( false, Session.CLIENT_ACKNOWLEDGE );
```

A message consumer that creates a `Session` with the `CLIENT_ACKNOWLEDGE` mode must acknowledge a message by calling its `acknowledge` method directly:

```
public void onMessage(Message message) {

    // process the message...

    message.acknowledge();
}
```

The message consumer's `Session` object retains each message until it is acknowledged, allowing the messages to be redelivered in the event of a listener failure. With client-based acknowledgment, this also means that a great deal of resources may be consumed if many messages go unacknowledged. Although it is acceptable for a client to receive more than one message before acknowledging them, it is not good practice to let a large number of messages go unacknowledged without good reason. It is also not good practice to close a `Session` object with unacknowledged messages, as they do not get automatically acknowledged. The result may be that the provider wastes resources keeping these messages around for a long period of time. This can lead to memory problems if this practice occurs frequently within a client application. For this reason, most JMS providers allow administrators to set limits on the number of messages retained with a `Session`.

Message Recovery

The sole purpose of message acknowledgment is to identify messages that have not been delivered so that they may be recovered by a message consumer. This is done by calling the `recover` method on the consumer's `Session` object. The result is that the Session is put back into a state just before the last unacknowledged message, and it resumes message delivery from that point. Each message that is being redelivered will have its JMSRedelivered property set to true by the Session object before it is delivered again.

Although message order is always guaranteed to be retained (this will be discussed in detail later), the order can change over time because of message expiration and the sending of higher priority messages. Therefore, although a recovered Session resumes from the point before the last unacknowledged message, the stream of messages sent after a recovery are not guaranteed to be identical to when the messages were first delivered.

Message Groups

Message acknowledgment is important to reliable messaging because it directly affects message recovery. It's the main indicator to the provider that your application has processed a message. It also allows you to control how messages are recovered in the event of a failure. For instance, with the use of the CLIENT_ACKNOWLEDGE mode, your application can hold off on acknowledging message delivery until a set of messages has been received. Perhaps because of the way information is gathered in your application, the data that makes up a complete set may be divided across multiple JMS messages. In this case, these messages act like a group, and your application can acknowledge them as a group when they all arrive by calling the acknowledge method for the last message received in the group.

Take for example a scenario where all the data your application needs to process as a whole is spread across three JMS messages. As the messages arrive, the data is used to fill out the properties of an object in memory. Assume that after the first two messages arrive (and are acknowledged) your application stops running because of a hardware failure. When your application recovers, the provider will determine that you have not yet received the third message and will deliver it now. However, since your application lost the data from the first two messages, you have an incomplete data set. In this case, the JMS provider did its job—all the messages were delivered reliably to your application. It knows that because each message was acknowledged. However, you still have an error scenario because data has been lost.

To solve the problem in this case, your application should *not* acknowledge any messages until *all* of the data for your object arrive—meaning all three JMS messages have arrived. This way if a failure were to occur before all three messages arrive, all three messages are assured to be delivered again after a recovery. Let's look at an example. Listing 4.5 contains the code for the onMessage implementation of a consumer that receives order information in a stock trading system. The data for the order arrives in three messages, and each message is given a sequence number by the sender for identification.

Notice that after the first two messages arrive, the stock ticker and the order type for the new order are retrieved respectively, and the method returns without acknowledging the messages. When the third message arrives, the order quantity is retrieved, and the order is placed in the trading system. However, before the order is placed, a failure occurs (via the contrived example's call to System.exit). Fortunately, the data is not lost because the message acknowledgment does not occur until after the order is successfully placed. Therefore, when the consumer recovers, all three messages will be delivered once again, resulting in a complete order in the trading system.

LISTING 4.5   Code to Acknowledge Message Groups

```
public void onMessage(Message message)
{
    try {
        String ticker;
        String type;
        int qty;

        MapMessage mapMsg = (MapMessage)message;

        int sequence = mapMsg.getIntProperty("Sequence");

        System.out.println( "Received a message, sequence="
                            + sequence );
        switch ( sequence )
        {
        case 1:
            ticker = mapMsg.getString("Ticker");
            order.setTicker(ticker);
            return;
        case 2:
            type = mapMsg.getString("OrderType");
            order.setType(type);
            return;
        case 3:
            qty = mapMsg.getInt("Quantity");
            order.setQuantity(qty);
            break;
        default:
            System.out.println("Error: unknown message sequence");
            return;
        }
```

```
                        // SIMULATE A FAILURE BEFORE THE ORDER IS PLACED
                        System.exit(0);

                        // Place the order and acknowledge the messages

                        mapMsg.acknowledge();
                    }
```

Client acknowledgment also allows your application to acknowledge a message *before* it's done processing it. This allows the JMS provider to continue message delivery while your application performs a potentially lengthy operation on the received message. In the code in Listing 4.6, the message consumer receives a message, safely stores it, and then acknowledges it before waiting for input from the user (a potentially long operation). Keep in mind that this has consequences in terms of message recovery. If the application were to crash at some point after acknowledging the message, but before it was completely processed, it would not be resent by the JMS provider.

LISTING 4.6   Code that Acknowledges a Message Before it is Completely Processed

```
            public void onMessage(Message message)
            {
                try {
                    MapMessage orderMsg = (MapMessage)message;

                    storeOrder(orderMsg);

                    orderMsg.acknowledge();

                    if ( getUserConfirmation() )
                        placeOrder( orderMsg );
                }
                catch( Exception e ) {
                    e.printStackTrace();
                }
            }
```

Message Order

In one of the previous sections, a statement was made that JMS guarantees that message order will be maintained. This is true, but many constraints are placed on this guarantee that make message ordering a tricky subject. To be precise, it should be stated that JMS guarantees that messages will be delivered in the order that they were sent through a *single* Session object. There are no guarantees for message order between different Session objects for the same destination.

If you were to look at a `Session` object's message stream at one point in time, the internal message ordering may change when compared at another point in time. This is due to the constraints placed on the ordering of messages:

Message expiration: Undelivered messages that exceed their given time-to-live value will be removed from the internal message stream.

Message priority: New messages that are sent to a destination will jump ahead of other existing messages in the `Session`'s message stream.

Delivery mode: Nonpersistent messages may be lost if a failure occurs. When the system recovers, the nonpersistent messages may be missing from the internal message stream.

Message ordering is further subdivided within a `Session` according to its delivery mode (persistent or nonpersistent). Message order will only be maintained within the delivery mode group, not across. To clarify, examine Figure 4.8. In this diagram, the absolute order that all four messages were sent in are A, A', B', and then B (where A' and B' are persistent, and A and B are nonpersistent). However, the order that the message consumer received them in was A, A', B, and then B'. Message B was delivered before message B' even though they were sent in the reverse order. This is not an error. It's a valid scenario because message B' was a persistent message, and message B was not. If you group the persistent and non-persistent messages separately, you will see that the order was preserved.

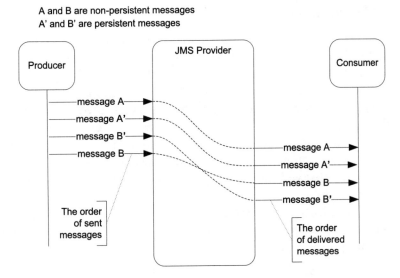

FIGURE 4.8   Messages are delivered in order only within their respective "mode"—persistent or nonpersistent.

> **Nonpersistent messages:**   Message A was sent and delivered before message B.
>
> **Persistent messages:**   Message A' was sent and delivered before message B'.

Because they were sent with different delivery modes, it is completely irrelevant that message B was received before message B' even though the order they were sent was the opposite.

MESSAGE DELIVERY SCENARIOS

To help clarify the choices provided by JMS messaging, let's explore the message delivery behavior with different messaging options chosen. The first option is the messaging domain: publish-and-subscribe or point-to-point (queues). The exact behavior of reliable message delivery varies slightly between these domains. Besides the obvious differences, such as the multicast nature of pub/sub and the single-consumer delivery of queues, the message delivery guarantees change in some not so obvious ways. Let's begin by looking at some scenarios common to both domains and then explore the exceptional cases in each domain.

 Use of synchronous versus asynchronous messaging does not affect the nature of reliable message delivery in any way. Therefore, most of the examples and figures use asynchronous messaging to be consistent in their illustration.

Domain-Independent Common Scenarios

This section examines messaging scenarios that work the same for both publish-and-subscribe and queue-based messaging. Therefore, the sequence diagrams used for illustration do not show Destination objects, and they refer to the *common* interfaces, Producer and Consumer. Each diagram also includes objects representing the JMS provider and a nonvolatile storage facility used to safely store messages. In the real world, this would most likely be a database or a flat-file system, which is an implementation detail that is specific to the JMS provider used and the administrative choices allowed. Regardless, this is meant to represent some long-term storage facility that will survive even if the JMS provider were to stop running for any reason.

Figure 4.9 contains a sequence diagram for a very basic messaging scenario; the sending of a nonpersistent message to either a Topic or a Queue. In this scenario, the following steps occur:

1. A message producer sends a nonpersistent message to the JMS provider for a Destination.
2. Since the message is nonpersistent, the provider immediately sends an acknowledgment to the sender's Session and simply keeps a copy of the message in memory. Nonvolatile storage (a database or a flat-file) is not used in this case.
3. The provider then delivers the message to a consumer for the message's Destination (in this example there is only one).
4. The consumer's Session acknowledges receipt of the message.

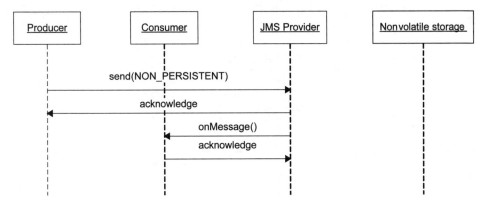

FIGURE 4.9   This call sequence for a nonpersistent message is common to both message domains.

Even with nonpersistent messaging, acknowledgments will be sent (and should be sent in the case of client-based acknowledgment) to ensure reliable message delivery if there are no JMS provider failures. However, because nonpersistent message delivery was chosen in this example, if a provider failure occurred somewhere in the process of message delivery—between steps 2 and 3 for instance—the message would likely be lost even after a recovery. To ensure the message will be delivered even if the JMS provider stops running, persistent messaging must be used.

The sequence diagram in Figure 4.10 represents the flow of events that occur when persistent messaging is used. In this scenario, the following steps occur:

1. A message producer sends a persistent message to the JMS provider for a Destination.

2. Upon receipt, the JMS provider persists the message to nonvolatile storage.
3. After the message is safely stored, the provider sends an acknowledgment to the message producer.
4. The provider then delivers the message to a consumer for the message's `Destination` (in this example there is only one).
5. The consumer's `Session` acknowledges receipt of the message.
6. Upon receipt of the message acknowledgment from the consumer, the persisted message is removed from persistent storage.

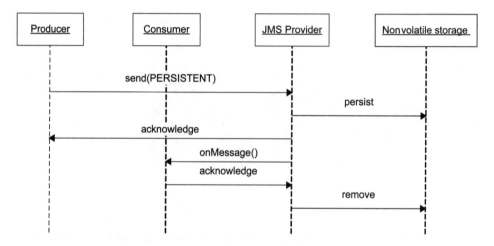

FIGURE 4.10   This call sequence for a persistent message is common to both message domains.

Since nonpersistent messaging is the default message mode, your client code must specifically set the mode to persistent as shown here:

```
Session session = connection.createSession(
                    false, Session.AUTO_ACKNOWLEDGE);
MessageProducer producer = session.createProducer(orderDest);
producer.setDeliveryMode(DeliveryMode.PERSISTENT);
```

There are two very important differences between the persistent and nonpersistent message scenarios we just examined. First, the JMS provider will *not* acknowledge the message producer until the message has been safely persisted. Therefore, after your producer gets an acknowledgment to a persistent message-send operation, you can be assured that the message will eventually be delivered. However, the lack of an acknowledgment indicates that the message may not have been received and/or persisted by the JMS provider. This may be because of a network error or a program error within the JMS provider. Either way, your JMS client code should use the acknowledgment (or lack thereof) to make intelligent choices about whether it should resend a message, rollback a transaction, or simply continue on with its normal processing.

Next, let's examine a scenario where a message consumer component fails, perhaps due to a hardware failure or some other failure of the JMS client application.

Figure 4.11 is a sequence diagram for a message scenario where the message consumer fails while processing a received message. Let's assume that the failure occurs before the consumer's onMessage method is called or after it is called but *before* it returns, as described in the steps that follow.

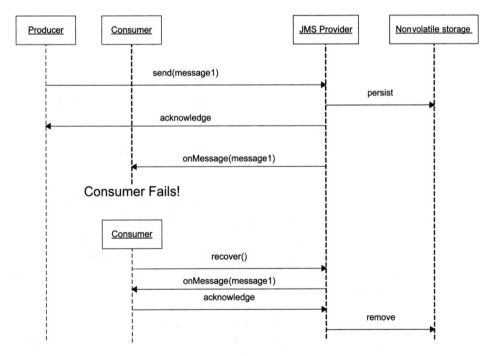

FIGURE 4.11 With a durable subscription, or a queue, message recovery is guaranteed.

1. A message producer sends a persistent message to the JMS provider for a destination.
2. Upon receipt, the JMS provider persists the message to nonvolatile storage.
3. Only after the message is safely stored, the provider sends an acknowledgment to the message producer.
4. The provider then delivers the message to a consumer for the message's `Destination`.
5. The message consumer fails while (or just prior to) processing the message.
6. Some time later, the message consumer recovers and calls the `Session` `recover` method.
7. Once again, the provider delivers the message to the consumer by calling its `onMessage` method.
8. This time, the consumer processes the message fully and sends an acknowledgment to the provider.
9. Upon receipt of the message acknowledgment from the consumer, the persisted message is removed from persistent storage.

The consumer's message acknowledgment plays a very important role in message recovery. In the previous scenario, the consumer failed while processing a message. However, even if the `onMessage` method did return, the message would remain a candidate for redelivery if the consumer failed to send an acknowledgment to the provider. Basically, JMS message recovery includes the redelivery of all messages that remain unacknowledged, which includes all messages that were delivered since the previous message acknowledgment was received from the consumer.

To best illustrate this scenario, follow the steps shown in the sequence diagram in Figure 4.12.

1–9. In the first nine steps, three messages are sent by the message producer, persisted, and acknowledged.
10. The provider delivers message1 to a consumer for the message's `Destination`.
11. The consumer's `Session` acknowledges receipt of the message.
12. Upon receipt of the message acknowledgment from the consumer, the persisted message is removed from persistent storage.
13. The provider delivers message2 to the consumer.
14. The provider delivers message3 to the consumer.
15. The message consumer fails while (or just prior to) processing message3.
16. Some time later, the message consumer recovers and calls the `Session` `recover` method.
17. The provider redelivers message2 to the consumer.
18. The provider redelivers message3 to the consumer.
19. The consumer sends a single acknowledgment, which applies to all unacknowledged messages up to that point (message2 and message3).

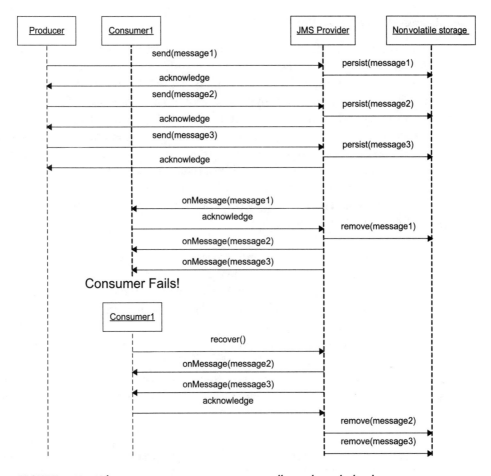

FIGURE 4.12 When a message recovery occurs, all unacknowledged messages are redelivered.

20. Upon receipt of the message acknowledgment from the consumer, the persisted messages, message2 and message3, are removed from persistent storage.

In this case, message1 was not included in the message recovery because the provider received an acknowledgment after it was delivered, prior to the failure of the consumer. Both message2 and message3 were delivered, but the provider never received a message acknowledgment for either message. After the message recovery began, message2 and message3 were redelivered to the consumer, but this time the consumer sent a single acknowledgment after receiving message3. This single acknowledgment covered all messages that were received (but unacknowledged) up to that point.

Publish-and-Subscribe Scenarios

According to the JMS specification, specifying persistent or nonpersistent message delivery with pub/sub messaging makes no difference for nondurable subscribers. There is no guarantee that persisted messages will be delivered to a subscriber in any failure condition, unless that subscriber has a durable subscription. What JMS does specify is that the message will be persisted until it is delivered to all known subscribers. Not only does this guarantee message recovery for durable subscribers, but it also opens the door to some form of message recovery for nondurable subscribers, although support for this is not required. Let's examine some examples.

Figure 4.13 contains a sequence diagram for a scenario where a persistent message is published and received by two known message subscribers. In this example, the following steps occur:

1. A message producer sends a persistent message.
2. The JMS provider saves the message to persistent storage.
3. The provider sends an acknowledgment to the message producer.
4–5. The message is delivered to the first consumer, and an acknowledgment is sent back to the provider.
6–7. The message is delivered to the second consumer, and an acknowledgment is sent back to the provider.
8. Now that the message has been delivered to all publish-and-subscribe consumers for this Destination, the message is removed from persistent storage.

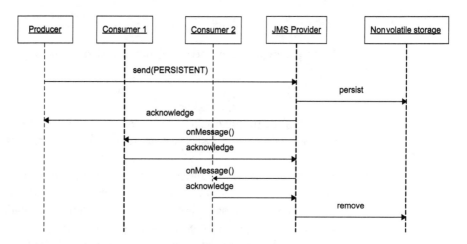

FIGURE 4.13 Multiple publish-and-subscribe consumers.

Notice that the message was not removed until after the message was delivered to all known subscribers. This helps ensure that the message will be delivered, but there is still no guarantee if one of the consumers failed while processing the message. This also means that the persistent message will not be available for consumers that subscribe later. If we were to change the scenario in Figure 4.13 slightly, so that Consumer2 was not created until after the message was delivered to Consumer1, it would never receive the message.

The sequence diagram in Figure 4.14 illustrates this scenario, in which the following steps occur:

1. A publish-and-subscribe message producer sends a message with a delivery mode of persistent, which is received by the JMS provider.
2. The provider safely stores the message into nonvolatile storage (either a database or flat-file storage).
3. The provider acknowledges the receipt of the message.
4. The message is delivered by the provider to a consumer (Consumer1 in this example). Durability does not matter here, as the consumer is online and available to receive the message.
5. After the onMessage method call returns, the consumer acknowledges receipt of the message.
6. Having delivered the persistent message to all available consumers, the JMS provider removes the message from storage.
7. Some time later, a nondurable subscriber comes online, but does *not* receive the persisted message.

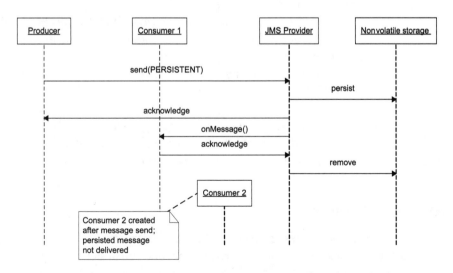

FIGURE 4.14 Regardless of delivery mode, a nondurable subscriber will not receive a missed message.

A durable subscription is the only way to guarantee that messages will be delivered to a consumer if a failure occurs. With durable subscriptions, there is almost no difference between a persistent or nonpersistent message: they will both be delivered to an offline subscriber once that subscriber comes online again. With nonpersistent messaging, however, there is a small period of time (between the sender acknowledgment and the persistence of the message) when a message could get lost. However, most JMS providers minimize this by persisting the message in all cases when durable subscriptions exist. Overall it is best to always create a durable subscription and send a message as persistent if the message is critical.

The sequence diagram in Figure 4.15 illustrates what happens when a message is sent while there is an existing durable subscription active. The scenario is as follows:

1. At some point prior to any messages being sent, a consumer creates a durable subscription.
2. Although the durable subscriber terminates, the durable subscription is still active inside the JMS provider.
3. A producer sends a message to the destination.
4. The provider stores the message to nonvolatile storage. This certainly will occur for persistent messages, and most providers will do this even for nonpersistent messages if a durable subscription is active.
5. The provider acknowledges the receipt of the message.
6. Some time later, the durable subscriber is created again. The provider recognizes the durable subscriber by the client ID provided here and earlier when the subscription was created.
7. Since its subscription was still active (identified by the client ID) the JMS provider sends it the messages it has missed (only one in this example) in that time period, if any.
8. The durable subscriber acknowledges receipt of the message
9. The JMS provider removes the delivered message from persistent storage.

It's very important to remember that sending a message with a delivery mode of persistent does not guarantee its delivery in the event of a failure unless the consumer uses a durable subscription or a queue to receive the messages.

Point-to-Point Scenarios

The point-to-point message scenarios don't differ much from publish-and-subscribe except that each message is delivered to only one consumer. Still, queue-based messaging is often chosen when reliable message delivery is desired, because its nature is to store messages for potentially long periods of time.

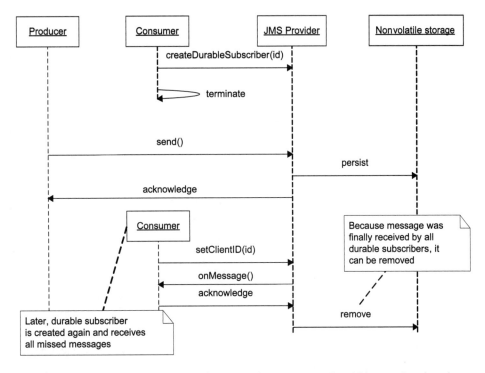

FIGURE 4.15 Regardless of the delivery mode, messages should be persisted and remain in storage until delivered when a durable subscription exists.

Let's explore a typical queue-based messaging scenario. The sequence diagram in Figure 4.16 illustrates what happens when a message is sent while there are multiple queue listeners active. Let's explore the steps that occur in this scenario (some of the steps we've seen in other scenarios have been summarized):

1–6. Two messages are sent by the message producer, persisted, and then acknowledged.
7–9. The first message is delivered to the consumer Consumer1, acknowledged, and then removed from persistent storage. The consumer Consumer2 does not receive this message.
10–12. The second message is delivered to the consumer Consumer2, acknowledged, and then removed from persistent storage. The consumer Consumer1 does not receive this message.

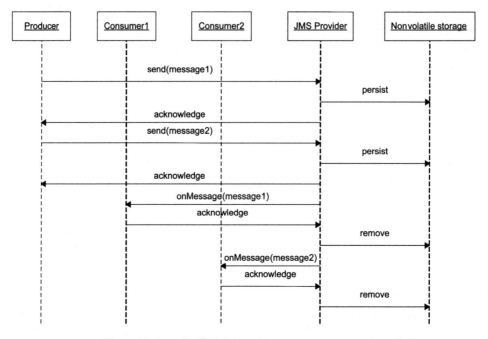

FIGURE 4.16 Unlike publish-and-subscribe, only one consumer receives each message when you use a queue.

With queue-based messaging, your messages are safe, even if the provider fails before the messages are delivered. Figure 4.17 contains a sequence diagram that illustrates a provider failure and subsequent recovery:

1. The producer sends a message to a queue.
2. The JMS provider saves the message to persistent storage.
3. The provider sends an acknowledgment to the message producer.
4. After sending the acknowledgment, the provider fails.
5. Some time later, the JMS provider process recovers.
6. Since the message sent in the first step was safely persisted, it is now delivered to the message consumer.
7. The consumer acknowledges receipt of the message.
8. Since the message was delivered to the consumer, it's removed from persistent storage.

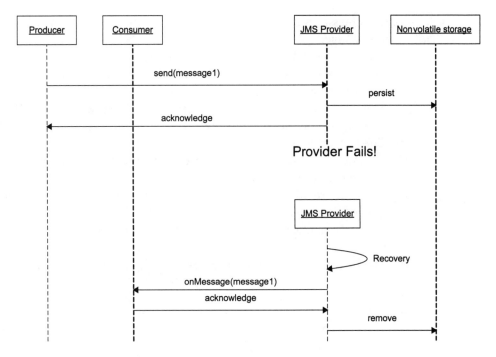

FIGURE 4.17 This sequence diagram illustrates queued message recovery.

Of course, the provider isn't the only component that has the potential to fail. As with publish-and-subscribe messaging, the provider will not remove a persisted message from its nonvolatile storage facility until it receives an acknowledgment from the message consumer. Therefore, if a consumer fails while processing a message, the message will be delivered to another consumer or to the original consumer when it recovers. The exact semantics depend on the timing of the failed consumer's recovery and the availability of other consumers for the same queue. However, it's important to realize that in the case of message recovery, the order in which messages are delivered is not guaranteed to be equivalent to the order in which the messages are placed on the queue.

Figure 4.18 shows a message recovery scenario that consists of two message consumers. In this case, one consumer fails and then quickly recovers. The following steps occur:

1–6. Two messages are sent by the message producer, persisted, and then acknowledged.

7. The first message, message1, is delivered to Consumer1. In this scenario, let's assume that this consumer fails while processing this message and does not send an acknowledgment.

8. The second message, message2, is delivered to Consumer2.

9. Consumer2 processes and acknowledges receipt of message2.

10. The JMS provider removes message2 from storage.

11. At some point quickly after it failed, and while Consumer2 was processing its message, Consumer1 recovers.

12. The JMS provider delivers the next remaining message (message1) on the queue to Consumer1.

13. This time Consumer1 processes the message fine and sends an acknowledgment.

14. The JMS provider removes message1 from storage.

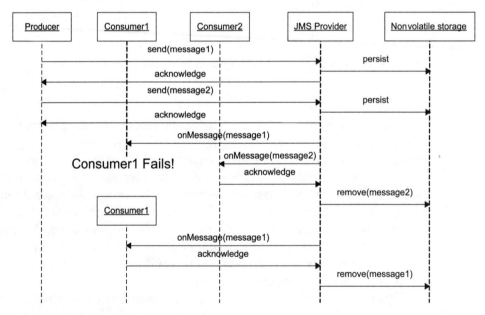

FIGURE 4.18 This sequence diagram shows how messages can be delivered in a different order than they were placed in the queue.

You can see in this scenario that the messages were ultimately delivered and processed out of order because of the failure of one of the consumers. message1 was delivered before message2, but because its consumer failed while receiving it, it was redelivered after message2 had been processed. Message delivery order is not guaranteed across consumers; it is only guaranteed for a single session. This means that in a scenario where a third message, message3, was sent after the first two messages, a single consumer will not receive message3 followed by message1 in a normal situation.

Other factors also affect message delivery order, such as message priority, the loss of nonpersistent messages because of a provider failure, and the use of transactions to treat sets of messages as one atomic unit of work. Finally, it's important to remember that persistent and nonpersistent messages are grouped separately; the provider will attempt to maintain delivery order within each group of messages. A nonpersistent message sent after a persistent message may arrive before the persistent message. However, all of the nonpersistent messages will be delivered in order relative to themselves, as will all of the persistent messages, but messages from both groups may be interleaved.

Transactions

Up until this point, we've explored the various messaging scenarios for publish-and-subscribe and point-to-point messaging, including message recovery, guaranteed delivery, and message acknowledgment. One more advanced messaging concept is important to understand regarding sending and receiving messages: transactions.

A JMS transaction is used to treat a series of message sends or message receives, or a combination of both as one atomic unit of work. When a transaction is committed that involves sending messages, the messages are sent as an atomic unit of work. When a transaction is committed that involves receiving messages, message acknowledgments are sent and the messages are considered delivered. In all cases, a rolled-back transaction reverses the scenario as though it never happened. Rolling back a transaction involving sent messages results in those messages being destroyed, never to be delivered to a consumer. Rolling back a transaction involving received messages results in the recovery of those messages, thereby placing them back in a queue or a pub/sub subscription, ready to be delivered again.

The use of transactions alters the message delivery scenarios from the previous sections in some obvious and not-so-obvious ways. For instance, transaction commits and rollbacks work in conjunction with message acknowledgment and are used by the provider to indicate when a persisted message can be removed.

The sequence diagram in Figure 4.19 shows an otherwise common message-send-and-receive scenario, but with two transactions. The first transaction is started by the message producer as it sends a message to the provider. The second transaction is started by the message consumer as it receives a message from the provider. Keep in mind that a transaction begins automatically with the first action on a transacted session and thereafter following each transaction's commit or rollback. This creates a virtual chain of transactions, where each one begins automatically as the previous one ends. Follow along with the steps below that trace the two transactions in this sample scenario:

1–3. In the first three steps, a message is sent by the message producer, persisted, and acknowledged. These steps are identical to the many scenarios explored earlier in this chapter.
4. The producer commits the transaction, which started in step 1.
5. The JMS provider delivers the message to the consumer. This step begins a new (separate) transaction for the message consumer.
6. The consumer acknowledges receipt of the message.
7. The consumer then commits the transaction started in step 5.
8. Now that the consumer's transaction has been committed, the message is removed from persistent storage. It was not removed upon receipt of the acknowledgment (in the previous step) because the transaction still had the potential to be rolled back.

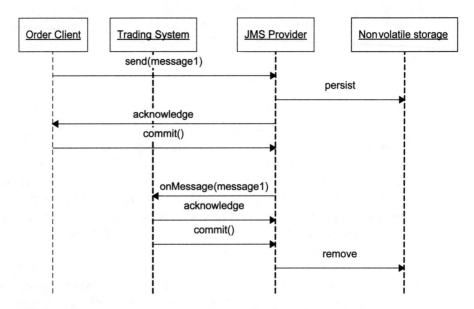

FIGURE 4.19   Two transactions, one for send and one for receive.

This relatively straightforward example illustrates how message acknowledgment, although still very important, is not the only signal used by the provider to indicate that the message processing is complete. With a transacted JMS session, a commit must be issued to indicate to the provider that it can follow through with message delivery or the removal of messages from the queue or topic (and persistent storage). However, this is a very simple example where a rollback of the sender's transaction would have resulted in the destruction of the message before it was ever delivered to a consumer. Additionally, the rollback of the consumer's session would have resulted in the provider recovering the message and placing it back on the queue. The scenario gets more interesting if a single transaction consists of a message receive *and* a message send.

Figure 4.20 shows a sequence diagram for a transaction that is started when a message is received by a consumer within a trading system software component, and includes its subsequently sent message. In this scenario, it's important that the client order not be removed from the queue until we're sure that the broker system has received the broker order. Therefore, the transaction is not committed until the trading system knows that the persistent message it has sent in response to the order request has been received by the JMS provider. This is outlined in the following steps:

1. The JMS provider delivers a message to the message consumer (the trading system). This starts a new transaction for the consumer.
2. The trading system acknowledges receipt of the message.
3. The trading system sends an order request message to a stock broker system to place the order on behalf of the client.
4. The provider persists the order request message.
5. The provider acknowledges receipt of the message.
6. The trading system commits the transaction started in step 1.
7. The order message is delivered to the stock broker system.

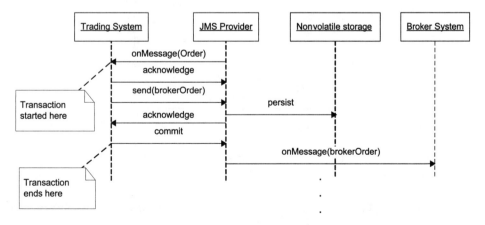

FIGURE 4.20 In this diagram, the receipt of a message starts a new transaction that is committed only when an order is placed.

A transaction does not need to be confined to just a single message send, a single message receive, or chained message-receive and -send operations. A single transaction can include multiple messages sent by a producer or the receipt of multiple messages by a consumer. As an example, let's assume that the trading system software needs to send a message indicating that a trade was executed. In this example, this also means a message must be sent to indicate that the previously placed order (which resulted in the trade) should be closed. Since each action depends on the other, it is not desirable for only one of the two messages to be sent; it must be guaranteed that both messages are sent as an atomic unit of work.

Figure 4.21 contains a sequence diagram outlining the steps involved in a transaction that contains two sent messages, which is similar to the example scenario just discussed. Follow along with the steps below that describe this transaction:

1–6. Two messages are sent by the message producer, persisted, and acknowledged.
7. The producer commits the transaction, which was started in step 1 and included both sent messages. If the transaction were rolled back, both messages would have been removed and not delivered.

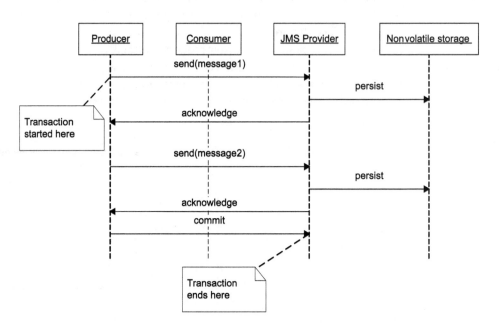

FIGURE 4.21 A message producer can roll multiple message sends into one transaction.

Since a combination of persistent messaging and a transaction are used, *both* messages are guaranteed to be delivered, which satisfies the requirement of the example scenario discussed previously. However, neither message will be delivered until the single transaction is committed by the message producer. If the transaction happens to be rolled back instead of committed, both messages will be removed from persistent storage and destroyed completely. Let's examine an example where two messages must be received as an atomic unit.

Assume that first message is a trade notification, and the second message is a trade ticket containing all of the details to the trade. In this example trading system, the first message is required to update an outstanding trade request, while the second is required to record the details of the trade and possibly clear the transaction with a bank.

Figure 4.22 shows a sequence diagram for the sample transaction involving two received messages. The following steps trace the transaction:

1. The JMS provider delivers a message to the message consumer. This starts a new transaction for the consumer.
2. The consumer acknowledges receipt of the message.
3. The JMS provider delivers a second message to the message consumer. This message is part of the same transaction started in step 1.
4. The consumer acknowledges receipt of the second message.
5. The consumer commits the transaction, which includes both received messages.
6–7. The JMS provider can now safely remove both messages from persistent storage (originally placed there in the previous sequence shown in Figure 4.21).

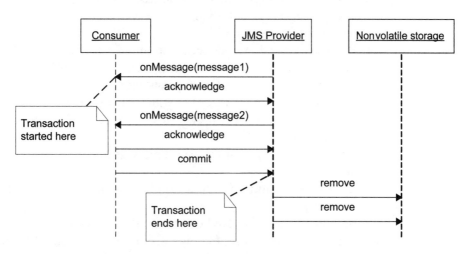

FIGURE 4.22 A message consumer can roll multiple message receives into one transaction.

The Trading System Order-Entry Example

We've spent a great deal of time examining detailed messaging scenarios that involve guaranteed messages and transactions. It's time to begin to implement a sample trading system based on the scenarios we've discussed so far. The example involves three main classes, each of which runs as its own application: the order client, the order manager, and the order broker. Because of the implied criticality of the example (someone's imminent stock trade is at stake here) and the complex interactions across the simulated software systems, this example serves as a good exercise in reliable, transaction-based messaging.

Figure 4.23 shows a sequence diagram that illustrates the message flow between the various systems involved in executing the simulated stock trade. With the combination of persistent messaging and the four chained queue-based transactions, the stock order executes in what is basically one *virtual* transaction. The four transactions are not truly nested within a transaction themselves. However, because of the semantics of transacted JMS reliable message delivery, the messages that trigger each stage of the order processing are guaranteed to be delivered, thereby guaranteeing the end-to-end order processing scenario as a whole. Let's examine the steps in this process in detail:

1–4. The order client sends an order request message; it is persisted and acknowledged by the JMS provider. Finally, the transaction is committed, ending transaction 1.

5–6. The provider delivers the message to the trading system consumer, and the trading system acknowledges its receipt. This begins transaction 2.

7–10. The trading system sends an order request message; it is persisted and acknowledged by the JMS provider. Finally, the transaction is committed, ending transaction 2.

11. Because transaction 2 has been committed, which included the processing of the client order message (from steps 1 through 4), the client order message can be removed from persistent storage.

12–13. The provider delivers the order request message to the stock broker system consumer and the broker acknowledges its receipt. This begins transaction 3.

14–15. The broker sends an order-placed message to the provider, and it is acknowledged.

16. The broker commits its transaction (transaction 3), which began in step 12.

17. Because transaction 3 has been committed, which included the processing of the broker order message (from steps 5 through 10), the broker order message can be removed from persistent storage.

18–19. The trading system receives the order-placed message and acknowledges its receipt. This starts transaction 4.

20–22. The trading system sends an order confirmation message for the order client, which is persisted and acknowledged by the JMS provider.

   23. The trading system commits transaction number 4.

24–26. The order client receives the order confirmation message and sends an acknowledgment. As a result, the provider removes the message from persistent storage.

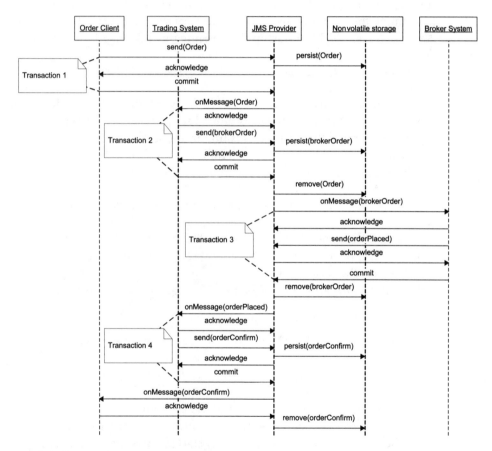

FIGURE 4.23   This diagram shows how JMS transactions can be chained to achieve one *virtual* atomic unit of work: placing a stock trade request.

This scenario represents a complex interaction between three components utilizing persistent messaging across two queues, with transacted sessions and a temporary topic. It may seem unlikely that a system with so many components and interactions could work reliably, but it does. To prove that it does, and that JMS does indeed deliver on its guarantees, let's examine this scenario in more detail as we implement it.

The complete source code for the trading system example can be found on the CD-ROM included with this book, in the folder labeled Chapter4. The example consists of three main applications: the order client, the order manager (a.k.a. the trading system), and the order broker. The order broker application can be started by running the Windows batch file runorderbroker.bat or UNIX command script runorderbroker.sh. Both startup files execute the following Java command:

```
> java -cp (classpath details here) com.TradingSystem.OrderBroker
```

The order manager can be started by executing the Windows batch file runordermanager2.bat or UNIX command script runordermanager2.sh. Notice the "2" in the name of the script; this is important, as the runordermanager.bat script from earlier in the chapter will run a different version of the order manager application. The startup files execute the following Java command:

```
> java -cp (classpath details here) com.TradingSystem.OrderManager2
```

Finally, the order client can be started by running the Windows batch file runorderclient2.bat or UNIX command script runorderclient2.sh. Again, make sure you run the script with the "2" in the name or you will run a version of the order client from earlier in the chapter. The startup files execute the following Java command:

```
> java -cp (classpath details here) com.TradingSystem.OrderClient2
```

Make sure your JMS provider is running before trying the sample application.

CAUTION

It is recommended that you run these components now by first starting the ActiveMQ message broker, then the order broker and order manager applications. Once these applications have completely started, start the order client application, which will send a buy order for 100 shares each of 10 different stocks. The order client application does not output any text until it receives an order confirmation reply message from the order manager, so let's focus on the order manager first. For each client order request received—which starts a new transaction—the order manager first outputs the following text:

```
Received a BUY order for 100 shares of IBM sequence=1
```

The code outputs the order type (buy or sell), the quantity, and the stock ticker for each order it receives. The sequence number is added to the message by the order client for accounting purposes. In response, the order manager sends a broker order request to the external stock broker system, where the stock trade actually takes place. When the order broker application receives a broker order, you will see the following message:

```
Received a BUY broker order for 100 shares of IBM sequence=1
```

The code outputs basically the same message as the order manager, except that it denotes the order as a broker order. The sequence number in this message was assigned by the order manager. It is not equivalent to the order client sequence number. In response, the order broker sends a message to the reply topic that was in the broker order message, informing the order manager that the order was placed. When this reply message is received, the order manager outputs the following text:

```
Broker reply received for ticker DELL
```

Finally, upon receiving the order-placed message from the order broker, the order manager sends an order confirmation message back to the order client, at which point it outputs the following:

```
Confirmation received: Order placed for ticker YHOO
```

This ends the order entry transaction envelope for one order. This will be repeated once for each of the 10 stocks the client application is coded to enter orders for. Let's examine the code for this example now.

The Order Client

The order client application (see Listing 4.7) contains a message producer component that sends new order request messages and a message consumer that listens for order confirmation messages in response to each order it places. The constructor contains the typical Java Naming and Directory Interface (JNDI) code to create a JMS provider connection and to create a transacted `Session` object. Although the acknowledgment mode, `AUTO_ACKNOWLEDGE`, is specified here, it is ignored, as each call to `Session.commit` serves as an acknowledgment.

Once the session is created, a reference to the `OrderQ Destination` is retrieved through JNDI, and a message producer is created with a message mode of `PERSISTENT`. Next, the temporary `Topic` and `Consumer` objects are created to receive order confirmation messages.

The bulk of the processing is done in the sendOrders method, where a loop sends out an order request for 100 shares of each stock in the stocks array. For each order, a MapMessage is created and populated with the stock ticker, the order type (buy or sell), the number of shares (quantity), and a sequence number. The reply Topic is set in the order's JMSReplyTo message property. Now that the order request is complete, the message is sent and the transaction is committed.

Each order confirmation message is received via the onMessage method as a TextMessage, and the text of the message is sent to the command line. Remember that each order confirmation message received is part of a new transaction. Therefore, as the last step in this method, the transaction is committed. If, however, an error occurs while processing this message, the transaction is rolled back so that it can be redelivered or otherwise handled differently.

LISTING 4.7 Code for the OrderClient2 Component

```java
package com.TradingSystem;

import javax.jms.*;
import javax.naming.InitialContext;

public class OrderClient2 implements MessageListener
{
    private static int sequence = 0;
    private Connection connection;
    private Session session;
    private MessageProducer producer;
    private MessageConsumer consumer;
    private Topic orderReplies;

    private String[] stocks = {
            "IBM", "MSFT", "SUNW", "ORCL", "SBL",
            "BEAS", "AAPL", "DELL", "GOOG", "YHOO" };

    public OrderClient2()
    {
        try {
            InitialContext jndi = new InitialContext();
            ConnectionFactory conFactory =
                (ConnectionFactory)jndi.lookup("ConnectionFactory");
            connection = conFactory.createConnection("","");
            session = connection.createSession(
                        true, // transacted session
                        Session.AUTO_ACKNOWLEDGE);
```

```
        // Create producer for order requests
        Destination orderDest =
            (Destination)jndi.lookup("OrderQ");
        producer = session.createProducer(orderDest);
        producer.setDeliveryMode(DeliveryMode.PERSISTENT);

        // Create temp topic and consumer for order replies
        orderReplies = (Topic)session.createTemporaryTopic();
        consumer = session.createConsumer(orderReplies);
        consumer.setMessageListener(this);

        connection.start();

        sendOrders();
    }
    catch ( Exception e ) {
        e.printStackTrace();
        try {
            session.rollback();
        }
        catch ( Exception e1 ) { }
    }
}

private void sendOrders() throws Exception
{
    // Place a buy order for 100 shares of each stock
    for ( int i = 0; i < stocks.length; i++ )
    {
        MapMessage msg = session.createMapMessage();
        msg.setString("Ticker", stocks[i]);
        msg.setString("OrderType", "BUY");
        msg.setInt("Quantity", 100);

        msg.setIntProperty("Sequence", ++sequence);

        msg.setJMSReplyTo(orderReplies);
        producer.send(msg);
        session.commit();
    }
}

public void onMessage(Message msg)
{
```

```
        try {
            TextMessage textMsg = (TextMessage)msg;
            System.out.println( "Confirmation received: "
                                + textMsg.getText());
            session.commit();
        }
        catch ( Exception e ) {
            e.printStackTrace();
            try {
                session.rollback();
            }
            catch ( Exception e1 ) { }
        }
    }


    public static void main(String[] args) throws Exception
    {
        OrderClient2 client = new OrderClient2();
        try {
            Thread.sleep(5000);
        }
        catch ( Exception e ) { }
        client.connection.close();
    }
}
```

The Order Manager (a.k.a. the Trading System)

The order manager application (see Listing 4.8) contains a message consumer to receive order request messages from the order client component, a message producer to send messages to the order broker component, and a temporary Topic to receive reply messages from the order broker. As with the order client, the constructor contains all the appropriate JNDI code to connect to the JMS provider. However, the order manager creates *two* transacted Session objects: one to receive client order requests and subsequently send broker order messages and another to receive reply messages from the order broker via asynchronous messaging.

After the appropriate destinations, message producer, and message consumer components are created, the order manager enters an infinite loop to receive client order request messages. Each received message automatically starts a new transaction. When an order is received, the code prepares to send a broker order message by increasing the broker order sequence number, and storing the client order message's reply-to Topic in a HashMap using the broker sequence number as the key.

Next, the order data is extracted from the message, logged, and then used to create a *broker order* message that is sent to the order broker. This message also contains a reply-to Topic, to which the order broker replies to the order manager. When the reply is received, the order manager uses the broker sequence number within the message to locate the order client's reply-to Topic from within the HashMap.

The end result is that the order manager does not reply to the order client until the order broker replies to the order manager. This processing occurs in the onMessage method, which handles the order broker reply messages. Each reply message starts a new transaction that includes the receipt of the order broker's message and the sending of a reply to the order client. After the client reply has been sent, this transaction is committed. The transaction rollback processing for this application will be discussed in detail later in the chapter in the section labeled "Queue Theory."

LISTING 4.8   Code for the Trading System's OrderManager2 Component

```
package com.TradingSystem;

import java.util.*;
import javax.jms.*;
import javax.naming.*;

public class OrderManager2 implements MessageListener
{
    private Connection connection;
    private Session session;
    private MessageConsumer consumer;
    private MessageProducer responder;
    private MessageProducer brokerOrderProd;

    private Session replySession;
    private Destination brokerReplies;
    private MessageConsumer brokerConsumer;

    private int brokerSequence = 0;
    private HashMap replyMap = new HashMap();

    public OrderManager2()
    {
        try {
            InitialContext jndi = new InitialContext();
            ConnectionFactory conFactory =
                (ConnectionFactory)jndi.lookup("ConnectionFactory");
            connection = conFactory.createConnection("","");
```

```
session = connection.createSession(
                    true, // transacted session
                    Session.AUTO_ACKNOWLEDGE);

// Client order queue
Destination orders =
  (Destination)jndi.lookup("OrderQ");
consumer = session.createConsumer(orders);
responder = session.createProducer(null);

// Broker order queue
Destination brokerOrders =
  (Destination)jndi.lookup("BrokerOrderQ");
brokerOrderProd =
  session.createProducer(brokerOrders);

// Broker order reply temporary topic
replySession = connection.createSession(
                    true, // transacted session
                    Session.AUTO_ACKNOWLEDGE);
brokerReplies =
  (Topic)replySession.createTemporaryTopic();
brokerConsumer =
  replySession.createConsumer(brokerReplies);
brokerConsumer.setMessageListener(this);

connection.start();

// Listen forever for new client orders
while ( true )
{
    try {
      ++brokerSequence;

      MapMessage mapMsg =
        (MapMessage)consumer.receive();
      Destination reply = mapMsg.getJMSReplyTo();
      replyMap.put(new Integer(brokerSequence),reply);
      String ticker = mapMsg.getString("Ticker");
      String type = mapMsg.getString("OrderType");
      int qty = mapMsg.getInt("Quantity");
      int clientSeq =
        mapMsg.getIntProperty("Sequence");
      System.out.println( "Received a "
```

```
                                  + type + " order for "
                                  + qty + " shares of "
                                  + ticker
                                  + " sequence="
                                  + clientSeq);

                MapMessage brokerOrder =
                   (MapMessage)session.createMapMessage();
                brokerOrder.setString("Ticker", ticker);
                brokerOrder.setString("OrderType", type);
                brokerOrder.setInt("Quantity", qty);
                brokerOrder.setIntProperty( "Sequence",
                                        brokerSequence);
                brokerOrder.setJMSReplyTo(brokerReplies);
                brokerOrderProd.send(brokerOrder);

                session.commit();
            }
            catch ( Exception e1) {
                e1.printStackTrace();
                try {
                    session.rollback();
                }
                catch ( Exception e2 ) { }
            }
        }
    }
    catch ( Exception e ) {
        e.printStackTrace();
    }
}

public void onMessage(Message msg)
{
    try {
        MapMessage mapMsg = (MapMessage)msg;
        String ticker = mapMsg.getString("Ticker");
        System.out.println( "Broker reply rcvd for ticker "
                            + ticker);

        // Send order client a reply
        Integer key = new Integer(mapMsg.getInt("Sequence"));
        Destination reply =
            (Destination)replyMap.get( key );
```

```
                    TextMessage replyMsg = session.createTextMessage();
                    replyMsg.setText( "Order placed for ticker "
                                      + ticker );
                    responder.send(reply, replyMsg);
                    session.commit();
                }
                catch ( Exception e ) {
                    e.printStackTrace();
                    try {
                        session.rollback();
                    }
                    catch ( Exception e2 ) { }
                }
            }

            public static void main(String[] args) throws Exception
            {
                OrderManager2 orderMgr = new OrderManager2();
            }
        }
```

The Order Broker

The order broker (see Listing 4.9) creates a transacted Session of its own, which it uses to receive messages from the BrokerOrderQ Destination and send reply messages to the order manager. After the Destination, Producer, and Consumer objects have been set up, the code enters an infinite loop where it receives broker order messages. When an order arrives, a transaction is automatically started, and the order broker extracts all of the data (as well as the reply-to Topic object) from the message. In a real implementation, the order would be executed here, but this is a sample application, so the message is simply logged. Next, a reply MapMessage is prepared, sent to the reply-to Topic from the order message, and the transaction is committed. The transaction rollback processing for this application will be discussed in detail in the section "Queue Theory."

LISTING 4.9 Code for the OrderBroker Component

```
        package com.TradingSystem;

        import javax.jms.*;
        import javax.naming.*;

        public class OrderBroker
        {
```

```
private Connection connection;
private Session session;
private MessageConsumer consumer;
private MessageProducer responder;

public OrderBroker()
{
    try {
        // Lookup a JMS connection factory
        InitialContext jndi = new InitialContext();
        ConnectionFactory conFactory =
          (ConnectionFactory)jndi.lookup("ConnectionFactory");

        // Create a JMS connection
        connection = conFactory.createConnection("","");

        session = connection.createSession(
                            true,
                            Session.AUTO_ACKNOWLEDGE);

        Destination orders =
            (Destination)jndi.lookup("BrokerOrderQ");

        consumer = session.createConsumer(orders);

        responder = session.createProducer(null);

        connection.start();

        while ( true )
        {
            try {
                MapMessage msg = (MapMessage)consumer.receive();
                Destination replyDest = msg.getJMSReplyTo();

                String ticker = msg.getString("Ticker");
                String type = msg.getString("OrderType");
                int qty = msg.getInt("Quantity");
                int sequence = msg.getIntProperty("Sequence");
                System.out.println( "Received a "
                                + type + " broker order for "
                                + qty + " shares of "
                                + ticker
                                + " sequence="
                                + sequence );
```

```
                              if ( replyDest != null )
                              {
                                  MapMessage reply =
                                      session.createMapMessage();
                                  reply.setString("Ticker", ticker);
                                  reply.setString("OrderType", type);
                                  reply.setInt("Quantity", qty);
                                  reply.setInt("Sequence", sequence);
                                  responder.send(replyDest, reply);
                              }

                              session.commit();
                          }
                          catch ( Exception e1 ) {
                              e1.printStackTrace();
                              try {
                                  session.rollback();
                              }
                              catch ( Exception e2 ) { }
                          }
                      }
                  }
                  catch ( Exception e ) {
                      e.printStackTrace();
                  }
              }

              public static void main(String[] args)
              {
                  OrderBroker orderBroker = new OrderBroker();
              }
          }
```

MESSAGE-DRIVEN BEANS

In the trading system sample application we've been discussing in this chapter, the broker system represents an outside stock broker software system that can make stock trades on our behalf. The example so far has assumed that it is just another standalone JMS client application like the others we have been writing, but in the real world, many sophisticated, mission-critical transaction systems like the broker system would be implemented as a J2EE enterprise application, capable of running on an application server. Deployed in a clustered environment using a multitier architecture, such an application would possess the robustness and scalability needed to match its requirements.

Where does JMS fit into a software system built using Enterprise JavaBeans (EJBs) running within an application server? Session and entity beans can receive messages synchronously, and they can even send messages, but only when they have been invoked by an outside caller, as shown in Figure 4.24. Since the lifetime of an EJB is not defined (objects are pooled, destroyed, and created from scratch all the time), there is simply no way to reliably keep a session or entity bean around long enough to listen asynchronously for messages. However, starting with the EJB 2.0 specification, Sun defined a new EJB, called the Message-Driven Bean (MDB), whose sole purpose is to asynchronously receive messages. An MDB is a stateless EJB that leverages the messaging, transaction, security, and concurrency and pooling facilities of the application server's EJB container [Monson-Haefel04]. An MDB cannot be accessed directly by clients; instead, the EJB container activates your MDB when a message arrives for it, as shown in Figure 4.25. The EJB specification indicates that an MDB can use any messaging system, not just those that are JMS compliant. If a messaging system other than JMS is to be used, it must provide a J2EE-compliant resource adapter to interface with the EJB container. However, we will focus on JMS and its interfaces in our discussion of message-driven beans.

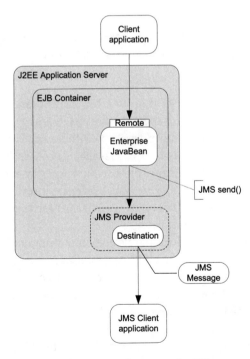

FIGURE 4.24 A session or entity EJB can send JMS messages, but they cannot receive JMS messages asynchronously.

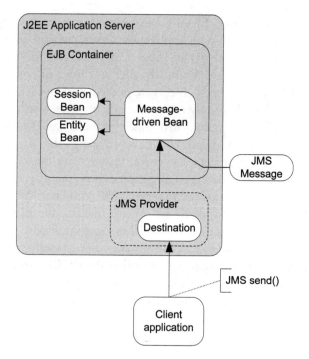

FIGURE 4.25 Message-driven Beans are activated by the EJB container when a JMS message arrives.

Developing an MDB is quite a bit easier than developing a session or entity bean. All that you need is the Bean class itself and a deployment descriptor; there is no need for home or remote classes as with Session or Entity beans. The MDB class must implement the javax.ejb.MessageDrivenBean interface, as well as a message listener interface for the appropriate messaging system it is to use. The MDB must implement the javax.jms.MessageListener interface to receive JMS messages. Figure 4.26 shows the MessageDrivenBean interface, and the interface javax.ejb. EnterpriseBean, which it extends.

Although the previous paragraph stated that an MDB is a stateless EJB, this is not entirely accurate. An MDB can maintain state in the form of a database connection or a connection to some other resource, but it cannot be something that is client specific. One resource that most message-driven Beans do store is a reference to its MessageDrivenContext object, which is provided to it by the EJB container through the setMessageDrivenContext method of the MessageDrivenBean interface. This object provides access to the runtime context held by the EJB container for the MDB. This interface (shown in Figure 4.27) provides access to the caller's transaction and security roles. It also allows an MDB to mark the current transaction to be rolled back.

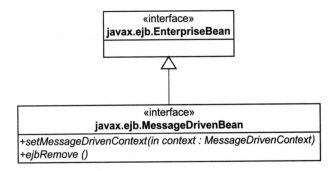

FIGURE 4.26 The methods for the MesageDrivenBean interface.

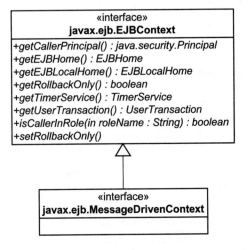

FIGURE 4.27 The methods for the MessageDrivenContext interface.

The methods on the MessageDrivenContext interface are inherited from the EJBContext interface, and are as follows:

getCallerPrincipal: Returns the java.security.Principal object that identifies the caller. A Principal object is used to identify a user login, an individual, or even a corporation.

getEJBHome and **getEJBLocalHome:**   Since message-driven beans do not implement home interfaces, these methods should never be called.

getRollbackOnly: This method returns true if the current transaction has been marked to be rolled back. It is only valid for container-managed transactions and can be used as an indicator if further processing can be abandoned for the current transcation.

getTimerService: This method provides access to the EJB timer service, which allows EJBs to register for timer-based callback events.

getUserTransaction: This method is to be invoked by MDBs with bean-managed transactions only. It returns a `javax.transaction.UserTransaction` object that the `Bean` can use to begin, commit, and rollback transactions.

isCallerInRole(java.security.Identity role):   This method is not to be called by a message-driven `Bean`.

setRollbackOnly: This method is to be invoked by MDBs with bean-managed transactions only. It notifies the EJB container that the current transaction is to be rolled back when complete.

Message Acknowledgment and Transactions

Message acknowledgment with message-driven `Beans` requires no special bean code; in *all* cases it's handled by the container. If an MDB is deployed to use container-managed transactions (as discussed shortly), a message acknowledgment is automatically sent if the transaction is committed; otherwise it is not sent. If transactions are not required at all, or if the MDB is deployed to use `Bean`-managed transactions, the bean can indicate exactly how message acknowledgments should be handled. For instance, for EJB 2.0 message-driven `Bean` deployment descriptors, the acknowledge mode tag can contain either the value `Auto-acknowledge` or `Dups-ok-acknowledge`. With the `Dups-ok-acknowledge` setting, the EJB container—working in conjunction with the JMS provider—may not send message acknowledgments with every delivered message. For optimization reasons, message acknowledgments may be deferred, and there is a possibility that messages may be redelivered if something goes wrong. If you want to ensure that each message is received once and only once, you must use the `Auto-acknowledge` setting.

The EJB 2.0 deployment descriptor denotes the acknowledgment mode to use as in this example:

```
<enterprise-beans>
    <message-driven>
        <ejb-name>OrderBrokerBean</ejb-name>
        <ejb-class>OrderBrokerBean</ejb-class>
        <transaction-type>Container</transaction-type>
        <acknowledge-mode>Auto-acknowledge</acknowledge-mode>
        ...
```

The EJB 2.1 deployment descriptor denotes the acknowledgment mode via an activation configuration property, as in this example:

```
<enterprise-beans>
    <message-driven>
        <ejb-name>OrderBrokerBean</ejb-name>
        <ejb-class>OrderBrokerBean</ejb-class>
        <transaction-type>Container</transaction-type>
        <activation-config>
            <activation-config-property-name>
                acknowledgeMode
            </activation-config-property-name>
            <activation-config-property-value>
                Auto-acknowledge
            </activation-config-property-value>
            ...
```

As with message acknowledgment, the MDB's transaction mode is configured in the Bean's deployment descriptor. If the message-driven Bean's deployment descriptor's trans-attribute tag is set to the value Required, container-managed transactions will be used for all message processing. In this case, there is nothing the MDB needs to do to commit a JMS transaction; the EJB container will take care of it automatically. This is one advantage to using a J2EE application server. However, if bean-managed transactions are chosen—where the trans-attribute tag is set to the value Bean—the MDB developer is responsible for beginning, committing, and potentially rolling back the transaction manually. This is done, not through the JMS Session object, but instead with a javax.transaction.UserTransaction object, as returned by the getUserTransaction method. However, the received message will not be part of the transaction; hence a rollback will not automatically place the received message back on the queue or topic for redelivery. To include the received message itself, the MDB must be deployed to use container-managed transactions.

Message-Driven Bean Message Destinations

A message-driven Bean needs to be associated with a specific JMS Destination in order to receive messages for that destination. However, neither the Bean code nor its deployment descriptor specifically mentions the destination name. Instead, the MDB is mapped to the applicable destination at deployment time—when the MDB is manually deployed to the EJB container. The only thing that can be specified in the deployment descriptor is an indicator that the MDB is to be associated with a Queue or a Topic. In EJB 2.0, an MDB deployment descriptor indicates this with the value javax.jms.Queue or javax.jms.Topic for the destination-type tag, nested within the message-destination-type tag:

```
<message-driven-destination>
    <destination-type>javax.jms.Queue</destination-type>
</message-driven-destination>
```

However, because the only acceptable values are javax.jms.Queue or javax.jms.Topic, there is not enough flexibility to support non-JMS message systems in the EJB 2.0 deployment descriptor. The EJB 2.1 specification addresses this by using activation configuration properties to specify destination types:

```
<activation-config>
    <activation-config-property-name>
        destinationType
    </activation-config-property-name>
    <activation-config-property-value>
        javax.jms.Queue
    </activation-config-property-value>
        . . .
```

Durable Subscriptions

In EJB 2.0, a subscription can be made durable by setting the subscription durability setting to the value Durable:

```
<message-driven-destination>
    <destination-type>javax.jms.Topic</destination-type>
    <subscription-durability>Durable</subscription-durability>
</message-driven-destination>
```

The EJB 2.1 specification addresses this by using activation configuration properties to specify a subscription's durability:

```
<activation-config>
    <activation-config-property-name>
        subscriptionDurability
    </activation-config-property-name>
    <activation-config-property-value>
        Durable
    </activation-config-property-value>
        . . .
```

Message Selectors

Finally, message selectors are specified in EJB 2.0 with the message-selector element, where the value is the filter criteria itself:

```
<message-selector>
    StockTicker IN ('IBM', 'MSFT', 'YHOO')
</message-selector >
```

Once again, the EJB 2.1 specification addresses this by using activation configuration properties:

```
<activation-config>
    <activation-config-property-name>
        messageSelector
    </activation-config-property-name>
    <activation-config-property-value>
        StockTicker IN ('IBM', 'MSFT', 'YHOO')
    </activation-config-property-value>
        ...
```

The Order Broker Message-Driven Bean

Developing a JMS message consumer as a message-driven Bean with message acknowledgment and full transaction support is, in many ways, easier than developing a standalone JMS client application. This is because the MDB is able to leverage the facilities of the J2EE application server, as we discussed in the previous sections. Rewriting the order broker sample application as an MDB (see Listing 4.10) is straightforward. Let's examine the code to see how an MDB works.

LISTING 4.10   Code for the Order Broker as a Message-Driven Bean

```
import javax.jms.*;
import javax.ejb.*;
import javax.naming.*;

public class OrderBrokerBean
    implements
        javax.ejb.MessageDrivenBean,
        javax.jms.MessageListener
{
    MessageDrivenContext context;
    Context jndi;

    public void setMessageDrivenContext(MessageDrivenContext mdc)
    {
        log("setMessageDrivenContext called");
        context = mdc;
        try {
```

```
            jndi = new InitialContext();
        }
        catch ( Exception e ) {
            e.printStackTrace();
        }
    }

    public void ejbCreate()
    {
        log("ejbCreate called");
    }

    public void ejbRemove()
    {
        try {
            jndi.close();
            context = null;
        }
        catch ( Exception e ) {
            e.printStackTrace();
        }
    }

    public void onMessage(Message message)
    {
        try {
            log("onMessage called");
            MapMessage msg = (MapMessage)message;
            Topic replyDest = (Topic)msg.getJMSReplyTo();

            String ticker = msg.getString("Ticker");
            String type = msg.getString("OrderType");
            int qty = msg.getInt("Quantity");
            int sequence = msg.getIntProperty("Sequence");
            log("Received a "
                + type + " broker order for "
                + qty + " shares of "
                + ticker
                + " sequence="
                + sequence );

            if ( replyDest != null )
            {
```

```
            TopicConnectionFactory factory =
                (TopicConnectionFactory)jndi.lookup(
                    "java:comp/env/jms/ConnectionFactory");

            TopicConnection conn =
                factory.createTopicConnection(
                    "weblogic","weblogic");

            TopicSession session = conn.createTopicSession(
                    false, Session.AUTO_ACKNOWLEDGE);

            TopicPublisher responder =
                session.createPublisher(null);

            MapMessage reply = session.createMapMessage();
            reply.setString("Ticker", ticker);
            reply.setString("OrderType", type);
            reply.setInt("Quantity", qty);
            reply.setInt("Sequence", sequence);
            responder.publish(replyDest, reply);
            conn.close();
        }
    }
    catch ( Exception e ) {
        e.printStackTrace();
        throw new EJBException(e);
    }
}

public static void log( String msg ) {
    System.out.println("[OrderBrokerBean]" + msg);
}
}
```

The setMessageDrivenContext method is written to store the MessageDriven Context object that is provided. It also creates a new InitialContext object that is used to access any JNDI resources, such as a ConnectionFactory or Destination object. This context object is cleaned up in the ejbRemove method, which is called when the MDB is being removed from the pool of available MDB objects, presumably to be destroyed. The ejbCreate method is called after the setMessageDriven Context method, allowing your Bean code to create or connect to any other resources it needs in order to operate. When this method returns, the MDB is placed into the pool of available MDB objects for the applicable destination.

The onMessage method is where all the real action takes place. First, the JMS message is cast to a MapMessage object, and all of the stock order data is extracted. This includes the Destination object within the message's JMSReplyTo property. In order to send a message to this reply destination, a new Session and MessageProducer object must be created for this destination. Since this MDB is stateless, each step to do this is performed with each message that is received:

1. Since the reply destination is known to be a Topic, a TopicConnection Factory is retrieved using the JNDI resource name "java:comp/env/jms/ConnectionFactory." This resource must be predefined within the J2EE application server before this code executes.
2. A TopicConnection object is created using a valid username and password for an authorized user for the application server in which the MDB is deployed.
3. A TopicSession is created.
4. A TopicPublisher object is created.

Finally, a new MapMessage object is created as a reply to the order request, indicating that the order broker has executed the order, and it's published to the reply topic. Once the method returns, the EJB container will take care of sending the message acknowledgment and committing the transaction on behalf of the MDB. If an Exception occurs within the processing of the message, the catch block not only logs it but throws an EJBException object. Upon receiving this exception, the EJB container will roll back the transaction, thereby placing the order request message back on the queue.

The OrderBrokerBean MDB Deployment Descriptor for EJB 2.0

The EJB 2.0–compatible deployment descriptor for the order broker MDB can be seen in Listing 4.11. The XML in this descriptor specifies an MDB that uses container-managed transactions, once-and-only-once message delivery, and a JMS Queue for its message delivery. It also specifies that a ConnectionFactory object will be accessed through the resource name "jms/ConnectionFactory," which when appended to the standard "java:comp/env/" results in a complete JNDI resource name.

LISTING 4.11 EJB 2.0 Deployment Descriptor for the OrderBrokerBean MDB

```
<?xml version="1.0"?>
<!DOCTYPE ejb-jar PUBLIC
    "-//Sun Microsystems, Inc.//DTD Enterprise JavaBeans 2.0//EN"
    "http://java.sun.com/dtd/ejb-jar_2_0.dtd">
<ejb-jar>
```

```
<enterprise-beans>
<message-driven>
    <ejb-name>OrderBrokerBean</ejb-name>
    <ejb-class>OrderBrokerBean</ejb-class>
    <transaction-type>Container</transaction-type>
    <acknowledge-mode>Auto-acknowledge</acknowledge-mode>
    <message-driven-destination>
        <destination-type>javax.jms.Queue</destination-type>
    </message-driven-destination>
    <security-identity>
        <use-caller-identity/>
    </security-identity>
    <resource-ref>
        <res-ref-name>jms/ConnectionFactory</res-ref-name>
        <res-type>javax.jms.ConnectionFactory</res-type>
        <res-auth>Container</res-auth>
    </resource-ref>
</message-driven>
</enterprise-beans>
<assembly-descriptor>
  <container-transaction>
    <method>
        <ejb-name>OrderBrokerBean</ejb-name>
        <method-name>*</method-name>
    </method>
    <trans-attribute>Required</trans-attribute>
  </container-transaction>
</assembly-descriptor>
</ejb-jar>
```

The `OrderBrokerBean` MDB Deployment Descriptor for EJB 2.1

Listing 4.12 contains the EJB 2.1–compatible deployment descriptor for the `OrderBrokerBean` message-driven `Bean`; the differences from the EJB 2.0 version are in bold text.

LISTING 4.12   EJB 2.1 Deployment Descriptor for the `OrderBrokerBean` MDB

```
<?xml version="1.0"?>
<ejb-jar
   xmlns="http://java.sun.com/xml/ns/j2ee"
   xmlns:xsi="http://www.w3.org/2001/XMLSchema-instance"
   xsi:schemaLocation="http://java.sun.com/xml/ns/j2ee
       http://java.sun.com/xml/ns/j2ee/ejb-jar_2_1.xsd"
```

```
        version="2.1">
    <enterprise-beans>
      <message-driven>
          <ejb-name>OrderBrokerBean</ejb-name>
          <ejb-class>OrderBrokerBean</ejb-class>
          <transaction-type>Container</transaction-type>
          <acknowledge-mode>auto-acknowledge</acknowledge-mode>
          <messaging-type>javax.jms.MessageListener</messaging-type>
          <activation-config>
              <activation-config-property-name>
                  destinationType
              </activation-config-property-name>
              <activation-config-property-value>
                  javax.jms.Queue
              </activation-config-property-value>
              <activation-config-property-name>
                  acknowledgeMode
              </activation-config-property-name>
              <activation-config-property-value>
                  Auto-acknowledge
              </activation-config-property-value>
          </activation-config>
          <security-identity>
              <use-caller-identity/>
          </security-identity>
          <resource-ref>
              <res-ref-name>jms/ConnectionFactory</res-ref-name>
              <res-type>javax.jms.ConnectionFactory</res-type>
              <res-auth>Container</res-auth>
          </resource-ref>
      </message-driven>
    </enterprise-beans>
    <assembly-descriptor>
      <container-transaction>
          <method>
              <ejb-name>OrderBrokerBean</ejb-name>
              <method-name>*</method-name>
          </method>
          <trans-attribute>Required</trans-attribute>
      </container-transaction>
    </assembly-descriptor>
</ejb-jar>
```

To deploy an MDB, as with any EJB, you should use the Java JAR utility to create a Java archive with the structure shown in Figure 4.28.

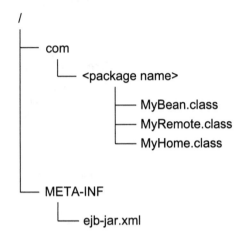

FIGURE 4.28   The correct JAR structure to deploy your EJBs.

Of course, the text <package name> should be replaced with the directory structure that matches your Bean's package, and your EJB classes probably won't have names like MyBean.class, but you get the idea. It's important that the deployment descriptor is named ejb-jar.xml, and that it be placed in a directory named META-INF at the root of the archive.

JCA MESSAGE INFLOW

The Java Connector Architecture (JCA) defines a series of *inflow contracts*, each of which defines a standard method of integration and communication into a J2EE application server. The intent is to provide a "plug-in" model to extend the functionality of an application server without upgrading it (see Figure 4.29). The inflow contracts also make it possible to communicate with and extend the application server dynamically, while it is running, without requiring a server restart. Components that are built to this standard are called JCA *resource adapters*. Resource adapters allow outside applications to initiate transactions, send messages to, and otherwise invoke components within J2EE applications running within an application server.

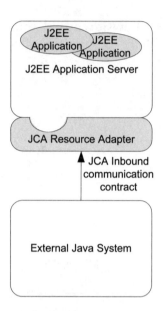

FIGURE 4.29 This diagram illustrates the standard JCA inflow contract architecture.

The JCA *message inflow* contract specifies a standard way for an application to build a resource adapter specifically to deliver messages to endpoints within a J2EE application server. More than a means to deliver messages, the message inflow contract defines a standard way to plug new message providers into existing application servers. The contract consists of sets of method calls made between the implementation of standard interfaces by both the resource adapter and the application server. It is also the way most application server vendors have implemented message-driven beans.

Figure 4.30 shows a message inflow resource adapter, the interfaces it needs to support, and some internal objects it needs to create. This design pattern benefits both the messaging system developer and the application server developer, since neither one needs to understand the internals of the other one's software. The result is a separation of concerns that is very important to maintain in distributed software development, as it helps limit complexity.

EJB activation is done transparently through the `javax.resource.spi.ResourceAdapter` and `javax.resource.spi.ActivationSpec` interface implementations. Message objects are created to encapsulate all message details and are sent via the `javax.resource.spi.endpoint.MessageEndpoint` interface implementation. Two-phase commit transactions are started and ended through the `javax.transaction.xa.`

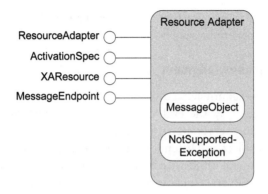

FIGURE 4.30 A resource adapter, by contract, must
implement a set of interfaces, and create certain objects.

XAResource interface implementation. Pattern-specific exceptions, such as the
javax.resource.NotSupportedException, are the standard way of informing the
application server of a resource adapter's limitations. For example, if the resource
adapter chooses not to support transactions, the NotSupportedException exception
object should be thrown back to the application server when it attempts to initiate
a transaction.

Inflow Message Delivery

Message delivery through a message inflow adapter can occur either serially or con-
currently by simply creating more MessageEndpoint objects. However, the application server may block concurrency altogether, or limit it, by throwing an exception
when more than one MessageObject object is created or by blocking the calling
thread inside message delivery methods.

When a message arrives from the external message provider, the resource
adapter must activate the listener EJB component, as prescribed by the EJB activation specification. The actual MessageEndpoint object created to deliver the message
is only a proxy to the actual message listener running within the application server.
The use of a proxy allows the application server to intercept message delivery,
which allows it to perform its own processing such as message routing, transactions, and message storage for recovery in case of an error. The resource adapter
can take part in the transactions the application server starts by passing its own
XAResource object in the MessageEndpointFactory.createEndpoint method call,
although this is optional.

Once message delivery is complete, the resource adapter may call the release
method on the endpoint, thereby indicating to the application server that its use of

the endpoint is over for the time being. The application server may choose to destroy the endpoint or save it for potential message delivery in the future.

Inflow Message Acknowledgment

A message is acknowledged when the resource adapter is certain the message has been processed by the endpoint inside the application server. For cases where the application server starts a transaction, the resource adapter must provide an XAResource object and listen for transaction commit notifications before it sends an acknowledgment. Otherwise it can send an acknowledgment after the call to deliver the message returns (such as the MessageListener.onMessage method). A resource adapter can determine whether or not a transaction will be used by the application servers by calling the MessageEndpointFactory.isDeliveryTransacted method.

Inflow Message Recovery

In cases where the application server crashes, or is shut down, before all sent messages are delivered, message recovery must be performed. This involves the following steps that are performed by the application server:

1. Each resource adapter that was active before the crash is re-instantiated and started.
2. For each resource adapter, the getXAResources method is called, where an array of ActivationSpec objects is provided. Each object in the array corresponds to a MessageEndpoint object that was active prior to the crash. The resource adapter may return null if it does not support transactions, or it may return an array of valid XAResource objects when this method is called.
3. The application server uses each XAResource object to report the outcome of each message transaction to the resource adapter. This information may be used by the message provider to attempt message redelivery of messages that were not successfully delivered before the application server crash.

Inflow Message Transactions

In cases where transactions are started by the message provider, the transaction information must be passed to the application server. It is the resource adapter's responsibility to push the provided external transaction (sometimes called a *source transaction*) to the application server via the JCA *transaction inflow* contract. The transaction must be capable of handling more than one message delivery cycle within the transaction begin/commit envelope. A committed transaction results in the acknowledged delivery of every message contained within the transaction. An aborted transaction results in the cancellation of every message contained within the transaction. Previously queued messages involved in the transaction are placed back on queues for future delivery, and sent messages are destroyed.

When a message endpoint component indicates that it requires transactions, the application server must use a sourced transaction object if it is provided; otherwise it must create its own. When the endpoint does not require a transaction, the application server can ignore source transaction objects and does not need to create its own internal transaction. The result can be improved performance and reduced memory usage.

QUEUE THEORY

The remainder of the chapter discusses what this book calls *queue theory*, which encompasses problems and trouble areas that almost all message-based applications will need to deal with. While some of the discussion is specific to JMS, most of it applies in general to the concept of messaging. As a developer of messaging-based software, you will likely come across some of these scenarios, and it's helpful to have some guidelines on how to deal with them.

Message Transaction Rollback

Review, if you will, the implementation of the order client, order manager, and order broker applications shown in Listing 4.7, Listing 4.8, and Listing 4.9, respectively. You should have noticed that in each application, if an error occurs during the processing of a received message or while sending a message, the active transaction is rolled-back. In this example, the rollback is performed within various `Exception` handling blocks via a call to `Session.rollback`. To test this code, and see how JMS handles rolled back transactions, we need to modify both the order client and order broker applications.

In the order client, we need to modify the `sendOrders` method to send only one order message. This makes the example simpler, and it's easier to follow the output. Modify the `for` loop by commenting it out and defining the variable `i`, as follows:

```
private void sendOrders() throws Exception
{
    // Place a buy order for 100 shares of each stock
    int i = 0;
    //for (i = 0; i < stocks.length; i++ )
    {
        ...
    }
}
```

Next, modify the main method by commenting out the call to `Thread.sleep` and the call to close the JMS connection, as follows:

```
public static void main(String[] args) throws Exception
{
    OrderClient2 client = new OrderClient2();
    /*
    try {
        Thread.sleep(5000);
    }
    catch ( Exception e ) { }
    client.connection.close();
    */
}
```

As for the order broker, we want to simulate an `Exception` within the broker order message-handling code. To do this, we need to add a line of code within the infinite loop, just before the call to `Session.commit`, that intentionally throws an `Exception`, as follows:

```
...
while ( true )
{
    try {
        ...

        if ( true )
            throw new Exception("Testing transaction code");

        session.commit();
    }
    catch ( Exception e ) {
        ...
    }
}
```

The `throw` call needs to be within an `if` statement because without it, the result would be a compiler error, as the call to `session.commit` would never get called. With the `if` statement, you can toggle the transaction testing code by simply changing the argument in the `if` statement to `true` or `false`. The `Exception` will cause the transaction to be rolled back, at which point the JMS provider should place the message back into the queue to be delivered once again. You can witness this yourself by starting the modified order broker. Of course, you need to ensure that your JMS provider and the order manager are also running.

Next start the modified order client application, which will send out a single order request message. You should see the effect of the Exception within the output of the order broker immediately: an endless loop of thrown Exceptions. This happens because again, when the Exception is thrown, the order message is placed back on the queue. The order broker then recovers from the Exception and calls consumer.receive to pull the next message off of the queue. (The next message happens to be the message that was just placed back on the queue.) When this message is delivered, the Exception is again thrown, the message is placed back on the queue, and the process starts all over again. This will continue endlessly until the order broker process is stopped.

Stop the order broker process. Next, locate the if statement where the Exception is thrown and change the argument to false. This will cause the order broker to process the message normally and not throw an Exception. When you restart the order broker, you should notice that it processes the broker order message and replies to the order manager, which subsequently sends an order confirmation to the order client. The chain of transactions is now complete, albeit a little delayed because of all of the Exceptions that occurred in the previous run. Altogether, this exercise should prove how resilient JMS transaction processing is and how reliable it is when combined with persistent messaging.

Message Recovery

It's important to note that JMS message transaction processing is different from JMS message recovery; as a matter of fact, they are mutually exclusive. Message recovery, as discussed earlier in this chapter, is the name of the process by which the JMS provider redelivers all unacknowledged messages to a message consumer. This is done automatically by the JMS provider after a failure scenario, and it can be made to happen if a client application calls the Session.recover method. If the recover method is called, the JMS provider will redeliver all unacknowledged messages to the consumer of the applicable Session. It is not legal for a client application to call the recover method on a transacted Session; the result will be an IllegalStateException.

The code in Listing 4.13 contains a message consumer that uses client-based acknowledgment to process and acknowledge groups of related JMS messages. In this example, the message consumer waits to receive both a stock trade notification message *and* an order state-change message before sending an acknowledgment to the JMS provider. Let's assume that in this system, a trade notification message *always* precedes an order state-change message.

LISTING 4.13   Stock Trade Message Handling Code

```java
public void onMessage(Message msg)
{
    String ticker;
    int quantity;
    String type; // 'buy' or 'sell'
    String state;
    int orderID;

    try {
        MapMessage mapMsg = (MapMessage)msg;
        int messageType = mapMsg.getByteProperty("Type");
        switch ( messageType )
        {
        case TRADE_NOTIFICATION:
            ticker = mapMsg.getString("Ticker");
            quantity = mapMsg.getInt("Quantity");
            type = mapMsg.getString("TradeType");
            orderID = mapMsg.getInt("RelatedOrderID");
            System.out.println("Trade notification:");
            System.out.println("   Type: " + type);
            System.out.println("   Stock: " + ticker);
            System.out.println("   Quantity: " + quantity);

            if ( mapMsg.getJMSRedelivered() )
                removeIncompleteTradeNotifications();

            // Store the trade notification data.
            // The trade's not complete until we
            // receive an order state change message
            storeTradeNotification( tradeType,
                                    ticker,
                                    quantity,
                                    orderID);
            break;

        case ORDER_STATE_CHANGE:
            orderID = mapMsg.getInt("OrderID");
            state = mapMsg.getString("OrderState");
            System.out.println("Order state change:");
            System.out.println("   New State: " + state);
```

```
            // Modify the order's state
            modifyOrderState( orderID, state );

            // Mark the trade notification as complete
            markTradeComplete( orderId );

            mapMsg.acknowledge();
            break;
        }
    }
    catch ( Exception e ) {
        e.printStackTrace();
        try {
            session.recover();
        }
        catch ( Exception e1 ) { }
    }
}
```

When a trade notification message arrives, all the trade data is pulled from the message, including the trade's related order identifier, the stock ticker, the number of shares traded, and the type (whether the trade was a buy or a sell). This information is stored in the database via a call to the method storeTradeNotification (implementation not shown here). However, this information is considered incomplete until we receive an order state-change message, and it is marked in the database as such. Shortly afterward, the order state-change message arrives containing the order identifier and the order's new state. The method modifyOrderState is then called to update the order's state in the database. Now that the order state-change message has been received and processed, the trade notification database entry is marked as complete via a call to the method markTradeComplete, and both messages are acknowledged via the call to mapMsg.acknowledge.

Let's assume that the application temporarily loses connectivity to the database, and calls to any one of the database modification methods (storeTradeNotification, modifyOrderState, or markTradeComplete) result in a SQLException. The exception handling code will call Session.recover, instructing JMS to redeliver all unacknowledged messages. Since trade notifications and order state changes are acknowledged in pairs, the redelivery will always include both messages. When the redelivered trade notification message is received, the call to mapMsg.getJMSRedelivered will return true causing the application to remove the previously incomplete trade notification entry(s) from the database. Assuming the database is now available, message processing should continue as normal; the trade notification data is added to the database, and the order state-change message arrives, resulting in message acknowledgment.

Poison Message Processing

If a message that is delivered to a message consumer causes the consumer to fail or throw an Exception, the JMS provider will mark the message for redelivery. If the message consumer fails each time it receives the redelivered message, presumably because of the content of the message, we have a serious problem. This endless loop of message redelivery and consumer failure can stall a message queue, affect the JMS provider's performance as a whole, and halt the client application's ability to function. Typically, a JMS provider will track the number of redelivery attempts made for a message. Once that number passes a threshold—which may be configurable by the JMS administrator—the message is declared a *poison message*.

Technically, it's the JMS client application's responsibility to track and handle poison message scenarios. Although it is tedious, the application can track messages by message ID and perform the following processing:

1. When a message arrives, a call is made to the message's getJMSRedelivered method.
2. If it is not being redelivered, the message is processed as normal, end of story.
3. If the message *is* being redelivered, perform the following steps:
   a. Look up the message in a database or an in-memory data structure using the message's identifier, as returned by the method getJMSMessageID.
   b. If the message is not in the database or data structure, make a new entry for it, using the message identifier.
   c. Increment a counter for that message.
   d. Check the counter; if it has exceeded an application-defined threshold for delivery attempts, do *not* process the message.

Once your application has detected a poison message using the above algorithm, it has a choice of what it can do with the message:

- The message can be discarded. Basically, the client does not process the message at all, but an acknowledgment is sent to the JMS provider, and for transacted sessions, commit is called as though it were processed normally.
- The message can be placed on a special queue (such as the dead-letter queue discussed in the next section) for offline inspection at a later time.
- All message delivery to your application can be halted (via a call to stop on your application's Connection object) because of concern that messages are being corrupted as the result of a system error.

Some JMS providers do provide support for detecting poison messages so that your applications do not have to. WebSphereMQ, for example, tracks the number of redelivery attempts per message and will place a repeatedly failed message onto the dead-letter queue (discussed in the next section), or what WebSphere calls a backout queue. A *backout queue* is a named queue that the JMS administrator sets up specifically for poison messages. You may configure a backout queue for each queue in your system or one that works system-wide. If attempts to en-queue the poison message on any queue fail entirely, the message may be removed from the system.

Dead-Letter Queues

On occasion a message cannot be delivered to consumers of a destination because of an error condition in either the JMS provider or the message itself. In this case, the provider may place messages on what is called a *dead-letter queue* (DLQ). Although the JMS specification does not specifically mention dead-letter queues, most JMS providers support the concept, albeit in their own ways. In each case, however, the provider, not necessarily the client application, is responsible for placing messages onto this queue.

Even though message delivery is guaranteed for persistent JMS messages, real-world factors may affect it. For instance, what happens to a persistent message that has expired? We already discussed the issue surrounding poison messages. They too may be persistent messages, but can still end up on a DLQ. In general, these are the factors that may cause a message to be placed on a DLQ:

Message expiration: The message was sent with an expiration time value and was not delivered in that time frame. Most providers will place the message on the DLQ for offline processing.

Poison message: The message repeatedly causes consumers to fail (discussed in the previous section). Most providers will place the message on the DLQ for offline processing.

Message nondelivery: Although messages that do not specify an expiration value technically should never timeout, it's not wise to have large numbers of undelivered messages in the system for long periods of time. Most providers will place undelivered messages in the DLQ regardless of their expiration status. This time period is usually provider specific, but may be configurable through the provider's administrative interface.

Error condition: The JMS provider experienced an internal error while delivering a message and has hence placed it on the DLQ.

Regardless of the details surrounding your provider's support and processing of dead-letter queues, the DLQ needs to be monitored regularly to ensure that important messages are getting delivered, and that the DLQ does not overflow with messages, thereby causing server resource issues. This is typically something that can be monitored through the administrative interface for your provider.

SUMMARY

This chapter explored the more advanced, and more involved, areas of JMS as well as JMS client application development. Combined with Chapter 3, this chapter should give you a complete picture of what JMS has to offer and how to tap into the full power of its feature-set. We've begun exploring the issues affecting the sample trading system which we will continue to build throughout this book. The next chapter will present tools and techniques to aid in the development of real-world JMS client applications, and they will be applied to the sample application for illustration.

5

JMS Development, Deployment, and Support

In This Chapter

- The Facade Design Pattern
- A JMS Facade
- Distributed JavaBean Events
- Component Distribution: The JMS Component Server

THE FACADE DESIGN PATTERN

Class hierarchies are the result of a design approach where components of an otherwise complex system are broken down into smaller, yet related, pieces. Although this approach does help the development process, there are times when using the classes and working with their relationships can be a complex task. Therefore, it is common for developers to look back at a system, a library, or an Application Programming Interface (API), and develop wrapper classes to encapsulate the relationships and dependencies that they would otherwise need to carry throughout their software. This approach has been formalized in a design pattern called the *facade* [Gamma95].

A facade conceptually hides the details and complexities of the lower-level software service for which it is written, making the service easier to use. A facade also provides a unified entry point into the layers of the software. This reduces your application's dependency on the software details and allows the facade to hide future changes in the software itself. In fact, the lower-level classes need not be classes at all. They can be an API in the form of a code library or a Web Service. The facade itself may be implemented as a Web Service that, for example, provides an XML/SOAP (Simple Object Access Protocol) interface into a legacy software system.

The Java Message Service (JMS) interface hierarchy is a good example of a structured design approach that leads to some added complexity for client applications. Figure 5.1 shows a JMS client application component, Client, which uses a subset of the JMS interfaces.

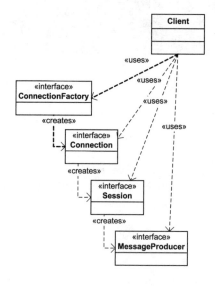

FIGURE 5.1   A single JMS client component must interact with many JMS interfaces.

Considering that your code will most likely contain *multiple* client components that use the JMS interfaces, the dependency tree can get very complex, very quickly. Additionally, each component may contain a lot of duplicate code to use the interfaces over and over again. What's needed is a facade class that hides the complexities of the JMS interfaces (see Figure 5.2). Although this diagram uses the JMS interfaces to illustrate a point, the pattern applies to any situation where the services of a complex system can be simplified with the creation of a facade class.

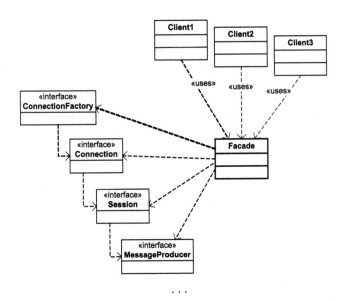

FIGURE 5.2 All of the code to use the services of a complex software system is encapsulated in one easy-to-use facade class.

The facade pattern is the author's personal favorite because it is a driver for software reuse. Unfortunately, too many software engineers view software reuse as the wholesale reuse of an entire software system. Instead, these engineers need to look at the class level and identify opportunities to build facades as either new classes or entire layers of software such as Web Services. This is where good developers achieve true software reuse.

For example, the author once worked for a company that decided to build a family of products that were to be browser based. This was a wise decision in itself. However, the software architects decided that since each application needed a set of similar functionality, the solution was to build a custom browser or container application that included the common functionality built in. When the development teams went off to build their products using the custom browser, they found themselves spending more time building adapters to fit (or contort) their software to fit into its software model. The custom browser created more work than it saved. It's unfortunate that the architects didn't create, instead, a family of facade classes to enable the software groups to reuse the common set of functionality, as intended.

A JMS FACADE

In the previous two chapters, we explored the JMS API, a Sun Microsystems specification for connecting Java programs to enterprise messaging middleware. We learned that JMS is composed of multiple object interfaces with a hierarchy of relationships. The JMS class hierarchy in particular is extensive and can seem complex and confusing at first glance. The relationships between the classes are straightforward, but they require a sequence of code that is often repeated within a JMS application. The complex relationships and patterns are necessary for JMS to:

- Abstract the implementation details of the underlying messaging software
- Interface with existing messaging systems such as IBM's WebSphereMQ, using familiar JavaBean paradigms
- Provide and enforce thread-safe code practices
- Maintain the fundamentals of the Java language, such as Java threading, and Exception handling

Although the reasons for its complexity are sound, the relationships among JMS classes make writing code to the JMS API tedious and confusing at times. Applying the facade pattern offers a solution to this problem.

The SimpleQuoteListener Class

The class JMSManager is a facade class for using the JMS interfaces. The purpose of this class is to make using JMS so simple that you *almost* don't know you're using JMS. Before we get into the details of the JMSManager implementation, let's first examine the code for a component that uses it. In this case, the component is the class SimpleQuoteListener, which is the QuoteListener class from Chapter 3 modified to use JMSManager. Listing 5.1 shows the entire SimpleQuoteListener class, which requires a lot less code than it did in Chapter 3.

LISTING 5.1   Code to Receive Stock Quote Messages Using the JMS Facade

```
package com.TradingSystem.StockTicker;

import javax.jms.*;
import com.toolkit.messaging.JMSManager;

public class SimpleQuoteListener implements MessageListener
{
    JMSManager jmsMgr = new JMSManager();

    public SimpleQuoteListener() throws Exception
    {
        jmsMgr.listen( "StockTrades", this );
    }

    public void onMessage(Message message)
    {
        try {
            TextMessage textMessage = (TextMessage)message;
            String text = textMessage.getText();
            System.out.println(text);
        }
        catch ( JMSException e ) {
            e.printStackTrace();
        }
    }

    public static void main(String args[]) throws Exception
    {
        SimpleQuoteListener jmsFacadeTest =
            new SimpleQuoteListener();
    }
}
```

To keep this example simple, the code to make the stock quote requests has been removed in this version of the class. However, it will be added back later in the chapter, where it will use the JMSManager class. This code simply listens for stock quote update messages.

The first thing you will notice is the import of the com.toolkit.messaging. JMSManager class. Next, the SimpleQuoteListener class creates an instance of the JMSManager class as a member variable. In the SimpleQuoteListener class constructor, a call is made to the method JMSManager.listen. The parameters to this call include the text "StockTrades," which represents the name of the destination to listen to and a reference to an object—itself in this case—that implements the `javax.jms.MessageListener` interface. This indicates that the `SimpleQuoteListener` class wants to listen asynchronously for messages. The implementation of the `MessageListener` interface, and the method `onMessage`, are the only obvious portions of JMS in this example. The rest of the JMS details are neatly tucked away in the `JMSManager` facade class. You can run this code by executing the Windows batch file `runsimplequotelistener.bat`, or UNIX command script `runsimplequotelistener.sh`. Both startup files (located on the CD-ROM in the `Chapter5` folder) execute the following Java command:

ON THE CD

```
java -cp (classpath details here) com.TradingSystem.StockTicker.SimpleQuoteListener
```

The output of this class is identical to the stock quote updates from the `QuoteListener` class. The client application saves a considerable amount of code through its use of the `JMSManager` facade class. How does the facade help when sending JMS messages? What benefit does the `JMSManager` class provide in this case? Let's explore this by examining a simple message producer application.

The `SimpleQuoteSender` Class

Listing 5.2 shows the code for the `SimpleQuoteSender` class, which sends stock quote update messages using JMS. This class is a simplified version of the `QuoteSender` class from Chapter 3, modified to use the `JMSManager` facade.

LISTING 5.2   Code to Send Stock Quote Messages Using the JMS Facade

```
package com.TradingSystem.StockTicker;

import java.text.NumberFormat;
import java.util.*;
import com.toolkit.messaging.JMSManager;

public class SimpleQuoteSender
{
    private JMSManager jmsMgr = new JMSManager();
    // ...

    public SimpleQuoteSender() throws Exception
    {
        while ( true )
        {
```

```
try {
    int stock = random.nextInt(10);
    String newPrice = getLastTradePrice( stock );
    String text = stocks[stock] + ": \t" + newPrice;

    jmsMgr.send("StockTrades", text );

    Thread.sleep(2000);
}
catch ( Exception e ) {
    e.printStackTrace();
}
        }
    }

    private String getLastTradePrice(int stockIndex) {
        // ...
    }

    private int getStockIndexFromName(String name) {
        // ...
    }

    public static void main(String[] args) throws Exception
    {
        SimpleQuoteSender sender = new SimpleQuoteSender();
    }
}
```

Methods such as getLastTradePrice and getStockIndexFromName have had their code omitted from this example for brevity. They are exactly the same as in the QuoteSender class and have nothing to do with JMS. As with the SimpleQuoteListener class, the SimpleQuoteSender class imports and instantiates JMSManager the same way. The class constructor contains the code to build the stock quote update text and to send it as a JMS message. This is achieved through a call to the method JMSManager.send, where the name of the Destination and the text to send are provided as parameters.

You can run this code by executing the Windows batch file runsimplequote-sender.bat or UNIX command script runsimplequotesender.sh. Both startup files (located on the CD-ROM in the Chapter5 folder) execute the following Java command:

```
java -cp (classpath details here) com.TradingSystem.StockTicker.SimpleQuoteSender
```

The JMSManager Class

As you've seen in the two previous sample applications, the JMSManager class is a facade that makes using JMS to send and receive messages much simpler. A lot of otherwise tedious code has been removed from the sample applications, yet the same apparent level of functionality remains. It's important that a facade class for any software doesn't prevent the programmer from using all of the wrapped software's functionality. The JMSManager class is no exception. Let's explore the implementation of this class and see how it simplifies the use of JMS, without blocking any of its features.

Listing 5.3 shows an overview of the JMSManager class. The method implementations have been omitted and will be discussed in detail as this chapter progresses. For now, let's concentrate on the methods themselves, both public and otherwise, as well as some other internals. The code for the full implementation of the JMSManager class can be found on the book's CD-ROM under the folder \Chapter5\ com\toolkit\messaging.

ON THE CD

LISTING 5.3   An Overview of the JMSManager Class

```
package com.toolkit.messaging;

import java.util.*;
import java.io.*;
import javax.jms.*;
import javax.naming.*;

public class JMSManager
{
    protected static Context jndi = null;
    protected static Connection connection = null;
    protected static boolean connected = false;
    protected Hashtable jmsDestinations = new Hashtable();

    // Nested class encapsulates JMS Destination objects
    class JMSDestination
    {
        Destination destination = null;
        Session session = null;
        MessageProducer producer = null;
        MessageConsumer consumer = null;

        public JMSDestination(  Destination destination,
                                Session session,
                                MessageProducer producer,
                                MessageConsumer consumer)
```

```
        {
            this.destination = destination;
            this.session = session;
            this.producer = producer;
            this.consumer = consumer;
        }
    }

    public JMSManager() throws Exception
    {
        connectToJMS();
    }

    public void createDestination(String name, Class type)
        throws Exception {
        //...
    }

    public void createDestination(String name, Class type,
                            boolean fTransacted, int ackMode)
        throws Exception {
        //...
    }

    public void listen(String destName, MessageListener callback)
        throws Exception {
        //...
    }

    public Message listen(String destName)
        throws Exception {
        //...
    }

    public void listen(Destination dest, MessageListener callback)
        throws Exception {
        //...
    }

    public Message listen(Destination dest)
        throws Exception {
        //...
    }
```

```
public void send(String destName, Message msg)
    throws Exception {
    //...
}

public void send(String destName, Serializable obj)
    throws Exception {
    //...
}

public void send(String destName, String messageText)
    throws Exception {
    //...
}

public void send(Destination dest, Message msg)
    throws Exception {
    //...
}

public void stop(String destName) {
    //...
}

public Session getSession(String destName) {
    //...
}

public Destination getDestination(String destName) {
    //...
}

public MessageProducer getProducer(String destName) {
    //...
}

public MessageConsumer getConsumer(String destName) {
    //...
}

protected void connectToJMS() {
    //...
}
```

```
    protected JMSDestination getJMSDestination(String name)
        throws Exception {
        //...
    }

    protected void setupProducer(JMSDestination jmsDest)
        throws Exception {
        //...
    }

    protected void setupAsynchConsumer( JMSDestination jmsDest,
                                        MessageListener callback)
        throws Exception {
        //...
    }

    protected Message setupSynchConsumer(JMSDestination jmsDest)
        throws Exception {
        //...
    }

    protected Message createJMSMessage( Serializable obj,
                                        Session session)
        throws Exception {
        //...
    }

    protected ConnectionFactory getConnectionFactory()
        throws Exception {
        //...
    }

    protected Object jndiLookup(String name)  {
        //...
    }
}
```

You may recall that once a JMS client application has an open reference to a JMS Connection object, that's usually enough for the entire application. Therefore, the JMSManager class maintains the Connection in a static member variable to be used by all instantiations of the class. Also static is the Java Naming and Directory Interface (JNDI) Context object, since this is also needed only once. Therefore it's safe to instantiate multiple instances of the JMSManager facade class in a client application; the resource-sensitive data will be shared across all of them.

Each `Destination` object created is encapsulated within objects of the nested class `JMSDestination`. This class also holds references to the destination's `Session`, `MessageProducer`, and `MessageConsumer` objects. Each `JMSDestination` object is stored in the `java.util.Hashtable` member variable called `jmsDestinations`, where the destination name is used as the key. This way, when a call is made to send a message, the appropriate object can be quickly located, and its `MessageProducer` can be used for the message send.

One of the benefits of using the facade is that you don't need to create destinations explicitly, even though the `JMSManager` does allow it. The facade creates `Destination` objects automatically when you call the `listen` or `send` methods. In this case, the class will attempt to locate the `Destination` using JNDI but will otherwise default and create a `Topic` destination. The only reason to call the `JMSManager.createDestination` method is to explicitly specify the destination type (`Topic` or `Queue`) to indicate whether its messages are to be transacted or to indicate whether acknowledgments will be sent automatically or not. There are two variations of `createDestination`: the first allows the caller to specify just the name and type of the destination, but defaults to nontransacted and auto-acknowledgment. The second allows the caller to also specify the transaction and acknowledgment settings. Listing 5.4 shows the implementation of the two `createDestination` methods.

LISTING 5.4 The `createDestination` Method Implementation

```
public void createDestination(String name, Class type)
    throws Exception
{
    this.createDestination( name, type,
                       false, Session.AUTO_ACKNOWLEDGE);
}

public void createDestination(String name, Class type,
                       boolean fTransacted, int ackMode)
    throws Exception
{
    if ( jmsDestinations.get(name) != null )
        return;

    Session session =
        connection.createSession(fTransacted, ackMode);

    Destination destination = (Destination)jndiLookup(name);
    if ( destination == null )
    {
```

```
        if ( type.getName().equals("javax.jms.Queue") )
            destination = session.createQueue(name);
        else
            destination = session.createTopic(name);
    }

    JMSDestination jmsDest = new JMSDestination(
                                destination, session,
                                null, null);

    jmsDestinations.put( name, jmsDest );
  }
```

Examining the code, you can see that if the destination already exists in the Hashtable, it isn't created again. If it's not found, it's looked up via JNDI or created explicitly using the parameters provided and stored in the Hashtable of JMSDestination objects. Notice that you can optionally specify the transaction and acknowledgment modes or use the defaults.

Receiving Messages

To receive messages for a particular destination, you simply call one of the two listen methods that the JMSManager class provides. To receive messages asynchronously, call the version of the listen method that requires both a destination name and a callback reference. This call returns right away, and your code is free to do whatever processing it needs to do. When a message arrives for the specified destination, the onMessage method is called on the provided object that implements the MessageListener interface. This method is continuously called for each message that arrives for this destination. To stop listening to messages for a destination, simply call the JMSManager.stop method and provide the applicable destination name as the parameter.

You don't have to create multiple instances of the JMSManager class to asynchronously listen to more than one destination at a time. One instance will do the job. However, your code will need to call listen once for each destination. You must choose one the six forms of the listen method:

listen(String destName, MessageListener callback):   This method listens asynchronously for messages for the specified destination name. When messages arrive, the onMessage method on the supplied MessageListener object will be called.

listen(String destName): This method listens synchronously to the destination specified. The call will block until a message arrives, and the Message object will be returned.

listen(String destName, int timeout): This method listens synchronously to the destination specified. The call will block until a message arrives or the timeout value is reached. If the call times out, null is returned.

listen(Destination dest, MessageListener callback): This method listens asynchronously for messages for the specified Destination object. When messages arrive, the onMessage method on the supplied MessageListener object will be called.

listen(Destination dest): This method listens synchronously to the Destination object supplied. The call will block until a message arrives; the Message object will be returned.

listen(Destination dest, int timeout): This method listens synchronously to the Destination object supplied. The call will block until a message arrives or the timeout value is reached. If the call times out, null is returned.

If your code has no other purpose but to process messages only when they arrive, you may choose to use one of the synchronous versions of the listen method. Simply provide the name of the destination to "listen to," and the call will not return until a message arrives for that destination (or the timeout is reached if specified). When a message does arrive, it is returned from the call in the form of a javax.jms.Message object. With synchronous message delivery, your code must call listen again after a message arrives in order to receive additional messages for the specified destination.

Let's examine how the listen methods do their work (see Listing 5.5). The first version delivers messages asynchronously using the provided MessageListener object, while the second delivers then synchronously and provides the Message object as the return value of the call. Again, there is no need to create a Destination object first; the call to getJMSDestination will return it if it already exists or it will create (and store) a new one for you.

LISTING 5.5 The JMS Facade listen Methods

```
// Asynchronous listen
public void listen(String destName, MessageListener callback)
    throws Exception
{
    JMSDestination jmsDest = getJMSDestination(destName);
    setupAsynchConsumer( jmsDest, callback );
}
```

```
// Synchronous listen with NO timeout
public Message listen(String destName)
    throws Exception
{
    JMSDestination jmsDest = getJMSDestination(destName);
    return setupSynchConsumer( jmsDest, 0 );
}

// Synchronous listen with timeout specified
public Message listen(String destName, int timeout)
    throws Exception
{
    JMSDestination jmsDest = getJMSDestination(destName);
    return setupSynchConsumer( jmsDest, 0 );
}

// Asynchronous listen with Destination object provided
public void listen(Destination dest, MessageListener callback)
    throws Exception
{
    Session s =
        connection.createSession(false, Session.AUTO_ACKNOWLEDGE);
    MessageConsumer c = s.createConsumer(dest);
    c.setMessageListener(callback);
}

// Synchronous listen with Destination Object supplied
public Message listen(Destination dest, int timeout)
    throws Exception
{
    Session s =
        connection.createSession(false, Session.AUTO_ACKNOWLEDGE);
    MessageConsumer c = s.createConsumer(dest);
    Message msg = null;
    if ( timeout > 0 )
        msg = c.receive(timeout);
    else
      msg = c.receive();
    s.close();
    return msg;
}

public Message listen(Destination dest)
    throws Exception
```

```
    {
        return this.listen(dest, 0);
    }
```

The `listen` methods that take a destination name call either `setupAsynch Consumer` or `setupSynchConsumer`. Since this is where most of the work is done, let's examine these methods now (Listing 5.6).

LISTING 5.6 Setting Up an Asynchronous Message Consumer

```
protected void setupAsynchConsumer( JMSDestination jmsDest,
                                    MessageListener callback)
    throws Exception
{
    if ( jmsDest.consumer == null )
    {
        jmsDest.consumer =
            jmsDest.session.createConsumer(jmsDest.destination);
    }
    jmsDest.consumer.setMessageListener(callback);
}

protected Message setupSynchConsumer(JMSDestination jmsDest
                                     int timeout )
    throws Exception
{
    if ( jmsDest.consumer == null )
    {
        jmsDest.consumer =
            jmsDest.session.createConsumer(jmsDest.destination);
    }
    if ( timeout > 0 )
        return jmsDest.consumer.receive();
    else
        return jmsDest.consumer.receive(timeout);
}
```

Both methods do as you might expect; they both create a `MessageConsumer` if they haven't already, and they are stored as part of the `JMSDestination` object that resides in the `Hashtable`. For the asynchronous call, the `setMessageListener` is called on the consumer with the given `MessageListener` interface. For the synchronous listen, a call is made to the method `receive`, which blocks until a message is received. The `JMSManager` class also contains a version of the listen method that takes a timeout value that is passed to the consumer's `receive` method.

Sending Messages

To provide flexibility, the JMSManager class defines four send methods. The difference between them is the type of message payload each carries:

send(String dest, String messageText): This method sends the message text as a JMS TextMessage object to the destination specified by name in the first parameter.

send(String dest, Serializable messageObj): This method sends the JMS ObjectMessage to the destination specified by name in the first parameter.

send(String dest, Message jmsMessage): This method sends the JMS Message provided to the destination specified by name in the first parameter.

send(Destination dest, Message jmsMessage): This methods sends the JMS Message object to the supplied Destination object. A Session object and a MessageProducer object will be created temporarily, just for this method call.

The first three send methods call JMSManager.getJMSDestination to retrieve the specified destination, first from the Hashtable of JMSDestination objects, then from JNDI. If it cannot be found, this method creates it and adds it to the Hashtable; the default is a Topic. Next, the method JMSManager.setupProducer is called. If a MessageProducer has not already been created for this Destination, one is created now and stored in the existing JMSDestination object. The fourth method takes a Destination object as its first parameter and therefore does not need to retrieve or create one. An example use of this method is to send a reply to a request Message that contains a valid Destination object in the JMSReplyTo property.

Besides the message payload type, the first three send methods work the same way. Each requires a destination name to send the message to. For the method that takes a JMS Message object as a parameter, the message is sent via the MessageProducer (see Listing 5.7).

LISTING 5.7 JMSManager Code to Send a JMS Message Object

```
public void send(String destName, Message msg)
    throws Exception
{
    JMSDestination jmsDest = getJMSDestination(destName);
    setupProducer( jmsDest );
    jmsDest.producer.send(msg);
}
```

For the send methods that take a String or Serializable object as a parameter, a JMS Message object is created to wrap it (see Listing 5.8). Since a Java String is a Serializable object, both send methods share one implementation.

LISTING 5.8 JMSManager Code to Send a String or Serializable Object

```
public void send(String destName, String messageText)
    throws Exception
{
    this.send(destName, (Serializable)messageText);
}

public void send(String destName, Serializable obj)
    throws Exception
{
    JMSDestination jmsDest = getJMSDestination(destName);
    setupProducer( jmsDest );
    Message msg = createJMSMessage(obj, jmsDest.session);
    jmsDest.producer.send( msg );
}
```

Because of this, an extra step needs to be done when the JMS Message object is created (see Listing 5.9). A check is made to see if the given object is a String. If so, a TextMessage is created and the setText method is called. Otherwise, an ObjectMessage is created and the setObject method is called.

LISTING 5.9 JMSManager Code to Create the Correct JMS Message Object

```
protected Message createJMSMessage(Serializable obj, Session session)
    throws Exception
{
    if ( obj instanceof String )
    {
        TextMessage textMsg = session.createTextMessage();
        textMsg.setText( (String)obj );
        return textMsg;
    }
    else
    {
        ObjectMessage objMsg = session.createObjectMessage();
        objMsg.setObject( obj );
        return objMsg;
    }
}
```

For completeness, a version of the send method exists that takes a Destination object instead of a destination name for which to send the message (see Listing 5.10). In this case, Session and MessageProducer objects are created for the given

`Destination`, but they exist only for the life of the method call. By the end of the call, the `Session` is closed, and the objects are candidates for garbage collection. Keep in mind that this method is provided for convenience, and it's not very efficient if used often since the JMS objects are created and torn down each time. The methods that take a destination name are more efficient since they create and use JMS objects that live *beyond* the send method call. Therefore you should try to use those methods where you can.

LISTING 5.10   Code for the `send` Method that Accepts a `Destination` Object

```
public void send(Destination dest, Message msg)
    throws Exception
{
    Session s = connection.createSession(false,
            Session.AUTO_ACKNOWLEDGE);
    MessageProducer p = s.createProducer( dest );
    p.send(msg);
    s.close();
}
```

The end result is convenience; each client application developed with the JMS facade is spared from doing all of this work each time it sends a message. Simply call the send method, specifying exactly what you want to send—a `String` or an object—and never be concerned with the underlying JMS `Message` used to transport it unless you want.

Access to the Underlying JMS Interfaces

Although the `JMSManager` shields your client application from the internals of JMS, your application can still perform detailed tasks such as setting the transaction mode, setting the acknowledgment mode, creating durable subscribers, using message selectors, commit, or rollback transactions, and so on. Access to the internal JMS objects is provided through the following `JMSManager` methods:

`getSession(String destName):`   Returns the `Session` object for the specified destination name

`getDestination(String destName):`   Returns the `Destination` object for the specified destination name

`getProducer(String destName):`   Returns the `MessageProducer` object for the specified destination name

`getConsumer(String destName):`   Returns the `MessageConsumer` object for the specified destination name

Modifying the SimpleQuoteListener class from Listing 5.1 to support transactions is quite easy. All you need to do is add two lines of code; one in the constructor, and one in the onMessage method (see Listing 5.11; the added lines are in bold text). The JMSManager class allows you to specifically create Destination objects, where you can optionally specify the transaction and acknoweldgment modes. In this example, transactions are set to true and AUTO_ACKNOWLEGDE is used. When a message is received, the Session for the "StockTrades" destination is retrieved via a call to JMSManager.getSession, and the Session.commit method is called to commit the transaction.

LISTING 5.11   Code that Adds Transaction Support to the SimpleQuoteListener Class

```
//...
public SimpleQuoteListener() throws Exception
{
    // Create a Destination with a transacted Session
    jmsMgr.createDestination(   "StockTrades", Topic.class,
                                true, Session.AUTO_ACKNOWLEDGE);

    jmsMgr.listen( "StockTrades", this );
}

public void onMessage(Message message)
{
    try {
        TextMessage textMessage = (TextMessage)message;
        String text = textMessage.getText();
        System.out.println(text);
        jmsMgr.getSession("StockTrades").commit();
    }
    catch ( JMSException e ) {
        e.printStackTrace();
    }
}
//...
```

The Complete Simple Stock Quote Example

Only one item is missing from both the SimpleQuoteListener and SimpleQuoteSender class: support for quote requests. In Chapter 3, the quote listener class, upon starting up, made quote requests to a queue for stocks it was interested in. The quote sender class listened to this queue and replied with the quote. Let's examine what it would take to add this support to the *simple* stock quote example in this chapter.

Listing 5.12 shows just the code for the SimpleQuoteListener class to send stock quote request messages. This code uses a combination of the JMSManager class from this chapter and the QuoteRequestor class from Chapter 3 to perform this task. You should notice that the code is simpler and more straightforward with the use of the facade class. No longer does the code call JNDI explicitly to get the Queue, nor does it explicitly create a Session object.

LISTING 5.12   Code to Send Stock Quote Requests with the JMS Facade

```
public SimpleQuoteListener() throws Exception
{
  for ( int i = 0; i < stocks.length; i++ )
  {
      GenericRequestor requestor =
          new GenericRequestor(
                  jmsMgr.getSession("RequestQuote"),
                  jmsMgr.getDestination("RequestQuote"),
                  TemporaryQueue.class);

      MapMessage mapMsg =
          jmsMgr.createMapMessage("RequestQuote");
      mapMsg.setString("ticker", stocks[i]);

      Message response = requestor.request(mapMsg, 2000);
      if ( response != null )
          onMessage(response);
  }
  // ...
}
```

The code to receive the quote requests is in Listing 5.13. This class, QuoteRequestListener, is a nested class of the SimpleQuoteSender class, similar to the quote sender example in Chapter 3. If you compare them, you should notice that this class has gotten much simpler and much smaller. The seven lines of code in the QuoteSender example are replaced by one call to the JMSManager.listen method in this example.

LISTING 5.13   The SimpleQuoteSender Object's Nested QuoteRequestListener Class

```
// ...
class QuoteRequestListener implements MessageListener
{
    public QuoteRequestListener() throws Exception{
        jmsMgr.listen("RequestQuote", this);
    }
```

```
public void onMessage(Message message)
{
    try {
        MapMessage mapMsg = (MapMessage)message;
        String ticker = mapMsg.getString("ticker");
        int stock = getStockIndexFromName( ticker );

        TextMessage textMsg =
            jmsMgr.createTextMessage("RequestQuote");

        if ( stock != -1 ) {
            String newPrice = getLastTradePrice( stock );
            textMsg.setText(stocks[stock]+": \t"+newPrice);
        }
        else {
            textMsg.setText("Stock ticker not supported");
        }

        jmsMgr.send( mapMsg.getJMSReplyTo(), textMsg);
    }
    catch ( Exception e ) {
        e.printStackTrace();
    }
}
}
```

When you run the SimpleQuoteListener and SimpleQuoteSender applications, the output will be identical to the sample applications from Chapter 3. You can run the SimpleQuoteListener application with the original QuoteSender application, and vice versa, and they will work together without a difference in behavior. The JMS facade, like any good facade class, doesn't change the expected behavior of JMS messaging, but instead makes it easier to use.

DISTRIBUTED JAVABEAN EVENTS

The idea of a facade class for JMS can be taken one step further. In this section, a class is presented that makes the use of JMS as easy as sending and receiving JavaBean events, called the *event distributor*. The event distributor is comprised of one main class, EventDistributor, which becomes a local listener of events for the source component, and a local sender of the same events for the remote listener. On the source component end, the event distributor uses Java reflection to dynamically create an object of the event source interface. On the listener end, the event distributor uses reflection to call the event interface as implemented by the listener components. In between, JMS messages are sent that encapsulate the event data as objects of the `DistEvent` class.

While the purpose of a facade class is to make it easier to use a software interface, it is not meant to obfuscate that interface. It should be obvious to the programmer who uses the JMS facade that he is using JMS. However, the point of the event distributor is to make the use of JMS transparent to the programmer. A technique such as this should be used sparingly, as it may "trick" the user into doing something in a way he may not have otherwise chosen, but since it was hidden, he has no idea of the true nature of the software. However, there are cases, as with the event distributor, where hiding the details of a technology is desirable and is not completely unknown to the user.

The Event Distributor

The goal is to create a wrapper class that extends JavaBean events across Java virtual machines by transparently using JMS as the transport. Applications written with the event distributor contain typical JavaBean event code and don't need any JMS code or knowledge to make them work. The only additions are two base classes: one to be extended by event source components and the other to be extended by event listener components. You can even configure it to use persistent or nonpersistent message delivery. Before we go into the details of how the event distributor works, let's look at how to use it.

Event Listener Components

To define a JavaBean event listener, you must implement the `java.util.EventListener` interface along with the event interfaces in which it is interested. Event source components deliver events by calling the methods defined by the event interface on each event listener component. Using the event distributor class from an event listener component is simple. Make the following two enhancements to your event listener code to receive remote Java events:

- `import` the `com.toolkit.messaging` package.
- `extend` the `com.toolkit.messaging.EventListenerDist` class.

These modifications are minor and they don't expose any implementation details about how the events will be received remotely. When your listener object is instantiated, the class constructor automatically calls the `EventListenerDist` constructor (because it `extended` it). This constructor gets a reference to the event distributor singleton object and calls the method, onNewListener, which notifies it about the new listener. Listing 5.14 shows the simple yet important EventListenerDist class that each event listener object must extend to receive distributed events.

LISTING 5.14 The EventListenerDist Base Class for Event Listeners

```
package com.toolkit.messaging;

public abstract class EventListenerDist
{
    private EventDistributor eventDistributor =
        EventDistributor.getInstance();

    public EventListenerDist()
    {
        eventDistributor.onNewListener( this );
    }
}
```

The event distributor then uses Java *reflection* to get the name of each interface the listener object implements (see Listing 5.15). Java reflection allows you to discover, at runtime, which interfaces are implemented by any arbitrary Java object. Figure 5.3 shows how the event distributor method onNewListener performs this task.

LISTING 5.15 This Code Uses Java Reflection to Discover a Listener's Implemented Interfaces

```
public void onNewListener(EventListenerDist listener)
{
    try {
        Class listenerClass = listener.getClass();
        Class[] interfaces = listenerClass.getInterfaces();
        String[] interfaceNames =
        new String[interfaces.length];

        for ( int i = 0; i < interfaces.length; i++ )
        {
            interfaceNames[i] = interfaces[i].getName();
            Vector listeners =
                (Vector)listenerMap.get( interfaceNames[i] );

            if ( listeners == null )
            {
```

```
                    listeners = new Vector();
                    listenerMap.put( interfaceNames[i], listeners );
                    EventConsumer eventConsumer =
                        new EventConsumer (interfaceNames[i]);
                }
                listeners.add(listener);
            }
        }
        catch ( Exception e ) {
            e.printStackTrace();
        }
    }
```

First, the `java.lang.Class` object for the given listener component is obtained. The `Class.getInterfaces` method returns an array of `Class` objects, one for each interface implemented by the listener. The code then iterates through the array and calls the `Class.getName` method for each array element. As a result, the code fills out an array of `Strings` that contains the names of the implemented interfaces. To avoid confusion, this detail has been left off the sequence diagram.

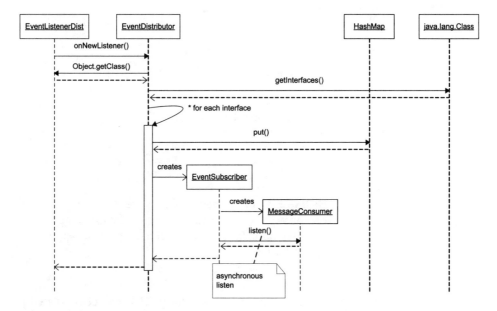

FIGURE 5.3   The call sequence that occurs when an event listener transparently registers with the event distributor.

A few steps from now, the interface name will be used in the JMS Destination name by which the events are distributed remotely for this event interface. For now, a check is made to see if any listeners already exist for this interface. The event distributor's listenerMap is a HashMap that contains one entry per interface name. Each HashMap entry is a reference to a Vector that contains all of the JavaBean listener objects that implement the interface (see Figure 5.4). If this is the first listener for this interface, an EventConsumer object is created. The EventConsumer object then uses the JMSManager class (from earlier in this chapter) to create a Destination and a MessageConsumer for the event interface and perform an asynchronous listen method call. The event listener is then stored in the list of listeners for this interface.

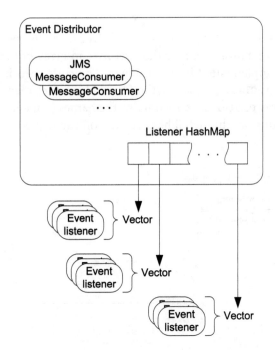

FIGURE 5.4 Event listener objects are stored in a Vector with other objects that implement the same event interface. Each Vector is stored in a HashMap by interface name.

Because only one EventConsumer (see Listing 5.16) object is created per interface, the event distributor creates only one JMS Destination and MessageProducer for an interface, regardless of how many listeners implement that interface. This class is nested within the event distributor's main class, EventDistributor. The interface name is used here as the `Destination` name by prepending the text "eventdist" to it, with a period as a separator. When a JMS message is received, the `EventDistributor.onEvent` method is called. The event distributor multicasts each message it receives to all the JavaBean listeners it has for that event interface.

LISTING 5.16   The Nested Class `EventConsumer`

```
// Nested class within Event Distributor
class EventConsumer implements MessageListener
{
    String interfaceName;

    public EventConsumer(String interfaceName)
    {
        try {
            this.interfaceName = interfaceName;
            jmsMgr.listen("eventdist." + interfaceName, this);
        }
        catch ( Exception e ) {
            e.printStackTrace();
        }
    }

    public void onMessage(Message message)
    {
        try {
            ObjectMessage objMsg = (ObjectMessage)message;
            DistEvent distEvent = (DistEvent)objMsg.getObject();
            // call the Event Distributor
            onEvent( distEvent );
        }
        catch ( Exception e ) {
            e.printStackTrace();
        }
    }
}
```

Event Source Components

The implementation of a listener registration method defines a JavaBean event source. This method accepts references to objects that implement a particular event interface. Make the following enhancements to your event source code to send remote events:

1. import the com.toolkit.messaging package.
2. extend the com.toolkit.messaging.EventSourceDist base class.
3. Define a method named getInterfaceNames that returns a String array. The array should contain the name of each interface for which the event source produces events.
4. Define a method named addListener, which allows listener objects to register for the events the source component produces. Regardless of whether you use the event distributor, your event source components need to define a similar method.
5. Define a method named removeListener, which allows listener objects to deregister for the events the component produces. Again, your event source components should define a similar method whether they use the event distributor or not.

These modifications are similar to those outlined for listener components, with three additional yet simple methods. Still, no implementation details about sending the events remotely via JMS are exposed. In the previous section, we learned that the event distributor uses Java reflection to get the name of each interface a listener object implements. A JMS Destination object is created in preparation for receiving a JMS message for each event that the event source fires. Now the event distributor must perform the similar, but reverse, task for the event source component. When a source object is instantiated, the class constructor automatically calls the EventSourceDist class constructor (because it extended it). The constructor gets a reference to the event distributor singleton object and calls the method, onNewSource, which notifies it about the new event source. Listing 5.17 shows the simple yet important EventSourceDist class that each event source object must extend to send distributed events.

LISTING 5.17 The EventSourceDist Base Class for Event Source Components

```
package com.toolkit.messaging;

public abstract class EventSourceDist implements SourceInterface
{
    private EventDistributor eventDistributor =
        EventDistributor.getInstance();

    public EventSourceDist()
    {
        eventDistributor.onNewSource( this );
    }
```

```
        public abstract String[] getInterfaceNames();
    }
```

Using Java reflection, the event distributor dynamically examines each interface for which the source component sources events and creates a proxy event listener object per interface (see Listing 5.18). Figure 5.5 shows how the event distributor method onNewSource performs this task.

LISTING 5.18   Java Reflection is Used to Register for a Source Component's Event Interfaces

```
public void onNewSource(EventSourceDist source)
{
    try {
        String[] interfaces = source.getInterfaceNames();

        for ( int i = 0; i < interfaces.length; i++)
        {
            Object proxy = createProxy( interfaces[i] );
            if ( proxy != null )
            {
                String destName = "eventdist." + interfaces[i];
                SourceInfo sourceInfo =
                    new SourceInfo(interfaces[i], destName);
                sourceMap.put( interfaces[i], sourceInfo );
                source.addListener( proxy );
            }
        }
    }
    catch ( Exception e ) {
        e.printStackTrace();
    }
}

protected Object createProxy(String interfaceName)
{
    try {
        InvocationHandler handler = new EventInvocationHandler();
        Class eventInterface = Class.forName( interfaceName );

        Object proxy =
            Proxy.newProxyInstance(
                    eventInterface.getClassLoader(),
```

```
                              new Class[] { eventInterface },
                              handler );

        return proxy;
    }
    catch ( Exception e ) {
        e.printStackTrace();
    }

    return null;
}
```

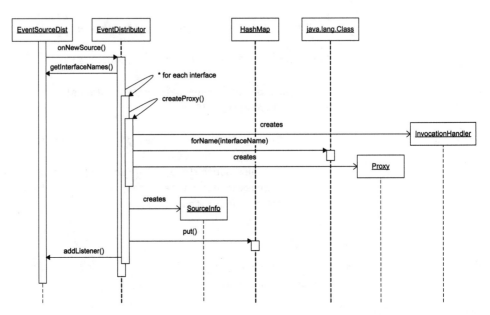

FIGURE 5.5 A Unified Modeling Language (UML) sequence diagram that shows the code flow when a new source component registers with the event distributor.

The event distributor retrieves the names of the event interfaces supported by the source component by calling its implementation of the method getInterface Names. The java.lang.reflect library contains the Proxy class and InvocationHandler interface. Using these together, you can create an object at runtime that implements any valid interface. This is done in the CreateProxy method, where the event distributor creates a proxy Java listener object for each event interface the source component sources. Each proxy listener object is stored in a HashMap (see Figure 5.6) and provided to the event source component (via the addListener method) so that it can receive JavaBean events like any other JavaBean listener. A SourceInfo object is created to encapsulate the interface and destination names for the proxy event listener.

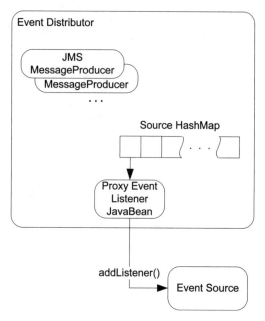

FIGURE 5.6   The event distributor creates a proxy listener for each event source interface.

At the end of this process, the event distributor registers with the event source as a listener for each event interface, and all the JMS plumbing is in place to remotely distribute the events. As a result, when an event source component produces an event, one of the listeners it calls is the proxy object that the event distributor created. All of the details of the event—the method name, parameters, and parameter types—are wrapped in a serializable object class and sent out over JMS (see Figure 5.7). This class is the DistEvent class (discussed later in this chapter) that is used to encapsulate each event's interface name, method name, and parameters.

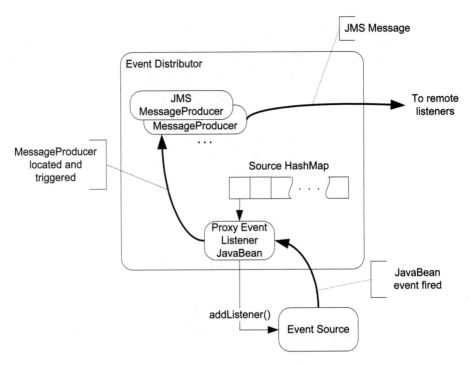

FIGURE 5.7 This diagram shows how an event from a local source component is propagated using JMS to remote event listeners.

Using Java Reflection

While JMS does the actual work in distributing JavaBean events, Java reflection makes it possible and transparent. Using reflection, the event distributor "intercepts" events by creating interface proxy classes. We've seen how reflection enables it to receive the events by discovering the interfaces implemented by event listener components, but the real magic is how reflection allows the event distributor to dissect and wrap the events themselves. All of this happens transparently and it is nonintrusive to the source and listener components. It's a real showcase of the power of Java and reflection.

The `InvocationHandler` Interface

An invocation handler is an object that implements the `InvocationHandler` interface. As discussed in the previous section, a reference to such an object is used in creating an interface proxy object. When a proxy object calls methods, the invocation handler's `invoke` method fields them. The `invoke` method provides three parameters: the proxy object on which the call was made, the actual method that was called, and the method's arguments. The event distributor's nested class EventInvocationHandler fields all method calls for the proxy listener objects (see Listing 5.19).

LISTING 5.19 The Event Distributor's Nested EventInvocationHandler Class

```
class EventInvocationHandler implements InvocationHandler
{
    public Object invoke(Object proxy, Method mthd, Object[] args)
        throws Throwable
    {
        try {
            Class proxyClass = proxy.getClass();
            Class[] interfaces = proxyClass.getInterfaces();
            String interfaceName = interfaces[0].getName();
            Class[] argTypes = mthd.getParameterTypes();
            String[] argNames = new String[argTypes.length];

            for ( int p = 0; p < argTypes.length; p++ )
                argNames[p] = argTypes[p].getName();

            SourceInfo srcInfo =
                (SourceInfo)sourceMap.get(interfaceName);

            if ( srcInfo != null )
            {
                DistEvent DistEvent =
                    new DistEvent(interfaceName,
                                  mthd.getName(),
                                  args, argNames );

                jmsMgr.send(srcInfo.destName, DistEvent );
            }
        }
        catch ( Exception e ) {
            e.printStackTrace();
        }
        return null;
    }
}
```

The first step is to get the Class object for the proxy by calling proxy.getClass. Next, call getInterfaces on the proxy Class object to retrieve the implemented interfaces as an array of `Class` objects. You can prove that the proxy's interface truly implemented the invoked method by calling `proxyClass.getMethods`. Iterating through the returned `Method` object array should find a match. Continuing with this example, the invoked method name is retrieved via a call to `Method.getName`. A call to `Method.getParameterTypes` then retrieves the argument types for the invoked method. The result is an array of `Class` objects, one for each argument of the method call.

By now you should have noticed a pattern to using Java reflection, which allows you to dive deeper into classes, methods, argument types, and argument values. The remainder of the example uses this pattern to output the details of the method call, the parameters, and the parameter types. The event's method name and parameters are wrapped into an object of class `DistEvent`, which is sent from JMS as a serializable object. Notice the use of the JMS facade class `JMSManager` to do the work of sending this object over JMS. When received, this object is dissected and the correct method on the real JavaBean event listener object(s) is called.

The `DistEvent` Object

The `DistEvent` class is meant to be analogous to the JavaBean `Event` interface, with the added functionality of working in a distributed (inter-JVM [Java Virtual Machine]) messaging environment. In order for JMS to send a `DistEvent` object between Java virtual machines and over the network, `DistEvent` must implement the `java.io.Serializable` interface. This interface simply identifies the implementing class as being `serializable`. Listing 5.20 shows the structure of a `DistEvent` object, which contains all of the information about the event (the method name, parameters, etc.) that was retrieved using Java reflection.

LISTING 5.20   The Event Distributor's `DistEvent` Class

```
package com.toolkit.messaging;
class DistEvent implements java.io.Serializable
{
    public String interfaceName;
    public String eventMethod;
    public Object[] eventArgs;
    public String[] argNames;
    public Class[] argTypes;

    public DistEvent(String name, String mthd,
                Object[] args, String[] argnames) { ... }

    public void setArgTypes(Class[] argtypes) { ... }
}
```

Calling Listeners

The event distributor uses the JMSManager class to implement a MessageConsumer for each event interface. The EventConsumer class implements the MessageListener interface to support asynchronous message notification. When a message arrives, JMS calls the EventConsumer object's onMessage method. This is where the DistEvent object is extracted from the JMS message, as shown in Listing 5.21.

LISTING 5.21   The EventConsumer Object's onMessage Method Implementation

```
public void onMessage(Message message)
{
    try {
        ObjectMessage objMsg = (ObjectMessage)message;
        DistEvent distEvent = (DistEvent)objMsg.getObject();
        // call the Event Distributor
        onEvent( distEvent );
    }
    catch ( Exception e ) {
        e.printStackTrace();
    }
}
```

In the next step, the nested class calls the event distributor's onEvent method, where the DistEvent object is dissected (see Listing 5.22).

LISTING 5.22   Code to Handle a Remote Event

```
protected void onEvent( DistEvent distEvent )
{
    try {
        // Deliver the event to each listener
        // of this event interface
        Vector listeners = (Vector)
            listenerMap.get( distEvent.interfaceName );

        if ( listeners == null )
            return;

        int count = listeners.size();
        for ( int i = 0; i < count; i++ )
        {
            EventListenerDist listener =
                (EventListenerDist)listeners.elementAt(i);
```

```
            deliverEvent( listener, distEvent );
        }
    }
    catch ( Exception e ) {
    }
}


protected void deliverEvent( EventListenerDist listener,
                            DistEvent distEvent)
{
    try {
        // Create the arg type array from the args array
        // This array is used to get the called method
        int argCount = distEvent.argNames.length;
        Class[] argTypes = new Class[argCount];
        for ( int p = 0; p < argCount; p++ )
            argTypes[p] = distEvent.eventArgs[p].getClass();

        Class listenerClass = listener.getClass();

        Method eventMethod =
            listenerClass.getMethod( distEvent.eventMethod,
                                    argTypes );

        // The following invokes the event method on
        // the actual event listener object
        eventMethod.invoke( listener, distEvent.eventArgs );
    }
    catch ( Exception e ) {
        e.printStackTrace();
    }
}
```

When the event distributor receives a JMS message, the onEvent method performs the following steps:

1. The real event listeners are located. The interface name is used as a key to the HashMap listenerMap, where each HashMap bucket points to a Vector containing the listener objects. If at least one listener for this event interface exists, the event distributor will return and traverse a Vector.
2. For each listener object in the Vector, the event distributor calls the deliver Event method to deliver the event.

3. The event distributor uses the `DistEvent` object to extract the method's arguments. It then creates an array of `Class` objects and populates it with each argument's type by calling `getClass` on each argument object. The event distributor uses this array, along with the given method name, to get a reference to the correct `Method` object.
4. To invoke the event method on the actual listener object, the `invoke` method of the `Method` object is called.

Figure 5.8 provides an overview for the sequence of calls that are made when an event source component fires an event, which is in turn received by a remote event listener component. Neither the source nor the listener is aware that JMS was used to transport the event remotely.

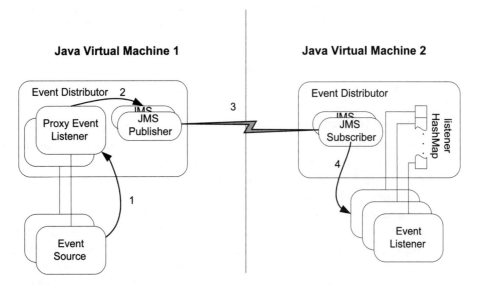

FIGURE 5.8 An overview of the entire remote JavaBean event sequence for the source and the remote listener.

The Stock Quote JavaBean Example

To prove how easy and transparent it is to use the event distributor for remote Java-Bean events, the stock quote example application has (once again) been modified for illustration. The sample application contains an event source component, `QuoteSourceBean`, an event listener component, `QuoteListenerBean`, and an event interface, `QuoteChangedEvent`, that the `QuoteListenerBean` implements.

The Event Interface: `QuoteChangedEvent`

An event interface meant for use with the event distributor is defined almost exactly like any JavaBean event interface. The interface still must extend the `java.util.EventListener` interface. The only difference is the addition of the fully qualified interface name added as a member variable of type `String`, named `interfaceName`, shown in bold in Listing 5.23.

LISTING 5.23 Code for the `QuoteChangedEvent` Interface

```
package com.TradingSystem.StockTicker;

public interface QuoteChangedEvent extends java.util.EventListener
{
    public static final String interfaceName =
        "com.TradingSystem.StockTicker.QuoteChangedEvent";
    public void onNewQuote(String stock, String quote);
}
```

This interface is to be implemented by any JavaBean component that wishes to receive the events as defined by the interface.

The Event Listener: `QuoteListenerBean`

The `QuoteListenerBean` component is like any other event listener JavaBean. It implements at least one event interface—`QuoteChangedEvent` in this case—and registers itself with the event source component. The event distributor requires one change: the event listener must extend the base class `EventListenerDist` and nothing else (see Listing 5.24). The purpose of extending this class is that its constructor is called automatically when the `QuoteListenerBean` class is created. It's in the `EventListenerDist` constructor that the event distributor is invoked transparently for the listener, and all of the Java reflection code described earlier is executed. No other method calls need to be made. The listener is automatically set up to receive remote events at this point.

LISTING 5.24 Code for the `QuoteListenerBean` Class

```
package com.TradingSystem.StockTicker;

import com.toolkit.messaging.*;

public class QuoteListenerBean
        extends EventListenerDist
        implements QuoteChangedEvent
{
```

```
public QuoteListenerBean()
{
    System.out.println("QuoteListenerBean created");
}

public void onNewQuote(String stock, String quote)
{
    System.out.println(stock + ": \t" + quote );
}
}
```

The Event Source: `QuoteSenderBean`

An event source component that wants to use the event distributor to support remote event listeners needs to make two minor changes when compared with normal JavaBean event source components (see Listing 5.25):

1. The event source class must extend the base class, `EventSourceDist`. The `EventSourceDist` constructor is automatically called, which transparently invokes the event distributor. At this point, the proxy listener object is created and later used to transport each event method call via JMS to remote listeners.
2. The class must override the method `getInterfaceNames` and return an array of `Strings`, where each `String` represents an event interface this source object fires events for. Even if one event interface is supported, an array with one element must be created and returned.

There are, technically, two other requirements to use the event distributor. The methods `addListener` and `removeListener` must be defined in the event source class to allow event listener components to register and deregister for events respectively. They are not on the previous list of changes because the JavaBean specification recommends that every event source component provide these methods.

LISTING 5.25 Code for the `QuoteSourceBean` Class

```
package com.TradingSystem.StockTicker;

import java.text.NumberFormat;
import java.util.*;
import com.toolkit.messaging.*;

public class QuoteSourceBean
        extends EventSourceDist
{
```

```
private Vector quoteEventListeners;

private Random random =
    new Random(System.currentTimeMillis());

private String[] stocks = {
        "IBM", "MSFT", "SUNW", "ORCL", "SBL",
        "BEAS", "AAPL", "DELL", "GOOG", "YHOO" };

private double[] prices = {
    91.79, 25.67, 4.09, 13.24, 17.41,
    8.50, 70.76, 40.12, 180.72, 33.93 };

public QuoteSourceBean()
{
}

public String[] getInterfaceNames()
{
    String[] interfaces = new String[1];
    interfaces[0] = QuoteChangedEvent.interfaceName;
    return interfaces;
}

public void addListener(Object obj)
{
    if ( quoteEventListeners == null )
        quoteEventListeners = new Vector();

    if ( obj == null )
        return;

    // Make sure the object implements the event interface
    Class cls = obj.getClass();
    Class[] ints = cls.getInterfaces();
    for ( int i = 0; i < ints.length; i++ )
    {
        if ( ints[i].getName().
            equals(QuoteChangedEvent.interfaceName) )
        {
            quoteEventListeners.add(obj);
        }
    }
}
```

```java
public void removeListener(Object obj) {
    // ...
}

private void fire_onNewQuote(String stock, String quote)
{
    // Notify all clients of the new quote
    Vector listeners;
    synchronized ( this ) {
        listeners = (Vector)quoteEventListeners.clone();
    }

    int cnt = listeners.size();
    for (int i = 0; i < cnt; i++)
    {
        QuoteChangedEvent client =
            (QuoteChangedEvent)listeners.elementAt(i);

        client.onNewQuote( stock, quote );
    }
}

public void sendLastTradeLoop()
{
    while ( true )
    {
        try {
            int stock = random.nextInt(10);

            String newPrice = getLastTradePrice( stock );

            fire_onNewQuote(stocks[stock], newPrice);

            Thread.sleep(2000);
        }
        catch ( Exception e ) {
            e.printStackTrace();
        }
    }
}

private String getLastTradePrice(int stockIndex) {
    // ...
}
```

```
        private int getStockIndexFromName(String name) {
            // ...
        }
    }
```

You can run this code by executing the Windows batch file runquotebeantest.bat or UNIX command script runquotebeantest.sh. Both startup files (located on the CD-ROM in the folder Chapter5) execute the following Java command:

```
java -cp (classpath details here) com.TradingSystem.StockTicker.QuoteEventTester
```

You do need to run this application twice: once to start the event source and the second time to start the event listener. In one command prompt, execute the following to start the event listener:

```
> runquotebeantest client
```

In a second command prompt, execute the following to start the event source:

```
> runquotebeantest source
```

The output of this example is identical to the stock quote update messages from the previous stock ticker examples. The difference is that the event distributor takes the JavaBean events and distributes them remotely (and transparently) to JavaBeans in other JVMs. Try running multiple event listener components, each in its own JVM; they will each receive the identical stock quote updates.

COMPONENT DISTRIBUTION: THE JMS COMPONENT SERVER

Most JMS providers on the market today deliver a robust messaging environment and guarantee reliable message delivery across local area networks (LANs), wide area networks (WANs), and even the Internet. Using a robust JMS provider the right way guarantees that your code will have its messages delivered, but this is where the JMS boundary ends. Your code is left as the weak link. What good is guaranteed message delivery if the component that needs to process it fails? Although a J2EE application server has built-in facilities to help with this problem, what about standalone JMS client applications?

This section proposes a solution in the form of a software system that monitors the MessageProducer and MessageConsumer objects within a client application and provides failover capabilities in the event of a failure. The solution is a software system called the *JMS Component Server* (JCS), which makes up an environment within which you can run your producer and consumer component classes. The JCS allows you to configure multiple servers on your network on which you can distribute your component objects. If an individual component fails, the JCS will detect it and restart it. If an entire server fails, for whatever reason, one of the other JCS servers running on your network will take over and instantiate the components that were running on the failed server. The JCS enables a cluster-like configuration for your JMS application code.

While your JMS provider works hard to guarantee the delivery of your messages, the JCS will make sure the components that generate them keep running under almost any conditions. Any number of servers can be configured in a JCS cluster; obviously at least two should be configured to be effective. Figure 5.9 shows two JCS servers configured to run different sets of JMS `MessageProducer` and `MessageConsumer` objects.

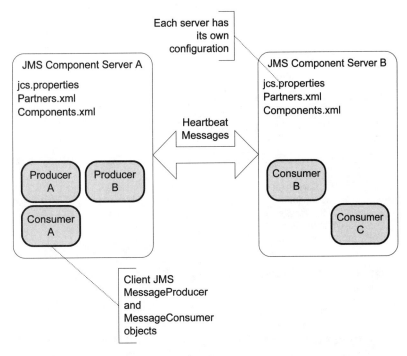

FIGURE 5.9 Two healthy JCS servers running with client components.

From this diagram we see that two JCSs (server A and server B) are running, exchanging heartbeats, and managing their respective JMS components. The functionality of the components themselves is an unimportant detail at this point. All we need to know is that they are client components that are actively producing and/or consuming JMS messages. Let's explore the scenario further and assume that the physical server that JCS server B is running on stops because of a hardware failure (Figure 5.10).

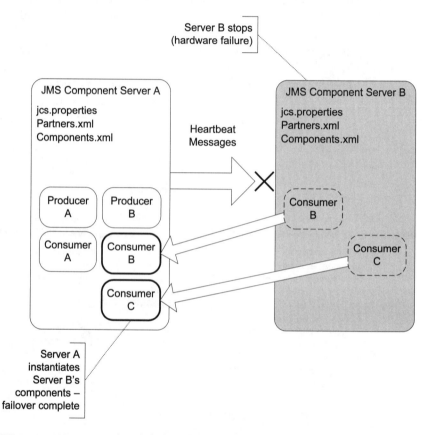

FIGURE 5.10 JCS server B has failed, and server A has instantiated its client components.

In this case, server A detects that server B is down because it has not received any heartbeat messages from it within a particular timeframe. Once the failure is detected, server A instantiates the components that were running within server B: consumer B and consumer C. Some time later, when server B recovers, heartbeat messages will resume and server A will realize that server B has recovered. At that point, server A will stop consumer B and consumer C, knowing that server B will instantiate them now, and all will be back to normal. The reverse situation is valid as well: server B will instantiate server A's components if server A fails.

JCS Configuration

Both servers know of each other's component classes because they share a common set of configuration files. These files list all of the components, the destinations they send to or receive from, and the JCS server (called a partner) they are intended to run on. Listing 5.26 is a sample JCS configuration file, in XML, that lists all of the component information, called Components.xml.

LISTING 5.26 The Components.xml JCS Configuration File

```
<Components>
    <Component>
        <Class>com.TradingSystem.StockTicker.QuoteSenderJCS</Class>
        <Destination>StockTrades</Destination>
    </Component>
    <Component>

<Class>com.TradingSystem.StockTicker.QuoteListenerJCS</Class>
        <Destination>StockTrades</Destination>
    </Component>
    <Component>
        <Class>com.TradingSystem.StockTicker.QuoteFinderJCS</Class>
        <Destination>QuoteRequests</Destination>
    </Component>
</Components>
```

The file contains the information for each component within repeated <Component> XML elements contained within the <Components> element. Each component section contains the component's class name in the <Class> element and the JMS Destination name in the <Destination> element. The example in this listing includes two components: one for the class com.TradingSystem. StockTicker.QuoteSenderJCS, and one for the class com.TradingSystem.StockTicker. QuoteListenerJCS. We will explore these classes later in this chapter. Notice that both classes share the same destination name. Everything that is needed to instantiate the components and to send and receive JMS messages is contained in this file.

Next we need to know how to distribute the components across multiple JCSs. Listing 5.27 shows a sample configuration file that contains the distribution information for all of the components, called Partners.xml.

LISTING 5.27 The Partners.xml JCS Configuration File

```
<PartnerList>
    <SystemName>Stock Quote System</SystemName>
```

```
    <Partner>
        <Name>ServerA</Name>
        <Address>192.168.1.1</Address>
        <Destinations>
            <Destination>StockTrades</Destination>
        </Destinations>
    </Partner>
    <Partner>
        <Name>ServerB</Name>
        <Address>192.168.1.2</Address>
        <Destinations>
            <Destination>QuoteRequests</Destination>
        </Destinations>
    </Partner>
</PartnerList>
```

This configuration file contains information for each JCS partner in the cluster contained within repeated `<Partner>` sections. There can be two or more partners, each containing its own `<Partner>` section. For each partner, the server's name is contained within the `<Name>` element; the server's host name or IP address is contained within the `<Address>` element; and the JMS `Destinations` the server handles are contained within the `<Destinations>` block in the XML.

When a JCS partner such as server A starts, it finds its `<Partner>` section in the `Partners.xml` file. The JMS destination names are then iterated from within the `<Destinations>` section. Each destination name is used to look up the appropriate components to create from within the `Components.xml` file. Each server will create every component that matches each of its assigned destination names. For example, with the configuration files listed above, server A handles the `StockTrades` destination name, and server B handles the `QuoteRequests` destination name. Server A will instantiate both the `com.TradingSystem.StockTicker.QuoteSenderJCS` class and the `com.TradingSystem.StockTicker.QuoteListenerJCS` class because they both use the `StockTrades` destination. Server B will instantiate only the `com.TradingSystem.StockTicker.QuoteFinderJCS` class because it is the only component listed for the `QuoteRequests` destination.

Each server identifies itself by reading its property file named `jcs.properties`. This file (see Listing 5.28) contains the server's name (`LocalNodeName`) and the port (`AdminPort`) to run the administrative server on. The JCS creates a small HTTP server on this port to provide a simple administrative front-end, accessible from a Web browser. The value for the property `LocalNodeName` is used as the server's name and as a cross-reference for the `Partners.xml` configuration file.

LISTING 5.28 The `jcs.properties` JCS Configuration File

```
LocalNodeName=ServerB
AdminPort=7981
```

JCS Internals

The JCS is an involved piece of software. Although it's not very complex, it does offer a lot of functionality in that it provides cluster-like failover capability to your JMS client components. There are three main classes: the `PartnerManager` class, the `ComponentManager` class, and the `StateManager` class. These classes work together to do all of the work of the JCS (see Figure 5.11 for a UML class diagram). Some classes are not shown on this diagram, such as those that parse the XML configuration files and perform logging. They have been left off because they're relatively unimportant to the design discussion. We'll begin our discussion with the `JCSMain` class, which is on the left-hand side of the diagram.

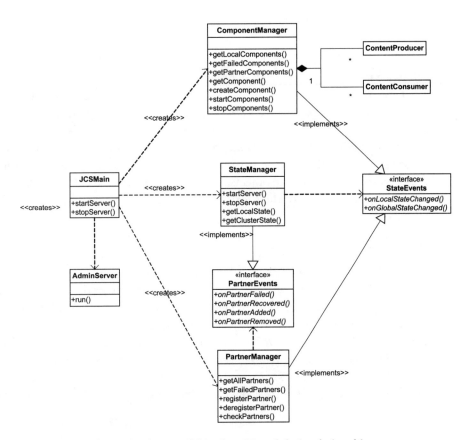

FIGURE 5.11 The main classes within the JCS and their relationships.

The `JCSMain` class contains the `main` method for the Java application, and it's here that the other classes are instantiated. `JCMain` is a singleton, although it's implemented slightly differently than those we've seen elsewhere in this book. The class has a public constructor and is instantiated with the keyword new in the application's `main` method. However, the class contains a `static` variable that is set, in the constructor, to a reference of the first `JCSMain` object created. A check is made to see that this `static` instance variable is `null`; otherwise it throws an `Exception` indicating that only one instance is allowed:

```
public JCSMain(String configDir) throws Exception
{
    if ( JCSMain.INSTANCE != null )
        throw new Exception ("Only one instance of JCSMain allowed");

    JCSMain.INSTANCE = this;

    // ...
}
```

The intent is for other classes to use the `static` `getInstance` method to get a reference to the singleton `JCSMain` object.

Next, the `jcs.properties` file is loaded by the `JCSProperties` class. This is where the server name is discovered. After some log messages are generated, instances of `ComponentManager`, `PartnerManager`, and `StateManager` are retrieved. These classes are true singletons whose objects are instantiated when the JVM is started. Next, the `Components.xml` and `Partners.xml` files are parsed, the gathered configuration data is passed to the appropriate objects, and the administrative HTTP server is started by creating an instance of the `AdminServer` class. The functionality provided by the administrative front-end is discussed later in the chapter.

JCS Client Component Classes

A JCS client component is defined as one that implements the `ContentComponent` interface, and therefore your components must implement this interface. The JCS defines two abstract base classes, `ContentProducer` and `ContentConsumer`, both of which implement the `ContentComponent` interface. Figure 5.12 shows a UML diagram of the classes, their common interface, and nested classes used for threading and JMS encapsulation. The `ContentProducer` and `ContentConsumer` classes are meant to act as base classes for your JMS components, although you do not need to use them. However, these base classes do provide functionality that you may find useful.

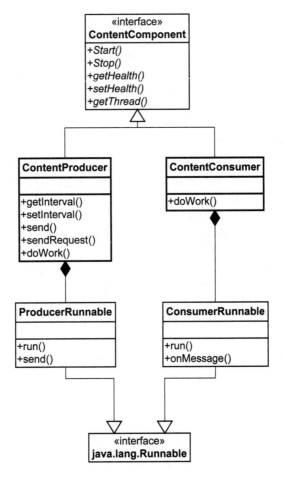

FIGURE 5.12   The UML class diagram for the client component base classes and interface.

For instance, both classes create a child thread, within which the JMSManager facade class is used to provide JMS message sending and receiving capabilities. Additionally, the ContentProducer class provides the option of calling the doWork method of your derived component at regular intervals. Although you don't need to use this feature, setting the interval (in milliseconds) to a nonzero value enables it. This feature is useful for components that need, for example, to periodically check a system object, such as a file in a directory, or some other system event that requires polling. You simply implement the doWork method to perform your component-specific functionality and call the send method when a message needs to be sent. The ContentConsumer base class is implemented to call the doWork method when a message arrives. Your component implements the doWork method to perform its specific task as each new message arrives. We'll talk more about these classes later in the chapter.

JCS State Management

The JCS is state driven. Many different events affect the overall system state, and the state changes drive other objects in the system to perform certain tasks. This leads to a level of predictability in the behavior of the system as a whole. It also allows for rule-based coordination between the many components in the system, which in turn ensures that the components remain as loosely coupled as possible. For instance, if the JCS is instructed to shut down, JCSMain does not call the ComponentManager object directly to instruct it to take action. Instead, it fires an event that is processed by the StateManager object, which in turn changes the system state. Upon receiving the system state change notification (in this case the STOPPED state), the Component Manager object stops all of the client components.

The StateManager class is an event source for the StateEvents interface, shown in Listing 5.29. There are only two event methods on this interface: onLocalState Changed and onGlobalStateChanged. Local state represents the state of the single JCS itself. Global state represents the state of the JCS cluster as a whole. The local JCS states are:

STARTING: The server state when it first starts up and is preparing to start

STARTED: The server state when it's up and functioning, with all components created

STOPPING: The server state when the server is shutting down, waiting for all components to stop

STOPPED: The server state when all client components have been stopped and their references discarded (marked for garbage collection).

The global state is boolean in nature, indicating whether the cluster is operating in a whole or partial state. The global states are:

WHOLE: Every server in the cluster is functioning normally.

PARTIAL: At least one server in the cluster has failed.

LISTING 5.29   The `StateManager`'s Event Interface, `StateEvents`

```
public interface StateEvents
{
    public static final String eventType = "StateEvents";

    public void onLocalStateChanged(Object StateEventObj);
    public void onGlobalStateChange(Object StateEventObj);
}
```

There are two ways the JCS system state is affected: first, the `StateManager` object is an event listener of the `PartnerEvents` interface, for which the `PartnerManager` object is the event source. Changes to the status of JCS partner servers affect global and local state. Second, the `JCSMain` class (and only this class) will call the `StateManager.StartServer` and `StateManager.StopServer` methods to transition the state to `STARTED` and `STOPPED`, respectively. Figure 5.13 shows the state transition diagram for local JCS state.

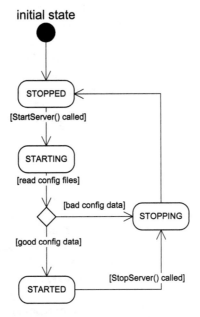

FIGURE 5.13   The UML state diagram for the JCS.

Starting the JMS Client Components

The sole purpose of the JCS is to create and manage client MessageProducer and MessageConsumer components. A JCS *client component* is defined as any class that implements the com.toolkit.messaging.componentserver.ContentComponent interface. For each component, two steps are performed in the start-up phase:

1. The component's class is instantiated and stored in a collection.
2. The component's ContentComponent.Start method is called, instructing it to begin its processing.

This work is done by the ComponentManager class and begins when the JCS state changes to STARTED. The JCS name is used as a cross-reference into the list of component data retrieved from the Components.xml file. The resulting sublist contains the components that are meant to run on this server. Using the component's class name, Java reflection enables the JCS to instantiate the component with the keyword new and to call the constructor that takes a String parameter. The component's destination name is passed in the constructor. Listing 5.30 shows the code that performs the steps just discussed. As long as the class is in the Java classpath and it contains a constructor that takes a String as a parameter, the object will be created. The resulting component is checked to ensure that it implements the ContentComponent interface, and if so, its reference is returned from the method call.

LISTING 5.30 The JCS Uses Java Reflection to Create ContentComponent Objects

```
public ContentComponent createComponent( String classname,
                                         String destination)
{
    try
    {
        Class compClass = Class.forName(classname );

        // Call the constructor that takes a String param
          Constructor[] con = compClass.getConstructors();
        Vector params = new Vector();
        params.add( destination );

        Object obj = (Object)con[0].newInstance( params.toArray() );

        if (obj instanceof ContentComponent )
        {
            ContentComponent component = (ContentComponent)obj;
            if ( component != null )
```

```
                    return component;
            }
        }
        catch ( Exception e ) {
            e.printStackTrace();
        }

        return null;
    }
```

The resulting component is added to a `Vector` that stores the object, class name, destination name, and intended partner name in a `ContentInfo` object. Each component created is then started with a call to the `Start` method. For each `ContentProducer` component, this is the time when its nested `ProducerRunnable` class is created on a new thread. It's from within this class that the `doWork` method will be called based on the interval specified in the base class's `setInterval` method. This means that all the processing your component performs will be done in the child thread created by this class. For each `ContentConsumer` component, the nested `ConsumerRunnable` class is created on a new thread. It's within this class that the `JMSManager` class's listen method is called with the component's specified destination name.

Both classes contain a nested class that implements the `Runnable` interface, as opposed to extending the `Thread` class, because it's intended that they be assigned a thread to run on. This opens the door to using some sort of thread-pooling algorithm in the future, thereby saving system resources by *not* creating a new thread per component. The components still maintain the concurrency and throughput of multithreading because they will be provided a thread to run on when a message arrives, or as a message needs to be sent. Although we won't explore that implementation here, this design choice does deserve some explanation.

Partner Heartbeats

Each JCS has a heartbeat that lets other JCS partner servers know it's alive. The heartbeats are JMS messages published to a `Topic`, named `JCS.partner.heartbeat`, which all JCS partners subscribe to. As soon as the JCS state changes to STARTED, the `PartnerManager` class instantiates two nested classes, `PartnerProducer` and `PartnerConsumer`, to send and receive partner heartbeat messages, respectively. `PartnerConsumer` also listens for three other partner-related messages, the SERVER_ STARTED, SERVER_REPLY, and PECKING_ORDER messages. We'll discuss these messages in the next section; for now let's focus on heartbeat processing.

The first time a heartbeat is received from a partner, the JCS adds it to a list of known partners and records the time it received the heartbeat message. This process is known as *partner registration*. Once a partner is registered, the `onPartnerAdded` event is fired, and the time between heartbeat messages is tracked. If the time since a heartbeat was last received from a partner has exceeded the time it takes to send three heartbeats, that partner is considered to have failed, at which point the `onPartnerFailed` event is fired. The next time a heartbeat message is received from a failed partner, the partner is considered to have recovered, and an `onPartnerRecovered` event is fired.

Of course, JCS partner servers that have not registered within a specific time frame—the time it takes to send four heartbeat messages—are also considered to have failed. However, when a heartbeat message is finally received for this component, which is considered failed, but has not yet registered, both the `onPartnerAdded` and the `onPartnerRecovered` events are fired.

The Active Supervisor

Determining the action a JCS server is to take when a partner fails is not straightforward. If every partner reacted to a failure by instantiating the failed partner's client components, there would be instances of the components running on every server but the one that failed. The desired outcome is to have only one of the remaining partners take over for the failed partner. To ensure this is the case, only one server at any point in time is marked as the one to take over in the event of a partner failure. This server is called the *active supervisor*, and there is an algorithm that is followed to determine which server it is.

Each JCS partner is provided an identical partner configuration file, `Partners.xml`, which identifies all of the partners within the system. The partner servers form a pecking order depending upon the order each server starts in. The first server that starts is at the top of the pecking order, the second server is next in the pecking order, and so on. The partner at the top of the pecking order is considered the active supervisor. This server has the responsibility of instantiating a partner's components if any partner fails. If the active supervisor fails, the next server in the pecking order takes over as the active supervisor. When using the JCS, you must carefully consider the number of servers to distribute your components on. It's wise to distribute the components across enough servers so that if one or two fail, the active supervisor will not be over-burdened with the failed server's (or servers') components.

The algorithm is implemented in such a way that every server will agree upon which server is the active supervisor. Figure 5.14 is a UML sequence diagram that shows the sequence of events that occur when the servers in a three-server JCS cluster start executing. Let's go step-by-step through this sequence, which is the implementation of the active supervisor algorithm.

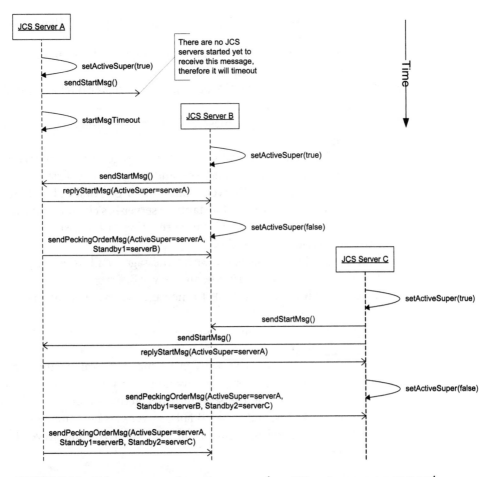

FIGURE 5.14 This sequence of events occurs when JCS partner servers start and determines which server is the active supervisor.

1. JCS server A starts executing before the other servers in the cluster. It assumes it is the active supervisor, which is something each server does when it's started. At this point, the fact that this server is the active supervisor is tentative.

2. Server A publishes a SERVER_STARTED JMS message to all listening partners. Since there are no listening partners, the message is never received.

3. Server A never hears back from any other partners in response to its message, so a timeout occurs. This indicates that server A truly is the active supervisor.

4. Some time later, server B starts executing. It too assumes that it's the active supervisor (tentatively).

5. Server B publishes a SERVER_STARTED message to all listening partners. In this case there is a listening partner: server A.

6. Server A publishes a SERVER_REPLY message to server B telling it that server A is the active supervisor.

7. Upon receiving the reply message, server B no longer assumes it is the active supervisor.

8. Server A then publishes a PECKING_ORDER message to all partners indicating that server A is the active supervisor, and server B is the first-order *standby server*. This means that if server A fails, server B is first in line to take over as the active supervisor (and instantiate server A's client components).

9. Some time later still, server C starts executing. It too assumes that it's the active supervisor (tentatively).

10. Server C publishes a SERVER_STARTED message to all listening partners. In this case there are two: server A, and server B.

11. Server A publishes a SERVER_REPLY message to server C telling it that server A is the active supervisor.

12. Upon receiving the reply message, server C no longer assumes it is the active supervisor.

13. Server A then publishes a PECKING_ORDER message to all partners indicating that server A is the active supervisor and server B is the first-order standby server, and server C is the second-order active supervisor. This means that if server A fails, and server B fails, server C is next in line to take over as the active supervisor (and instantiate server A's and server B's client components).

You can see that a pattern of messages is followed when each new server is started. Therefore, whether a JCS cluster contains 2 servers or 22 (or more), the outcome is always the same: the first server started is the active supervisor, and the pecking order continues according to each server's start time. It's important to realize that once a server is the active supervisor, that status is not revoked unless that server fails. Therefore, in the scenario we just discussed, if server A fails and server B takes over as the active supervisor, server B will remain the active supervisor even when server A recovers. At that point, server A is considered the last server to have started and it goes to the bottom of the pecking order.

The previous section spoke about partner failure scenarios caused by missed heartbeats. This section discussed the concepts of the active supervisor and the server pecking order. Now let's discuss what action is taken by the active supervisor when a JCS partner fails.

Partner Failure

When a JCS partner server fails, the components for the failed partner are created and started using the same methods as the server's local components. The only exception is that they are stored in the failedPartnerComponents Vector using the failed partner's name so that they can be isolated, and stopped, when the partner recovers. Each component that is instantiated is started via a call to its ContentComponent.Start method.

Although the components are stored in a different list than the local components, they are treated the same. The periodic health checks that occur for local components now also include the components of the failed partner.

One important item needs to be discussed here. Consider the following scenario: the active supervisor (server A) in a JCS cluster containing three servers fails, leaving server B as the active supervisor. This of course means that server B now contains its own components, as well as server A's components. Some time later, server B fails, leaving server C as the active supervisor. What does server C do? If it simply instantiates server B's components, there is a major problem (see Figure 5.15).

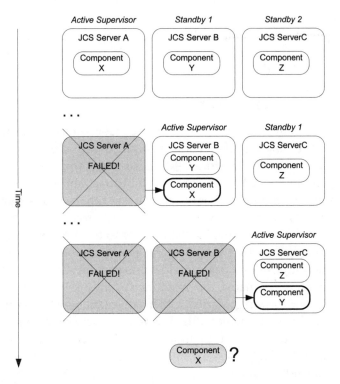

FIGURE 5.15 Cluster failover must be carefully implemented to ensure that all components continue to run when multiple failures occur.

In this scenario, the result is that server C is now running its own components, and server B's components, but server A's components are no longer running. This is an incomplete—and unacceptable—failover scenario. This is solved by each server in the cluster tracking all of its partners. Therefore, even if a partner is not the active supervisor, it tracks partner heartbeats and knows when a partner fails. Since each partner knows which server is the active supervisor, it can safely assume that server has taken over for the failed partner. By tracking this continuously per partner, each server in the cluster knows what set of components the other partners are running, even after partner failures. Therefore, in the original scenario, when server C takes over for server B, it instantiates the components for server B *and* server A because it knew that server B had previously taken over for server A.

Partner Recovery

Partner recovery is a much more straightforward process then partner failure. When a failed partner recovers, the other JCS servers in the cluster recognize this because they receive the recovered partner's heartbeat messages once again. At this point the failed partner is considered recovered, and the `PartnerManager` class fires an `onPartnerRecovered` event. When the active supervisor's `ComponentManager` class receives this event, it simply calls the `ContentComponent.Stop` methods for all the components that belong to the recovered partner, and it discards all references to the components. The components' threads will terminate, and the objects will be garbage collected.

The JCS Administrative Front-End

Simple JCS administrative functions are made available through a built-in HTTP server. The port that it runs on is specified with the `AdminPort` property in the `jcs.properties` file. When the JCS is running, you can view the administrative front-end interface by opening a Web browser and browsing to the port on the machine it's running on. For instance, if you run the browser on the same machine on which you run the JCS, and the administrative port is configured to be 7980, the URL is *http://localhost:7980*. Browsing to this URL will result in a page similar to that in Figure 5.16.

The administrative page provides information about the JCS, such as the server version, the server name, the operating system (OS) that the server is running on, and the time the server started. Other information includes the JVM version, total and available JVM memory, the JCS active supervisor status, and the JCS partner pecking order. Through the administrative interface, certain operations can be performed on the JCS. These operations are listed at the bottom of the Web page as HTTP hyperlinks and include:

View server configuration: View the server configuration, which includes the local server name, address, administrative port, log file, and min and max JVM heap size settings.

View clustered servers: This page lists the other partners in the JCS cluster. For each partner, information such as the partner's name, address, registration status, and server status (good or failed) is displayed (see Figure 5.17).

View hosted components: This page lists all of the client components that are currently running in the local JCS. For each component, information such as the component class name, destination name, component health, and intended host partner is displayed (see Figure 5.18). Each component entry in the list contains a link to either start or stop the component, depending upon its state. There are also two links provided above the list that allow you to stop or start *all* of the components at once.

Shutdown this server: This link causes the JCS to shut down, hence stopping all hosted client components as well.

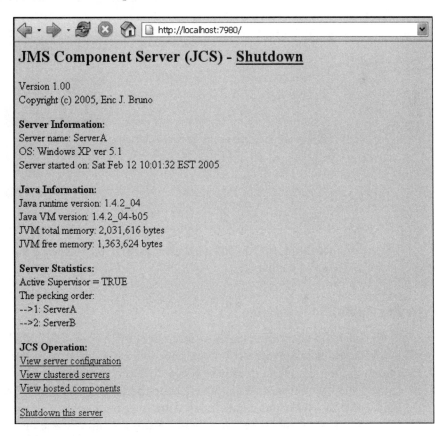

FIGURE 5.16 The JCS administrative front-end main HTTP page.

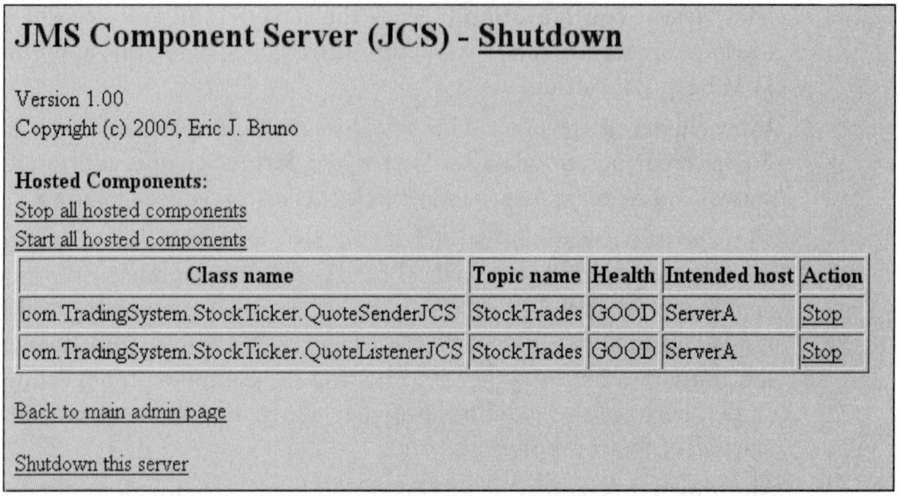

JMS Component Server (JCS) - <u>Shutdown</u>

Version 1.00
Copyright (c) 2005, Eric J. Bruno

Hosted Components:
Stop all hosted components
Start all hosted components

Class name	Topic name	Health	Intended host	Action
com.TradingSystem.StockTicker.QuoteSenderJCS	StockTrades	GOOD	ServerA	Stop
com.TradingSystem.StockTicker.QuoteListenerJCS	StockTrades	GOOD	ServerA	Stop

Back to main admin page

Shutdown this server

FIGURE 5.17   The JCS administrative HTTP page showing the hosted client components.

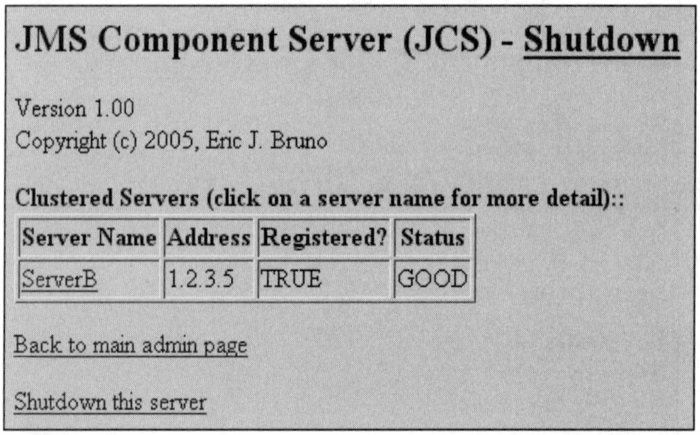

JMS Component Server (JCS) - <u>Shutdown</u>

Version 1.00
Copyright (c) 2005, Eric J. Bruno

Clustered Servers (click on a server name for more detail)::

Server Name	Address	Registered?	Status
ServerB	1.2.3.5	TRUE	GOOD

Back to main admin page

Shutdown this server

FIGURE 5.18   The JCS administrative HTTP page showing the cluster partner JCS.

Developing Applications with the JCS

While the main goal of the JCS is to add reliability to your distributed applications by providing failover support to your components, it also makes it easier to build those components. First of all, the JCS serves as a container application for your components. You don't need to worry about adding a main method or instantiating all of your JMS component classes. Also, by extending the ContentProducer and ContentConsumer base classes, you benefit from the built-in use of the JMSManager facade class, which makes it easier to send and receive JMS messages.

As stated earlier in the chapter, a JCS client component is defined as a class that implements the `com.toolkit.messaging.componentserver.ContentComponent` interface, shown in Listing 5.31. Your code does not have to extend the base classes `ContentProducer` and `ContentConsumer`, but it does have to implement this interface. By extending the base classes, your code will have implemented this interface implicitly. Let's examine the details of the `ContentComponent` interface now.

LISTING 5.31   The JCS `ContentComponent` Interface

```
package com.toolkit.messaging.componentserver;

public interface ContentComponent
{
    final String HEALTH_GOOD = "GOOD";
    final String HEALTH_BAD = "BAD";
    final String HEALTH_STOPPED = "STOPPED";

    public void Start() throws Exception;

    public void Stop();

    public String getHealth();

    public void setHealth(String health);

    public Thread getThread();
}
```

Each component is responsible for maintaining an indicator of its health. The possible health values are defined as `String` constants at the top if the interface. These include `HEALTH_GOOD`, `HEALTH_BAD`, and `HEALTH_STOPPED`, and they are mostly self-explanatory. When a component is instantiated, but has not yet been started via a call to its `Start` method, its health is by default set to the `HEALTH_STOPPED` value. When `Start` is called, the component should set its health value to either the `HEALTH_GOOD` or `HEALTH_BAD`, depending upon the success or failure of the code in the implementation of the `Start` method. The health can be set at any time by calling the `setHealth` method with one of the health `String` constants provided as a parameter. When the `Stop` method is called, your component should stop its processing and set its health to `HEALTH_STOPPED`.

When the JCS calls the `Start` method, the component should enter its normal operating state. After this call, the component is ready to send or receive JMS messages. When the JCS calls the `Stop` method, the component should stop sending JMS messages, and it will not be able to receive JMS messages. The `getHealth` method is called by the JCS periodically to ensure that the child thread (for JMS message processing) is still running.

The `ContentProducer` Base Class

Developers who are comfortable with the JMS interfaces and its internals can develop components that implement the `ContentComponent` interface and provide their own JMS client implementation. However, a lot of this work can be saved by extending the helper classes that the JCS provides: the `ContentProducer` abstract base class in one example. Using it can save you from repeating a lot of JMS-specific code in your `MessageProducer` client components. First of all, this class (see Listing 5.32) encapsulates the use of `JMSManager`, which makes sending JMS messages quite simple. Second, the class automatically creates a child thread for you within which it sends the JMS messages. Third, the class supports an optional interval-based callback method, `doWork`, which was described earlier in the section titled "JCS Client Component Classes."

LISTING 5.32 The JCS `ContentProducer` Base Class

```
package com.toolkit.messaging.componentserver;

import java.io.*;
import com.toolkit.messaging.*;

public abstract class ContentProducer implements ContentComponent
{
    protected JMSManager jmsMgr = null;
    protected String destName;
    protected Thread m_thread = null;
    protected boolean m_continueSending = false;
    protected long m_interval = 0;
    protected String mHealth = null;

    class ProducerThread implements Runnable
    {
        public ProducerThread()
        {
        }

        public void run()
        {
            try {
                m_continueSending = true;
```

```
        while ( m_continueSending )
        {
            if ( m_interval > 0 )
            {
                try {
                    doWork();
                }
                catch( Exception e ){ }
            }
            else
            {
                Thread.sleep(1000);
            }

            Thread.sleep( m_interval );
        }
    }
    catch ( Exception e ) {
        e.printStackTrace();
    }
}

public synchronized boolean send( String textToSend )
{
    try {
        jmsMgr.send(destName, textToSend);
        return true;
    }
    catch ( Exception e ) {
        e.printStackTrace();
    }

    return false;
}

public synchronized boolean send( Serializable obj )
{
    try {
        jmsMgr.send(destName, obj);
        return true;
    }
    catch ( Exception e ) {
        e.printStackTrace();
    }
```

```
                return false;
        }
    }

    protected ProducerThread producer;

    public ContentProducer(String name)
    {
        try {
            jmsMgr = new JMSManager();

            setHealth( HEALTH_GOOD );

            destName = name;
        }
        catch ( Exception e ) {
            e.printStackTrace();
        }
    }

    public final void Start() throws Exception
    {
        producer = new ProducerThread();

        m_thread = new Thread( producer );
        m_thread.start();

        setHealth( HEALTH_GOOD );
    }

    public final void Stop()
    {
        m_continueSending = false;
        jmsMgr.stop(destName);
        mHealth = HEALTH_STOPPED;
    }

    public final String getHealth()
    {
        return mHealth;
    }

    public final void setHealth(String health)
    {
```

```
            mHealth = health;
        }

        public final Thread getThread()
        {
            return m_thread;
        }

        public final void setInterval(long interval)
        {
            m_interval = interval;
        }

        public void doWork() throws Exception { }

        public final synchronized boolean send(String s)
        {
            return producer.send( s );
        }

        public final synchronized boolean send(Object obj)
        {
            return producer.send( (Serializable)obj );
        }

        public final synchronized void sendRequest( Object obj )
        {
            producer.send( (Serializable)obj );
        }
    }
```

The class supports versions of the send method that take a String or a Serial izable object. Because it uses the JMSManager to do the actual work, a TextMessage or ObjectMessage instance will be created for the String or object provided, respectively. Your component can, however, send its own JMS Message object, such as a MapMessage object, by calling the send message that takes a Java object. Internally, the JMSManager checks if the object is already one of the JMS Message types before it creates one itself.

The ContentConsumer Base Class

The ContentConsumer class (see Listing 5.33) saves you from repeating the code required to listen for JMS messages within your JCS MessageConsumer components. This class doesn't support an interval-based callback method, as your component is assumed to not need it (most message consumer components are driven by the receipt of messages). However, it does automatically create a child thread on which it runs the MessageListener object used to receive JMS messages. When a message does arrive for your component, the type of Message object is checked. For a TextMessage and an ObjectMessage, the payload of the message (a String or Object, respectively) is extracted from the message and passed to your component by calling the doWork method. Any other type of JMS Message type (such as a MapMessage) is passed as-is to your component.

LISTING 5.33   The JCS ContentConsumer Base Class

```
package com.toolkit.messaging.componentserver;

import javax.jms.*;
import com.toolkit.messaging.*;

public abstract class ContentConsumer implements ContentComponent
{
    protected JMSManager jmsMgr = null;
    protected String destinationName;
    protected Thread m_thread = null;
    protected boolean mThreadRun = true;
    protected String mHealth = null;

    class ConsumerRunnable
        implements Runnable, javax.jms.MessageListener
    {
        public ConsumerRunnable()
        {
        }

        public void run()
        {
            try {
                jmsMgr.listen(destinationName, this);
                m_thread.join();
            }
            catch ( InterruptedException ie ) {
                // thread was told to stop
            }
            catch ( Exception e ) {
                e.printStackTrace();
            }
        }
```

```
    public void onMessage(Message msg)
    {
        try {
            if ( msg instanceof TextMessage )
            {
                TextMessage text =(TextMessage)msg;
                doWork(text.getText());
            }
            else if ( msg instanceof ObjectMessage )
            {
                ObjectMessage objMsg = (ObjectMessage)msg;
                dowWork( objMsg.getObject() );
            }
            else
              {
                doWork( msg );
            }
        }
        catch (JMSException jmse) {
            jmse.printStackTrace();
        }
    }
}

// Methods

public ContentConsumer(String destination)
{
    try {
        jmsMgr = new JMSManager();

        setHealth( HEALTH_GOOD );

        this.destinationName = destination;
    }
    catch ( Exception e ) {
        e.printStackTrace();
    }
}

public final void Start() throws Exception
{
    mThreadRun = true;

    ConsumerRunnable listener = new ConsumerRunnable();
```

```
        m_thread = new Thread( listener );
        m_thread.setPriority(Thread.MAX_PRIORITY);
        m_thread.start();

        setHealth( HEALTH_GOOD );
    }

    public final void Stop()
    {
        mThreadRun = false;
        jmsMgr.stop(destinationName);
        m_thread.interrupt();
        setHealth( HEALTH_STOPPED );
    }

    public final String getHealth()
    {
        return mHealth;
    }

    public final void setHealth(String health)
    {
        mHealth = health;
    }

    public final Thread getThread()
    {
        return m_thread;
    }

    public void doWork( Object obj ) throws Exception { }
}
```

The child thread, implemented by the class ContentRunnable, joins the main class to ensure that it will continue for as long as the application runs or until it is explicitly interrupted. The ContentConsumer.Stop method stops the thread by calling the Thread.interrupt method, at which point the ContentRunnable object's run method will receive an InterruptedException and return, causing the thread to terminate.

The JCS Stock Quote Sample Classes

The stock quote sample application is a prime candidate to use the JCS. It makes sense to distribute the components across servers to balance the load, and the service should be as reliable as possible. Using the JCS across multiple servers provides failover for the quote publisher component, as well as the component that handles quote requests. If one server fails, the other takes over and handles both quote updates and quote requests, but in the normal state, the work is distributed across the servers to improve scalability.

Let's begin with the configuration files needed to implement this design. Listing 5.34 contains the Partners.xml configuration file, which defines a JCS cluster of two servers, server A and server B. Server A is designated as the partner that runs the components to support the StockQuotes destination. Server B runs the components that support the QuoteRequests destination. For each server's address, you can set them *both* to your computer's IP address (or simply localhost) to run both JCS partners on one computer for illustrative purposes.

LISTING 5.34 The Stock Quote System's Partner.xml Configuration File

```
<PartnerList>
    <SystemName>Stock Quote System</SystemName>
    <Partner>
        <Name>ServerA</Name>
        <Address>1.2.3.4</Address>
        <Destinations>
            <Destination>StockTrades</Destination>
        </Destinations>
    </Partner>
    <Partner>
        <Name>ServerB</Name>
        <Address>1.2.3.5</Address>
        <Destinations>
            <Destination>QuoteRequests</Destination>
        </Destinations>
    </Partner>
</PartnerList>
```

The component classes that need to be created for the destinations listed in Partners.xml are found in the Components.xml configuration file (see Listing 5.35). For the StockTrades destination, the classes QuoteSenderJCS and QuoteListenerJCS are created in server A. In reality the quote listener component would most likely be part of another software system, but for the sake of this example it runs in the JCS. Server B instantiates the QuoteFinderJCS class, which listens for quote requests and responds accordingly.

LISTING 5.35 The Stock Quote System's `Component.xml` Configuration File

```
<Components>
    <Component>
        <Class>com.TradingSystem.StockTicker.QuoteSenderJCS</Class>
        <Destination>StockTrades</Destination>
    </Component>
    <Component>
        <Class>com.TradingSystem.StockTicker.QuoteListenerJCS</Class>
        <Destination>StockTrades</Destination>
    </Component>
    <Component>
        <Class>com.TradingSystem.StockTicker.QuoteFinderJCS</Class>
        <Destination>QuoteRequests</Destination>
    </Component>
</Components>
```

The Stock Quote Sender

When you examine the code for the stock quote sender class, `QuoteSenderJCS` (see Listing 5.36), you will notice that almost all of the code is business logic. In this example, the `doWork` method is utilized to periodically generate a new quote for a random stock. Only one line of code is needed to send the quote update JMS message, and that's the call to the base class's `send` method, where the new quote text is provided. All of the JMS `Session`, `Destination`, and `MessageProducer` implementation details, and the component failover capability the JCS provides, come with this one JCS method call.

LISTING 5.36 The Sample Stock Quote Sender Class, `QuoteSenderJCS`

```
package com.TradingSystem.StockTicker;

import java.text.NumberFormat;
import java.util.Random;
import com.toolkit.messaging.componentserver.*;

public class QuoteSenderJCS extends ContentProducer
{
    private Random random =
        new Random(System.currentTimeMillis());

    private String[] stocks = {
        "IBM", "MSFT", "SUNW", "ORCL", "SBL",
        "BEAS", "AAPL", "DELL", "GOOG", "YHOO" };
```

```
private double[] prices = {
    91.79, 25.67, 4.09, 13.24, 17.41,
    8.50, 70.76, 40.12, 180.72, 33.93 };

public QuoteSenderJCS(String destName)
{
    super(destName);
    this.setInterval(2000);
}

public void doWork() throws Exception
{
    int stock = random.nextInt(10);

    String newPrice = getLastTradePrice( stock );

    String text = stocks[stock] + ": \t" + newPrice;

    this.send(text);
}

private String getLastTradePrice(int stockIndex) {
    // ...
}

private int getStockIndexFromName(String name) {
    // ...
}
}
```

The Stock Quote Listener

Listing 5.37 shows the code for stock quote listener class, QuoteListenerJCS. In this example, the doWork method is called by the JCS when a message arrives for the component's destination. Again, the JMS implementation details are completely hidden from the component developer. The result is that you get a lot of benefit for very little effort.

LISTING 5.37   The Sample Stock Quote Sender Class, QuoteListenerJCS

```
package com.TradingSystem.StockTicker;

import com.toolkit.messaging.componentserver.*;
```

```
public class QuoteListenerJCS extends ContentConsumer
{
    public QuoteListenerJCS(String destName)
    {
        super(destName);
    }

    public void doWork( Object obj )
    {
        System.out.println((String)obj);
    }
}
```

The Quote Request Listener

Listing 5.38 shows the code for the class QuoteFinderJCS, which listens for quote requests and replies to them. Technically this component is both a listener and a producer, but since it spends most of its time listening for quote request messages, the class extends the ContentConsumer base class. This situation does not pose a problem because QuoteFinderJCS still has access to the JMSManager object reference from its base class. Therefore, when a JMS MapMessage object is received in the doWork method, the class uses the JMSManager object to send the reply message to the reply destination. Because this example is more involved than a simple producer or consumer component, some of the underlying JMS details are visible in the component's code. However, since the component's base class uses, and exposes, the JMSManager class, replying to the request message is still very straightforward.

LISTING 5.38   The Sample Stock Quote Sender Class, QuoteFinderJCS

```
package com.TradingSystem.StockTicker;

import java.text.NumberFormat;
import java.util.Random;

import javax.jms.*;

import com.toolkit.messaging.componentserver.*;

public class QuoteFinderJCS extends ContentConsumer
{
    private Random random =
        new Random(System.currentTimeMillis());
```

```
private String[] stocks = { //... };
private double[] prices = { //... };

public QuoteFinderJCS(String destName)
{
    super(destName);
}

public void doWork( Object obj )
{
    try {
        MapMessage mapMsg = (MapMessage)obj;
        String ticker = mapMsg.getString("ticker");
        int stock = getStockIndexFromName( ticker );

        TextMessage textMsg =
        jmsMgr.createTextMessage("RequestQuote");
        if ( stock != -1 ) {
            String newPrice = getLastTradePrice( stock );
            textMsg.setText(stocks[stock] + ": \t" + newPrice);
        }
        else {
            textMsg.setText("Stock ticker not supported");
        }

        System.out.println("Sending a quote reply");
        jmsMgr.send( mapMsg.getJMSReplyTo(), textMsg);
    }
    catch ( Exception e) {
        e.printStackTrace();
    }
}
private String getLastTradePrice(int stockIndex) {
    // ...
}

private int getStockIndexFromName(String name) {
    // ...
}
}
```

Running the Sample Application

The true power of the JCS is best illustrated by running the sample quote system. The entire stock quote sample application to run within the JCS is contained on the CD-ROM in the folder named Chapter5. The sample application is composed of two startup scripts, each of which starts the same JCS class, but with different configuration files. Each startup script starts the class JCSMain and provides as an argument the path name that contains the configuration files. The Windows batch file runjcstestA.bat (and runjcstestB.sh on UNIX) executes the following command:

```
> java -cp (classpath here) com.toolkit.messaging.componentserver.JCSMain
ServerA
```

The text in bold, ServerA, is the folder name (relative to the Chapter5 folder from which it is run) where it can find the configuration files for server A. The batch file runjcstestB.bat (and runjcstestB.sh) executes the following command:

```
> java -cp (classpath here) com.toolkit.messaging.componentserver.JCSMain
ServerB
```

In this case, the configuration files can be found in the folder ServerB. Start each server in a different command prompt and watch them start up. The messages you see should indicate that each server has started its components, received a registration from the other partner, and established a pecking order. The following is a snapshot of the output from server B (some unimportant output has been omitted):

```
JCS: Info - ----------
JCS: Info - JMS Component Server (JCS)
JCS: Info - ----------
JCS: Info - Started Mon Feb 14 00:16:51 EST 2005
JCS: Info - Version 1.00
JCS: Info - Java Runtime Version: 1.4.2
JCS: Info - Java VM Version: 1.4.2-b28
JCS: Info - ----------
JCS: Info - Local Server Name: ServerB
JCS: Info - StateManager created
JCS: Info - PartnerManager created, server name: ServerB
JCS: Info - ComponentManager created
JCS: Info - JCS starting
JCS: Info - Reading Component list config file
JCS: Info - Reading Partner list config file
JCS: Info - PartnerManager - Other JCS Partners:
```

```
JCS: Info -      Partner name: ServerA
JCS: Info - StateMgr - changing state from 'STOPPED' to 'STARTED'
...
JCS: Info - PartnerMgr - new partner registered: ServerA
JCS: Info - ComponentManager: Partner added event received
JCS: Info -    for partner=ServerA
JCS: Info - ComponentManager - State changed to STARTED
JCS: Info - ContentConsumer listening on destination RequestQuote
JCS: Info - ComponentManager - Created component
JCS: Info -    com.TradingSystem.StockTicker.QuoteFinderJCS
JCS: Info -    for destination RequestQuote
JCS: Info - JCS: I - Received REPLY_START_MESSAGE from ServerA
JCS: Info - JCS: I - ServerA is the Active Supervisor
JCS: Info - Started Admin server on port 7981
JCS: Info - Accepting connections on port 7981
JCS: Info - Admin server request processor running
JCS: Info - JCS: I - Received PECKING_ORDER_MESSAGE
JCS: Info -       Server 0: ServerA
JCS: Info -       Server 1: ServerB
JCS: Info - JCS started
```

Once both JCS partners are running, server A should output stock quote messages as its listener receives them. At this point start the simple quote listener application from earlier in this chapter by executing the runsimplequotelistener. bat (or runsimplequotelistener.sh) script from a third command prompt.

You should notice that the simple quote listener receives replies to its quote requests and begins displaying quote update messages as it should. You should also notice that the QuoteFinderJCS component in server B has sent a message to the command prompt window for each request it replied to. Now comes the interesting part: stop server B by issuing a CTRL-C from within its command prompt window. After several seconds, server A should notice that server B has failed and will take over for it by instantiating the QuoteFinderJCS component within its process. At this point, stop the simple quote listener application and run it again. You should see that it still receives replies to its quote requests, as well as quote updates thereafter. Looking at the output from server A should indicate that the QuoteFinderJCS component running there handled the requests, whereas before it was on server B.

The example is not over yet. At this point, restart server B in its original command prompt by executing the runjcstestB.bat (or runjcstestB.sh) script again. You will notice that as server B starts, server A detects this and stops the QuoteFinderJCS component from running. Once again, stop and restart the simple quote listener application, and you should notice that the quote requests are handled by server B once again. Try the reverse scenario, where server A is stopped and server B is allowed to take over for it, and you will see that the simple quote listener application will still continue to receive updates. This is the power of the JCS.

SUMMARY

This chapter has applied the messaging concepts learned in the previous two chapters to build actual JMS applications. Presented in this chapter are tools and utilities to help make the construction and deployment of JMS-based applications easier, and less tedious. This includes a class that distributes JavaBean events remotely by transparently using JMS, a facade class to make JMS easier to use, and a runtime environment for JMS application components. The JCS serves as a solid runtime environment for JMS applications while providing startup and failover capabilities to the software components built to use JMS. The JCS offers a level of reliability and administration for the code that runs on top of a JMS provider: your applications.

6

Web Services and Messaging

In This Chapter

- XML Overview
- Web Services
- XML-RPC
- SOAP

XML OVERVIEW

The *eXtensible Markup Language* (XML) specifies a platform-neutral syntax for expressing data in human-readable, text form. The main purpose of XML is to describe data in such a way that any piece of software running on any computer, or even a human, can interpret it. XML is derived from the Standard Generalized Markup Language (SGML), and by definition XML documents conform to the SGML specification. Being composed of text, XML is easily transmitted over the Internet and it can be encrypted and compressed using standard algorithms.

XML is made up of three main pieces, called *entities*: elements (sometimes called tags), attributes, and the data (also called values) that the elements and attributes describe. Look at the XML document in Listing 6.1 as an example. An element is always enclosed in angle brackets (< >) and can consist of any piece of text, such as `<Address>`. Attributes are additional name–value pairs placed within an element's brackets, but after the element's tag name, such as `<Employee type="Developer">`. The attribute name is always followed by an equal sign (=) and then the value in quotes. An element can contain zero or more attributes, where each attribute name–value pair is separated by white space. Elements and attributes themselves make up what is called meta-data, which is data that describes data.

LISTING 6.1   Sample XML Document for Employee Data

```xml
<?xml version="1.0" encoding="utf-8"?>
<Employee type="Developer">
    <Lastname>Bruno</Lastname>
    <Firstname>Eric</Firstname>
    <Id>XXX-XX-XXXX</Id>
    <Address>
        <Street>123 Anywhere Street</Street>
        <City>Anytown</City>
        <State>NY</State><Zip>11111</Zip>
    <Address>
    <Spouse>
        <Lastname>Bruno</Lastname>
        <Firstname>Christine</Firstname>
        <Id>XXX-XX-XXXX</Id>
    </Spouse>
    <Children>
        <Child>
            <Lastname>Bruno</Lastname>
            <Firstname>Ashley</Firstname>
            <Id>XXX-XX-XXXX</Id>
        </Child>
```

```
<Child>
    <Lastname>Bruno</Lastname>
    <Firstname>Brandon</Firstname>
    <Id>XXX-XX-XXXX</Id>
</Child>
</Children>
</Employee>
```

Each element within an XML document can contain at most one text value and must have a matching closing element that consists of the element's name preceded by a "/," as in:

```
<Address>
    ...
</Address>
```

The first element in an XML document is called the *root element*. A document can contain no more than one root element; additional elements are not allowed at this level. However, elements can be nested, meaning they can contain other elements, but they cannot overlap. For instance, the following is proper XML with a nested element:

```
<Stock>
    SUNW
    <Name>
        Sun Microsystems, Inc.
    </Name>
</Stock>
```

The following is *not* proper XML because the tags overlap:

```
<Stock>
    SUNW
<Name>
    Sun Microsystems, Inc.
</Stock>
</Name>
```

In other words, `</Name>` should come *before* `</Stock>`. It is also good practice to include a header in your XML documents, where additional XML parser directives can be included. One use of an XML header is to specify the character set encoding that should be used when parsing your XML document, such as "UTF-8," "ISO-8859-1," and so on. (See *http://www.w3.org/International/O-charset.html* for more on character set encoding.) The first line of the XML in Listing 6.1 is a common XML header.

Sometimes an XML document will need to contain another XML document, or an HTML document, as data. In these cases, it is usually desired to *not* have this data interpreted as markup, although it contains entities that look like markup to the parser. For instance, look at the sample XML document in Listing 6.2, which contains an HTML document embedded within it. Notice that the element <Data> contains an HTML document as its data entity. The intent is for the receiving application to use the data returned in the XML document, as well as to display this HTML as a response to a user request. However, this document won't parse because, as is the case with most HTML pages or data that is otherwise in a raw form, the text of the data contains entities that the parser will attempt to process and fail.

LISTING 6.2 Failed Attempt to Encompass HTML in an XML Document

```
<?xml version="1.0" encoding="utf-8"?>
<Response>
    <Status>OK</Status>
    <Data>
        <HTML>
            <Head><Title>A Response HTML Page</Title></Head>
            <body>
              <h1>My Web Site<p>
              <h2>This is a response to a request for information:
              <p>The answer is 41
            </body>
        </html>
    </Data>
</Response>
```

You can see the error this XML generates if you attempt to open it from within a Web browser. To communicate the true intent of this XML document to the parser, the data portion of the <Data> element must be tagged in such a way that the parser will not interpret the data as markup. This is done by enclosing the data within a *character data* (CDATA) section, as shown in Listing 6.3. Within a CDATA section, angle brackets, ampersands, and other characters that would otherwise be interpreted by the parser will be ignored, except for the end marker ("]]>") itself.

LISTING 6.3 Using a CDATA Section within an XML Document

```
<?xml version="1.0" encoding="utf-8"?>
<Response>
```

```
<Status>OK</Status>
<Data>
    <![CDATA[
    <HTML>
        <Head><Title>A Response HTML Page</Title></Head>
        <body>
            <h1>My Web Site<p>
            <h2>This is a response to a request for information:
            <p>The answer is 41
        </body>
    </html>
    ]]>
</Data>
</Response>
```

If you include an XML header, use CDATA sections where needed, and follow the rule of correctly nesting elements within a document, you will have what is called *well-formed* XML. This means that the XML complies with the XML specification and hence can be parsed by any standard XML parser. However, since XML element and attribute names can be any arbitrary text, how can you be sure that an XML document your application receives contains all of the data it expects? There needs to be a way to pre-parse an XML document to ensure that it is not just well-formed, but *valid* as well. This is where an XML document type definition (DTD) is used.

XML Document Type Definition (DTD)

To make XML truly useful to an application, it's important to communicate to parsers and other applications exactly what you are expecting an XML document to contain when your application receives it. For example, if an XML document is sent to your application to perform a login function, you will require it to contain data such as a user identifier and a password. Perhaps, for the user identifier, your application may accept a user ID in the form of a number (i.e., a database key) or a string of characters (i.e., a user name). To help your application determine the type of user identifier provided, an attribute for the user identifier element is required.

A *document type definition* (DTD), although not itself XML, describes the rules that an XML document follows. The DTD can be contained completely within an XML document (an internal subset of the DTD) or it can exist on its own, within its own file (an external subset of the DTD). An external DTD is a definition of rules followed by XML documents that reference it. An XML document optionally specifies a DTD within its document type declaration section, which is located immediately after the XML header, and before the root tag of the document.

A DTD must specify the document's required root element and usually includes all of the elements expected within the document. For each element, the type of data expected can be specified, along with required or optional attributes and their data types. To clarify, look at the sample XML with an internal DTD in Listing 6.4.

LISTING 6.4 An XML Document with an Internal DTD

```
<?xml version="1.0" encoding="utf-8"?>
<!DOCTYPE Login [
  <!ELEMENT Login (UserID,Password)>
  <!ELEMENT UserID (#PCDATA)>
  <!ELEMENT Password (#PCDATA)>
  <!ATTLIST UserID
    id      ID        #IMPLIED
    name    CDATA     #IMPLIED>
]>
<Login>
    <UserID type="name">ebruno</UserID>
    <Password>my_password</Password>
</Login>
```

The lines in bold encompass the DTD. The !DOCTYPE element signals the beginning of the DTD and contains its entire definition. First, the document's root tag is specified. Next, the elements expected within the document are listed, each with its expected content. For instance, the Login element as specified is expected to contain two nested elements: UserID and Password. Both of these elements are expected to contain parsed character data (PCDATA) as their value, but UserID is expected to also contain an attribute; either id or name. If the DTD for this XML document were contained within an external file, it would be referenced as follows:

```
<?xml version="1.0" encoding="utf-8"?>
<!DOCTYPE Login SYSTEM "login.dtd">
<Login>...
</Login>
```

XML Namespaces

As you can imagine, many applications implement a login function. Therefore, the XML document from Listing 6.4 contains element names that can conflict with elements within documents sent and received by multitudes of other applications deployed in the world. Because of this, it's useful to be able to further constrain elements as belonging to a particular application. The standard way to do this in XML is to declare an XML *namespace*, as shown in Listing 6.5.

LISTING 6.5 A Sample XML Namespace

```
<?xml version="1.0" encoding="utf-8"?>
<!DOCTYPE Login SYSTEM "login.dtd">
<MyApp:Login xmlns:MyApp="http://myapplication.com">
    <MyApp:UserID type="name">ebruno</MyApp:UserID>
    <MyApp:Password>my_password</MyApp:Password>
</MyApp:Login>
```

In this example, the namespace used is MyApp, although it can be any name that you find useful, relevant, and somewhat unique to your application. The namespace is formally declared using the xmlns attribute in the document's root element. The xmlns attribute is combined with the actual name of your namespace and is defined to point to a location that is absolutely unique, such as a Web URL. This URL does not really need to be valid, just unique, although pointing to a valid URL (owned by the company defining the namespace, for instance) helps to ensure this. From this point onward, all element names are prefixed with the namespace name itself along with a colon (:) in between.

XML Schema

XML DTDs have multiple shortcomings, such as the complexity of their syntax, the lack of hierarchy, problems with namespaces, the lack of XML document linking, the fact that they are not object-oriented, and the fact that they are not expressed using XML. For these reasons, many XML developers have found DTDs to be limiting, and in many cases not applicable. The *XML Schema* specification has been developed to solve each of these problems. With XML Schema, XML developers can express rules and constraints for their XML documents using XML itself. See Listing 6.6 for an XML Schema that applies to the XML from Listing 6.5. XML schemas can be used to validate documents and process them. A detailed discussion of XML Schema is beyond the scope of this book, but you can study it further, starting with the specification at *http://www.w3.org/XML/Schema*.

LISTING 6.6 Sample XML Schema

```
<xsd:schema xmlns:xsd="http://www.w3.org/2001/XMLSchema">
    <xsd:element name="UserID" type="xsd:anyType"/>
    <xsd:element name="Password" type="xsd:string"/>
    <xsd:attribute name="name" type="xsd:string"/>
    <xsd:attribute name="id" type="xsd:ID"/>
</xsd:schema>
```

eXtensible Stylesheet Language (XSL)

The *eXtensible Stylesheet Language (XSL)* specification (*http://www.w3.org/TR/xsl11*) defines a language and XML vocabulary for transforming XML documents. The transformation includes structuring data into alternative XML formats, as well as for presentation in Web browsers or other output media such as Adobe® Portable Document Format (PDF) files. An *XSL Transformation* (XSLT) is the result of providing a source XML document, along with an XSL style sheet, to an XSL processor to produce an internal result tree. This result tree is then formatted into its final presentation form, such as an HTML page (see Figure 6.1).

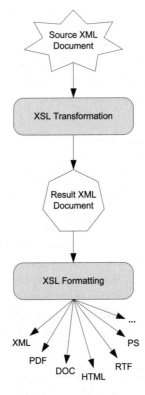

FIGURE 6.1 XSLT involves two steps: the data transform and the data formatting.

The resulting XML from the first step in the transformation, but before the formatting is performed, can be returned from the XSL processor. However, this XML will contain formatting objects and properties that most XML clients will not know how to handle. Therefore, its use is discouraged. Instead, if the requirement is to transform the source XML to an alternate XML format, the proper XSL formatter should be used.

As with XML Schema, a detailed discussion of XSL transformations is beyond the scope of this book. The remainder of this chapter will focus on the role of XML in building distributed software systems using components called services.

WEB SERVICES

What exactly is a Web Service? It's an important question, because not everyone understands the distinction between a service-oriented architecture (SOA) and a Web Service. Quite often, people tend to get them confused. A *service-oriented architecture* is one that integrates the services of multiple applications to produce a new, distinct application. This does not preclude the use of any particular technology; the services may be integrated using Application Programming Interfaces (APIs), network sockets, or even a proprietary communications protocol. It's not until the services communicate over HTTP, with the data being in XML form, that we call them *Web Services*. Technically, a Web Service does not need to conform to the simple object access protocol (SOAP) and it does not need to support the Web Service description language (WSDL) or the universal description, discovery, and integration (UDDI) standard. As long as your service can communicate over the Web via HTTP and can communicate in a platform-independent manner (i.e., XML), it is a Web Service.

Figure 6.2 shows a client communicating with a service over the Web using HTTP. Each service request is made using XML, and likewise, each response is returned in XML. Because the underlying transport used is HTTP, the request/response message cycle can be asynchronous in nature. This allows the client application to remain responsive to the user even while a server request is outstanding. The use of XML in the messages helps abstract the underlying platform and language used to build and deploy both the client application and the Web Service. Hence, the client may be a C++ application running on Windows, and the Web Service may be a Java application running on UNIX.

It's important to note that although the HTTP request/response cycle is by nature asynchronous, most Web Service infrastructures (such as those that come with Sun's Java Web Service Developer's Pack) make the communication behave in a synchronous manner. This is something that will be discussed in more detail in Chapters 7 and 8.

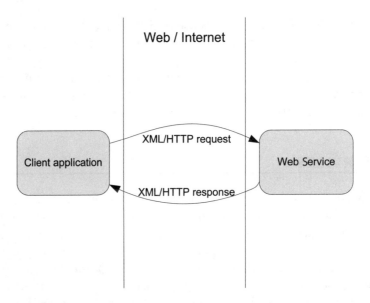

FIGURE 6.2 This diagram summarizes client and Web Service communication.

HTTP URL Query-Based Web Services

A simple (albeit borderline) Web Service can be implemented using HTTP query URLs. In this service, requests arrive as query parameters within a URL, and the result is served back as XML as it should for any Web Service (see Figure 6.3). Some may not consider this a true Web Service, as the requests are not formatted as XML. However, it does lend itself well to situations where requests are so straightforward and simple that formatting them as XML is overly complex and in some ways unnatural. The service can be implemented as a CGI application running within a Web Server, hence maintaining language and platform independence. A useful example of this type of service is an application that serves as a front-end to a database, where SQL query results are returned as XML instead of a database result-set. The result is a language-independent database query application.

In this example, calling applications will make simple requests of the service to retrieve user credentials as they log in to a remote system. Let's assume that the service accepts a primary key, a user name, or a wildcard to retrieve database information, as in the following examples.

Retrieve by primary key:

http://myservice.com/GetUserData?userid=2341

Retrieve by user name:

http://myservice.com/GetUserData?username=ebruno

Retrieve all:

http://myservice.com/GetUserData?all=true&sortby=username

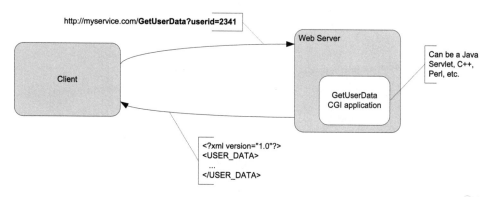

FIGURE 6.3   Requests arrive as URL queries; responses are sent as XML.

All three requests call a common base URL, *http://myservice.com/GetUserData*, which is implemented by a CGI application, such as a Java Servlet, a Perl script, Python, and so on. The differentiating factors in all of the requests are the parameters. The first two requests take only one parameter each: userid or username. The third request takes two parameters; the first tells the application to return all users; the second tells it to sort the results by user name. Listing 6.7 shows a Java Servlet implementation of the application that serves these sample requests.

LISTING 6.7   A Servlet that Handles URL Query-Based Requests

```
import javax.servlet.*;
import javax.servlet.http.*;
import java.util.*;
import java.io.*;
import java.lang.*;
import java.sql.*;

public class UserQueryService extends HttpServlet
{
    public void init( ServletConfig config )
        throws ServletException
```

```
    {
        super.init(config);

        try {
            connectToDb();
        }
        catch ( Exception e ) {
            e.printStackTrace();
        }
    }

    public void destroy() {
        // ...
    }

    public void doGet(  HttpServletRequest request,
                        HttpServletResponse response)
        throws ServletException, IOException
    {
        String xmlOutput = "";

        // Get parameters
        String userid = request.getParameter( "userid" );
        String username = request.getParameter( "username" );
        String all = request.getParameter( "all" );

        ResultSet rs = null;
        if ( userid != null )
        {
            rs = getUserData( new Long(userid) );
        }
        else if ( username != null )
        {
            rs = getUserData( username );
        }
        else if ( all != null )
        {
            String sortby = request.getParameter( "sortby" );
            rs = getAllUserData( sortby );
        }

        // Create XML from the ResultSet
        xmlOutput = formatXML( rs );
```

```
        // set content type
        response.setContentType("text/xml");

        // Write and send the UTF-8 XML response
        PrintWriter out =
            new PrintWriter(
                new OutputStreamWriter( response.getOutputStream(),
                                        "UTF8"),
                true);

        out.println( xmlOutput );
        out.flush();
    }

    // Actual implementation left out for brevity
    private void connectToDb() { ... }
    private ResultSet getUserData(Long userid ) { ... }
    private ResultSet getUserData(String username ) { ... }
    private ResultSet getAllUserData(String sortby ) { ... }
    private String formatXML(ResultSet rs) { ... }
}
```

The database request code and the XML formatting code have been left out of this code for simplicity. Listing 6.8 is an example of the XML that would be sent in response to a single user request (either by primary key or user name). In this example, the XML element names are intended to match database table and column names. The actual XML structure is up to the developer to define.

LISTING 6.8 Sample User Request XML Response Output

```
<?xml version="1.0"?>
<USER_DATA>
    <USER_ID>2341</USER_ID>
    <USER_NAME>ebruno</USER_NAME>
    <PASSWORD>a_secure_password</PASSWORD>
    <FIRST_NAME>Eric</FIRST_NAME>
    <LAST_NAME>Bruno</LAST_NAME>
    <EMAIL>eric@ericbruno.com</EMAIL>
</USER_DATA>
```

Applications built this way are truly based on an SOA. This approach can be used to quickly and easily create a service front-end to a legacy application. However, as stated previously, some may consider that this implementation is not a Web Service in the strictest sense because the requests are not made using XML. One can argue against this point because the requests are made using a URL query language supported by all Web Servers running in the Internet today. The argument is moot, however, when you consider that not all requests fit nicely into the URL query structure. There are requests, such as those that contain structured data or those that require encryption, where XML makes more sense as the protocol.

XML Structure Issues

However, stating that an SOA will use XML is not nearly enough; the structure of the XML quickly becomes an issue. A client must express its service requests with an XML format that the service can understand, and the response must be in a format that the client expects in return. Of course, you can easily define an arbitrary format for your service's XML and publish it to the world, but put yourself in the client's shoes for a moment. What if your service is *not* the only one your client needs to communicate with? The client application code would need to format its requests to your service differently than to the other services, leading to a situation similar to that illustrated in Figure 6.4.

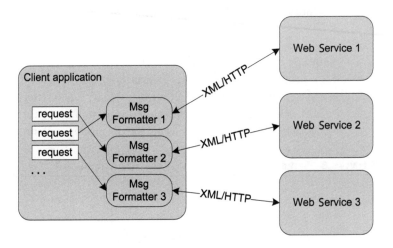

FIGURE 6.4 Custom message formats lead to custom message formatting code.

As each service request is made, the client code must first determine which service the request is destined for. Next the message must be formatted to meet the requirements of the applicable service. Then the request message must be sent to the correct service, and finally, the response, after it is received, must be parsed using code specific to the service that sent it. For each service, a separate implementation for message formatting must be in place. This means that with each new service to be integrated, a new body of code must be written to format the messages accordingly. This is really not efficient, as code that performs similar tasks must be re-implemented each time a new service is used. The time it takes to write this code could be better spent implementing new features and functionality in the application. There must be a way to optimize this.

If you examine the scenario again, you will see that each service has something basic in common: the concept of a request and a response. Once you identify a commonality, you should be able to generalize the implementation. What we need is a standard way to format XML requests and responses. Then the client code will need to concern itself only with the important pieces of the requests and responses: the data. A basic message formatter that conforms to the standard can be built once, or acquired, as a black box, and the message format can forever be ignored, as shown in Figure 6.5.

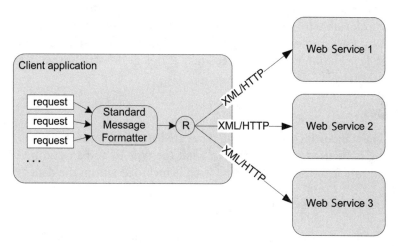

FIGURE 6.5 Standard message formatting for all services leads to simpler, reusable code.

In this diagram you see that each request is formatted the same way using a standard implementation. Each request is then routed to the proper service over HTTP. The responses can be handled in much the same way. The client code can now express a request—regardless of the service that will receive it—as a request name such as "login," and the parameters, such as the user name and password. Subsequently, the standard response message parser can deliver just the returned data to the client. No message formatting details are exposed to the client code. As long as each service implements the standard, requests to new services can be added without impact to the client code. This discussion has come down to defining a standard remote procedure call (RPC) protocol that uses XML and HTTP for its transport. Fortunately, such a standard exists, called XML-RPC.

XML-RPC

XML-RPC is a standard that allows you to make remote procedure calls to servers over the Internet using XML over HTTP. The body of each request message, and its subsequent response message, is in XML. Procedure names, parameters, return values, and value data types are all expressed in XML with standard tag names. The specification for XML-RPC can be found at *http://www.xmlrpc.com/spec*, and we will go over the details in this section. There is support for Java, C/C++, .NET, ASP, PHP, Python, Perl, and Ruby. Because XML-RPC is language and platform independent, you can choose the language and operating environment that is most comfortable to you or your development group. A C++/.NET client running on Windows can seamlessly make calls to, and receive responses from, a server written in Java running on Linux. Let's take a look at the structure of XML-RPC calls and data types.

Data Types

The standard XML-RPC data types are listed in Table 6.1, which includes the XML tag to be used, a description of what the type is, and an example for further illustration. The value for the data itself is included within the data-type tag:

```
<int>65536</int>
```

The data-type tag can be omitted completely from the XML, in which case it defaults to the <string> type. The next two sections describe the <struct> and <array> data types in more detail.

Data Structures

An XML-RPC data structure is similar to a C/C++ struct or a Java class with data members only. The point of it is to group related data into one structured element within the XML payload of an XML-RPC message. A structure contains one or more <member> elements, each of which contains a <name> and <value> pair, as shown in Listing 6.9.

TABLE 6.1 XML-RPC Standard Data Types

Tag	Type	Example
<int>	A four-byte signed integer	−500
<i4>	A four-byte signed integer	−500
<string>	A character string	"Java Messaging"
<double>	A signed floating point number	49.99
<boolean>	False (0) or true (1)	0
<base64>	Base64-encoded binary	N/A
<dateTime.iso8601>	Date/time value	20050101T:23:14:00
<struct>	A data structure	N/A
<array>	An array of values	N/A

LISTING 6.9 An XML-RPC Data Structure

```
<struct>
    <member>
        <name>Price</name>
        <value><double>49.99</double></value>
    </member>
    <member>
        <name>State</name>
        <value><string>New York</string></value>
    </member>
</struct>
```

A structure can also contain an embedded structure with a <value> element. The fact that the data is tagged as a structure is an indicator to the receiving process that the data should be handled a certain way. Perhaps it indicates that a class should be instantiated to contain the data or that it should be placed into a database table that matches the structure. The actual implementation is application specific and up to the developer.

Data Arrays

A data value can also be tagged as an array, which itself can contain any number of <value> elements, including structs and other arrays of data as well. The data types of the values within the array can be mixed, as shown in Listing 6.10.

LISTING 6.10 An XML-RPC Data Array

```
<array>
    <data>
        <value><string>Alabama</string></value>
        <value><double>4.74</double></value>
        <value><string>Alaska</string></value>
        <value><double>0</double></value>
        <value><string>Arizona</string></value>
        <value><double>5.6</double></value>

        ...
    </data>
</array>
```

This example contains an array of state names (each as a `string`) with each state's sales tax percentage (as a `double`).

Method Calls

The whole point of XML-RPC is to make remote procedure (or method) calls to a service. Therefore, all of the XML-RPC elements we've examined so far will be contained within an XML payload for either a method call, or a method response. A method call is denoted by the existence of a `<methodCall>` root tag, while a response is denoted by a `<methodResponse>` root tag. The `<methodCall>` must contain a `<methodName>` tag, indicating the remote method to invoke, and a `<params>` tag, which contains the parameters to the remote method call, as shown in Listing 6.11.

LISTING 6.11 Sample XML-RPC Remote Method Call XML

```
<?xml version="1.0"?>
<methodCall>
    <methodName>addSalesTax</methodName>
    <params>
        <param>
            <value>
                <double>49.99</double>
            </value>
        </param>
        <param>
            <value>
                <string>New York</string>
            </value>
        </param>
    </params>
</methodCall>
```

In this example, the remote method to invoke is named `addSalesTax`, which takes two parameters: the price to add sales tax to, and the state in which the sale was made. There is an implied order to the parameters, and reversing the order can lead to problems. To avoid issues like this, an XML-RPC structure can be used as the sole parameter, where each member of the structure has a name. Because the data within the structure is named, the server can read the data in any order without a problem.

The `<methodResponse>` tag can contain either a return value or an error indicator and never both. The return value is embedded within the correct XML-RPC value type, such as `<double>`, within a `<value>` tag, within a single `<param>` tag, within a `<params>` tag. The response cannot contain more than one `<param>` and `<value>` combination. Listing 6.12 shows a sample XML-RPC method return for the earlier method call in Listing 6.11.

LISTING 6.12   Sample XML-RPC Remote Method Response XML

```
<?xml version="1.0"?>
<methodResponse>
    <params>
        <param>
            <value>
                <double>52.11</double>
            </value>
        </param>
    </params>
</methodResponse>
```

If the call fails, the server can indicate this by returning XML with a `<fault>` tag in place of the `<params>` tag. The fault contains a `<struct>`, which itself contains two `<member>` tags; the first one, named `faultCode`, contains an `<int>` tag within a `<value>` tag that provides the caller with a numeric representation of the error. The second member, named `faultString`, contains a `<string>` tag within a `<value>` tag that provides a text description of the error that has occurred. It should be much clearer when you look at the sample fault response XML shown in Listing 6.13.

It's important to note that a fault's `<struct>` *should not contain any members other than the two shown here.*

LISTING 6.13   XML-RPC Remote Method Response Fault XML

```
<?xml version="1.0"?>
<methodResponse>
```

```
            <fault>
                <value>
                    <struct>
                        <member>
                            <name>faultCode</name>
                            <value>
                                <int>1</int>
                            </value>
                        </member>
                        <member>
                            <name>faultString</name>
                            <value>
                                <string>Bad State Name</string>
                            </value>
                        </member>
                    </struct>
                </value>
            </fault>
        </methodResponse>
```

XML-RPC Servers

Apache offers an excellent XML-RPC implementation in Java at *http://ws.apache. org/xmlrpc*. When you download the code, you get everything you need to build XML-RPC client and server applications in Java. There are three main server classes: org.apache.xmlrpc.XmlRpcServer, org.apache.xmlrpc.WebServer, and org. apache.xmlrpc.SecureWebServer. The last two classes are full-blown HTTP server implementations, while the first is meant to run within an existing Servlet engine such as Apache Tomcat.

For any XML-RPC server, the Apache software uses Java reflection to expose a class's public methods to remote callers. Put another way, when a client sends an XML-RPC request to a server, the Apache implementation uses Java reflection to find a matching public member method on the server class. The return value from the Java method call is automatically wrapped as an XML-RPC response message and delivered back to the original caller.

To use the WebServer and SecureWebServer classes, simply instantiate an object of either type, optionally specify the port and/or IP address, and provide a reference to the class whose public methods you'd like to expose via XML-RPC by calling the addHandler method:

```
server = new WebServer(80); // port 80
server.addHandler("$default", salesTaxService );
```

To use the Apache XML-RPC classes within an existing Servlet engine, first you must create and store an instance of the XmlRpcServer class. As in the previous example, provide a reference to the class whose public methods you'd like to expose via XML-RPC with a call to the addHandler method:

```
XmlRpcServer server = new XmlRpcServer();
server.addHandler("$default", salesTaxService );
```

When an incoming HTTP request arrives, it should be in XML form. Therefore, all you need to do is grab the input as an InputStream object and pass it to the execute method of the XmlRpcServer object instance. The return of this call is a byte array that you must wrap as an OutputStream object and return as an HTTP response, as shown in Listing 6.14.

LISTING 6.14   Calling an XmlRpcServer Object in a Servlet

```
public void doPost( HttpServletRequest request,
                    HttpServletResponse response )
    throws ServletException, IOException
{
    byte[] result = server.execute( request.getInputStream() );
    response.setContentType( "text/xml" );
    response.setContentLength( result.length() );
    OutputStream out = response.getOutputStream();
    out.write( result );
    out.flush();
}
```

Server Security

Basic security for XML-RPC servers that use the Apache classes includes username and password authentication, IP address validation, and java.net.Socket-based validation. To use a username and password method of authentication, the server class that handles incoming XML-RPC requests must implement the org. apache.xmlrpc.AuthenticatedXmlRpcHandler interface. This interface requires your handler class to implement an execute method that takes a String as the method name, a Vector as a container for the method's parameters, and two more String objects for the caller's username and password.

The WebServer and SecureWebServer classes implement a method, acceptClient, which you can call as many times as you wish to add servers to the list of clients to accept requests from. The parameter to the call is a String that represents an IP address, where the wildcard character (*) can be used anywhere in the address. For instance, you can provide "*" as the parameter to specify all addresses, or you can used the "*" anywhere in the address (such as "66.94.234.*" or "216.251.*.*"). Conversely, you can call the denyClient method to specify exactly which clients to *not* accept requests from. The IP address String follows the same rules as with the acceptClient method, as previously discussed.

The SecureWebServer class has the added benefit of handling requests over a secure channel, such as Secure HTTP. To use this class, you must first set the security values, such as a key store, a trust store, the appropriate passwords, and so on. Additionally, you can call the createServerSocket method to provide an SSLServerSocket object for further security.

XML-RPC Clients

A client application that uses the Apache XML-RPC package has the choice of instantiating an XmlRpcClient, SecureXmlRpcClient, or XmlRpcClientLite class. The first two classes are complete HTTP-client implementations that use the java. net.URLConnection class to provide authentication, cookie, and proxy-server support. The third class is a bare-bones implementation that can serve as a faster, smaller implementation of an HTTP client if more advanced client options are not required.

Regardless of which client class is used, you must specify the server's address and port number in one of the constructors. You can provide the entire URL as a String or java.net.URL object, or you can specify the server's host name and port separately as a String and int respectively. Optional user authentication is handled via the setBasicAuthentication method, which takes two String values for the caller's username and password. To call a remote method synchronously via XML-RPC, use the execute method with the remote procedure name as a String and the procedure's parameters contained within a Vector. The call's return value can be any valid Java object.

Asynchronous Method Calls

Asynchronous method calls are supported via a second execute method that takes the method name and parameters as previously described, plus a third parameter that can be any object that implements the org.apache.xmlrpc.AsyncCallback interface. This version of the execute method will return immediately, and the callback object will be called later with the remote procedure's resulting XML. If the remote call was successful, the callback's handleResult method will be called with the returned object, the URL of the server that handled the request, and the name of the original method that was called. This allows your code to implement one callback object for all of its remote procedure calls and still know the context of each call when the results arrive asynchronously.

If an error occurs during the call (resulting from either a bad or missing parameter or some other problem), the callback's handleError method will be called. As with the handleResult method, the server's URL and method name are included. However, the error that occurred is provided through an Exception object as the first parameter. A call to getMessage on the Exception object will result in a String that describes the error that has occurred.

A Java XML-RPC Example

Let's explore the XML-RPC implementation details as we build a simple server (see Listing 6.15) that calculates sales tax when given a price and a state name (such as New York). The method that performs this calculation is called addSalesTax. The price that is returned is the original price plus sales tax, calculated according to the state given. The server class is simply a Java class that imports the org.apache. xmlrpc package and instantiates an object of type org.apache.xmlrpc.WebServer. When you instantiate the WebServer object, you need to pass a valid TCP/IP port number in the constructor. Next, when you call the start method, the server will begin listening for requests on the provided port. The Apache XML-RPC classes handle the parsing of incoming requests, routing those requests to the correct method, and wrapping the return as an XML-RPC response. You don't need to implement any code to get this functionality.

LISTING 6.15   Code for the XML-RPC Sales Tax Web Service

```
package com.myservices;

import java.util.*;
import org.apache.xmlrpc.*;

public class SalesTaxService
{
    private HashMap salesTaxTable = new HashMap();

    // the xml-rpc webserver
    private static WebServer server;
    private final int port = 8181;

    public SalesTaxService()
    {
        populateSalesTaxTable();

        // Start web server to handle requests
        server = new WebServer( port );
```

```
            server.addHandler ("$default", this);
            server.start();
            System.err.println ("Listening on port " + port);
        }


        // This method is invoked via XML-RPC using Reflection
        public String addSalesTax(String state, String priceStr)
        {
            // Locate state sales tax
            Double Tax = (Double)salesTaxTable.get(state);
            if ( Tax == null )
                return priceStr;

            // Calculate and return price with sales tax included
            double price = new Double(priceStr).doubleValue();
            double tax = Tax.doubleValue();
            price += (price * (tax/100));

            return new Double(price).toString();
        }

        private void populateSalesTaxTable()
        {
            salesTaxTable.put("Alabama", new Double(4));
            ...
            salesTaxTable.put("Washington D.C.", new Double(5.75));
        }

        public static void main(String[] args)
        {
            SalesTaxService service = new SalesTaxService();
        }
    }
```

Creating an XML-RPC client application is as straightforward as creating a server. Your client code needs to import the org.apache.xmlrpc package, and instantiate an object of type org.apache.xmlrpc.XmlRpcClient. Listing 6.16 contains the implementation of a client for the sales tax XML-RPC server from the previous section. When you want to make a call to an XML-RPC server, you must first place the parameters to the call in a Vector object. Next, to invoke the remote procedure, you must call the execute method of the XmlRpcClient object, where you provide the name of the method to call as a String and the Vector that contains the parameters. The object returned from the call must be cast to the expected Java Object subtype, such as a String in this example.

LISTING 6.16 Code for the XML-RPC Sales Tax Client

```java
import java.util.*;
import java.io.*;
import org.apache.xmlrpc.*;

public class Client
{
    // the xml-rpc client
    XmlRpcClient rpcClient;

    public Client() throws Exception
    {
        rpcClient = new XmlRpcClient("http://localhost:8181");

        BufferedReader d =
            new BufferedReader(
                    new InputStreamReader(System.in) );

        while ( true )
        {
            System.out.println("Enter price:");
            String price = d.readLine();
            System.out.println("Enter state:");
            String state = d.readLine();

            Vector params = new Vector();
            params.add(state);
            params.add(price);

            String result = (String)
                rpcClient.execute("addSalesTax", params);

            System.out.println("Price with sales tax: "+result);
            System.out.println(" ");
        }
    }

    public static void main(String[] args)
        throws Exception
    {
        Client client = new Client();
    }
}
```

ON THE CD
The code for the sales tax example can be found on the CD-ROM in the Chapter6\SalesTaxService folder. You can start the XML-RPC server by executing the Windows batch file named server.bat (or server.sh for UNIX). To start the client, execute the Windows batch file client.bat (or client.sh for UNIX). Once started, you will be prompted to enter a price (i.e., "99.99"). Next, you will be prompted to enter a state name (i.e., "New York"). The request will then be sent, via XML-RPC, to the server, and the response will be displayed. If you typed "99.99" and "New York" in the steps described, you should receive the value "104.239575" in return. In the real implementation, the precision would be two decimal places, but this is just an example.

SOAP

XML-RPC is a derivative of the work done by Dave Winer from Userland Software, Bob Atkinson and Mohsen Al-Ghosein from Microsoft, and Don Box (then from Developmentor, now from Microsoft) [St. Laurent01]. The Simple Object Access Protocol (SOAP) was the ultimate result. Like XML-RPC, SOAP is a lightweight protocol designed to be used for communication in heterogeneous distributed application architectures. The remainder of this chapter will discuss SOAP in reasonable detail, but you can get all of the details from the specifications available on the World Wide Web Consortium's Web site at *http://www.w3.org/2000/xp/Group*. This particular URL is for the XML protocol working group and contains links to specifications on many different SOAP-related topics.

SOAP and XML-RPC have common roots as an XML-based definition for making remote procedure calls and handling the subsequent responses. SOAP goes much further, however, in its definition of the following:

Message Structure: The SOAP message is rigidly structured and uses a "letter in the mail" analogy. Every message has an envelope that contains all of the individual SOAP parts, such as an optional header, the body, and zero or more attachments (see Figure 6.6). The message not only contains the payload, but can also contain instructions on who the message is for and how to process it.

Message Encoding: SOAP messages support scalar data types, arrays and sparse arrays, enumerations, polymorphism, compound types, and data references. SOAP defines a message XML namespace to eliminate ambiguity.

To begin, let's examine a SOAP message and make sense of its parts. Listing 6.17 contains a sample SOAP message that describes a method call to get stock-related data for Microsoft. Every SOAP message must contain an Envelope element

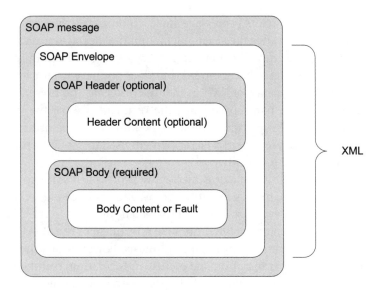

FIGURE 6.6 A visual representation of the SOAP message structure.

and should (but does not have to) use an XML namespace. Within the SOAP message envelope, the message may contain a `Header` element. This is optional, but a header is generally used for communication between the message sender and receiver. It can be used to convey processing instructions for the message itself or to help other software systems route the message to the correct recipient. If a SOAP message does contain a `Header` element, it must appear first, after the `Envelope` element within the message.

LISTING 6.17 A SOAP Message

```
<env:Envelope
  xmlns:env="http://www.w3.org/2003/05/soap-envelope"
  xmlns:rpc="http://www.w3.org/2003/05/soap-rpc"
  env:encodingStyle="http://schemas.xmlsoap.org/soap/encoding">
    <env:Header/>
    <env:Body>
        <m:GetStockData xmlns:m="http://myservice.com/">
            <symbol>MSFT</symbol>
            <CIK>0000789019</CIK>
        </m:GetStockData >
    </env:Body>
</env:Envelope>
```

Next, every SOAP message must contain exactly one Body element. It must appear directly after the Header element if the message contains a header; otherwise it must appear directly after the Envelope element. Each immediate child element within the message body should (but does not have to) use an XML namespace for clarity. The elegance of XML is that the ordering and presence of data is not mandated. Using a namespace helps the recipient discern the various pieces of data within a SOAP message without depending on their order to figure it out. The SOAP namespace defines a Fault element used to convey error-related information to the message recipient.

SOAP itself is a stateless messaging protocol. It's not concerned with application semantics, message routing, transaction processing, reliability, or even security. It is, however, a paradigm upon which solutions to these issues can be layered. Applications that use SOAP can take advantage of the SOAP message structure to create more complex messaging solutions. For example, the SOAP header can be used to convey transaction and security information, routing instructions, and object state. Nodes in a distributed system can be dynamically deployed to intercept and route messages as a system grows in complexity. By inserting nodes that append or modify the contents of SOAP messages, a deployed system can be extended without modifying all the components of the system.

Perhaps the intercepting node simply logs all SOAP messages it sees, or perhaps it takes a more active role in the transaction itself in some way. Either way, a message sender can use the message structure defined by SOAP to accurately define how a message is to be processed once it reaches its recipient. Still, this is done independently of programming language, platform, and other implementation details of the various parties involved in processing the SOAP messages along the way. SOAP messages can be sent over application socket connections, HTTP, or even over email. For more information on this, see the SOAP email-binding specification at *http://www.w3.org/TR/2002/NOTE-soap12-email-20020626*.

SOAP Headers

In the previous section, we learned that adding a SOAP header to a message is optional. However, using a header allows the message sender to include process control information with the message that is not technically part of the message's payload. This can be any information that ensures the message is processed by the proper component, with the right context, and in the correct state. If a header is used, the first level subelements must be qualified with a namespace. Child elements of those subelements are not required to be namespace qualified, but it is good practice to do so. Header subelements may have optional attributes, among which the following are defined by SOAP to have special meaning:

encodingStyle: Contains a URL to the rules for serializing the header data.

mustUnderstand: Indicates that the processing of the header is mandatory by all recipients. If a particular node does not understand the header information, it must either pass the message along to the next node (if it is not an endpoint) or send a SOAP fault message as a reply. The omission of this attribute is equal to adding it with the value of false.

role: Indicates the role the intended processing node should be operating under. The omission of this attribute is equal to adding it with the value of http://www.w3.org/2003/05/soap-envelope/role/ultimateReceiver.

relay: Indicates whether this message should be sent along to another node if the current node cannot process it . The omission of this attribute is equal to adding it with the value of false.

Listing 6.18 contains a SOAP message with an optional header that includes transaction information required for processing this message. Although the header in this example contains one subelement, t:transaction, there is quite a bit of information here. First, the attribute env:mustUnderstand with a value of true means that the receiving node must understand this particular element. In this case, the intent is that the receiver must be able to enlist in the distributed transaction before processing this message. If not, the message should not be processed, and a SOAP fault indicating this should be returned to the sender. Finally, the transaction identifier itself is sent and must be stored for later reference (for a possible commit or rollback). This state information is not part of the message itself; therefore, it belongs in the header as this example illustrates, not in the body.

LISTING 6.18   SOAP Message with Transaction Information in the Header

```
<env:Envelope
  xmlns:env="http://www.w3.org/2003/05/soap-envelope"
  xmlns:rpc="http://www.w3.org/2003/05/soap-rpc"
  env:encodingStyle="http://schemas.xmlsoap.org/soap/encoding">
    <env:Header>
        <t:transaction
          xmlns:t="http://myservice.com/transaction"
          env:mustUnderstand="true" >
            14764366
        </t:transaction>
    </env:Header>
    <env:Body>
        <m:Buy xmlns:m="http://myservice.com/">
            <symbol>SUNW</symbol>
            <quantity>1000</quantity>
```

```
            </m:Buy >
          </env:Body>
        </env:Envelope>
```

The message header can contain any information a SOAP application feels it requires. Message expiration, time-to-live, priority, sequence number, transaction identifiers, redelivery flag, references to other messages—these are all examples of reasonable SOAP header entries. Specific nodes can be targeted by including an env:role attribute with a role name. Any nodes operating under that role can assume the message is intended for them.

SOAP Faults

SOAP faults, communicated as a Fault element within a SOAP message, are typically used in a response message to convey that a server error has occurred while processing a SOAP request. If a message contains a Fault element, it must contain the following two mandatory subelements:

env:Code: Mandatory; the env:Code element is used to convey the actual error that has occurred. It must contain one env:Value subelement, which contains a SOAP namespace-defined error value. The code value must be one of the following: env:VersionMismatch, env:MustUnderstand, env:DataEncodingUnknown, env:Sender, or env:Receiver. These values will be described later in this section. The env:Code element may also contain an optional env:Subcode subelement to refine the error code. The env:Subcode element itself must contain an env:Value subelement, and may contain an option env:Subcode subelement of its own. Confusing? The example later in this section will help clear it all up.

env:Reason: Mandatory; a one-line, human-readable explanation of the error that has occurred. The explanation text must be placed within an env:Text subelement of the env:Reason element. For multilanguage support, each env:Text subelement should contain an xml:lang attribute with the correct language code for the text.

The Fault element may also contain the following two *optional* subelements:

env:Detail: Optional; an application-defined section that contains more detail related to the error. The details themselves should be placed within application-specific subelements within the env:Detail element.

env:Node: Optional when from the ultimate recipient, mandatory when from a middle party; this element is inserted by an application that processed the SOAP message before it arrived at its ultimate recipient yet experienced an error while doing so. If the application (the node) is the intended recipient, this element should not be added even if an error occurs.

In the list above, the description of the `env:Code` element mentioned five possible `env:Value` subelement data values. These values are described here:

`env:VersionMismatch:`   The XML-namespace used does match that of the message recipient's namespace.

`env:MustUnderstand:`   A header attribute marked as mandatory was not understood and/or processed by the recipient.

`env:DataEncodingUnknown:`   The recipient does not support the encoding specified in the SOAP message part.

`env:Receiver:`   The message could not be processed because the recipient experienced an error not related to the message's contents or structure. Perhaps the recipient depends upon a resource (such as a database or another SOAP node) that was not available at the time the request was received. A subsequent retry of the same request message may succeed at a later time.

`env:Sender:`   The message could not be processed because the sender did not include all the needed information or the request was in some way malformed. Simply resending the message as-is will not solve the problem; it needs to be reformed correctly.

Although the rigid structure for SOAP fault reporting may seem overly complex and confusing at this point, an example is sure to help clarify the situation. Listing 6.19 shows a sample SOAP fault message in response to a SOAP request for stock data where the company symbol was missing. The `env:Fault` contains one `env:Code` subelement, one `env:Reason` subelement, and one `env:Detail` subelement. `env:Code` contains a mandatory `env:Value` subelement (indicating that the sender was to blame) and an optional `env:Subcode` subelement (indicating that bad arguments were sent with the request).

LISTING 6.19   A SOAP Fault Response Message

```
<env:Envelope
  xmlns:env="http://www.w3.org/2003/05/soap-envelope"
  xmlns:rpc='http://www.w3.org/2003/05/soap-rpc'
  env:encodingStyle="http://schemas.xmlsoap.org/soap/encoding">
    <env:Body>
        <env:Fault>
            <env:Code>
              <env:Value>env:Sender</env:Value>
```

```
            <env:Subcode>
              <env:Value>rpc:BadArguments</env:Value>
            </env:Subcode>
          </env:Code>
          <env:Reason>
            <env:Text xml:lang="en-US">Bad arguments</env:Text>
          </env:Reason>
          <env:Detail>
            <err:myFaultDetails
              xmlns:err="http://myservice.com/faults">
                <err:message>
                  The request for stock data was missing a
                  valid company symbol
                </err:message>
                <err:errorcode>1</err:errorcode>
            </err:myFaultDetails>
          </env:Detail>
        </env:Fault>
      </env:Body>
    </env:Envelope>
```

The env:Reason element contains the required env:Text element with the human-readable error summary. Finally, the env:Detail element contains the application-specific err:myFaultDetails, with its own subelements that describe the error in more detail, including a text description and an error code. This part of the SOAP fault is defined by the SOAP application developer.

SOAP Attachments

So far our discussion of Web Services and SOAP has centered on a common concept: XML. However, there are times when an application needs to send information that cannot be easily or naturally transmitted via XML, such as images or binary data. Just as you would add image or binary attachments to an email message that otherwise would be nothing but text, you can do the same with SOAP. To be precise, the *SOAP with attachments* specification is an add-on to the original SOAP specification. But since it builds upon the existing SOAP protocol with virtually no change and uses the same facilities and mechanisms used to send and receive SOAP messages, it is generally accepted to be part of SOAP in general. You can find the SOAP message with attachment specification at *http://www.w3.org/TR/SOAP-attachments*.

Attachments are sent with SOAP messages using a multipart, multipurpose Internet mail extensions (MIME) structure called the MIME Multipart/Related Content type (*http://www.ietf.org/rfc/rfc2387.txt*). This MIME structure is combined with the SOAP message definition as explored in the previous chapter and is known as the *SOAP Message Package* (see Figure 6.7), which is also known as a *compound SOAP structure*. The specification purposely does not define an additional XML structure for the message package. It is, instead, more of a concept than a physical entity itself. Within the SOAP message package, zero or more attachments (also known as secondary SOAP message parts) are defined as MIME parts and are appended to the end of a SOAP message, after the message body (the primary SOAP message part). The attachments themselves can even be referenced within the SOAP message that contains them.

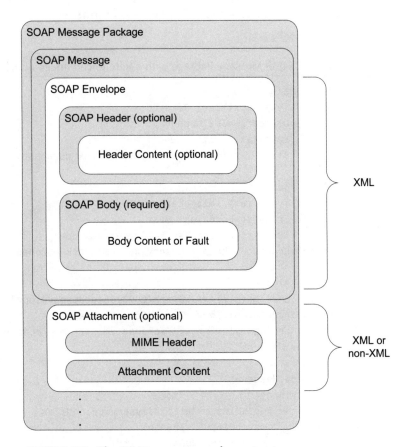

FIGURE 6.7 The SOAP message package structure.

The SOAP message is contained as the root of the multipart/related message structure, with a MIME Content-type of text/xml. Attachments are added using a MIME boundary and are given the MIME Content-type appropriate to the data type, such as image/jpg. Referencing attachments within the body of a SOAP message is optional. However, when they are referenced, they must be referenced by the MIME Content-ID defined in the attachment's MIME structure. The SOAP message package in Listing 6.20 shows an example of this. Notice that the attachment in this message (an image) is referenced by Content-ID and has a Content-Location entry for its location.

Keep in mind that although the content-type in the header of the SOAP message package shown in Listing 6.20 is broken up into multiple lines, in reality it is sent as only one line. It has been split up here for illustrative purposes only.

LISTING 6.20   A SOAP Message Package with a Referenced Image Attachment

```
MIME-Version: 1.0
Content-Type: Multipart/Related;
        boundary=MIME_boundary;
        type=text/xml;
        start="<http://myservice.com/stock_purchase.xml>"

--MIME_boundary
Content-Type: text/xml; charset=UTF-8
Content-Transfer-Encoding: 8bit
Content-ID: <stock_purchase.xml@myservice.com>
Content-Location: http://myservice.com/stock_purchase.xml

<env:Envelope
  xmlns:env="http://www.w3.org/2003/05/soap-envelope"
  xmlns:rpc="http://www.w3.org/2003/05/soap-rpc"
  env:encodingStyle="http://schemas.xmlsoap.org/soap/encoding">
    <env:Header>

        ...
    </env:Header>
    <env:Body>
        <m:Buy xmlns:m="http://myservice.com/">
            <symbol>SUNW</symbol>
            <quantity>1000</quantity>
            <aggreement_form
                href="cid:stock_aggreement.jpg@myservice.com"/>
        </m:Buy >
    </env:Body>
</env:Envelope>
```

```
--MIME_boundary
Content-Type: image/jpg
Content-Transfer-Encoding: binary
Content-ID: <stock_aggreement.jpg@myservice.com>
Content-Location: http://myservice.com/stock_aggreement.jpg
```

When transferring a SOAP message package over HTTP, the multipart/related MIME header (the one at the beginning of this example) essentially becomes the HTTP header (as shown in Listing 6.21). The remainder of the SOAP message and the attachments become the HTTP message body.

LISTING 6.21   An HTTP Header for a SOAP Message Package

```
POST /StockPurchase HTTP/1.1
Host: www.myservice.com
Content-Type: Multipart/Related;
        boundary=MIME_boundary;
        type=text/xml;
        start="<http://myservice.com/stock_purchase.xml>"
Content-Length: 1234
SOAPAction: http:// myservice.com/stock_purchase
```

SUMMARY

This chapter began with an overview of XML, its uses, and its related technologies. We then explored service-oriented architectures implemented with XML as the protocol and with HTTP as the transport. This RPC combination is more commonly referred to as a Web Service. We started by exploring a simple URL query-based Web Service that can be implemented by a CGI application written in almost any language. After uncovering the shortcomings of URL-based services, the XML-RPC standard (a precursor to the SOAP specification) was explored and discussed as a way of implementing a true Web Service. After examining a working XML-RPC sample application, the discussion moved to SOAP-based Web Services. This chapter mainly provided an overview of the SOAP and SOAP with attachments specifications; the next chapter will explore how to implement SOAP-based Web Services using the Java Web Service Development Pack (JWSDP).

7 Web Services Specifications

In This Chapter

- Reliable Messaging
- Events
- Coordination
- Security

IBM, Microsoft, BEA, Sun, TIBCO, and various other companies teamed up to develop Web Service specifications to help form a common understanding of how Web Service technologies can be applied to various areas of distributed application development. Although most of them are fairly short, a relatively large number of standards documents are available, with new ones released occasionally. This chapter is a review and summary of the standards that apply to messaging software, namely:

WS-ReliableMessaging: Discusses a transport-independent protocol for reliable message delivery

WS-Eventing: Discusses a protocol for simple event notification messages that can be used or sent by Web Services and the applications that use them

WS-Coordination: Discusses a protocol for coordinating distributed application activities that span two or more Web Services, to ensure a reasonable outcome

WS-Security: Discusses improvements to the Simple Object Access Protocol (SOAP) protocol to support the authentication, confidentiality, and integrity of SOAP messages

Other specifications not discussed here but still recommended to further enhance your understanding of the latest standards in the world of messaging and Web Services are:

WS-AtomicTransactions: Discusses a protocol for performing atomic transactions across Web Service nodes, including support for two-phase commit (2PC), as well as short- and long-lived transactions.

WS-BusinessActivity: Discusses a business activity protocol that builds upon the standards for transactions and coordinated activities to create distributed operations that have permanent affects. This protocol is meant to be used by existing business process and work flow orchestration systems, allowing for the interoperation of otherwise noncompliant vendor offerings.

WS-Addressing: Describes the use of XML to define unique, transport-independent names for Web Service endpoints on the Internet.

WS-SecureConversation: Built on top of the security and policy specifications, this specification describes a way to apply security contexts to the activities that occur between Web Service endpoints involved in a long-running messaging conversation.

WS-Manageability: Defines an approach to identify, configure, and monitor Web Service endpoints. Also included are standard mechanisms for measuring performance and application state.

WS-Notification: Defines methods to use the messaging paradigms of message-oriented middleware (MOM) systems such as JMS, including publish-and-subscribe messaging, filtered messages, and the use of queues.

For a complete list of Web Service standards, and to keep up to date with updates, visit *http://www-128.ibm.com/developerworks/views/webservices/libraryview. jsp?type_by=Standards/.*

RELIABLE MESSAGING

The *WS-ReliableMessaging* (RM) specification defines a Web Service messaging protocol to identify, track, and manage the reliable delivery of messages between exactly two parties: a source and a destination [Bilorusets04]. The specification describes a model to guarantee to source and destination Web Service applications that messages sent from one side will be delivered on the other. This delivery assurance is obtained via the addition of a reliable messaging source (*RM source*) and destination (*RM destination*) used by the SOAP client and Web Service, respectively, which encapsulate the process of transporting the messages (see Figure 7.1). This concept is what the JMSSOAPConnection class from Chapter 8 is based on.

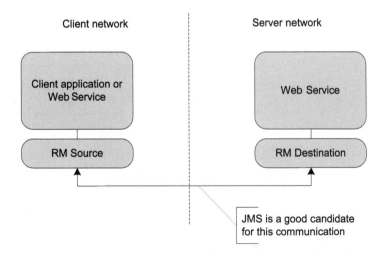

FIGURE 7.1 The Web Service and its client use reliable messaging components called an RM destination and RM source, respectively.

The RM specification describes all messages as being explicitly sequenced by the RM source and acknowledged by the RM destination (see Figure 7.2). Further, the RM destination must include the last n sequence numbers from the messages received with each acknowledgment sent. The number of messages, n, is configurable. If there are sequence numbers missing from the list in an acknowledgment, those missing represent messages that need to be resent by the RM source. In general, an acknowledgment message is not sent until the sender indicates it is done sending (at least for this sequence of messages). To enable delivery assurance, the source application must support message correlation, and the sending application must adhere to the service's message protocol (for example, using Web Service Description Language [WSDL] to form the correct SOAP requests).

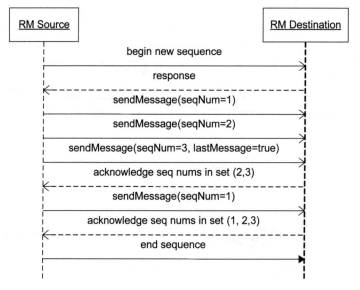

FIGURE 7.2 This sequence diagram illustrates a message exchange between an RM source and an RM destination.

Message Sequences

Reliable messaging requires that messages be sent by the source in *sequences* that are acknowledged by the destination. Message sequences may contain one or more messages, and they represent a series of messages in time that must be guaranteed to be delivered. Since we're talking about Web Service messaging, all messages are sent as XML. Therefore, the message sequence, its creation, acknowledgment, and termination are all described using XML.

To begin, a sequence must be started, or created. This is performed by the RM source (the client) when it sends an XML document to the RM destination with the root element `<wsrm:CreateSequence>`. The RM destination, upon receipt of this message, will send a response containing the `<wsrm:CreateSequenceResponse>` element that contains a unique message sequence number in the form of a universal resource identifier (URI) (see Listing 7.1). The destination may determine that it cannot start a new sequence at this time (because of an error or some other circumstance). In this case, it will return an XML document with the element `<wsrm:CreateSequenceRefused>`.

LISTING 7.1   A Create Message Sequence Response

```
<wsrm:CreateSequenceResponse>
  <wsu:Identifier>http://myservice.com/sequence1</wsu:Identifier>
</wsrm:CreateSequenceResponse>
```

Each message that is sent as part of a sequence must contain a `<wsrm:Sequence>` element within its header. The header must also contain the message sequence identifier provided when the sequence was created, and each message must contain a unique sequence number that increases by one with each message, starting from one (see Listing 7.2). Additionally, the `<wsrm:Sequence>` header can also contain a `<wsu:Expires>` element, indicating a message expiration time. When the last message of a sequence is sent by the RM source, it must contain the `<wsrm:LastMessage>` element, which informs the RM destination that this concludes this message sequence.

LISTING 7.2   An RM Message with a Sequence Header

```
<wsrm:Sequence>
  <wsu:Identifier>http://myservice.com/sequence1</wsu:Identifier>
  <wsrm:MessageNumber>1</wsrm:MessageNumber>
</wsrm:Sequence>
...
```

Upon receipt of the last message, the RM destination sends a sequence acknowledgment either as a standalone message, or as a header to a response message, which contains the `<wsrm:SequenceAcknowledgment>` element. Acknowledgments can be sent at any time, but they are typically only sent after the last message is received or after any message that contains the `<wsrm:AckRequested>` element is received, even if it is *not* the last message. The acknowledgment message contains the range of sequence numbers for all messages that have been received. Missing messages can be deduced from gaps in the range of numbers. In the example in Listing 7.3, the acknowledgment contains two groups of acknowledged messages—one through three and five through eight—because the message with sequence number four was never received.

LISTING 7.3   A Message Sequence Acknowledgment

```
<wsrm:SequenceAcknowledgment>
  <wsu:Identifier>http://myservice.com/sequence1</wsu:Identifier>
  <wsrm:AcknowledgmentRange Lower="1" Upper="3"/>
  <wsrm:AcknowledgmentRange Lower="5" Upper="8"/>
</wsrm:SequenceAcknowledgment>
```

Upon receiving this acknowledgment, the RM source will deduce that message four was not received, and it must resend it. Once an acknowledgment for *all* messages is received by the RM source, it will send a message containing the `<wsrm:TerminateSequence>` element back to the RM destination to terminate the sequence. This message (see Listing 7.4) indicates that the RM source will no longer send messages for this sequence; a new message sequence will need to be opened to send additional messages in the future.

LISTING 7.4   A Terminate Sequence Message

```
<wsrm:TerminateSequence>
   <wsu:Identifier>http://myservice.com/sequence1</wsu:Identifier>
</wsrm:TerminateSequence>
```

Namespace and Schema

What we've discussed so far has been an overview of the important aspects of the WS-ReliableMessaging specification. There are some more details you will need to know, such as sequence and message expiration, inactivity timeouts, message retransmission intervals, policy assertions, sequence faults for error conditions, and security. You can examine the full RM specification and XML schema to gain a complete understanding of the XML message structures required. The standard XML namespace and schema for the WS-ReliableMessaging specification is available at *http://schemas.xmlsoap.org/ws/2004/03/rm/wsrm.xsd* (see Listing 7.5).

LISTING 7.5   The WS-ReliableMessaging XML Schema and Namespace

```
<?xml version="1.0" encoding="UTF-8"?>
<!--
(c) 2002-2004 BEA Systems Inc., International Business Machines
 Corporation, Microsoft Corporation, Inc., and TIBCO Software Inc.
 All rights reserved.
```

```
-->
<xs:schema
  targetNamespace="http://schemas.xmlsoap.org/ws/2004/03/rm"
  xmlns:xs="http://www.w3.org/2001/XMLSchema"
  xmlns:wsrm="http://schemas.xmlsoap.org/ws/2004/03/rm"
  xmlns:wsu="http://schemas.xmlsoap.org/ws/2002/07/utility"
  elementFormDefault="qualified"
```

```
                    attributeFormDefault="unqualified">
            <xs:import
              namespace="http://schemas.xmlsoap.org/ws/2002/07/utility"
              schemaLocation="http://schemas.xmlsoap.org/ws/2002/07/utility"/>
            <!-- Protocol Elements -->
            <xs:complexType name="SequenceType">
              <xs:sequence>
                <xs:element ref="wsu:Identifier"/>
                <xs:element name="MessageNumber" type="xs:unsignedLong"/>
                <xs:element name="LastMessage" minOccurs="0"/>
                <xs:any namespace="##other" processContents="lax"
                  minOccurs="0" maxOccurs="unbounded"/>
              </xs:sequence>
              <xs:anyAttribute namespace="##other" processContents="lax"/>
            </xs:complexType>
            <xs:element name="Sequence" type="wsrm:SequenceType"/>
            <xs:element name="SequenceTerminate">
              <xs:complexType>
                <xs:sequence>
                  <xs:element ref="wsu:Identifier"/>
                  <xs:any namespace="##other" processContents="lax"
                    minOccurs="0" maxOccurs="unbounded"/>
                </xs:sequence>
                <xs:anyAttribute namespace="##other" processContents="lax"/>
              </xs:complexType>
            </xs:element>
            <xs:element name="SequenceAcknowledgment">
              <xs:complexType>
                <xs:sequence>
                  <xs:element ref="wsu:Identifier"/>
                  <xs:choice>
                    <xs:element name="AcknowledgmentRange"
                      maxOccurs="unbounded">
                      <xs:complexType>
                        <xs:sequence/>
                        <xs:attribute name="Upper" type="xs:unsignedLong"
                          use="required"/>
                        <xs:attribute name="Lower" type="xs:unsignedLong"
                          use="required"/>
                      </xs:complexType>
                    </xs:element>
                    <xs:element name="Nack" type="xs:unsignedLong"
                      maxOccurs="unbounded"/>
                  </xs:choice>
```

```
        <xs:any namespace="##other" processContents="lax"
          minOccurs="0" maxOccurs="unbounded"/>
      </xs:sequence>
      <xs:anyAttribute namespace="##other" processContents="lax"/>
    </xs:complexType>
</xs:element>
<xs:complexType name="AckRequestedType">
  <xs:sequence>
    <xs:element ref="wsu:Identifier"/>
    <xs:element name="MaxMessageNumberUsed"
      type="xs:unsignedLong" minOccurs="0"/>
    <xs:any namespace="##other" processContents="lax"
      minOccurs="0" maxOccurs="unbounded"/>
  </xs:sequence>
  <xs:anyAttribute namespace="##other" processContents="lax"/>
</xs:complexType>
<xs:element name="AckRequested" type="wsrm:AckRequestedType"/>
<!-- Policy Assertions -->
<xs:element name="InactivityTimeout">
  <xs:complexType>
    <xs:complexContent>
      <xs:extension base="wsrm:PolicyAssertionType">
        <xs:attribute name="Milliseconds"
          type="xs:unsignedLong" use="required"/>
      </xs:extension>
    </xs:complexContent>
  </xs:complexType>
</xs:element>
<xs:element name="BaseRetransmissionInterval">
  <xs:complexType>
    <xs:complexContent>
      <xs:extension base="wsrm:PolicyAssertionType">
        <xs:attribute name="Milliseconds"
          type="xs:unsignedLong" use="required"/>
      </xs:extension>
    </xs:complexContent>
  </xs:complexType>
</xs:element>
<xs:element name="ExponentialBackoff"
  type="wsrm:PolicyAssertionType"/>
<xs:element name="AcknowledgmentInterval">
  <xs:complexType>
    <xs:complexContent>
      <xs:extension base="wsrm:PolicyAssertionType">
```

```
                  <xs:attribute name="Milliseconds"
                    type="xs:unsignedLong" use="required"/>
                </xs:extension>
              </xs:complexContent>
            </xs:complexType>
          </xs:element>
          <xs:complexType name="PolicyAssertionType">
            <xs:sequence>
              <xs:any namespace="##other" processContents="lax"
                minOccurs="0" maxOccurs="unbounded"/>
            </xs:sequence>
            <xs:anyAttribute namespace="##other"/>
          </xs:complexType>
          <xs:element name="SequenceCreation">
            <xs:complexType>
              <xs:complexContent>
                <xs:extension base="wsrm:PolicyAssertionType">
                  <xs:attribute name="Value" type="xs:QName"
                    use="required"/>
                </xs:extension>
              </xs:complexContent>
            </xs:complexType>
          </xs:element>
          <!-- Fault Container and Codes -->
          <xs:simpleType name="FaultCodes">
            <xs:restriction base="xs:QName">
              <xs:enumeration value="wsrm:UnknownSequence"/>
              <xs:enumeration value="wsrm:SequenceTerminated"/>
              <xs:enumeration value="wsrm:InvalidAcknowledgment"/>
              <xs:enumeration value="wsrm:MessageNumberRollover"/>
            </xs:restriction>
          </xs:simpleType>
          <xs:simpleType name="Direction">
            <xs:restriction base="xs:QName">
              <xs:enumeration value="wsrm:Inbound"/>
              <xs:enumeration value="wsrm:Outbound"/>
              <xs:enumeration value="wsrm:Bidirectional"/>
            </xs:restriction>
          </xs:simpleType>
          <xs:complexType name="SequenceFaultType">
            <xs:sequence>
              <xs:element name="FaultCode" type="xs:QName"/>
              <xs:any namespace="##any" processContents="lax"
                minOccurs="0" maxOccurs="unbounded"/>
```

```
      </xs:sequence>
      <xs:anyAttribute namespace="##any" processContents="lax"/>
   </xs:complexType>
   <xs:element name="SequenceFault" type="wsrm:SequenceFaultType"/>
   <!-- Sequence Reference Domain Expression -->
   <xs:complexType name="SequenceRefType">
      <xs:sequence>
         <xs:any namespace="##other" processContents="lax"
            minOccurs="0" maxOccurs="unbounded"/>
      </xs:sequence>
      <xs:attribute name="Identifier" type="xs:anyURI"
         use="required"/>
      <xs:attribute name="Match" type="wsrm:MatchChoiceType"
         use="optional"/>
      <xs:anyAttribute/>
   </xs:complexType>
   <xs:simpleType name="MatchChoiceType">
      <xs:restriction base="xs:QName">
         <xs:enumeration value="wsrm:Exact"/>
         <xs:enumeration value="wsrm:Prefix"/>
      </xs:restriction>
   </xs:simpleType>
   <xs:element name="SequenceRef" type="wsrm:SequenceRefType"/>
   <xs:element name="CreateSequence">
      <xs:complexType>
         <xs:sequence>
            <xs:any namespace="##other" processContents="lax"
               minOccurs="0" maxOccurs="unbounded"/>
         </xs:sequence>
         <xs:anyAttribute namespace="##other"/>
      </xs:complexType>
   </xs:element>
   <xs:element name="CreateSequenceResponse"
      type="wsrm:HandshakeType"/>
   <xs:element name="TerminateSequence" type="wsrm:HandshakeType"/>
   <xs:complexType name="HandshakeType">
      <xs:sequence>
         <xs:element ref="wsu:Identifier"/>
         <xs:any namespace="##other" processContents="lax"
            minOccurs="0" maxOccurs="unbounded"/>
      </xs:sequence>
      <xs:anyAttribute namespace="##other" processContents="lax"/>
   </xs:complexType>
</xs:schema>
```

EVENTS

The *WS-Eventing* specification defines a protocol for one Web Service (a *subscriber*) to register interest (a *subscription*) with another Web Service (an *event source*) to receive messages about events (also called *notifications* or *event messages*) [Box04]. A *subscription manager*, which is a Web Service that manages event source subscriptions for events, is made available for the following reasons:

1. It may not be known at development time exactly which services will offer the events a client service is interested in.
2. Subscriptions may be leased and they can be configured to expire over time.
3. The number of subscriptions may be limited because of performance reasons.

The specification offers a lot of flexibility in terms of event message delivery. For instance, there is support for asynchronous events (push model), but clients may also poll for events (pull model). The event messaging can be combined with reliable messaging (as defined in the WS-ReliableMessaging specification), transactions (WS-AtomicTransaction), and security (WS-Security). Most of the time, the event messages are delivered in a standard SOAP envelope, but this does not have to be the case. WS-Eventing allows subscribers to define their own event message wrappers by extending the XML schema.

The XML in Listing 7.6 is a sample event subscription request for a Web Service at *http://myservice.com*, to the event source at *http://yourservice.com*. This SOAP message contains a header that indicates the action being performed in the `<wsa:Action>` element, the message destination (the event source) in the `<wsa:To>` element, and the message source (the event receiver) in the `<ReplyTo>` element. The SOAP body contains the URI for the event listener in the `<was:Address>` element, along with a subscription number in `<ew:MySubscription>`.

LISTING 7.6   A WS-Eventing Subscription Request

```
<s12:Envelope
  xmlns:s12='http://www.w3.org/2003/05/soap-envelope'
  xmlns:wsa='http://schemas.xmlsoap.org/ws/2004/08/addressing'
  xmlns:wse='http://schemas.xmlsoap.org/ws/2004/08/eventing'
  xmlns:ew='http://myservice.com' >
    <s12:Header>
      <wsa:Action>http://.../Subscribe</wsa:Action>
      <wsa:MessageID>uuid:...</wsa:MessageID>
      <wsa:ReplyTo>
        <wsa:Address>http://myservice.com/MyListener</wsa:Address>
```

```
          </wsa:ReplyTo>
          <wsa:To>http://yourservice.com/QuoteSource</wsa:To>
        </s12:Header>
        <s12:Body>
          <wse:Subscribe>
            <wse:Delivery>
              <wse:NotifyTo>
                <wsa:Address>
                   http://myservice.com/MyListener/onQuoteUpdate
                </wsa:Address>
                <wsa:ReferenceProperties>
                   <ew:MySubscription>120</ew:MySubscription>
                </wsa:ReferenceProperties>
              </wse:NotifyTo>
            </wse:Delivery>
          </wse:Subscribe>
        </s12:Body>
      </s12:Envelope>
```

The set of actions defined in the WS-Eventing specification include:

Subscribe: Sent by an event listener to subscribe for an event on the event source.

Renew: Sent by an event listener to renew a subscription that is about to expire.

GetStatus: Sent by an event listener to see if a current subscription is still valid, or if it has expired.

Unsubscribe: Sent by an event listener to terminate a current event subscription.

SubscriptionEnd: Sent by an event source to inform an event listener that its subscription has ended. The reason for the message is *not* an expiration or an unsubscribe request. Instead, valid reasons for terminating the subscription are "DeliveryFailure," in cases where the source cannot send any more events, "SourceShuttingDown," for obvious reasons, and "SourceCanceling," for any other reason besides the two previously listed. These values must be set in the <status> element of the event message. The message will also contain a <reason> element, and should contain locale-specific text describing the reason for the termination.

SubscribeResponse: Sent by the event source in response to a request to create a new subscription, this message indicates that a subscription has begun, along with the subscription's expiration.

RenewResponse: Sent by the event source in response to a request to renew a subscription, this message indicates whether or not the subscription was renewed; if so, a new expiration value is provided.

GetStatusResponse: Sent by the event source in response to a request to get the status of a subscription.

UnsubscripeResponse: Sent by the event source in response to a request to terminate a current subscription.

A typical event notification is sent as a SOAP message, as illustrated by the example in Listing 7.7. The action in this case is defined by the event itself. Each notification contains the URI of the event destination, the subscriber's subscription number, and a unique message identifier.

LISTING 7.7 An Event Notification SOAP Message

```
<s12:Envelope
  xmlns:s12="http://www.w3.org/2003/05/soap-envelope"
  xmlns:wsa="http://schemas.xmlsoap.org/ws/2004/08/addressing"
  xmlns:ew="http://yourservice.com/quotes"
  xmlns:ow="http://myservice.com">
  <s12:Header>
    <wsa:Action>http://.../QuoteUpdate</wsa:Action>
    <wsa:MessageID>uuid:...</wsa:MessageID>
    <wsa:To>http://myservice.com/OnQuoteUpdate</wsa:To>
    <ew:MySubscription>120</ew:MySubscription>
    <ow:EventTopics>stock.quote.update</ow:EventTopics>
  </s12:Header>
  <s12:Body>
    <ow:QuoteUpdate>
      <ow:Symbol>SUNW</ow:Symbol>
      <ow:Last>3.93</ow:Last>
      <ow:Volume>20993320</ow:Volume>
      <ow:Time>13:23</ow:Time>
    </ow:QuoteUpdate>
  </s12:Body>
</s12:Envelope>
```

In addition to events that are sent during the normal operation of a Web Service, faults may be sent because of error conditions. Each fault message must contain the following information:

Code: This is the general error category code for which the fault applies, such as to indicate that a network error has occurred.

Subcode: A more specific error, under the category specified in the fault code, such as to indicate that a network peer is unavailable.

Reason: A locale-specific text reason for the fault, such as "The peer Web Service for quote data is unavailable."

Detail: An optional field to indicate specific details about the fault, such as "The peer node addressed 10.1.32.2 is not responding to requests on port 80."

The WS-Eventing specification suggests that Web Service event notification security be implemented by complying with the WS-Security specification, which is discussed later in this chapter.

Namespace and Schema

You can examine the full WS-Eventing specification and XML schema to gain a complete understanding of the XML message structures required. The standard XML namespace and schema for the WS-Eventing specification is available at *http://schemas.xmlsoap.org/ws/2004/08/eventing/* (see Listing 7.8), and the WSDL document is available at *http://schemas.xmlsoap.org/ws/2004/08/eventing/eventing.wsdl* (see Listing 7.9). The full copyright notice for the schema and WSDL is the same as the one shown in Listing 7.5.

LISTING 7.8   The WS-Eventing XML Schema and Namespace

```
<?xml version="1.0" encoding="UTF-8" ?>
<!--
(c) 2004 BEA Systems Inc., International Business Machines
Corporation, Microsoft Corporation, Inc, Sun Microsystems,
Inc, and TIBCO Software Inc. All rights reserved.
FOR THE FULL COPYRIGHT, SEE LISTING 7.5 IN THIS CHAPTER
-->
<xs:schema
  targetNamespace="http://schemas.xmlsoap.org/ws/2004/08/eventing"
  xmlns:tns="http://schemas.xmlsoap.org/ws/2004/08/eventing"
  xmlns:wsa="http://schemas.xmlsoap.org/ws/2004/08/addressing"
  xmlns:xs="http://www.w3.org/2001/XMLSchema"
  elementFormDefault="qualified"
  blockDefault="#all">
```

```
<xs:import
  namespace="http://www.w3.org/XML/1998/namespace"
  schemaLocation="http://www.w3.org/2001/xml.xsd" />
<xs:import
  namespace="http://schemas.xmlsoap.org/ws/2004/08/addressing"
  schemaLocation=.../>

<!-- Types and global elements -->
<xs:complexType name="DeliveryType" mixed="true">
  <xs:sequence>
    <xs:any namespace="##any" processContents="lax"
      minOccurs="0" maxOccurs="unbounded" />
  </xs:sequence>
  <xs:attribute name="Mode" type="xs:anyURI" use="optional" />
  <xs:anyAttribute namespace="##other" processContents="lax" />
</xs:complexType>

<xs:element name="NotifyTo" type="wsa:EndpointReferenceType" />

<xs:simpleType name="NonNegativeDurationType">
  <xs:restriction base="xs:duration">
    <xs:minInclusive value="POYOMODTOHOMOS" />
  </xs:restriction>
</xs:simpleType>

<xs:simpleType name="ExpirationType">
    <xs:union memberTypes="xs:dateTime
      tns:NonNegativeDurationType" />
</xs:simpleType>

<xs:complexType name="FilterType" mixed="true">
  <xs:sequence>
    <xs:any namespace="##other" processContents="lax"
      minOccurs="0" maxOccurs="unbounded" />
  </xs:sequence>
  <xs:attribute name="Dialect" type="xs:anyURI" use="optional"/>
  <xs:anyAttribute namespace="##other" processContents="lax"/>
</xs:complexType>

<xs:complexType name="LanguageSpecificStringType">
  <xs:simpleContent>
    <xs:extension base="xs:string">
      <xs:attribute ref="xml:lang" />
      <xs:anyAttribute namespace="##other"
```

```
            processContents="lax" />
      </xs:extension>
    </xs:simpleContent>
</xs:complexType>

<!-- Subscribe request -->
<xs:element name="Subscribe">
  <xs:complexType>
    <xs:sequence>
      <xs:element name="EndTo" type="wsa:EndpointReferenceType"
         minOccurs="0" />
      <xs:element name="Delivery" type="tns:DeliveryType" />
      <xs:element name="Expires" type="tns:ExpirationType"
         minOccurs="0" />
      <xs:element name="Filter" type="tns:FilterType"
         minOccurs="0" />
      <xs:any namespace="##other" processContents="lax"
         minOccurs="0" maxOccurs="unbounded" />
    </xs:sequence>
    <xs:anyAttribute namespace="##other" processContents="lax"/>
  </xs:complexType>
</xs:element>

<xs:element name="Identifier" type="xs:anyURI" />

<!-- Subscribe response -->
<xs:element name="SubscribeResponse">
  <xs:complexType>
    <xs:sequence>
    <xs:element name="SubscriptionManager"
                type="wsa:EndpointReferenceType" />
      <xs:element name="Expires" type="tns:ExpirationType"/>
      <xs:any namespace="##other" processContents="lax"
        minOccurs="0" maxOccurs="unbounded" />
    </xs:sequence>
    <xs:anyAttribute namespace="##other" processContents="lax"/>
  </xs:complexType>
</xs:element>

<!-- Used in a fault if there's an unsupported dialect -->
<xs:element name="SupportedDialect" type="xs:anyURI" />

<!-- Used in a fault if there's an unsupported delivery mode-->
<xs:element name="SupportedDeliveryMode" type="xs:anyURI" />
```

```xml
<!-- Renew request -->
<xs:element name="Renew">
  <xs:complexType>
    <xs:sequence>
      <xs:element name="Expires" type="tns:ExpirationType"
        minOccurs="0" />
      <xs:any namespace="##other" processContents="lax"
        minOccurs="0" maxOccurs="unbounded" />
    </xs:sequence>
    <xs:anyAttribute namespace="##other" processContents="lax"/>
  </xs:complexType>
</xs:element>

<!-- Renew response -->
<xs:element name="RenewResponse">
  <xs:complexType>
    <xs:sequence>
      <xs:element name="Expires" type="tns:ExpirationType"
        minOccurs="0" />
      <xs:any namespace="##other" processContents="lax"
        minOccurs="0" maxOccurs="unbounded" />
    </xs:sequence>
    <xs:anyAttribute namespace="##other" processContents="lax"/>
  </xs:complexType>
</xs:element>

<!-- GetStatus request -->
<xs:element name="GetStatus">
  <xs:complexType>
    <xs:sequence>
      <xs:any namespace="##other" processContents="lax"
        minOccurs="0" maxOccurs="unbounded" />
    </xs:sequence>
    <xs:anyAttribute namespace="##other" processContents="lax"/>
  </xs:complexType>
</xs:element>

<!-- GetStatus response -->
<xs:element name="GetStatusResponse">
  <xs:complexType>
    <xs:sequence>
      <xs:element name="Expires" type="tns:ExpirationType"
        minOccurs="0" />
      <xs:any namespace="##other" processContents="lax"
```

```
          minOccurs="0" maxOccurs="unbounded" />
      </xs:sequence>
      <xs:anyAttribute namespace="##other" processContents="lax"/>
    </xs:complexType>
</xs:element>

<!-- Unsubscribe request -->
<xs:element name="Unsubscribe">
  <xs:complexType>
    <xs:sequence>
      <xs:any namespace="##other" processContents="lax"
        minOccurs="0" maxOccurs="unbounded" />
    </xs:sequence>
    <xs:anyAttribute namespace="##other" processContents="lax"/>
  </xs:complexType>
</xs:element>

<!-- count(/s:Envelope/s:Body/*) = 0 for Unsubscribe response-->

<!-- SubscriptionEnd message -->
<xs:element name="SubscriptionEnd">
  <xs:complexType>
    <xs:sequence>
      <xs:element name="SubscriptionManager"
                  type="wsa:EndpointReferenceType" />
      <xs:element name="Status"
        type="tns:OpenSubscriptionEndCodeType"/>
      <xs:element name="Reason"
        type="tns:LanguageSpecificStringType"
        minOccurs="0" maxOccurs="unbounded" />
      <xs:any namespace="##other" processContents="lax"
        minOccurs="0" maxOccurs="unbounded" />
    </xs:sequence>
    <xs:anyAttribute namespace="##other" processContents="lax"/>
  </xs:complexType>
</xs:element>

<xs:simpleType name="SubscriptionEndCodeType">
  <xs:restriction base="xs:anyURI">
    <xs:enumeration value="http://.../DeliveryFailure"/>
    <xs:enumeration value="http://.../SourceShuttingDown"/>
    <xs:enumeration value="http://.../SourceCancelling"/>
  </xs:restriction>
</xs:simpleType>
```

```
          <xs:simpleType name="OpenSubscriptionEndCodeType">
            <xs:union
              memberTypes="tns:SubscriptionEndCodeType xs:anyURI"/>
          </xs:simpleType>


          <xs:attribute name="EventSource" type="xs:boolean" />


        </xs:schema>
```

LISTING 7.9   The WS-Eventing WSDL Document

```
<?xml version="1.0" encoding="UTF-8"?>
<!--
(c) 2001-2004 BEA Systems, International Business Machines
Corporation, Microsoft Corporation, Inc. All rights reserved.
FOR THE FULL COPYRIGHT, SEE LISTING 7.5 IN THIS CHAPTER
-->
<wsdl:definitions
  targetNamespace='http://schemas.xmlsoap.org/ws/2004/08/eventing'
  xmlns:wse='http://schemas.xmlsoap.org/ws/2004/08/eventing'
  xmlns:wsdl='http://schemas.xmlsoap.org/wsdl/'
  xmlns:xs='http://www.w3.org/2001/XMLSchema' >

  <wsdl:types>
    <xs:schema
      targetNamespace='http://...eventing'>
      <xs:include schemaLocation='eventing.xsd' />
    </xs:schema>
  </wsdl:types>

  <wsdl:message name='SubscribeMsg' >
    <wsdl:part name='body' element='wse:Subscribe' />
  </wsdl:message>
  <wsdl:message name='SubscribeResponseMsg' >
    <wsdl:part name='body' element='wse:SubscribeResponse' />
  </wsdl:message>

  <wsdl:message name='RenewMsg' >
    <wsdl:part name='body' element='wse:Renew' />
  </wsdl:message>
  <wsdl:message name='RenewResponseMsg' >
    <wsdl:part name='body' element='wse:RenewResponse' />
  </wsdl:message>
```

```
<wsdl:message name='GetStatusMsg' >
  <wsdl:part name='body' element='wse:GetStatus' />
</wsdl:message>
<wsdl:message name='GetStatusResponseMsg' >
  <wsdl:part name='body' element='wse:GetStatusResponse' />
</wsdl:message>

<wsdl:message name='UnsubscribeMsg' >
  <wsdl:part name='body' element='wse:Unsubscribe' />
</wsdl:message>
<wsdl:message name='UnsubscribeResponseMsg' />

<wsdl:message name='SubscriptionEnd' >
  <wsdl:part name='body' element='wse:SubscriptionEnd' />
</wsdl:message>

<wsdl:portType name='EventSource' >
  <wsdl:operation name='SubscribeOp' >
    <wsdl:input message='wse:SubscribeMsg' />
    <wsdl:output message='wse:SubscribeResponseMsg' />
  </wsdl:operation>
  <wsdl:operation name='SubscriptionEnd' >
    <wsdl:output message='wse:SubscriptionEnd' />
  </wsdl:operation>
</wsdl:portType>

<wsdl:portType name='SubscriptionManager' >
  <wsdl:operation name='RenewOp' >
    <wsdl:input message='wse:RenewMsg' />
    <wsdl:output message='wse:RenewResponseMsg' />
  </wsdl:operation>
  <wsdl:operation name='GetStatusOp' >
    <wsdl:input message='wse:GetStatusMsg' />
    <wsdl:output message='wse:GetStatusResponseMsg' />
  </wsdl:operation>
  <wsdl:operation name='UnsubscribeOp' >
    <wsdl:input message='wse:UnsubscribeMsg' />
    <wsdl:output message='wse:UnsubscribeResponseMsg' />
  </wsdl:operation>
</wsdl:portType>
</wsdl:definitions>
```

COORDINATION

The *WS-Coordination* specification defines an extensible framework for coordinating activities using a coordinator and a set of coordination protocols. This framework enables participants to reach consistent agreement on the outcome of distributed activities. The coordination protocols that can be defined in this framework can accommodate a wide variety of activities, including protocols for simple short-lived operations and protocols for complex long-lived business activities [Cabrera04].

As stated in previous chapters, component dependencies translate directly into complexity. As you build software that depends on Web Services, and those Web Services are built to depend on other services, the complexities grow quickly. The need to coordinate and control the activities implemented using this potentially intricate web of services is growing each day, as more Web Services are built, deployed, and used globally. The WS-Coordination specification describes a means to build software that can control these activities, called a *coordination service*. The coordination service supports operations that allow clients to create new coordination contexts (for some distributed activity), and that allow other clients to participate in that activity by registering for the coordination context.

NOTE

Although the terms and definitions used in the description of the coordination protocol may seem very formal and rigid, the WS-Coordination specification is really quite straightforward. The sole intent of the protocol is to make sure all parties in a distributed operation (activity) are known, that their processing occurs when it should, and that their state is known at each step of the operation. Providing awareness of these pieces of information to all components in the operation at each step allows them to work around problems and be more resilient to the numerous problems that can plague distributed software.

Coordination Context

A *coordination context* is an abstract piece of information describing a business activity that is to be coordinated. The context itself is an XML document that contains the URI for the context registration service (which clients use to join the activity), the type of coordination that is performed, and any other extensions to the standard coordination context XML schema required. Each message that is sent as part of the activity must include a valid coordination context for that activity.

Activation Service

A new business activity is started when a Web Service sends a `CreateCoordination Context` message to an activation service implementation (see Listing 7.10). The request can be very simple and mainly specifies an activity as a coordination type. The result is that a new coordination context for the activity is created, and a CreateCoordinationContextResponse message is sent back. The response that is sent back contains a coordination context with the same coordination type, a unique identifier, and the URI of the registration service that is used to join the activity.

LISTING 7.10   A Sample CreateCoordinationContext **Message**

```
<CreateCoordinationContext>
    <CoordinationType>
        http://myservice/coordType
    </CoordinationType>
</CreateCoordinationContext>
```

Registration Service

Once a Web Service has obtained its coordination context, it can take part in the activity when it registers itself with a registration service. The requesting Web Service first sends a Register message with its coordination context information, along with the URI of its activity-specific message handler, called the protocol-specific endpoint reference. This is really just a URI to the software that can handle the SOAP messages that make up the distributed operation. The registration service should respond with a RegistrationResponse message, which provides its own protocol-specific endpoint reference. Both sides of the activity are now ready to participate in an activity, as defined by the coordination context.

What happens next is application specific but generally involves sending SOAP messages to and from the remote Web Services that are part of the coordinated activity. The entire process may be governed by policies, as implemented to the WS-Policy specification, and rights checking, as implemented to the WS-Trust and WS-SecureConversation specifications. Further security for the activity and message integrity is suggested to be implemented according to the WS-Security specification, discussed in the next section.

Namespace and Schema

You can examine the full WS-Coordination specification and XML schema to gain a complete understanding of the XML message structures required. The standard XML namespace and schema for the WS-Coordination specification is available at *http://schemas.xmlsoap.org/ws/2004/10/wscoor/wscoor.xsd* (see Listing 7.11), and the WSDL document is available at *http://schemas.xmlsoap.org/ws/2004/10/wscoor/ wscoor.wsdl* (see Listing 7.12). The full copyright notice for the schema and WSDL is the same as the one shown in Listing 7.5 earlier in this chapter.

LISTING 7.11 The WS-Coordination XML Schema and Namespace

```xml
<?xml version="1.0" encoding="UTF-8"?>
<!--
(c) 2001-2004 BEA Systems, International Business Machines
Corporation, Microsoft Corporation, Inc. All rights reserved.
FOR THE FULL COPYRIGHT, SEE LISTING 7.5 IN THIS CHAPTER
-->
<xsd:schema
  targetNamespace="http://schemas.xmlsoap.org/ws/2004/10/wscoor"
  xmlns:wsa="http://schemas.xmlsoap.org/ws/2004/08/addressing"
  xmlns:wscoor="http://schemas.xmlsoap.org/ws/2004/10/wscoor"
  xmlns:xsd="http://www.w3.org/2001/XMLSchema"
  elementFormDefault="qualified"
  attributeFormDefault="unqualified" version="1.0">

  <xsd:import
    namespace="http://schemas.xmlsoap.org/ws/2004/08/addressing"
    schemaLocation="http://.../addressing"/>

  <xsd:element name="Expires">
    <xsd:complexType>
      <xsd:simpleContent>
        <xsd:extension base="xsd:unsignedInt">
          <xsd:anyAttribute namespace="##other"/>
        </xsd:extension>
      </xsd:simpleContent>
    </xsd:complexType>
  </xsd:element>

  <xsd:complexType name="CoordinationContextType">
    <xsd:sequence>
      <xsd:element name="Identifier">
        <xsd:complexType>
          <xsd:simpleContent>
            <xsd:extension base="xsd:anyURI">
              <xsd:anyAttribute namespace="##other"/>
            </xsd:extension>
          </xsd:simpleContent>
        </xsd:complexType>
      </xsd:element>
      <xsd:element ref="wscoor:Expires" minOccurs="0"/>
      <xsd:element name="CoordinationType" type="xsd:anyURI"/>
      <xsd:element name="RegistrationService"
```

```
          type="wsa:EndpointReferenceType"/>
    </xsd:sequence>
</xsd:complexType>

<xsd:element name="CoordinationContext">
  <xsd:complexType>
    <xsd:complexContent>
      <xsd:extension base="wscoor:CoordinationContextType">
        <xsd:sequence>
          <xsd:any namespace="##other" processContents="lax"
            minOccurs="0" maxOccurs="unbounded"/>
        </xsd:sequence>
      </xsd:extension>
    </xsd:complexContent>
  </xsd:complexType>
</xsd:element>

<xsd:complexType name="CreateCoordinationContextType">
  <xsd:sequence>
    <xsd:element ref="wscoor:Expires" minOccurs="0"/>
    <xsd:element name="CurrentContext" minOccurs="0">
      <xsd:complexType>
        <xsd:complexContent>
          <xsd:extension base="wscoor:CoordinationContextType">
            <xsd:sequence>
              <xsd:any namespace="##other" processContents="lax"
                minOccurs="0" maxOccurs="unbounded"/>
            </xsd:sequence>
          </xsd:extension>
        </xsd:complexContent>
      </xsd:complexType>
    </xsd:element>
    <xsd:element name="CoordinationType" type="xsd:anyURI"/>
    <xsd:any namespace="##any" processContents="lax"
      minOccurs="0" maxOccurs="unbounded"/>
  </xsd:sequence>
  <xsd:anyAttribute namespace="##other" processContents="lax"/>
</xsd:complexType>

<xsd:element name="CreateCoordinationContext"
  type="wscoor:CreateCoordinationContextType"/>
<xsd:complexType name="CreateCoordinationContextResponseType">
  <xsd:sequence>
    <xsd:element ref="wscoor:CoordinationContext"/>
```

```xsd
      <xsd:any namespace="##other" processContents="lax"
        minOccurs="0" maxOccurs="unbounded"/>
    </xsd:sequence>
    <xsd:anyAttribute namespace="##other" processContents="lax"/>
  </xsd:complexType>

  <xsd:element name="CreateCoordinationContextResponse"
    type="wscoor:CreateCoordinationContextResponseType"/>
  <xsd:complexType name="RegisterType">
    <xsd:sequence>
      <xsd:element name="ProtocolIdentifier" type="xsd:anyURI"/>
      <xsd:element name="ParticipantProtocolService"
        type="wsa:EndpointReferenceType"/>
      <xsd:any namespace="##any" processContents="lax"
        minOccurs="0" maxOccurs="unbounded"/>
    </xsd:sequence>
    <xsd:anyAttribute namespace="##other" processContents="lax"/>
  </xsd:complexType>

  <xsd:element name="Register" type="wscoor:RegisterType"/>
  <xsd:complexType name="RegisterResponseType">
    <xsd:sequence>
      <xsd:element name="CoordinatorProtocolService"
        type="wsa:EndpointReferenceType"/>
      <xsd:any namespace="##any" processContents="lax"
        minOccurs="0" maxOccurs="unbounded"/>
    </xsd:sequence>
    <xsd:anyAttribute namespace="##other" processContents="lax"/>
  </xsd:complexType>

  <xsd:element name="RegisterResponse"
    type="wscoor:RegisterResponseType"/>
  <xsd:simpleType name="ErrorCodes">
    <xsd:restriction base="xsd:QName">
      <xsd:enumeration value="wscoor:AlreadyRegistered"/>
      <xsd:enumeration value="wscoor:InvalidState"/>
      <xsd:enumeration value="wscoor:InvalidProtocol"/>
      <xsd:enumeration value="wscoor:NoActivity"/>
      <xsd:enumeration value="wscoor:InvalidCreateParameters"/>
    </xsd:restriction>
  </xsd:simpleType>
</xsd:schema>
```

LISTING 7.12   The WS-Coordination WSDL Document

```
<?xml version="1.0" encoding="utf-8"?>
<!--
(c) 2004 BEA Systems Inc., International Business Machines
Corporation, Microsoft Corporation, Inc, Sun Microsystems,
Inc, and TIBCO Software Inc. All rights reserved.
FOR THE FULL COPYRIGHT, SEE LISTING 7.5 IN THIS CHAPTER
-->
<wsdl:definitions
  xmlns:wsdl="http://schemas.xmlsoap.org/wsdl/"
  xmlns:soap="http://schemas.xmlsoap.org/wsdl/soap/"
  xmlns:xs="http://www.w3.org/2001/XMLSchema"
  xmlns:wsa="http://schemas.xmlsoap.org/ws/2004/08/addressing"
  xmlns:wscoor="http://schemas.xmlsoap.org/ws/2004/10/wscoor"
  targetNamespace="http://schemas.xmlsoap.org/ws/2004/10/wscoor">
    <wsdl:types>
      <xs:schema>
        <xs:import
          namespace='http://...addressing'
          schemaLocation='http://...addressing' />
        <xs:import
          namespace='http://schemas.xmlsoap.org/ws/2004/10/wscoor'
          schemaLocation='http://.../wscoor'/>
      </xs:schema>
    </wsdl:types>

  <!-- Messages -->
  <wsdl:message name="CreateCoordinationContext">
    <wsdl:part name="parameters"
      element="wscoor:CreateCoordinationContext"/>
  </wsdl:message>

  <wsdl:message name="CreateCoordinationContextResponse">
    <wsdl:part name="parameters"
      element="wscoor:CreateCoordinationContextResponse"/>
  </wsdl:message>

  <wsdl:message name="Register">
    <wsdl:part name="parameters" element="wscoor:Register"/>
  </wsdl:message>
```

```
<wsdl:message name="RegisterResponse">
  <wsdl:part name="parameters"
    element="wscoor:RegisterResponse"/>
</wsdl:message>

<!-- Manditory Asyncronous PortTypes -->
<wsdl:portType name="ActivationCoordinatorPortType">
  <wsdl:operation name="CreateCoordinationContextOperation">
    <wsdl:input message="wscoor:CreateCoordinationContext"
      wsa:Action="http://.../wscoor/CreateCoordinationContext"/>
  </wsdl:operation>
</wsdl:portType>

<wsdl:portType name="ActivationRequesterPortType">
  <wsdl:operation
    name="CreateCoordinationContextResponseOperation">
    <wsdl:input
    message="wscoor:CreateCoordinationContextResponse"
    wsa:Action=".../wscoor/CreateCoordinationContextResponse"/>
  </wsdl:operation>
</wsdl:portType>

<wsdl:portType name="RegistrationCoordinatorPortType">
  <wsdl:operation name="RegisterOperation">
    <wsdl:input message="wscoor:Register"
      wsa:Action="http://.../wscoor/Register"/>
  </wsdl:operation>
</wsdl:portType>

<wsdl:portType name="RegistrationRequesterPortType">
  <wsdl:operation name="RegisterResponseOperation">
    <wsdl:input message="wscoor:RegisterResponse"
      wsa:Action="http://.../wscoor/RegisterResponse"/>
  </wsdl:operation>
</wsdl:portType>

<!-- Optional Syncronous RPC Port Types -->
<wsdl:portType name="ActivationPortTypeRPC">
  <wsdl:operation name="CreateCoordinationContextOperation">
    <wsdl:input message="wscoor:CreateCoordinationContext"
      wsa:Action="http://.../wscoor/CreateCoordinationContext"/>
    <wsdl:output
```

```
        message="wscoor:CreateCoordinationContextResponse"
        wsa:Action=".../wscoor/CreateCoordinationContextResponse"/>
    </wsdl:operation>
  </wsdl:portType>

  <wsdl:portType name="RegistrationPortTypeRPC">
    <wsdl:operation name="RegisterOperation">
      <wsdl:input message="wscoor:Register"
        wsa:Action="http://.../wscoor/Register"/>
      <wsdl:output message="wscoor:RegisterResponse"
        wsa:Action="http://.../wscoor/RegisterResponse"/>
    </wsdl:operation>
  </wsdl:portType>
</wsdl:definitions>
```

SECURITY

The *WS-Security* specification is flexible and is designed to be used as the basis for the construction of a wide variety of security models including public key infrastructure (PKI), Kerberos, and Secure Sockets Layer (SSL). WS-Security provides support for multiple security tokens, multiple trust domains, multiple signature formats, and multiple encryption technologies. This specification provides three main mechanisms: security token propagation, message integrity, and message confidentiality. WS-Security is a building block that can be used in conjunction with extensions and application-specific protocols to accommodate a wide variety of security models and encryption technologies [Atkinson02].

The primary concerns of WS-Security are to protect message integrity and to limit who can acquire and read the messages sent to and from Web Services. This is mainly implemented through the encryption of either the entire message or just through its body and/or attachments along with digital signatures that serve as checksums for the message's contents. Security information is placed within a SOAP message's header through the addition of one or more <Security> elements. The number of these elements generally matches the number of intended message receivers. Only one <Security> element instance may exist with the s:actor attribute, which indicates the ultimate receiver of the message.

The specification provides support for user authentication via the <Username Token> element, which contains a user's username and password information (see Listing 7.13). Of course, you will only want to include password information when using a secure protocol for communication, such as HTTPS.

LISTING 7.13   The WS-Security `UsernameToken` **Element**

```
<wsse:UsernameToken Id="ServiceUser">
    <wsse:Username>joeuser</Username>
    <wsse:Password wsse:Type="PasswordText">
     joespassword
    </wsse:Password>
</wsse:UsernameToken>
```

Security tokens can be added in XML form or can be in binary form for others such as Kerberos tickets. For binary security tokens, the encoding type and the name of the binary standard (the value type) must be included. For custom binary types and support for future binary standards, the `<ds:KeyInfo>` element is used to access the key.

As stated earlier in this section, the messages can be signed to ensure they were not altered somewhere between the sender and receiver. This is achieved with the addition of a `<sd:Signature>` element within the `<Security>` element in the message's header. Additionally, multiple signatures can be added to various parts of the message.

For message encryption, a `<xenc:ReferenceList>` element is added as meta-data about the various portions of the message that are encrypted. Each encrypted portion of the message must contain an `<xenc:EncryptedData>` element indicating that it is encrypted, along with information about the encryption algorithm used. Each encrypted portion of the message should also have a matching `<xenc:EncryptedKey>` element, referenced within the `<xenc:ReferenceList>` element.

Namespace and Schema

You can examine the full WS-Security specification and XML schema to gain a complete understanding of the XML message structures required. The standard XML namespace and schema for the WS-Security specification is available at *http://schemas.xmlsoap.org/ws/2002/04/secext/secext.xsd*.

SUMMARY

This chapter described some of the latest specifications for Web Services related to messaging and coordination. These specifications represent some of the latest trends in distributed application development, and it is suggested that you have at least a cursory understanding of those presented here and as many of the total specifications available as possible.

8

The Java Web Service Developer Pack (JWSDP)

In This Chapter

- Java API for XML Parsing (JAXP)
- Java API for XML Binding (JAXB)
- Java API for XML Messaging (JAXM)
- SOAP with Attachments API for Java (SAAJ)
- Java API for XML-Based Web Services (JAX-WS, formerly JAX-RPC)
- Java API for XML Registry (JAXR)

J ava has long been the leading choice for Web application development. Sun positioned Java as a powerful platform with which to build Web Services when it introduced the Java Web Service Developer Pack (JWSDP) two years ago. Now at version 1.5, the JWSDP provides all of the APIs, tools, and infrastructure needed to build Web Services that support the following important standards [Sun04]:

- SOAP with attachments
- Web Services Description Language (WSDL)
- Universal Description, Discovery, and Integration registry (UDDI)
- Web Services Interoperability (WS-I)
- Web Services Security (WSS); and XWS-Security
- Security Assertion Markup Language (SAML)
- XML Digital Signatures

ON THE CD

You can find the latest JWSDP software downloads at *http://java.sun.com/ webservices/index.jsp*, as well on the CD-ROM in the folder named java/jwsdp. There are download bundles available for Sun's J2EE 1.4–compatible application server, Sun's Java Web Server, and Apache's Tomcat Web Server/Servlet container. The bundle that includes the Tomcat container, which is an open source project from Apache-Jakarta (*http://jakarta.apache.org/tomcat/*), is included on the CD-ROM and was used in the development of this chapter's sample applications. It's free, it works well, and it's available on many platforms.

The JWSDP integrates XML parsing using JAXP, XML to Java binding using JAXB, WSDL and low-level SOAP messaging using JAX-WS, UDDI using JAXR, and high-level SOAP messaging with attachments using SAAJ. It also includes the Sun Java streaming XML parser and the JWSDP Registry Server. This chapter will provide a working overview of JWSDP; it should be enough to get you started using the main components to build Web Services, and applications that use Web Services. It is not meant as a replacement or a duplication of the specifications or Javadocs for the libraries that the JWSDP contains. Instead, this chapter will walk you through the important parts of the specifications, and it will use small sample applications (in the context of the book's online trading system application) to illustrate usage.

JAVA API FOR XML PROCESSING (JAXP)

You can parse XML from your Java code using either an event-based, callback model with the *Simple API for XML Parsing* (SAX) or you can traverse it using an object-model via the *Document Object Model* (DOM). SAX and DOM parsers are available from multiple sources, such as Microsoft (*http://msdn.microsoft.com/XML/XMLDownloads/default.aspx*), Apache (*http://xml.apache.org*), and others. Most application servers come with their own implementations of these parsers. *JAXP* is a thin abstraction layer (defined by the javax.xml.parsers package) on top of the SAX, DOM, and XSLT APIs that allows you to write vendor-neutral code, leaving your choice of parser as a configuration option, not a code change. It accomplishes this by providing a *pluggability layer* of vendor-neutral factory objects to retrieve instances of a SAX or DOM parser from any provider. You can also plug in *eXtensible Stylesheet Language* (XSL) processors into your code to transform XML data into other XML formats or HTML for display purposes. JAXP has built-in support for document type definition (DTD) definitions and XML namespaces, along with XML validation operations.

SAX provides an event-based paradigm for traversing XML. With SAX, the given XML is traversed sequentially in its entirety, from top to bottom. As the XML is processed, methods are called on your class that provide information for each node, its attributes, and data, in the order they appear in the XML. With SAX, you must traverse an entire document, even if you are only interested in a portion of it. DOM parsing provides an alternative to SAX, allowing your code to locate a specific node in an XML document while ignoring the rest. The DOM also supports creating XML documents within your code, which you can serialize as a file on disk.

Although these two features make DOM parsing seem much more appealing than SAX processing, they come with a price. DOM parsing typically uses more memory and time to process XML, as it must create an object hierarchy in memory for the entire XML document before your application can use it. If the XML you are parsing is particularly large, this may not be an option. In most cases, however, DOM parsing is the most efficient and useful way of working with XML in an application. This is especially true if your application needs to create XML documents from its own generated data.

The Simple API for XML Processing (SAX)

JAXP uses the org.xml.sax package to define all of the SAX-related classes and interfaces. As mentioned in the previous section, SAX defines an event-based paradigm, where callback methods are called on an application's implementing class. The classes and interfaces that make up SAX are straightforward and relatively easy to use (see Figure 8.1). To parse an XML document using SAX, an application first creates an instance of the SAXParserFactory class (see Listing 8.1).

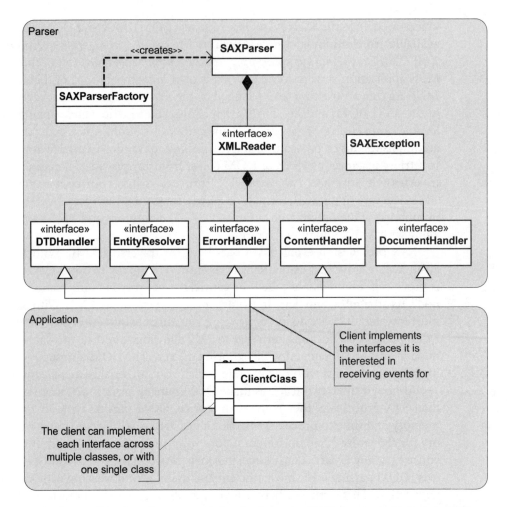

FIGURE 8.1 This class diagram contains the important SAX classes and interfaces with which to write a client application.

The factory is used to create an instance of the SAXParser class that does all the work as it validates and parses the document and then calls the client application's callback methods. In this example, validation is turned off, resulting in slightly faster parse performance. Of course, the risk is that errors can occur if the XML is not structured the way your application requires it. Next, the XMLReader object is retrieved, and the classes that implement the ContentHandler and ErrorHandler interfaces are provided. In this case, they are both implemented by the class MyXmlClass. Next, the file that contains the XML to parse is opened and provided to the XMLReader object to begin the parsing process. As the XML is parsed, the appropriate callback method implementations will be called as the matching XML structures are read.

LISTING 8.1 SAX Code to Parse and Process an XML Document

```
public class MyXmlClass implements ContentHandler, ErrorHandler
{
    public MyXmlClass ( String xmlFilename,
                        TopicFileParserEvents listeners)
    {
        try {
            // create a JAXP SAXParser
            SAXParserFactory spf = SAXParserFactory.newInstance();
            spf.setValidating(false);
            SAXParser parser = spf.newSAXParser();
            XMLReader xmlReader = parser.getXMLReader();
            xmlReader.setContentHandler( this );
            xmlReader.setErrorHandler( this );

            // load from the classpath
            InputStream is =
                getClass().getResourceAsStream(xmlFilename);
            InputSource isource = new InputSource(is);

            // start the parsing process
            xmlReader.parse(isource);
        }
        catch (Exception e) {
            e.printStackTrace();
        }
    }

    // ContentHandler interface implementation
    public void processingInstruction(String target, String data)
        throws SAXException { ... }

    public void startDocument() throws SAXException { ... }

    public void startElement( String namespace, String localName,
        String qName, Attributes atts) throws SAXException { ... }

    public void characters(char[] ch, int start, int end)
        throws SAXException { ... }
```

```
        public void startPrefixMapping(String prefix, String uri)
        { ... }

        public void endPrefixMapping(String prefix)
        { ... }

        public void ignorableWhitespace(char[] ch, int start, int end)
            throws SAXException { ... }

        public void skippedEntity(String name)
            throws SAXException { ... }

        public void endElement( String namespace, String localName,
            String qName) throws SAXException { ... }

        public void endDocument() throws SAXException { ... }

        // ErrorHandler interface implementation
        public void warning(SAXParseException exception) { ... }

        public void error(SAXParseException exception) { ... }

        public void fatalError(SAXParseException exception) { ... }
    }
```

Although you don't have to implement all of the callback interfaces, there are times when you may not want to implement every method even on the ones you do. On those occasions, your application class can extend the `org.xml.sax.helpers.DefaultHandler` class. This class implements all of the interfaces and generally does nothing in its callback method implementations. Your class, however, can override and implement only the methods you need. Even with this helper class, parsing and processing XML documents in a serial, event-driven way may feel unnatural to some. Parsing XML using the DOM is the alternative.

The Document Object Model (DOM)

JAXP uses the `org.w3c.dom` package to define all of the DOM-related classes and interfaces. When an XML document is processed using a DOM parser, the output is an object hierarchy, or tree, in the form of a `Document` object. This object serves as the root of the tree, which contains NODE objects that can be traversed recursively to inspect the contents of the XML. Every object in the DOM tree implements the node interface and can be treated as a node object, including the root `Document` object. Each node contains a list of child node objects, each representing either an XML tag, attribute, value, and so on. This allows you to write one method to recursively traverse the tree and process the contents of the entire XML document. A Unified Modeling Language (UML) class diagram for the Node interface is shown in Figure 8.2.

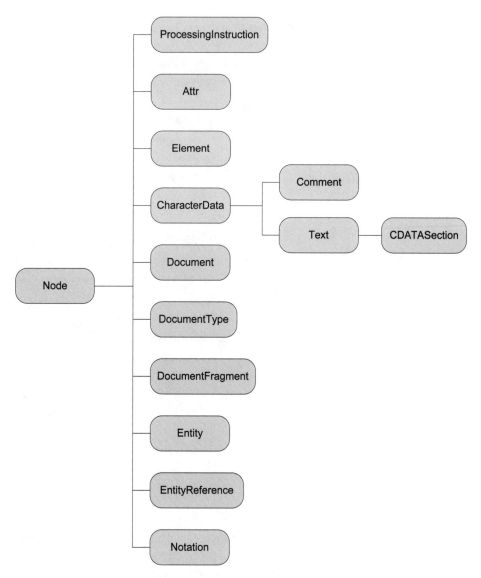

FIGURE 8.2   The UML class diagram for the DOM node interface.

DOM `Node` Types

Every node in a DOM tree has a type, which can be queried. The `NODE` types and their descriptions are listed in Table 8.1. The first node in the tree is always a node of type `DOCUMENT_NODE`, but the most common type encountered is `ELEMENT_NODE`. This `NODE` type and some of the other common types are discussed here.

TABLE 8.1   The Document Object Model `Node` Types

DOM Node Type	Description
TEXT_NODE	The text content within an XML element or attribute Example: `<StockPrice>3.28</StockPrice>`
ATTRIBUTE_NODE	An attribute of an XML element Example: `<Transaction type="buy">`
CDATA_SECTION_NODE	Data that is not to be interpreted as markup
COMMENT_NODE	A comment within the XML Example: `<!-- This is a comment -->`
DOCUMENT_FRAGMENT_NODE	A lightweight `Document` object
DOCUMENT_NODE	The XML `Document` root
DOCUMENT_TYPE_NODE	The XML document type attribute
ELEMENT_NODE	An XML element tag Example: `<Stock>SUNW</Stock>`
ENTITY_NODE	A basic piece of XML data
ENTITY_REFERENCE_NODE	An XML entity reference, which is a substitution for another character Example: `<command>java -cp &lt;classpath&gt;</command>`
NOTATION_NODE	Data
PROCESSING_INSTRUCTION_NODE	Data

The first element `NODE` in the tree is the root node of the parsed XML text. The name of an element `NODE` is the text located within the "<" and ">" characters in the XML. For the XML in Listing 8.2, the root element `NODE` name is `StockTrade`. Traversing the list of child nodes of an element will yield the element's textual content, attributes, and other elements—with their children and so on—if they exist. The

StockTrade element NODE in Listing 8.2 has three child nodes, Company, LastTrade Price, and Quantity, all of which are element NODEs themselves. The Company node does not contain any textual content, but the LastTradePrice element NODE does. Textual content—in this case "3.58"—is identified as having the node type TEXT_NODE. Nodes that represent XML attributes, such as the type attribute of the StockTrade node, have the node type ATTRIBUTE_NODE.

LISTING 8.2   Sample Stock Trade XML

```
<StockTrade type="Buy">
    <Company>
        <Stock>SUNW</Stock>
        <Name>Sun Microsystems, Inc.</Name>
    </Company>
    <LastTradePrice>3.58</LastTradePrice>
    <Quantity>500</Quantity>
</StockTrade>
```

Creating XML Documents

Besides parsing existing XML files, the DOM allows you to create new XML documents and serialize them to disk. This is useful when your application needs to generate an XML response to a request, or even the request itself. In the sample explored in this chapter, a server generates a stock order response after parsing an XML request from a client. Before getting into the details of the code, let's go over the general algorithm for parsing and creating XML using the DOM.

Building a DOM object hierarchy starts with a document factory object. In Java this is the DocumentBuilder object, which allows you to either parse an existing document or create a new document from scratch. First, obtain a reference to this class by calling DOMBuilderFactory.newDocumentBuilder. Next, create a Document object by calling DocumentBuilder.newDocument. The result is a new Document object, which is really a Node object of type DOCUMENT_NODE. The Document object is used to create Element node objects, which can be added as children of other Element nodes via the call appendChild. You have a complete DOM hierarchy when your code has created every element, text, and attribute node it needs and has added each as children of the proper parents.

The DOM can then be serialized to disk using a DOM serializer object. Serialization of the XML begins with a java.io.FileOutputStream object, which specifies the file name. This object is passed into the constructor of a new org.apache.xml. serialize.XMLSerializer object. A call to XMLSerialize.serialize is all it takes to write the XML DOM to a file on disk. The complete process of creating a DOM in Java can be seen in Listing 8.3.

LISTING 8.3   Sample Java Code that Uses a DOM to Create an XML File

```
DocumentBuilderFactory builderFactory =
    DocumentBuilderFactory.newInstance();

builderFactory.setExpandEntityReferences(false);
DocumentBuilder builder = builderFactory.newDocumentBuilder();
Document doc = builder.newDocument();

Node root = doc.createElement("StockPurchase");
doc.appendChild(root);
addElem(doc, root, "Status", "SUCCESS");
addElem(doc, root, "Quantity", quantity);
addElem(doc, root, "Price", price);

String filename = GetFilename();
FileOutputStream fos
    = new FileOutputStream("\\myFiles\\"+filename);

XMLSerializer out = new XMLSerializer( fos, null );
out.serialize(doc);
```

Traversing the DOM

Parsing an existing XML file in Java is straightforward. First, obtain a DOMBuilder object by calling createDOMBuilder on the DOMImplementation class. Next, call the DOMBuilder.parseURI method to parse the document, passing in the file name and path in URI format. For instance, to parse the file myDocument.xml, in the folder \myFiles, the URI is *file:///myFiles/MyDocument.xml*. Listing 8.4 contains the Java code for parsing an XML file. After creating a DOMParser object, the specified XML file is processed by calling the parse method. Calling DOMParser.getDocument returns the Document object.

LISTING 8.4   Java Code to Parse an XML File

```
// Create a DOMParser
DOMParser parser = new DOMParser();
// Parse the specified file
parser.parse("/myFiles/myDocument.xml");
Document doc = parser.getDocument();
NodeList nodes = doc.getChildNodes();
// ...
```

To traverse the DOM, your Java code must iterate recursively through the document elements. Starting with the root element, each element's type is checked and child elements are retrieved. The process continues up the tree until the elements needed are found and their values are retrieved. Listing 8.5 shows the Java code to iterate through the DOM, searching for the XML element StockPrice. The name of each child node of the root element is compared to the text "StockPrice." This is done by first calling DOMNode::GetFirstSibling, then GetNextSibling, in a loop. When the matching element has been found, its child nodes are retrieved and iterated through. In this case, the code is searching for the textual contents of the StockPrice node; therefore, it is searching for an element of type TEXT_NODE. Once found, the content is retrieved via a call to getNodeValue on the text node.

LISTING 8.5   Java Code to Traverse DOM-Parsed XML

```
// Start with the root element
Element elem = doc.getDocumentElement();

// Iterate through the child elements
Node child = elem.getFirstChild()
while ( child != null )
{
    // Look for the "StockPrice" element
    if ( node.getNodeName().equalsIgnoreCase( "StockPrice" ) )
    {
        // Found the element, now go through its
        // children and find the text value
        NodeList childNodes = node.getChildNodes();
        for (int y = 0;
             y < childNodes.getLength();
             y++ )
        {
            Node data = childNodes.item(y);
            if ( data.getNodeType() == Node.TEXT_NODE )
                return data.getNodeValue();
        }
    }

    child = child.getNextSibling();
}

// ...
```

The sample code and applications used in this book often contain helper methods to make it easier to work with the DOM, and to eliminate redundant code. For example, the getNode method shown in Listing 8.6 returns the DOM Node object for the tag name provided, within the document represented by the Iterator object, also provided. This object can then be used to get the element's attributes, text value, or children Node objects if they are part of a larger hierarchy.

LISTING 8.6 A Helper Method to Return a DOM Node Object

```
protected Element getNode(String tagName, Iterator iter )
{
    try {
        while ( iter.hasNext() )
        {
            Element node = (Element)iter.next();
            if ( node.getNodeName().equalsIgnoreCase(tagName) )
                return node;
        }
    }
    catch ( Exception e ) {
        e.printStackTrace();
    }

    return null;
}
```

In cases where your application simply wants to retrieve an element's text value, the getNodeValue method shown in Listing 8.7 returns it when provided with the element's tag name and a Node tree to search within.

LISTING 8.7 A Helper Method to Return a DOM Node Object's Text Value

```
protected String getNodeValue(String elementName, NodeList nodes )
{
    try {
        // Iterate through all of the nodes in the list.
        // The data will be found within the child nodes
        // of each node in the list
        for ( int x = 0; x < nodes.getLength(); x++ )
        {
            Node node = nodes.item(x);
            // Compare this node name to the one being searched for
            if ( node.getNodeName().equalsIgnoreCase( elementName ) )
            {
```

```
            // The data is a child 'text' node of the tag we
            // have located. Locate that node type now
            NodeList childNodes = node.getChildNodes();
            for (int y = 0; y < childNodes.getLength(); y++ )
            {
                Node data = childNodes.item(y);
                if ( data.getNodeType() == Node.TEXT_NODE )
                    return data.getNodeValue();
            }
        }
    }
}
catch ( Exception e ) {
    e.printStackTrace();
}

return "";
}
```

Feel free to use these methods within your XML application as you wish. The sample applications with this book use them extensively when parsing XML and processing SOAP messages as seen in later chapters.

JAVA API FOR XML BINDING (JAXB)

The *Java API for XML Binding* (JAXB) framework allows you to build applications with classes generated to match an XML schema that you provide [Armstrong04]. When XML source documents (that match the schema) are provided to your application at runtime, JAXB uses the generated classes to build a matching tree structure that is, in many ways, easier to use and more lightweight than DOM or SAX. The result is that you write code that is devoid of XML processing details. You simply use Java in an object-oriented manner to process, manipulate, and even generate XML without knowing any of the XML-related details.

JAXB takes as input an XML schema document to create Java classes that match the structures described within. When XML documents that adhere to the matching XML schema are provided to the JAXB compiler, the document is unmarshalled into an object tree structure. JAXB will even validate the XML documents against the schema, if you choose. The resulting tree structure matches the source XML document and uses the classes created from the XML schema. To follow the steps visually, examine Figure 8.3. JAXB will take, as input, File objects, DOM Node objects, SAX SAXSource objects, StringBuffer objects, InputStream objects, and URLs.

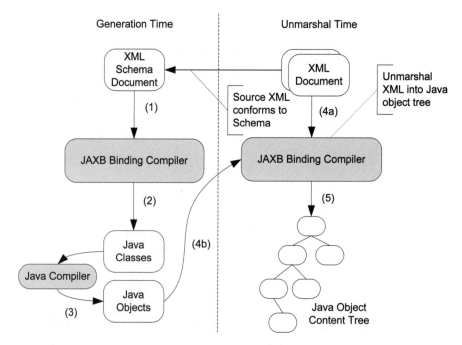

FIGURE 8.3   JAXB generates classes that are used later when XML documents are unmarshalled into Java object trees.

The JAXB implementation contains three main packages:

javax.xml.bind: This is the main package of interfaces and classes for JAXB. To begin using JAXB, you must acquire a reference to the class JAXBContext, which is part of this package. This class is a factory for the classes that handle XML marshalling, unmarshalling, validation, and exceptions (see Figure 8.4).

javax.xml.bind.helper: While the javax.xml.bind package defines mostly interfaces, the javax.xml.bind.helper package provides default class implementations for some of them. This package is not meant to be used by applications that use JAXB, but by software that implements JAXB (called a JAXB provider).

javax.xml.bind.util: Utility classes that can optionally be used by JAXB applications.

Unmarshalling XML to Content Trees

The intent of JAXB is to enable you to write applications that can parse and use XML documents in an object-oriented way. The process of parsing XML into a tree

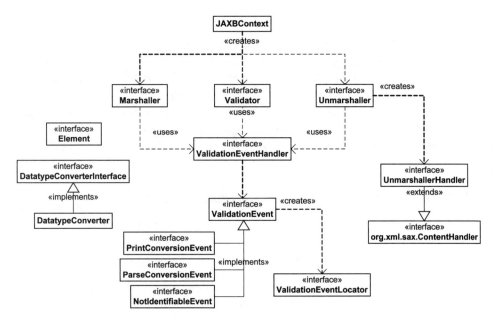

FIGURE 8.4 This UML class diagram shows the contents of and relationships for the JAXB `javax.xml.bind` package.

structure of Java objects that match the XML's schema is called *unmarshalling*. The `javax.xml.bind.Unmarshaller` class takes XML that adheres to the appropriate XML schema and creates a Java object tree from it. These objects are of classes that were generated from the XML schema you must provide prior to building the application that uses them. The first step is to run the JAXB binding compiler on your application's XML schema. Next, write an application that uses JAXB, along with the classes you have generated. For the most part, you do not need to deal with the details of XML; you simply use the generated classes without regard to how they were instantiated or how they were populated with data. The default JAXB binding compiler that comes with the Java Web Service Developer Pack is called XJC, and its package name is `com.sun.tools.xjc`.

JAXB allows you to generate a unified set of Java classes for more than one XML schema, called a schema set. With schema sets, you should ensure that the schemas and matching XML documents use proper XML namespaces to avoid naming collisions. To use the generated classes within an application, you must reference the packages for each set of generated classes, separated by a colon, when you obtain a reference to the JAXB context. This will be discussed in detail later in this section as we walk through the sample application code.

XML Schema Usage

To further understand how to use JAXB, we will explore a simple stock order processing sample application. In this example, stock orders arrive to the server as XML documents that need to be parsed in order to execute the order. In this scenario, assume we have chosen to implement the server with JAXB so that we can process the orders the same way, whether they arrive as XML in a JMS TextMessage object or as data fields within a JMS MapMessage object. To begin, let's define an XML schema that expresses the data expected, and in the types required, regardless of the form it is delivered in (see Listing 8.8).

LISTING 8.8   The Sample Application's XML Schema File (order.xsd)

```
<xs:schema xmlns:xs="http://www.w3.org/2001/XMLSchema"
           xmlns:jaxb="http://java.sun.com/xml/ns/jaxb"
           jaxb:version="1.0">

    <xs:element name="StockOrder" type="StockOrderType"/>
    <xs:complexType name="StockOrderType">
        <xs:sequence>
            <xs:element name="CustomerID" type="xs:int"/>
            <xs:element name="StockTicker" type="xs:string"/>
            <xs:element name="Quantity" type="xs:int"/>
        </xs:sequence>
        <xs:attribute name="type" type="xs:string"/>
    </xs:complexType>

    <xs:group name="ModelGroupChoice">
      <xs:choice>
        <xs:element name="bool" type="xs:boolean"/>
        <xs:element name="comment" type="xs:string"/>
        <xs:element name="value" type="xs:int"/>
      </xs:choice>
    </xs:group>

</xs:schema>
```

First, the element StockOrder is defined with the complex type, StockOrderType. The schema goes on to define this type as a sequence of elements, CustomerID, StockTicker, and Quantity, including the attribute, type, which is used to describe the order type (buy or sell). Each element and attribute defined in the schema is given a type, such as xs:string, xs:int, xs:boolean, and so on. This instructs the XML parser to first ensure that the data for these elements matches these types. This is done during the parser's validation phase when it parses XML documents that reference a schema.

Sample JAXB Unmarshalling Code

The sample order-processing JAXB application used to illustrate JAXB unmarshalling can be found on the CD-ROM, in the folder /Chapter8/JAXBOrder.

The file build.xml located in this folder is an Apache Ant script that is used to run the JAXB binding compiler to generate the proper classes, compile all of the resulting code as well as the application, and run the application. These steps are defined as individual Ant tasks within the build script, which we will go over, starting with the next paragraph. In summary, Apache Ant is a tool that is used mainly to build, deploy, and execute Java applications. You tell Ant what to do via XML files called Ant scripts. You can get more information on Apache Ant, and download it, at *http://ant.apache.org*. The book's CD-ROM contains Ant version 1.6.3 (the latest as of this writing) in the folder /java/ant.

First, you must tell Ant where to locate the JAXB tools and libraries. To do this, make sure the Ant build script's JWSDP path information is correct for your installation. You need to set the jwsdp.home property to the correct directory path, as shown in the following section (taken from /Chapter8/JAXBOrder/build.xml):

```
<property name="jwsdp.home" value="/jwsdp_1_4" />
<path id="classpath">
  <pathelement path="src" />
  <pathelement path="classes" />
  <fileset dir="${jwsdp.home}" includes="jaxb/lib/*.jar"/>
  <fileset dir="${jwsdp.home}" includes="jwsdp-shared/lib/*.jar"/>
  <fileset dir="${jwsdp.home}" includes="jaxp/lib/**/*.jar"/>
</path>
```

The JAXB binding compiler that's used to generate the Java classes from the sample's XML schema is the com.sun.tools.xjc tool that comes with JAXB. The next section of the Ant script is what you will modify if you'd like to use a different binding compiler, as shown here:

```
<taskdef name="xjc" classname="com.sun.tools.xjc.XJCTask">
    <classpath refid="classpath" />
</taskdef>
```

The section in the Ant script that generates the classes, and then compiles them along with the sample application that uses them, is shown in Listing 8.9. First, the directory gen-src is created if it does not exist. Next, the JAXB binding compiler, xjc, is launched to generate the Java classes from the schema and is placed in this directory. Then, the `classes` directory is created if it doesn't exist. All of the Java code is compiled next, using `javac`, including the generated classes and the sample application class, `com.TradingSystem.OrderProcessor`. Finally, the artifacts are copied to the correct output directories in preparation to execute the application.

LISTING 8.9   The Ant Target that Generates and Compiles the Java Code

```
<target name="compile" description="Compile the Java source">

  <echo message="Binding from the schema" />
  <mkdir dir="gen-src" />
  <xjc schema="order.xsd" binding="binding.xjb" target="gen-src">
    <produces dir="gen-src" includes="**/*.java" />
  </xjc>

  <echo message="Compiling the java code" />
  <mkdir dir="classes" />
  <javac destdir="classes" debug="on">
    <src path="." />
    <src path="gen-src" />
    <classpath refid="classpath" />
  </javac>

  <copy todir="classes">
    <fileset dir="gen-src">
      <include name="**/*.properties" />
      <include name="**/bgm.ser" />
    </fileset>
  </copy>

  <echo message="Done" />
</target>
```

The sample order processing JAXB application consists of the class `com.TradingSystem.OrderProcessor` (see Listing 8.10). An instance of the `JAXBContext` class is obtained in the class constructor. This class is the starting point for JAXB and must be obtained before you attempt to marshal or unmarshal XML. To communicate the schema classes to use, you provide the fully qualified class package name as a parameter to the `newInstance` method. If you want to specify a schema set (multiple schemas and hence multiple sets of Java classes), you simply include each package name in the `String` parameter, separated by a colon, as in:

```
JAXBContext.newInstance( "com.mycode.doThis:com.mycode.doThat" );
```

LISTING 8.10   Sample JAXB Order-Processing Application

```java
package com.TradingSystem;

import java.io.*;
import javax.xml.bind.*;
import order.*;

public class OrderProcessor
{
    private JAXBContext jc = null;

    public OrderProcessor() throws JAXBException
    {
        // create a JAXBContext for the generated order classes
        jc = JAXBContext.newInstance( "order" );
    }

    public void unmarshallOrderXml(String filename)
    {
        try {
            Unmarshaller u = jc.createUnmarshaller();

            StockOrder order =
                (StockOrder)u.unmarshal(
                        new FileInputStream( filename ) );

            System.out.println("Customer ID: " +
                                order.getCustomerID());
            System.out.println("Stock: " + order.getStockTicker());
            System.out.println(      order.getType() +
                                " " +
                                order.getQuantity() +
                                " of Stock " +
                                order.getStockTicker() );
        }
        catch ( Exception e ) {
            e.printStackTrace();
        }
    }

    public void marshallOrder(String xml)
    {
        //...
    }
```

```
public static void main( String[] args )
    throws Exception
{
    OrderProcessor orderProcessor = new OrderProcessor();
    orderProcessor.unmarshallOrderXml("order.xml");
}
}
```

All of the work involved in parsing the XML, and unmarshalling it into Java objects, occurs in the method unmarshallOrderXml. A reference to the Unmarshaller object is obtained by using the JAXBContext created in the constructor. Next, the call to the unmarshal method parses the XML file and results in a StockOrder object that represents the root node of the XML. This method takes the following types as input:

java.io.File: A Java reference to an XML file

java.io.InputStream: Any Java input stream that contains the XML data

org.xml.sax.InputSource: A SAX input source for an XML entity

org.w3c.dom.Node: A single node in a DOM document tree

javax.xml.transform.Source: A SAX or DOM input source

java.net.URL: A URL from which to get XML data

The remainder of the method outputs the contents of the XML file by calling methods on the resulting object. The method names match the data that is being pulled from the XML (such as getCustomerID), resulting in object-oriented code to read XML data. Once the XML is unmarshalled into an object tree, the remainder of the application code is devoid of any XML details. It's possible to create an application that uses an adapter-like front-end written with JAXB to completely abstract the data source (in this case XML) from the remainder of the business logic (see Figure 8.5). Since the business logic is so well encapsulated, it can be called from one of many front-end adapters, such as one for JMS, another for SOAP, and so on.

The combination of the business logic, the Java object content tree, and the adapters makes up the overall application. Changes to, or the addition of, adapters does not affect the business logic code. Additionally, business logic code is isolated to that which uses the Java object tree. The result is loosely coupled, yet well integrated, application components. When software is designed this way, the general result is easily maintainable, robust code. Not only is this design pattern desirable for *any* software development, but it is crucial to the success of distributed software development, which is where XML is used most.

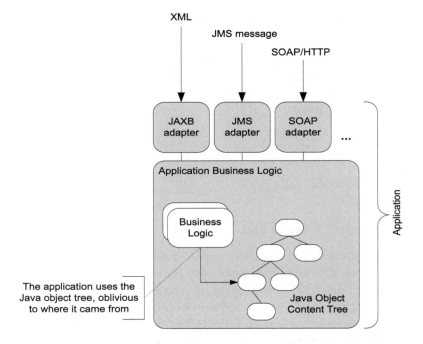

FIGURE 8.5 JAXB, used with the appropriate adapters, can completely hide the details of XML data and where it comes from.

Building the Sample JAXB Application

You can compile the application by starting the Ant tool from within the /Chapter8/ JAXBOrder folder by typing

```
> ant compile
```

When you start the compile, messages will be displayed as each step of the compilation phase occurs (generating the classes, compiling the classes, and copying the artifacts). If there are compilation errors, you will see them; otherwise you should see the text "BUILD SUCCESSFUL." If all goes well, you can execute the application by typing

```
> ant run
```

When run, the application parses the XML document in the file order.xml (see Listing 8.11). The XML contains an order type ("buy" in this case), a customer ID (to identify the party placing the order), the symbol of the stock for the transaction, and the quantity of shares to buy or sell. The application then pretends to place the order and simply writes out the order details to prove that JAXB did its job.

LISTING 8.11   The Order XML Document

```
<StockOrder type="buy">
    <CustomerID>11001</CustomerID>
    <StockTicker>SUNW</StockTicker>
    <Quantity>500</Quantity>
</StockOrder>
```

When you start the Ant tool, and provide "run" as the parameter, Ant will also build the application if a source file has changed. This occurs because the "compile" Ant task is listed as a dependency for the "run" task.

Marshalling Content Trees to XML

The previous section described how JAXB unmarshalling converts XML into a Java object tree. This section describes *marshalling*, which is when a Java object tree is converted into XML. This implies that the object tree uses the classes generated by the JAXB binding compiler, and the resulting XML conforms to the XML schema used to generate the classes. It doesn't matter where the object tree came from; it can be the result of an existing XML document that was unmarshalled or it can be created from scratch within a Java application that imports the JAXB generated classes.

As with unmarshalling, the advantage of using JAXB is that the application does not need XML-related code in order to generate XML documents for the appropriate schema. It simply uses the generated classes as plain old Java objects and populates data within them via the various set methods. The classes that are used are those that were generated from the XML schema provided to the JAXB binding compiler. Looking back at the XML schema from Listing 8.8 in the previous section, we need to add the definition of a stock order response XML structure (see Listing 8.12). A document of this XML structure will be sent back to the original order request client.

LISTING 8.12   The StockOrderResponse XML Definition for Order.xsd

```
<xs:element name="StockOrderResponse" type="StockOrderResponseType"/>
<xs:complexType name="StockOrderResponseType">
    <xs:sequence>
        <xs:element name="TransactionID" type="xs:int"/>
        <xs:element name="StockTicker" type="xs:string"/>
        <xs:element name="Price" type="xs:string"/>
        <xs:element name="Quantity" type="xs:int"/>
        <xs:element name="Status" type="xs:string"/>
```

```
        </xs:sequence>
        <xs:attribute name="type" type="xs:string"/>
    </xs:complexType>
```

Once the classes are regenerated by the JAXB binding compiler using the modified XML schema, we can modify the sample order-processing application to generate a response. Listing 8.13 shows the marshallOrder method implementation from the order processing application we began looking at in the previous section. In this code, a simulated stock order response is generated, as XML, to be sent to the original order request client.

LISTING 8.13 Application Code to Marshal JAXB Classes into XML

```
public void marshallOrder(String xml)
{
    try {
        System.out.println("Order processed, sending a response:");
        java.util.Random rand =
            new java.util.Random(System.currentTimeMillis());

        ObjectFactory factory = new ObjectFactory();
        StockOrderResponse response =
        factory.createStockOrderResponse();
        response.setQuantity(420);
        response.setStatus("SUCCESS");
        response.setStockTicker("SUNW");
        response.setTransactionID( rand.nextInt(1000000) );
        response.setType("buy");
        response.setPrice("3.89");

        Marshaller m = jc.createMarshaller();
        m.setProperty( Marshaller.JAXB_FORMATTED_OUTPUT,
                    Boolean.TRUE );
        m.marshal( response, System.out );
    }
    catch ( Exception e ) {
        e.printStackTrace();
    }
}
```

The code in bold type is the code to focus on; a transaction identifier is randomly generated for illustration only. To create objects from the generated classes, you must use the OrderFactory class for the appropriate generated classes' package.

For instance, in our sample application, we would use `order.OrderFactory`. If your code is using multiple schema sets (hence multiple generated class packages), then it is essential to use the proper package name to avoid ambiguity. The resulting `OrderFactory` object (`factory` in this example) is then used to create *all* new objects of this package. The resulting object is a plain-old Java object that can be modified via its mutator methods (such as `setQuantity`). Finally, the object tree you assemble in your code must be marshaled back to XML.

A reference to the `javax.xml.bind.Marshaller` class is obtained from the `JAXBContent` object's `createMarshaller` method. Before you tell JAXB to generate the XML, you need to get some other important details out of the way. For instance, you can specify the XML encoding to use, the XML schema location, and how to format the XML. The following properties can be set:

JAXB_ENCODING: Use this property to specify the character encoding to use for the XML that is generated (the default is UTF-8).

JAXB_FORMATTED_OUTPUT: Used to specify if the XML should be formatted with line-breaks and indentation to appear more readable. The value of `Boolean.TRUE` turns formatting on, while `Boolean.FALSE` turns it off.

JAXB_NO_NAMESPACE_SCHEMA_LOCATION: Used to specify the `xsi:noName spaceSchemaLocation` attribute value to place in the XML.

JAXB_SCHEMA_LOCATION: Used to specify the `xsi:schemaLocation` attribute value to place in the XML.

Once the properties are set, tell JAXB to create the XML from the object tree via the `marshal` method. This method can marshal the XML to one of the following output types:

- `System.output`
- SAX2 event objects
- A DOM `Node` object
- An `OutputStream` object (such as `FileOutputStream`)
- A `javax.xml.transform.Result` object such as `SAXResult`, `DOMResult`, or `StreamResult`
- A `java.io.Writer` object

This example sends the XML to the command line for illustration. However, sending the XML to a file is straightforward and can be accomplished with a `FileOutputStream` object, as shown here:

```
File file =  new File("response.xml");
FileOutputStream fos = new FileOutputStream(file);
m.marshal( response, fos );
```

Keep in mind that JAXB does not require the Java object trees to be validated before the parser begins the marshalling process. Therefore, there is no guarantee that the resulting XML will be valid, or will be created at all, if the provided object tree is not valid (does not conform to the rules of the XML schema). However, it is guaranteed that a valid object tree will always result in a valid XML document. If problems are encountered during the marshalling process, validation events will be sent to the validation handler objects that were registered with JAXB.

JAVA API FOR XML MESSAGING (JAXM)

The *Java API for XML Messaging* is similar to JAXP in that it is a specification and an API that is used to develop applications. In this case, JAXM is a lightweight API for writing Java messaging applications that use XML as the transport. To be clear, a JAXM application uses the JAXM API to send and receive XML messages, while a JAXM provider implements the API to perform the actual transmission of messages between senders and receivers. JAXM providers are encouraged (not strictly required) to use standard message transport protocols, but they *are* required to support the SOAP 1.1 and SOAP with Attachments specifications (discussed in Chapter 6). This requirement includes the ability to transport SOAP/XML messages over HTTP but does not preclude the use of other protocols such as FTP, SCP, or even JMS. When HTTP is used as the protocol, JAXM has the added advantage that applications built using it can interoperate with SOAP applications that both do and do *not* use JAXM. JAXM also has built-in support for the Electronic Business XML (ebXML) Message Handling Service 1.0 (MHS), as well as the SOAP Routing Protocol.

To JAXM applications, the semantics of message delivery are similar to those related to JMS, as discussed in Chapter 3. For instance, JAXM supports both synchronous and asynchronous message delivery and supports reliable messaging in the form of message acknowledgments when messages are received. The largest differentiator is that the messages must be SOAP 1.1 messages. Sender applications are not required to send SOAP messages with attachments, but when a message that contains at least one attachment is sent, the receiving application is required to process it, which is accomplished with the JavaBeans Activation Framework (JAF) [Shannon03]. Application developers should use JAXM when they need to consume or produce SOAP messages over HTTP but do not want to be exposed to the underlying software that sends the messages.

It's this level of abstraction that many developers strive for when building large-scale, distributed applications because it separates the various *concerns* from one another. Just as the concept of loose coupling has led to the creation and use of Web Services within modern application architecture, it can aid in the design and construction of the components of the application. The decision to transport the SOAP messages of HTTP, FTP, or JMS, and the details of how this is done, is not of concern to the application developer. This is, instead, a concern of the application architects, network administrators, and the business that uses the overall system. The choice to use one transport over the other, or even switch transport methods, is done at application deployment time by choosing and/or configuring the correct JAXM provider. The application should not be affected by these decisions and should never need to be changed because of them. JAXM helps to maintain this separation.

JAXM Client Application Models

There are two main types of JAXM client applications: those that use a messaging provider and those that do not. Clients that use a messaging provider typically run within a managed software environment, such as a J2EE Servlet container or J2EE/EJB application server. In this environment, the J2EE container works with the JAXM provider to provide a complete, robust, and reliable messaging system. In this model, messages can be sent both synchronously and asynchronously. The second type of JAXM client is a standalone Java application that does *not* use a JAXM provider but instead uses JAXM only in the capacity of a synchronous messaging client. When requests are made of other messaging services, the responses are handled synchronously. A standalone JAXM client application cannot be a Web Service; it can only be a client of one.

An application that uses a JAXM provider is free to act as both a Web Service and/or a client. However, some requirements that are placed on the server should be mentioned. First, the application must be able to serve as a complete Web Service and handle *all* SOAP 1.1 messages that are sent its way, whether from a JAXM client or not. The JAXM service developer must also choose to implement a request/response application, or a one-way message server, but not both. Finally, for the JAXM application that is built as a Servlet, HTTP must be chosen as the transport for the SOAP messages.

JAXM is made up of the following packages:

javax.xml.messaging: Contains the JAXM-specific classes and interfaces to access JAXM providers and Web Services.

javax.xml.soap: Contains the definitions of classes and interfaces for assembling and disassembling SOAP messages in Java. This package and its classes are *not* specific to JAXM. This package has been officially made a part of the SOAP with Attachments API for Java (SAAJ), discussed later in this chapter.

Sample JAXM Service Application

To get familiar with using JAXM, let's examine a sample JAXM service application. This example is an alternate implementation of the order-processing application explored in the section on JAXB. We will use JAXM to build a servlet that listens for new stock order requests that arrive as SOAP messages. The order will be processed (simulated) and a response will be sent as a SOAP message. The next section will deal with the standalone JAXM client application that sends these requests and handles the subsequent responses.

The JAXM order processor will be implemented as a Java servlet, so it will extend the `javax.xml.messaging.JAXMServlet` class (see Listing 8.14). Since we are building a request/response Web Service (as opposed to a one-way messaging server), the `OrderProcessor` class implements the `ReqRespListener` interface. This interface defines the `onMessage` method, which the `OrderProcessor` class implements to receive new stock order–request SOAP messages.

LISTING 8.14   A Sample JAXM Order-Processing Web Service

```
package com.TradingSystem;

import javax.xml.messaging.*;
import javax.xml.soap.*;
import javax.servlet.*;

public class OrderProcessor extends JAXMServlet
    implements ReqRespListener
{

    MessageFactory msgFact = null;

    public OrderProcessor()
    {
        try {
            msgFact = MessageFactory.newInstance();
        }
        catch (Exception e) {
            e.printStackTrace();
        }
    }
```

```java
public void init( ServletConfig config )
    throws ServletException
{
    super.init( config );
}

public SOAPMessage onMessage(SOAPMessage message)
{
    try {
        // Handle the stock order request
        message.writeTo(System.out);

        java.util.Random rand =
            new java.util.Random(System.currentTimeMillis());
        String transId =
            new StringBuffer(rand.nextInt(1000000)).toString();

        // Generate the stock order response
        SOAPMessage msg = msgFact.createMessage();
        SOAPEnvelope env = msg.getSOAPPart().getEnvelope();
        SOAPBody body = env.getBody();

        body.addChildElement(
            env.createName("Status"))
                .addTextNode( "SUCCESS" );
        body.addChildElement(
            env.createName("Price"))
                .addTextNode( "3.89" );
        body.addChildElement(
            env.createName("Quantity"))
                .addTextNode( "420" );
        body.addChildElement(
            env.createName("StockTicker"))
                .addTextNode( "SUNW" );
        body.addChildElement(
            env.createName("TransactionID"))
                .addTextNode( transId );
        body.addChildElement(
            env.createName("Type"))
                .addTextNode( "buy" );

        return msg;
    }
    catch ( Exception e ) {
```

```
                    e.printStackTrace();
            }

            return null;
        }
    }
```

The class constructor gets a reference to the javax.xml.soap.MessageFactory singleton object. The onMessage method is where the order request is processed, and an order response SOAP message is created and sent in response. First, using the SOAP message factory, a new message is created. Once a reference to the message's SOAPBody object is attained, child text elements are added via sequential calls to addChildElement, createName, and addTextNode. The first method creates a new SOAPElement object; the second gives it a name (such as "Price"); the third assigns it a text value and returns another SOAPElement object. Finally, the entire SOAP message is sent to the caller via the return from the onMessage method.

ON THE CD

The code for the JAXM order-processing servlet can be found on the CD-ROM in the /Chapter8/JAXMOrder folder. All of the files needed to deploy the servlet within any servlet container (such as Apache Tomcat) are included in this folder.

Sample JAXM Standalone Client

The order client application is implemented as a standalone Java application. This application uses JAXM to send new stock order requests as SOAP messages to the JAXM Web Service (see Listing 8.15). The first difference you will notice about this client application compared to the previous client application is that it doesn't extend any JAXM classes or implement any of its interfaces. The next difference is in regard to the use of the SOAPConnectionFactory class (shown in bold type) to send a request SOAP message to the Web Service. Otherwise the code to build the SOAP message is similar to the previous example.

LISTING 8.15   A Sample Web Service Implemented with JAXM

```
package com.TradingSystem;

import java.net.*;
import java.util.*;
import javax.xml.soap.*;

public class OrderSender
{
    private SOAPConnection conn;
    private String server =
        "http://localhost:8080/jaxmorder/orderprocessor";
```

```
public OrderSender()
{
    try {
        SOAPConnectionFactory fact =
            SOAPConnectionFactory.newInstance();
        conn = fact.createConnection();
        MessageFactory mf = MessageFactory.newInstance();

        // Create an Order Request SOAP message
        SOAPMessage msg = mf.createMessage();
        SOAPPart sp = msg.getSOAPPart();
        SOAPEnvelope envelope = sp.getEnvelope();
        SOAPHeader hdr = envelope.getHeader();
        SOAPBody bdy = envelope.getBody();
        SOAPBodyElement bdyElem
            = bdy.addBodyElement(
                envelope.createName("StockOrder"));
        bdyElem.addChildElement(
          envelope.createName("CustomerID"))
              .addTextNode( "123" );
        bdyElem.addChildElement(
          envelope.createName("StockTicker"))
              .addTextNode( "SUNW" );
        bdyElem.addChildElement(
          envelope.createName("Quantity"))
              .addTextNode( "300" );

        // Send the message
        URL urlEndpoint = new URL(server);
        SOAPMessage reply = conn.call(msg, urlEndpoint);

        // Handle the Order Response
        if (reply != null) {
            SOAPEnvelope env =
                reply.getSOAPPart().getEnvelope();

            bdy = env.getBody();
            Iterator iter = bdy.getChildElements();
            System.out.println( "Status: " +
                    getNodeValue( "Status", iter ) );
            System.out.println( "Price: " +
                    getNodeValue("Price", iter) );
            System.out.println( "Quantity: " +
                    getNodeValue("Quantity", iter) );
```

```
                    System.out.println( "Type: " +
                            getNodeValue("Type", iter) );
                    System.out.println( "TransactionID: " +
                            getNodeValue("TransactionID", iter) );
            }
        }
        catch ( Exception e ) {
            e.printStackTrace();
        }
    }

    protected SOAPElement getNode(String tagName, Iterator iter){
        //...
    }
    protected String getNodeValue(String tagName, Iterator iter){
        //...
    }

    public static void main( String[] args )
    {
        OrderSender sender = new OrderSender();
    }
}
```

When the time comes to send the message, the client application first instantiates a java.net.URL object, and provides it with the URL for the Web Service. In this example, the URL is *http://localhost:8080/jaxmorder/orderprocessor*, but this can be any valid local or Web URL. Next, the SOAP message is sent to the Web Service over HTTP via the SOAPConnection.call method. The SOAP message and URL object are given as parameters to this call, which blocks until a response message is received or the request times out without a response. The response message arrives in the form of a SOAPMessage object, which is easily parsed, and the data extracted.

Earlier it was mentioned that SOAP attachments are processed using the JavaBeans Activation Framework (JAF). JAF can be used by applications that handle data in many forms; it helps to determine the type of the data, and it abstracts access to the data. Additionally, JAF will instantiate the proper software component(s) to perform operations on the data. For example, a SOAP attachment in the form of an HTML document may be added to a SOAP message via the javax.activation.DataHandler object:

```
URL url = new URL("http://myserver.com/mydoc.html");
DataHandler dh = new DataHandler(url);
```

```
// Create the attachment
AttachmentPart attach = soapMsg.createAttachmentPart(dh);
attach.setContentType("text/xml");

// Add the attachment
soapMsg.addAttachmentPart(attach);
```

The DataHandler object manages the details of acquiring the data, which is then added to the SOAP attachment seamlessly without the need for HTTP-specific code in the application. The DataHandler class is used the same way in the receiving application to obtain the actual attachment data.

JAXM is no longer officially part of the Java Web Service Developer Pack and it is not included with the latest download; it's a separate download available from Sun at http://java.sun.com/xml/downloads/jaxm.html/. *However, since it's still a supported specification and it's very much related to building Java messaging software, this chapter was written to include it. Sun's choice to remove it from the JWSDP may have been motivated by the popularity of the more flexible SOAP with Attachments API for Java (SAAJ).*

SOAP WITH ATTACHMENTS API FOR JAVA (SAAJ)

While JAXM is a high-level interface for all XML-based messaging, including SOAP, the SAAJ API is *specific* to Java/SOAP development. Because of this, the javax.xml.soap package was removed from JAXM and was officially made a part of SAAJ. (This may cause some initial confusion, as SAAJ and JAXM application code appear similar in many respects, as we will see in this section.) In cases where you want, or are required, to create and manipulate SOAP messages directly, the SAAJ API is a good choice. The SAAJ class model directly extends the DOM class model, which makes sense since SOAP documents are true XML documents. In the end, the SAAJ document model is completely interchangeable with the DOM Level 2 model and hence should work with existing DOM processing code and tools.

Let's review the various parts of a SOAP message (see Figure 8.6). As illustrated in this diagram, SAAJ contains classes that map directly to the parts of a SOAP message, which follows a *has a*, or *contains*, model:

SOAP Message: Maps to the SAAJ javax.xml.soap.SOAPMessage class. This class contains zero to many attachment parts and one mandatory SOAP part of the message.

SOAP Part: Maps to the SAAJ `javax.xml.soap.SOAPPart` class and contains all of the message's SOAP-related data. In particular, this class contains the SOAP message envelope.

SOAP Envelope: Maps to the SAAJ `javax.xml.soap.SOAPEnvelope` class, which contains the SOAP header and body.

SOAP Header: Maps to the SAAJ `javax.xml.soap.SOAPHeader` class, which contains the content of the SOAP message header.

SOAP Header Content: Maps to the SAAJ `javax.xml.soap.SOAPHeaderElement` class, which references an element in the message's XML header document.

SOAP Body: Maps to the SAAJ `javax.xml.soap.SOAPBody` class, which contains the content of the SOAP message body document, or payload, as body elements.

SOAP Body Content: Maps to the SAAJ `javax.xml.soap.SOAPBodyElement`, which references an element in the message's XML body document.

SOAP Attachment: Maps to the SAAJ `javax.xml.soap.AttachmentPart` class, which contains attachment data.

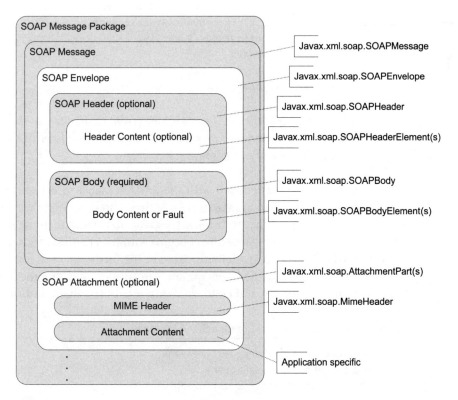

FIGURE 8.6   The SOAP message package structure with SAAJ class mapping.

Let's begin to explore SAAJ with a simple SOAP request message, one with only a body, as shown in Listing 8.16. In this example, a stock purchase request is being made of the order processor Web Service. The contents of the SOAP body are in bold and contain the type of stock order being made, the customer's identification number, the stock ticker in question, and the quantity of shares in the transaction. In this section, we will build a sample Web Service that processes stock transaction requests using the SAAJ API. This application will be implemented as a Java servlet by extending the class `com.sun.xml.messaging.soap.server.SAAJServlet`, which is part of the `saaj-coms.jar` library. When SOAP messages are received, they are processed via the implementing class's `onMessage` method.

LISTING 8.16   The Sample Stock Purchase SOAP Request Message

```
<SOAP-ENV:Envelope xmlns:SOAP
ENV="http://schemas.xmlsoap.org/soap/envelope/">
    <SOAP-ENV:Header />
    <SOAP-ENV:Body>
        <StockOrder type="buy">
            <CustomerID>11001</CustomerID>
            <StockTicker>SUNW</StockTicker>
            <Quantity>500</Quantity>
        </StockOrder>
    </SOAP-ENV:Body>
</SOAP-ENV:Envelope>
```

You should notice that the SAAJ sample code is almost identical to the sample code from the previous section that uses JAXM. This is because both JAXM and SAAJ use the same package of classes (`javax.xml.soap`).

The SOAP message is created with the SAAJ `MessageFactory` singleton object (see Listing 8.17). A call to `createMessage` returns a new `SOAPMessage` object, from which you can get a reference to the `SOAPEnvelope` object and then the `SOAPBody` object. Adding data to the `SOAPBody` object begins with the creation of `SOAPBodyElement` objects, to which you add an element name in the form of a `Name` object. Remember that the body, like any XML document, can contain only one root element. To this new element, you can add child elements, attribute values, and/or text nodes.

LISTING 8.17   SAAJ Code to Create a SOAP Message

```
// Create a SOAP request message
MessageFactory msgFactory
    = MessageFactory.newInstance();
```

```
SOAPMessage soapMsg
    = msgFactory.createMessage();
SOAPEnvelope envelope
    = soapMsg.getSOAPPart().getEnvelope();
SOAPBody bdy
    = env.getBody();

// Add the request data to the SOAP body
SOAPBodyElement bdyElem
    = bdy.addBodyElement(
        envelope.createName("StockOrder"));
bdyElem.addChildElement(
  envelope.createName("CustomerID"))
    .addTextNode( custID );
bdyElem.addChildElement(
  envelope.createName("StockTicker"))
    .addTextNode( stockTicker );
bdyElem.addChildElement(
  envelope.createName("Quantity"))
    .addTextNode( qty );

SOAPConnectionFactory scf
  = SOAPConnectionFactory.newInstance();

con = scf.createConnection();

// Send the request to the Order Broker Service
URL urlEndpoint
  = new URL( "http://localhost:8080/OrderBroker" );
SOAPMessage fundReply
  = con.call( soapMsg, urlEndpoint );
```

It may seem tedious at first, but there is a general pattern to follow that repeats itself. The steps below apply when adding data to a SOAP message header, as well as a SOAP message body (simply swap references to SOAPBodyElement with SOAP HeaderElement):

1. Create a javax.xml.soap.Name object by calling SOAPEnvelope.createName.
2. Create a SOAPBodyElement object with the SOAPBody.addBodyElement method, providing the Name object from the previous step.
3. Optionally add an attribute by creating another Name object, followed by a call to SOAPBodyElement.addAttribute to which you provide new Name object.

4. Optionally add a text value by calling SOAPElement.addTextNode (which can also be called on a SOAPBodyElement object). You provide the String value of the node as a parameter to the call.

5. Optionally add a child element by calling SOAPBodyElement.addChild Element, where you provide yet another Name object as the element name.

6. Repeat from step 3, as needed.

When the order processor Web Service receives a SOAP request, it is parsed and checked to ensure that it contains all of the necessary data. Listing 8.18 shows the code that receives and parses the simple SOAP request message. After the request is parsed, the Web Service simulates the execution of the order and sends a contrived SOAP response message back to the client.

LISTING 8.18 SAAJ Calls Your Application's onMessage Method to Process a SOAP Message

```java
public SOAPMessage onMessage(SOAPMessage message)
{
    // Process the message
    try {
        // The envelope contains the message
        // header, body, and attachments
        SOAPEnvelope env =
            message.getSOAPPart().getEnvelope();

        SOAPBody bdy =
            env.getBody();

        // Get the ticker symbol
        Iterator iter = bdy.getChildElements();
        SOAPElement node = getNode("StockOrder", iter);
        if ( node != null )
        {
            String type =
                node.getAttributeValue( env.createName("type") );

            iter = node.getChildElements();

            String ticker = getNodeValue("StockTicker", iter);
            String quantity = getNodeValue("Quantity", iter);
            String customerId = getNodeValue("CustomerID", iter);

            // ...
        }
```

```
        }
        catch(Exception e) {
            return null;
        }
    }
```

The onMessage method (see Listing 8.19) provides the Web Service application with each newly received SOAPMessage object. First, the SOAPEnvelope is extracted, from which we get a reference to the SOAPBody part of the message. The transaction type is set as an attribute to the StockOrder root element, which is retrieved through the call to getAttributeValue. The method getNodeValue from earlier in this chapter is used to extract the additional data for the stock transaction. In this simple example, the XML is only one level deep below the root element. However, if the data were stored deeper within a larger tree of child nodes, the calls to SOAPElement.getChildElements and getNodeValue would have to be made recursively as we traversed further into the tree.

Once the request is processed by the Web Service, it will want to send a response message in the form of a transaction acknowledgement. To do this, a SOAPMessage object is created in similar fashion to the earlier code in Listing 8.17. When the message is complete, the service implementation simply returns the object in the onMessage call, and from there SAAJ handles the delivery of the message to the client.

LISTING 8.19   This Code Creates a SOAP Reply Message with SAAJ

```
public SOAPMessage onMessage(SOAPMessage message)
{
    // Process the message
    ...

    // Create the SOAP reply message
    SOAPMessage replyMsg
        = msgFactory.createMessage();
    SOAPEnvelope env
        = replyMsg.getSOAPPart().getEnvelope();
    SOAPBody bdy
        = env.getBody();

    // Add data to the reply message
    ...

    return replyMsg;
}
```

Before the reply message is sent, let's assume that the Web Service wants to return an HTML document that describes the legal terms and conditions of the stock trade. Since HTML itself is markup, it cannot be easily added to the body of the XML SOAP message. It could be added within an XML CDATA section, but that is not very elegant, and the HTML is technically not part of the data specific to this transaction. It is simply an item that the Web Service wants to send along with the trade, which is generic in nature. The ideal solution is to send the HTML as an attachment to the reply message.

After the SOAPMessage object is created, and the data added to it, a javax. xml.soap.AttachmentPart object is created (see Listing 8.20). The HTML document is provided as a String parameter to the constructor, along with the attachment's MIME type (in this case text/html). Each attachment can be given an identifier via a call to AttachmentPart.setContentId. To attach data other than String data, the SOAPMessage.createAttachmentPart method takes the following parameters:

DataHandler: The DataHandler class is part of the javax.activation package, which supports the XML information set specification that encapsulates where the data comes from and how it is retrieved.

ByteArrayInputStream: Allows binary data such as images (.JPG, .GIF, etc.), PDF files, and other formats to be attached as a BYTE array. By setting the MIME type properly (such as to text/jpeg), the receiver should know how to treat the BYTE array and then unmarshal it back into its original form.

LISTING 8.20   This Code Adds a SOAP Attachment to a SOAP Reply Message

```
// Create the SOAP reply message
SOAPMessage replyMsg
    = msgFactory.createMessage();
SOAPEnvelope env
    = replyMsg.getSOAPPart().getEnvelope();
SOAPBody bdy
    = env.getBody();

// Add data to the reply message
...

// Add the "legal" HTML as a SOAP Attachment
AttachmentPart attach
    = replyMsg.
        createAttachmentPart(legalHTML,"text/html");
```

```
attach.setContentId("terms_conditions");
replyMsg.addAttachmentPart(attach);

return replyMsg;
```

An SAAJ Connection

The code samples examined so far work nicely within a class that extends the SAAJServlet base class. This class, however, does some important work for you, such as gaining a connection to an SAAJ provider. To gain a complete understanding of SAAJ, let's go over the missing details now.

To perform the request-and-response messaging that most Web Service client applications require, you need to create a connection to SAAJ. As with most of the Java messaging-related technologies, the code follows the factory design pattern, where one object creates another. In this case, the SOAPConnectionFactory class is used to create a new SOAPConnection object, and hence a connection to SAAJ itself, as seen here:

```
SOAPConnectionFactory factory =
    SOAPConnectionFactory.newInstance();

SOAPConnection con = factory.createConnection();
```

The connection is used when the client wants to send a SOAP message. The message is sent via a SOAPConnection.call method, which takes as parameters the SOAPMessage object to send and a java.net.URL object that specifies where to send it. With SAAJ, this call is required to support a URLEndpoint object as the destination; otherwise it will accept either a String or a URL object, both of which specify a Web Service to send the message to, as seen here:

```
SOAPMessage msg = msgFactory.createMessage();
...
URL serviceUrl = new URL("http://localhost:8080/orderbroker");
SOAPMessage reply = con.call( msg, serviceUrl );
```

Support for SOAP Faults

As discussed in Chapter 6, SOAP faults are used in a response message to convey that a server error has occurred while processing a SOAP request. The error can be the result of a malformed request, missing data, or bad data (such as an invalid parameter value or range, etc.). It can also be used to inform the requester that some unrelated error occurred within the server at the time the request was processed, such as an out-of-memory error, or the failure of a dependent system. Whatever the cause, there can be, at most, one SOAP fault element, and no other elements, contained within the response SOAP message itself.

With SAAJ, a SOAP fault is added to a message when you create an instance of the SOAPFault class (see Listing 8.21) via a call to the SOAPBody.addFault method. The fault is given a valid SOAP 1.1 fault code, such as Client, used in this example, represented by a Name object. This fault code indicates that the error was caused by something the client (calling) application did or, in this case, failed to do. As shown next in this example, a fault String containing a simple description of the problem is added to the message. To provide more detail, a Detail object is created via a call to SOAPFault.addDetail. This example provides it a Name that represents the request's missing element. A DetailEntry object is added to the Detail object, which contains a more complete explanation of the error that occurred. Although it may seem tedious, this code creates the SOAP fault XML structure required to communicate errors to calling applications in a platform-independent manner.

LISTING 8.21   SAAJ Code to Add a SOAP Fault Element to a Response

```
SOAPMessage msg = msgFactory.createMessage();
SOAPEnvelope env = msg.getSOAPPart().getEnvelope();
SOAPBody body = env.getBody();
SOAPFactory factory = SOAPFactory.newInstance();
...

SOAPFault fault = body.addFault();
Name code = factory.createName( "Client", "",
                SOAPConstants.URI_NS_SOAP_ENVELOPE);
fault.setFaultCode(code);
fault.setFaultString("Missing request element");
Detail detail = fault.addDetail();
Name param = factory.createName( "StockTicker" );
DetailEntry entry = detail.addDetailEntry(param);
entry.addTextNode("The request was missing a stock ticker");
```

When the fault arrives at the client, there is no immediate indication that an error occurred; the fault arrives just as any normal SOAP response message would. The client needs to explicitly check for a fault with a call to the SOAPBody.hasFault method on the response message (see Listing 8.22). If the call returns true, the SOAPFault object is retrieved via a call to SOAPBody.getFault. The components of the fault are then pulled out in a sequence of steps similar to how they were added:

- The method getFaultCodeAsName returns the Name object that represents the fault code.
- The method getFaultString returns the short fault description.
- The method getDetail returns the Detail object.
- Any DetailEntry objects contained within the Detail object are retrieved using an Iterator object returned from the getDetailEntries method.
- The text of each entry is retrieved via the getValue method.

LISTING 8.22 Handling a SOAP Fault with SAAJ

```
SOAPEnvelope env = reply.getSOAPPart().getEnvelope();
SOAPBody bdy = env.getBody();
if ( bdy.hasFault() )
{
    SOAPFault fault = bdy.getFault();
    Name code = fault.getFaultCodeAsName();
    String string = fault.getFaultString();
    Detail detail = fault.getDetail();
    if (detail != null)
    {
        Iterator entries = detail.getDetailEntries();
        while ( entries.hasNext() )
        {
            DetailEntry entry =
                (DetailEntry)entries.next();
            String text = entry.getValue();
            System.out.println("fault entry: " + text);
        }
    }
}
...
```

JAVA API FOR XML-BASED WEB SERVICES (JAX-WS, FORMERLY JAX-RPC)

The act of sending and receiving SOAP messages between a server and a client application in order to accomplish some task is *the* point of a Web Service, and a service-oriented architecture. However, some structure needs to be defined and put into place; namely the format of the SOAP messages and the location of the Web Services that process them. The *Web-services description language* (WSDL) specification, available at *http://www.w3.org/TR/wsdl*, defines an XML format that is used to describe any available network service that uses XML as its transport. These network services are called *endpoints*, and although WSDL is not specific to any particular message formats or network protocols, it is typically used to define SOAP messages sent over the Internet using HTTP. Before getting into the details of JAX-WS specifically, let's take a closer look at WSDL.

WSDL

WSDL is an XML document that describes other XML documents that are used as messages sent between remote pieces of software. In particular, WSDL is used to describe the operations and data types sent between a client application and a Web Service. The operations and data are described using XML in a platform-independent manner, and therefore applications can be written in any language, so long as they adhere to the WSDL specification. The same applies to the Web Service itself: the language and platform used to implement it are irrelevant.

WSDL defines many abstract components that allow software services to be deployed independently of their definition:

Data Type: Acceptable type definitions for data exchanged between client and server

Message: A grouping of data

Operation: A direct mapping between an action (a remote call), and two messages: one for input and another for output

Port Type: A grouping of operations supported by a service (also called an *endpoint*)

Binding: The definition of the protocol used by an endpoint

Port: The combination of a binding with a network location

Service: A grouping of one or more endpoints

The WSDL specification goes into great detail on the structure of a WSDL document, which can be located at *http://www.w3.org/TR/wsdl*. For a quick overview, examine the WSDL document in Listing 8.23 for a sample order processing Web Service similar to the one we have been exploring in this chapter. This document defines two messages: `placeMarketOrderMessageMsg` and `place MarketOrderResponseMsg`. A message definition specifies a name, along with the data that belongs in it. Next, a `portType` element is defined that contains a group of related operations. In this case the port type is `OrderProcessorInt`, which contains one operation, `placeMarketOrder`, which itself contains the messages `placeMarket OrderMessageMsg` and `placeMarketOrderResponseMsg` as their input and output, respectively. Next, the port type is bound to the SOAP protocol with HTTP as the

transport. Finally, the port and binding are defined as belonging to the Order
ProcessorService Web Service via the service element.

LISTING 8.23   A Sample WSDL Document

```
<?xml version="1.0" encoding="UTF-8"?>
<definitions name="OrderProcessorService"
    targetNamespace="urn:StockOrder"
    xmlns:tns="urn:StockOrder"
    xmlns="http://schemas.xmlsoap.org/wsdl/"
    xmlns:xsd="http://www.w3.org/2001/XMLSchema"
    xmlns:soap="http://schemas.xmlsoap.org/wsdl/soap/">
  <types/>

  <message name="placeMarketOrderMsg">
    <part name="type" type="xsd:byte"/>
    <part name="StockTicker" type="xsd:string"/>
    <part name="Quantity" type="xsd:int"/>
    <part name="CustomerID" type="xsd:long"/>
  </message>

  <message name="placeMarketOrderResponseMsg">
    <part name="result" type="xsd:double"/>
  </message>

  <portType name="OrderProcessorInt">
    <operation name="placeMarketOrder"
        parameterOrder="type StockTicker Quantity CustomerID">
      <input message=
        "tns:placeMarketOrderMsg"/>
      <output message=
        "tns:placeMarketOrderResponseMsg"/>
    </operation>
  </portType>

  <binding name="OrderProcessorIntBinding"
        type="tns:OrderProcessorInt">
    <soap:binding transport="http://schemas.xmlsoap.org/soap/http"
        style="rpc"/>
    <operation name="placeMarketOrder">
      <soap:operation soapAction=""/>
      <input>
        <soap:body encodingStyle=
            "http://schemas.xmlsoap.org/soap/encoding/"
```

```
                        use="encoded"
                        namespace="urn:StockOrder"/>
                </input>
                <output>
                  <soap:body encodingStyle=
                        "http://schemas.xmlsoap.org/soap/encoding/"
                        use="encoded"
                        namespace="urn:StockOrder"/>
                </output>
              </operation>
            </binding>

            <service name="OrderProcessorService">
              <port name="OrderProcessorIntPort"
                  binding="tns:OrderProcessorIntBinding">
                <soap:address location="REPLACE_WITH_ACTUAL_URL"/>
              </port>
            </service>
          </definitions>
```

In summary, WSDL is a set of definitions, where each definition builds upon the other to describe sets of Web Services, each of which supports sets of operations, where each operation is defined to send and receive well-defined messages.

If the thought of defining WSDL documents for every service you implement seems tedious, there is a solution. Sun has defined the JAX-WS specification (part of the JWSDP) that encapsulates the generation and consumption of WSDL to help you build Web Services using nothing more than Java.

Using JAX-WS

It's important to note here that JAX-WS was previously called JAX-RPC and is still referred to as such in most of Sun's documentation and libraries.

JAX-WS is a specification and a library that allows you to create and use Web Services in an object-oriented way. Just as JAXB encapsulates XML and allows you to read and write XML documents as Java objects, JAX-WS allows you to call Java methods (and have your object's methods called remotely) that are translated to and from SOAP messages. JAX-WS hides all of the SOAP-related messaging details from the Java developer. This is similar to the way the Apache XML-RPC library (discussed in Chapter 6) makes RPC calls, except that JAX-WS uses true SOAP messages for communication. The concept is the same in that Java reflection is used to translate method calls to and from XML-based messages that are transported over HTTP (see Figure 8.7).

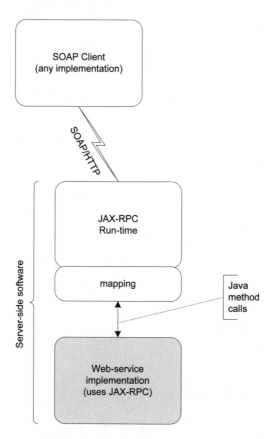

FIGURE 8.7 A JAX-WS Web Service is implemented to handle Java method calls only; SOAP messages are completely encapsulated.

JAX-WS can also generate the WSDL for a Java object that you want to expose as a Web Service. The WSDL, and your JAX-WS Web Service, can subsequently be used by any SOAP client regardless of language and platform. Conversely, JAX-WS consumes WSDL to generate stub objects that can be used by a Java client to call any Web Service, regardless of its language and platform. Each method's parameter list and return value is transparently mapped into a SOAP message. Table 8.2 lists the supported Java classes and primitive types and the SOAP types that JAX-WS maps them to.

TABLE 8.2 The JAX-WS SOAP to Java Type Mapping

SOAP Type	Java Type
xsd:boolean	boolean, java.lang.Boolean
xsd:byte	byte, java.lang.Byte
xsd:unsignedByte	short, java.lang.Short
xsd:short	short, java.lang.Short
xsd:int	int, java.lang.Integer
xsd:unsignedShort	int, java.lang.Integer
xsd:long	long, java.lang.Long
xsd:unsignedInt	long, java.lang.Long
xsd:integer	java.math.BigInteger
xsd:nonPositiveInteger	java.math.BigInteger
xsd:negativeInteger	java.math.BigInteger
xsd:nonNegativeInteger	java.math.BigInteger
xsd:unsignedLong	java.math.BigInteger
xsd:postiveInteger	java.math.BigInteger
xsd:float	float, java.lang.Float
xsd:double	double, java.lang.Double
xsd:decimal	java.math.BigDecimal
xsd:string	java.lang.String
xsd:normalizedString	java.lang.String
xsd:ID	java.lang.String
xsd:Name	java.lang.String
xsd:NCName	java.lang.String
xsd:language	java.lang.String
xsd:token	java.lang.String
xsd:NMTOKEN	java.lang.String
xsd:NMTOKENS	java.lang.String
xsd:duration	java.lang.String
xsd:gYear	java.lang.String
xsd:gMonth	java.lang.String

SOAP Type	Java Type
xsd:gDay	java.lang.String
xsd:gYearMonth	java.lang.String
xsd:gMonthDay	java.lang.String
xsd:date	java.lang.Date, java.lang.Calender
xsd:time	java.lang.Calender
xsd:dateTime	java.lang.Calender
xsd:anyURI	java.net.URI
xsd:base64Binary	byte[]
xsd:hexBinary	byte[]

JAX-WS supports arrays of any of the supported Java types as parameters. You can even pass custom Java objects (called *value types*), so long as the object's data fields are in the set of supported types and they are not defined as final or transient. If any of the data fields are *not* declared as public, they must have matching get and set methods. Additionally, the object must not implement the java.rmi.Remote interface, and it must have a public default constructor. So long as all of these rules are met, value types can be passed as method parameters and return values.

A Sample JAX-WS Web Service

To build a Web Service with JAX-WS, you begin with a Java interface that you define. The methods on the interface are made available remotely via SOAP, and the WSDL to describe them is generated as well. As a JAX-WS Web Service developer, you will never need to write code to parse or create SOAP messages directly. This is done for you transparently by the JAX-WS run-time.

The JWSDP comes with a reference implementation of JAX-WS. Most implementations support the use of JAX-WS in standalone J2SE applications, a J2EE servlet container, or a J2EE EJB container. A servlet is the typical choice for a JAX-WS Web Service implementation, and therefore the sample Web Service application explored here is implemented as one.

You start with the definition of a Java interface, which contains the methods you wish to expose as a Web Service. Remember, the parameters and return values of the methods on this interface must adhere to the list of types from Table 8.2. The interface we define for this example is com.TradingSystem.OrderProcessorInt, shown in Listing 8.24. The interface contains four methods:

placeMarketOrder: Supply your customer ID, a stock ticker, and a quantity to place an order at the market trading price.

placeLimitOrder: Supply your customer ID, a stock ticker, a quantity, and a price to buy or sell at if the market price reaches it.

getPosition: Returns the number of shares owned for the supplied stock ticker.

getValue: Returns the amount of money you have gained, or lost, for the supplied stock.

ON THE CD

You can find the interface, the implementing class, and all of the code for this sample application on the CD-ROM in the /Chapter8/JAXRPCOrder folder.

LISTING 8.24 The JAX-WS-Compliant Order Processor Interface

```
package com.TradingSystem;
import java.rmi.*;

public interface OrderProcessorInt extends Remote
{
    public double placeMarketOrder( byte type, String ticker,
                                    int quantity, long customerId)
        throws RemoteException;

    public boolean placeLimitOrder( byte type, String ticker,
                                    double price,
                                    int quantity, long customerId)
        throws RemoteException;

    public int getPosition(String ticker, long customerId)
        throws RemoteException;

    public double getValue(String ticker, long customerId)
        throws RemoteException;
}
```

You must also supply an implementation of this interface that will ultimately become the Web Service itself. This class (see Listing 8.25) contains the business logic for the methods in the interface and does not need to contain any Web Service or XML-specific code at all; the JAX-WS run-time takes care of that for you. A portion of the class is shown here to illustrate the point.

LISTING 8.25   The Order Processor Implementation

```java
package com.TradingSystem;
import java.util.*;

public class OrderProcessor implements OrderProcessorInt
{
    class CustomerOrder {
        public long customerId;
        public String ticker;
        public int position;
        public double purchasePrice;
        public double currentValue;
    }
    private HashMap orders = new HashMap();

    public OrderProcessor() {
    }

    public double placeMarketOrder( byte type, String ticker,
                                    int quantity, long customerId)
    {
        // execute order
        double price = executeOrder(type, ticker, quantity);

        // store order
        CustomerOrder order = new CustomerOrder();
        order.purchasePrice = price;
        order.position = quantity;
        order.currentValue = 0;
        order.ticker = ticker;
        order.customerId = customerId;
        orders.put(order, new Long(customerId));

        return price;
    }

    public boolean placeLimitOrder( /*...*/ ) { /*...*/ }
    public int getPosition( /*...*/ ) { /*...*/ }
    public double getValue( /*...*/ ) { /*...*/ }
    private double executeOrder( /*...*/ ) { /*...*/ }
    private boolean executeLimitOrder( /*...*/ ) { /*...*/ }
}
```

In order to turn this plain old Java object into a full-fledged Web Service, you must first run the JAX-WS wscompile utility to create the WSDL file and the mapping.xml file that is used at deploy time. The wscompile utility comes with JAX-WS and is located in the jwsdp/jaxrpc/bin folder of your JWSDP installation. There are two versions: wscompile.bat for Windows and wscompile.sh for UNIX. When you run this utility, you must supply the location of the output folder and the class-path that contains the class files. You must also provide a file, named config-interface.xml, which tells wscompile how to create the WSDL. Listing 8.26 shows the contents of this file for the order-processor sample application. For this example, you can execute the mk_wsdl.bat file in the /Chapter8/JAXRPCOrder/OrderProcessor folder, which invokes the following command to create both the WSDL and mapping files:

```
> wscompile -define -mapping build/mapping.xml -d build -nd build -
classpath build;./ config-interface.xml
```

LISTING 8.26   A Sample JAX-WS config-interface.xml File

```xml
<?xml version="1.0" encoding="UTF-8"?>
<configuration
  xmlns="http://java.sun.com/xml/ns/jax-rpc/ri/config">
  <service
      name="OrderProcessorService"
      targetNamespace="urn:JAXRPCOrder"
      typeNamespace="urn:JAXRPCOrder"
      packageName="JAXRPCOrder">
      <interface name="com.TradingSystem.OrderProcessorInt"/>
  </service>
</configuration>
```

JAX-WS uses the value of the attribute, name, as the WSDL filename (in this case it is OrderProcessorService.wsdl). Next, you specify the namespace for the generated XML files to avoid conflicts with other Web Services and deployed software. Finally, you specify the interface name for which the utility will use Java reflection and generate the matching WSDL. The resulting WSDL will include all of the data types and SOAP operations for the Web Service.

Now that the JAX-WS Web Service has been defined and the WSDL generated, the generated mapping.xml file is used to deploy it. The most straightforward way to deploy your Web Service is as a servlet, using the generic J2EE deploytool utility. This utility should work with most application servers and servlet engines, such as the Sun Java System Application Server, which comes with the J2EE installation package. As an alternative to running the wscompile and deploytool utilities manually, the J2EE tutorial and sample applications contain Apache Ant scripts that will build your project's Java code, run the `wscompile` utility, and deploy the Web Service for you. These Ant scripts are meant to be easily adapted to your own projects.

A Sample JAX-WS Client

A JAX-WS Web Service client application is written to use *stub* classes that represent the remote Web Service. The stubs are generated from the Web Service's WSDL, which describes the remote methods as XML messages. When you make method calls on the proxy object, the JAX-WS run-time is invoked to translate them into SOAP messages, which are then sent to the remote Web Service. When the SOAP response is received, it is translated back into a Java object and provided as the return value from the proxy method call, as shown in Figure 8.8.

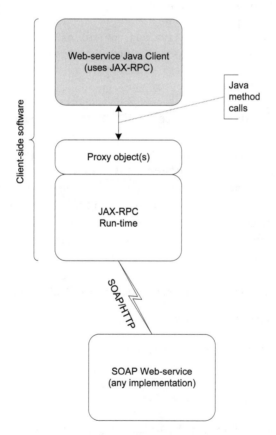

FIGURE 8.8 A JAX-WS Web Service client makes Java method calls that are translated to SOAP messages by the JAX-WS run-time.

To generate the stub classes, you again run the `wscompile` utility, but this time you supply a `config-wsdl.xml` file, which tells the utility where to find the WSDL and what package name to use for the generated stub classes. In this example (see Listing 8.27) the configuration file points to the `OrderProcessorService.wsdl` file generated in the previous section and uses the package name `staticstubs` for all generated stub classes. For this example, you can execute the `mk_stub.bat` file, in the `/Chapter8/JAXRPCOrder/OrderProcessor` folder, which invokes the following command to create the stub classes:

```
> wscompile -gen:client -d build -classpath build config-wsdl.xml
```

LISTING 8.27 A Sample JAX-WS `config-wsdl.xml` File

```xml
<?xml version="1.0" encoding="UTF-8"?>
<configuration
  xmlns="http://java.sun.com/xml/ns/jax-rpc/ri/config">
  <wsdl location="build/OrderProcessorService.wsdl"
        packageName="staticstubs"/>
</configuration>
```

Now that the Web Service has been built and deployed, and the stubs for it have been created, we can go ahead and develop the client application to use it (see Listing 8.28). To begin, import the `javax.xml.rpc.Stub` package, as well as the package for the stub classes generated above. In this example, that package name is `staticstubs`. The very first thing the client application needs to do is create an instance of the stub object. This occurs in the `createProxy` method in this example, where an instance of the `OrderProcessorService_Impl` class is created and returned. In general, for any JAX-WS client application, the stub class will follow the naming convention `<WebServiceName>_impl.class`.

LISTING 8.28 The Order-Processor Web Service Static-Stub Client Implementation

```java
package com.TradingSystem;

import javax.xml.rpc.Stub;
import staticstubs.*;

public class OrderClient
{
    public static String endpointAddress =
        "http://localhost:8080/JAXRPCOrder/orderservice";
```

```
public static final byte BUY = 1;
public static final byte SELL = 2;
public static final long id = 12345;

public static void main( String[] args )
{
    try {
        Stub stub = createProxy();

        stub._setProperty(
            javax.xml.rpc.Stub.ENDPOINT_ADDRESS_PROPERTY,
            endpointAddress);

        OrderProcessorInt_Stub orderProc =
            (OrderProcessorInt_Stub)stub;

        double price =
            orderProc.placeMarketOrder(BUY, "SUNW", 400, id);

        System.out.println("Stock bought at: $" + price);
    }
    catch (Exception ex) {
        ex.printStackTrace();
    }
}

private static Stub createProxy()
{
    OrderProcessorService_Impl impl =
        new OrderProcessorService_Impl();

    return (Stub)impl.getOrderProcessorIntPort();
}
}
```

Next, the stub object is cast to an object of class `OrderProcessorInt_Stub`. This class contains the stub method calls that we can make to the order processor Web Service. This is illustrated with the call to `placeMarketOrder`, with the appropriate parameters. JAX-WS will convert this method call into a SOAP request message and send it to the Web Service. The SOAP response message sent back from the server is then converted, by JAX-WS, into the method's return value (a `double` in this case).

In our example, the Web Service is running as a Java servlet and is therefore accessible via a URL as seen in this sample client. However, if the Web Service were deployed as an EJB running within an application server somewhere on your network, your client code would need to use Java Naming and Directory Interface (JNDI) to access it. In this case, you would need to use the generated Service object, as shown here:

```
Context context = new InitialContext();
OrderProcessorService orderService = (OrderProcessorService)
  context.lookup("java:comp/env/service/MyOrderProcessorServer");
OrderProcessorInt orderProc =
  (OrderProcessorInt)orderService.getOrderProcessorIntPort();
((Stub)orderProc)._setProperty(
  ENDPOINT_ADDRESS_PROPERTY, endpointAddress);
double price = orderProc.placeMarketBid( /*...*/ );
```

A JAX-WS Dynamic Proxy Client

The sample client application from the previous section was an example of a *static stub client*, because it used classes that represent a snapshot of the Web Service at the time they were created. What happens if the Web Service is updated with new methods or changes to existing methods, and is redeployed? The static stub client application will most likely break, as the Web Service method signatures have changed. Building a JAX-WS *dynamic proxy* client solves this problem.

To generate the dynamic proxy classes, you again run the wscompile utility, but this time with a slightly modified version of the config-wsdl.xml file. This file contains the URL to the running Web Service to load the WSDL and the package name to use for the generated classes. In this example (see Listing 8.29) the configuration file points to *http://localhost:8080/JAXRPCOrder/orderservice?wsdl* and uses the package name dynamicproxy for all generated classes. For this example, you can execute the mk_dynproxy.bat file, in the /Chapter8/JAXRPCOrder/OrderProcessor folder, which invokes the following command to create the stub classes:

```
> wscompile -import -d build -classpath build config-wsdl-dyn.xml
```

LISTING 8.29   A Sample JAX-WS config-wsdl-dyn.xml File

```
<?xml version="1.0" encoding="UTF-8"?>
<configuration
    xmlns="http://java.sun.com/xml/ns/jax-rpc/ri/config">
  <wsdl location="http://localhost:8080/JAXRPCOrder/
                  orderservice?wsdl"
        packageName="dynamicproxy"/>
</configuration>
```

Once the dynamic proxy classes are generated, we can write the client application that uses them to access the order processor Web Service (see Listing 8.30). First, you must import the package that includes the dynamic proxy classes (dynamicproxy.*), as well as the JAX-WS packages, javax.xml.rpc.ServiceFactory and javax.xml.rpc.Service. Next, create an instance of the Service class, using the ServiceFactory class, the Web Service name, namespace, and URL. Although it's hard-coded in this example, this information can be read from the WSDL file at run-time to remain a truly dynamic client application. Next, a proxy to the order processor Web Service's interface, represented by the Java interface OrderProcessorInt, is retrieved via the Service.getPort method. Finally, the client application is ready to make calls to the service through the proxy, such as the call to placeMarketOrder, shown in this example. As with the static stub client, all calls to the Web Service, and all responses back, are sent and received as SOAP messages; JAX-WS performs the translation to and from method calls for you.

LISTING 8.30 The Order Processor Web Service Dynamic-Proxy Client Implementation

```java
package com.TradingSystem;

import java.net.URL;
import javax.xml.rpc.*;
import javax.xml.namespace.QName;
import dynamicproxy.*;

public class OrderClient
{
    //...

    public static void main( String[] args )
    {
        try {
            String UrlString = endpointAddress + "?WSDL";
            String nameSpaceUri = "urn:JAXRPCOrder";
            String serviceName = "OrderProcessorService";
            String portName = "OrderProcessorIntPort";

            URL orderWsdlUrl = new URL(UrlString);

            ServiceFactory serviceFactory =
                ServiceFactory.newInstance();

            QName qname = new QName(nameSpaceUri, serviceName);
            Service helloService =
```

```
                    serviceFactory.createService(
                                  orderWsdlUrl,
                                  qname);

            qname = new QName(nameSpaceUri, portName);
            OrderProcessorInt orderProxy =
                (OrderProcessorInt)helloService.getPort(
                                  qname,
                                  OrderProcessorInt.class);

            double price =
                orderProc.placeMarketOrder(BUY, "SUNW", 400, id);

            System.out.println("Stock bought at: $" + price);
        }
        catch ( Exception e ) {
            e.printStackTrace();
        }
    }
}
```

A JAX-WS Dynamic Invocation Interface Client

JAX-WS makes it possible to write an entirely generic client application that does not reference static stubs *or* dynamic proxy classes at all. This client, called a *dynamic invocation interface* (DII) client, defines method calls to a Web Service dynamically at run-time. The resulting code is rather tedious and quite a bit more complex when compared to the prior two client applications we explored. However, the benefit is that it's possible to develop a generic client application that can be used to call *any* Web Service by reading the required method setup data from a property file. The client application in Listing 8.31 is a DII client that is specific to the order processor Web Service we have been exploring. It doesn't require you to import the stub or proxy classes generated earlier.

LISTING 8.31   A JAX-WS Dynamic Invocation Interface Client Implementation

```
package com.TradingSystem;

import javax.xml.rpc.Call;
import javax.xml.rpc.Service;
import javax.xml.namespace.QName;
import javax.xml.rpc.ServiceFactory;
import javax.xml.rpc.ParameterMode;
```

```
public class OrderClient
{
    //...
    public static String ENCODING_STYLE_PROPERTY =
        "javax.xml.rpc.encodingstyle.namespace.uri";
    public static String NS_XSD =
        "http://www.w3.org/2001/XMLSchema";
    public static String URI_ENCODING =
        "http://schemas.xmlsoap.org/soap/encoding/";

    public static void main(String[] args) {
        try {
            String nameSpaceUri = "urn:JAXRPCOrder";
            String serviceName = "OrderProcessorService";
            String portName = "OrderProcessorIntPort";

            ServiceFactory factory =
                ServiceFactory.newInstance();
            QName qname = new QName(serviceName);
            Service service = factory.createService(qname);
            QName port = new QName(portName);

            Call call = service.createCall(port);
            call.setTargetEndpointAddress(endpointAddress);
            call.setProperty(Call.SOAPACTION_USE_PROPERTY,
                            new Boolean(true));
            call.setProperty(Call.SOAPACTION_URI_PROPERTY,
                            "");
            call.setProperty(ENCODING_STYLE_PROPERTY,
                            URI_ENCODING);

            QName QNAME_TYPE_STRING = new QName(NS_XSD, "string");
            QName QNAME_TYPE_BYTE = new QName(NS_XSD, "byte");
            QName QNAME_TYPE_INT = new QName(NS_XSD, "int");
            QName QNAME_TYPE_LONG = new QName(NS_XSD, "long");
            QName QNAME_TYPE_DOUBLE = new QName(NS_XSD, "double");

            // Create a method call object with the method's name
            QName operation = new QName(nameSpaceUri,
                                    "placeMarketOrder");
            call.setOperationName(operation);
```

```
                    // Add parameter names and types
                    call.addParameter(  "byte_1",
                            QNAME_TYPE_BYTE, ParameterMode.IN);
                    call.addParameter(  "String_2",
                            QNAME_TYPE_STRING, ParameterMode.IN);
                    call.addParameter(  "int_3",
                            QNAME_TYPE_INT, ParameterMode.IN);
                    call.addParameter(  "long_4",
                            QNAME_TYPE_LONG, ParameterMode.IN);

                    // Set the return value type
                    call.setReturnType(QNAME_TYPE_DOUBLE);

                    // Add the parameter values
                    Object[] paramVals = {  BUY, "SUNW",
                                            new Integer(400),
                                            new Long(12345) };

                    // Invoke the Web Service call
                    Double price = (Double)call.invoke(paramVals);
                    System.out.println("Price bought at: $" + price);
                }
            catch ( Exception e ) {
                    e.printStackTrace();
                }
            }
        }
    }
```

First, an instance of the Service class is created. Next, a javax.xml.rpc.Call object is created for this Web Service. Next, some properties are set to tell JAX-WS to use SOAP for the method calls and provide the URI encoding style. Next, javax.xml.namespace.QName objects are created for each of the data types to be used in the calls to the Web Service. Finally, after the method name, parameter types, return type, and parameter values are supplied, the call is made via the Call.invoke method.

JAVA API FOR XML REGISTRY (JAXR)

Since a URL is the standard convention used for client-to-Web-Service communication, this implies that both the client and service can exist anywhere (logically and physically) on the Internet. To enable the discovery, lookup, and publication of globally deployed Web Services, various registry standards have been created (such as UDDI: *http://www.uddi.org*). The *Java API for XML Registry (JAXR)* is a standard API for accessing Web Service application registries such as UDDI and ebXML (*http://www.ebxml.org*). Not only does JAXR provide a universal API that can be used with any JAXR-compliant registry provider, but it defines a plug-in architecture that allows support for a wide range of registry software and standards (see Figure 8.9). This chapter, and the remainder of this book, will focus mainly on the UDDI standard as a Web Service registry.

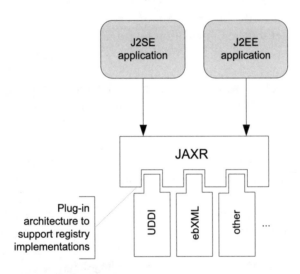

FIGURE 8.9   JAXR, through its plug-in architecture, supports multiple directory standards.

Following the pattern seen with JMS and JAXM, the JAXR specification defines a JAXR provider as software that implements access to a registry via the JAXR API and a JAXR client application as software that uses the JAXR API to access a registry. There are two main JAXR packages: `javax.xml.registry` and `javax.xml.registry.infomodel`. The first package defines a model of classes and interfaces that allow access to a registry. The second package defines a model of classes and interfaces that describe the contents of a registry.

This section provides a very quick glance at the JAXR API; for more detailed information, download the JAXR specification from Sun at http://java.sun.com/ xml/downloads/jaxr.html.

Writing a JAXR Client Application

Let's explore how to use JAXR as we examine a simple client application. The basic steps that are followed for any application that wants to locate a service are as follows:

1. Create a connection to a registry.
2. Query the registry by organization name, business classification, or service name.
3. Query the organization for contact information.
4. Query the organization for services.
5. Get service information for an organization, such as its URI (from which you can query for WSDL, etc.).

ON THE CD

The code listings used in this section come from a simple JAXR client application located on the book's CD-ROM in the /Chapter8/JAXRTest folder.

Create a Connection

The first thing a JAXR client must do is connect to a registry provider (see Listing 8.32). You start with a javax.xml.registry.ConnectionFactory object, on which you set properties such as the registry URL. In this example, the registry to connect to is the IBM test registry, *http://uddi.ibm.com/testregistry/inquiryapi.* If successful, the createConnection call will return a valid javax.xml.registry.Connection object.

LISTING 8.32   JAXR Code to Connect to a Registry

```
public void createConnection(String url)
{
    try {
        ConnectionFactory factory =
            ConnectionFactory.newInstance();

        Properties props = new Properties();
        props.setProperty(
            "javax.xml.registry.queryManagerURL", queryUrl);
        props.setProperty(
            "javax.xml.registry.lifeCycleManagerURL", publishURL);
        factory.setProperties(props);

        connection = factory.createConnection();

        log("Opened connection");
    }
```

```
        catch (Exception e) {
            e.printStackTrace();
        }
    }
```

A client can alternatively connect to registry via JNDI, as shown here:

```
Context context = new InitialContext();
ConnectionFactory factory =
    (ConnectionFactory)context.lookup("java:comp/env/eis/JAXR");
```

Find an Organization

Regardless of how it is obtained, once you have a `Connection` object you may begin using it to query for organizations and services (see Listing 8.33). First, you get a reference to a `RegistryService` object, which is then used to get a reference to a `BusinessQueryManager` object. With this object, you form a query by providing search qualifiers and a text pattern to search for. Search qualifiers specify sorting (by name or publish date, for instance) and filtering criteria. The code in this simple example tells JAXR to find all organizations that match the given text pattern and sort them by name, via the call to `findOrganizations`.

LISTING 8.33   Query a JAXR Registry Connection

```
public BulkResponse makeQuery(String query)
{
    BulkResponse response = null;

    try {
        // Get registry service and query manager
        RegistryService rs =
            connection.getRegistryService();
        BusinessQueryManager bqm =
            rs.getBusinessQueryManager();

        // Find using the name
        Collection findQual = new ArrayList();
        Collection namePatterns = new ArrayList();
        findQual.add(FindQualifier.SORT_BY_NAME_DESC);
        namePatterns.add("%" + query + "%");
        response = bqm.findOrganizations(
                    findQual,
                    namePatterns,
                    null, null, null, null);
```

```
                    return response;
              }
              catch (Exception e) {
                  e.printStackTrace();
              }


              return response;
          }
```

If nothing could be found to match your criteria, a null is returned. If your query is successful, the result will be a BulkResponse object that contains a Java Collection of one or more javax.xml.registry.infomodel.Organization objects. Your code can iterate through the collection to access each Organization object within (see Listing 8.34) and extract information such as the organization's name, description, contact information (phone numbers and email addresses), and the services it offers.

LISTING 8.34   Iterate through the Returned Organizations

```
          public void displayOrganizations(Collection orgs)
          {
              try {
                  Iterator orgIter = orgs.iterator();
                  while ( orgIter.hasNext() )
                  {
                      Organization org = (Organization)orgIter.next();
                      log("Organization Found");
                      log("name: " + getName(org));
                      log("description: " + getDesc(org));
                      log("key: " + getKey(org));

                      // Display primary contact information
                      User contact = org.getPrimaryContact();
                      displayContact(contact);

                      // Display service and binding information
                      Collection services = org.getServices();
                      displayServices(services);
                  }
              }
              catch ( Exception e ) {
                  e.printStackTrace();
              }
          }
```

Find a Service

The point of using a registry is to locate a service (such as a Web Service) that your client can use. Although this example so far simply iterates through a list of organizations and their available services, in reality, your application is more likely to search for a specific classification of services or an organization that implements a specific WSDL. Regardless of a client application's specific intent, most of the code seen so far will be needed.

A call to the `Organization.getServices` method returns a Java `Collection` of `Service` objects—one for each service that organization implements (see Listing 8.35). A `Service` object contains meta-data such as a name and a description of the service itself. It also contains a list of child `ServiceBinding` objects that map to UDDI `bindingTemplate` structures (each of which represents a Web Service). Each `ServiceBinding` has its own meta-data, as well as a URI for its location.

LISTING 8.35   Iterate through an Organization's Available Services

```
public void displayServices(Collection services)
{
    try {
        Iterator serviceIter = services.iterator();
        while (serviceIter.hasNext())
        {
            Service service = (Service)serviceIter.next();
            log("Service Found");
            log("name: " + getName(service));
            log("description: " + getDesc(service));

            Collection serviceBindings =
                service.getServiceBindings();

            Iterator bindIter = serviceBindings.iterator();
            while (bindIter.hasNext())
            {
                ServiceBinding bind =
                    (ServiceBinding)bindIter.next();
                log("Binding Found");
                log("description: " + getDesc(bind));
                log("URI: " + bind.getAccessURI() );
            }
        }
    }
```

```
        catch ( Exception e ) {
            e.printStackTrace();
        }
    }
}
```

Create an Organization

So far, the discussion has focused on the discovery and retrieval of organizations and services within a registry using JAXR. Let's turn our focus to publishing a service to an available registry. The JAXR `javax.xml.registry.BusinessLifeCycle Management` class allows you to create (and remove) organizations, associations, services, classifications, and concepts for a registry. The sample code in Listing 8.36 uses JAXR to perform the following steps:

1. Obtain a reference to the `BusinessLifeCycleManagement` class from the `RegistryService` class.
2. Provide the proper credentials (a `PasswordAuthentication` object) to the registry connection.
3. Create an `Organization` object.
4. Create user contact information.
5. Find a classification scheme such as the WSDL classification, the North American Industry Classification System (NAICS), the Universal Standard Products and Services Classification (UNSPSC), or the ISO 3166 classification for country codes.
6. Create one or more organization `Concept` objects to store URLs to the service's WSDL documents.
7. Create one or more organization `Service` objects and bind them to service implementations.
8. Save the new organization in the registry.

The code to create the `Concept` and `Service` objects for the order processor Web Service is covered in the next two sections.

LISTING 8.36   JAXR Code to Create an Organization

```
public Organization createOrg()
{
    Organization org = null;
    try {
        RegistryService rs =
            connection.getRegistryService();
        BusinessLifeCycleManager blcm =
            rs.getBusinessLifeCycleManager();
```

```
BusinessQueryManager bqm =
    rs.getBusinessQueryManager();

// authorization
PasswordAuthentication auth =
    new PasswordAuthentication(
        username, password.toCharArray());
Set creds = new HashSet();
creds.add(auth);
connection.setCredentials(creds);

org = blcm.createOrganization("My Organization");
InternationalString desc =
    blcm.createInternationalString(
            "A Web-services Company");
org.setDescription(desc);

// Create primary contact
User contact = blcm.createUser();
//...
org.setPrimaryContact(contact);

// Create concept and classification here...

// Create service here...

// Add organization and submit
Collection orgs = new ArrayList();
orgs.add(org);
BulkResponse response = blcm.saveOrganizations(orgs);
Collection exceptions = response.getExceptions();
}
catch ( Exception e ) {
    e.printStackTrace();
}
return org;
}
```

Create a Concept

A JAXR Concept object is used to reference a service's technical specification, such as a WSDL document, through the containment of an ExternalLink object. An ExternalLink object contains the URL for the service specification. The code in Listing 8.37 contains the code (left out of the previous sample code) that creates a Concept object for the order-processor Web Service's WSDL document.

LISTING 8.37   JAXR Code to Create a `Concept` Object

```
// Create a concept
Concept specConcept =
    blcm.createConcept(null, "OrderConcept", "");
desc = blcm.createInternationalString(
    "Concept for Order Processor Service");
specConcept.setDescription(s);
ExternalLink wsdlLink =
    blcm.createExternalLink(
        "http://localhost:8080/JAXRPCOrder/orderservice?wsdl",
        "Orfer Processor WSDL document");
specConcept.addExternalLink(wsdlLink);

String schemeName = "uddi-org:types";
ClassificationScheme uddiOrgTypes =
bqm.findClassificationSchemeByName(null, schemeName);

Collection concepts = new ArrayList();
concepts.add(specConcept);
BulkResponse concResponse = blcm.saveConcepts(concepts);

Classification classification =
    blcm.createClassification(
        uddiOrgTypes,"wsdlSpec", "wsdlSpec");
specConcept.addClassification(classification);
```

Create a Service

Finally, the organization's services are defined as JAXR `Service` objects. The code in Listing 8.38 creates a new service with a name and description and adds it to the list of services for the newly created `Organization` object. `ServiceBinding` objects are created and added to the `Service` object to describe the service and how to access it.

LISTING 8.38   JAXR Code to Create a Service

```
// Create service bindings
Collection bindings = new ArrayList();
ServiceBinding bind = blcm.createServiceBinding();
is = blcm.createInternationalString("Binding Description");
bind.setDescription(is);
bind.setValidateURI(false);
bind.setAccessURI(
    "http://localhost:8080/JAXRPCOrder/orderservice/sb");
bindings.add(bind);
```

```
// Create a service
Collection services = new ArrayList();
Service service = blcm.createService("My Service");
InternationalString is =
    blcm.createInternationalString(
        "My Service Description");
service.setDescription(is);
service.addServiceBindings(bindings);
services.addService(service);
org.addServices(services);
```

SUMMARY

This chapter provided a comprehensive study of the technologies available in the Java Web Service Developer Pack, including JAXP, JAXB, JAXM, SAAJ, JAX-WS, and JAXR. We explored each area of technology with sample Java code that included XML documents, XML schema, WSDL, and UDDI, where applicable. From the simple parsing of XML with SAX and DOM, to the construction of an entire Web Service, this chapter forms the foundation to combine JMS with the XML-based Web Service development concepts learned in this chapter. This form of reliable distributed application architecture is explored in detail in the next chapter.

9

Distributed Application Architecture

In This Chapter

- The Complete Trading System Sample Application
- JMS and the Internet
- JMS + SOAP = Reliability
- Loosely Coupled Components (The Company Data Web Service)
- Building for Scale (The Quotes Web Service)
- Reliability (The Order Processor Web Service)
- Deploying and Running the Trading System

THE COMPLETE TRADING SYSTEM SAMPLE APPLICATION

In this chapter, most of the Java messaging concepts we've discussed so far will be combined into one distributed application (see Figure 9.1). The application combines the use of Java Message Service (JMS) and Simple Object Access Protocol (SOAP) messaging (using both SOAP with Attachments API for Java [SAAJ] and Java API for XML-Based Remote Procedure Calls [JAX-RPC]) to demonstrate how these two areas of technology can be used together. The application, a sample trading system, will combine a sophisticated quotes service to retrieve the latest (delayed) stock quote data for a requested company, a component to retrieve fundamental company data for user research, and an order-processing component that simulates the buying and selling of company stock.

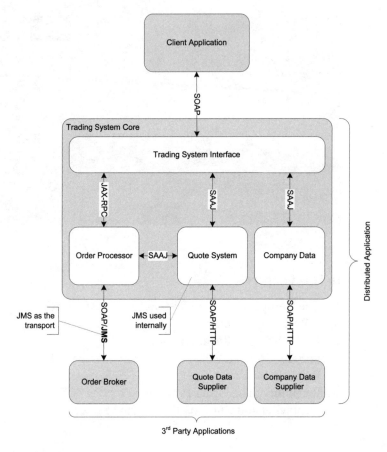

FIGURE 9.1 An overview of the components of the sample trading system application.

The order processor service is the JAX-WS application we examined in Chapter 8 with some enhancements:

- The use of SAAJ to get the latest quotes from the quotes service
- The transport of SOAP messages over JMS to reliably execute stock buy and sell transactions with a third-party system

The company data service uses SAAJ to return data about a company in XML form in a SOAP message with HTML attachments that contain the company's cash flow, income statement, and balance sheet. The quotes service uses JMS internally to queue stock quote requests, which are handled by one of multiple deployed order request applications for redundancy. The quotes service itself can be deployed across multiple load-balanced Web Servers such as Apache Tomcat for scalability and failover. The objective of using the various APIs and designs for the Web Services that make up this application is to demonstrate how to build reliable, scalable, distributed applications using the material you've learned in this book.

JMS AND THE INTERNET

JMS is a useful technology when you want to communicate between applications running on a network. The first thing that comes to mind is that JMS communication can be used between applications on a LAN in data center. This type of environment is controlled, isolated, and predictable; you can measure and maintain messaging performance very well—but will this design work on a WAN, or even the Internet? Most JMS providers do support WAN operation, and many distributed applications run in a WAN environment.

An example may be an application running in a data center in New York that places messages on a queue in a server running in London. If both data centers are owned by the same company, dedicated lines of communication can be leased to ensure secure, reliable connectivity between the two locations. However, if the Internet is chosen as the path of communication, the situation changes for the following reasons:

- Connectivity is not guaranteed (connections may be lost unexpectedly).
- Communication performance cannot be guaranteed.
- Network latency can vary by geographic region.
- Network and application security can be compromised.

Since the Internet is a web of networks connected together, where hundreds of network nodes can be involved in the relay of packets from a client to a server, network connectivity is far from a guarantee. Similar factors affect performance as well:

- Messages to and from the same nodes may be routed differently, resulting in different transmission times.
- Usage trends during the day may affect network traffic and hence performance.
- The telecommunication infrastructure in different areas of the world are not as advanced or reliable as others.

Maintaining a constant JMS connection over the Internet is certain to be troublesome at times, although it may be stable at other times. This lack of dependability is what reliable messaging is supposed to help you avoid. Besides, opening up client and server networks for JMS communication is a security risk; most Internet-facing networks employ layers of network firewalls to close all but a few necessary ports (such as HTTP port 80). However, the Internet is too convenient and omnipresent to dismiss; there's no reason why JMS shouldn't work to *some degree* over the Internet.

SOAP + JMS = Reliability

To enable JMS applications to use the Internet as a viable communications link, most JMS providers support the routing of messages over HTTP (see Figure 9.2). The communication between the JMS application and JMS provider remain the same; the provider encapsulates the communication over the Internet by effectively tunneling over port 80 (HTTP). The result is that JMS messages are translated and sent as stateless HTTP requests. Although this may not be ideal in all cases, it works well enough for most. A JMS application can depend on missed acknowledgments and transaction timeouts to know when to resend messages caused by broken Internet connectivity.

Besides using HTTP tunneling techniques, JMS can be combined with Web Services in other ways to build reliable distributed applications. For instance:

1. JMS can be used *within* the implementation of a Web Service to allow for the reliability and redundancy of the service itself. This ensures that the Web Service is available more often for its users.
2. JMS can be used natively as the message transport between components of a service-oriented architecture.
3. JMS can be tunneled through HTTP as the message transport between components of a service-oriented architecture.
4. SOAP messages can be transported over JMS for reliability and to ensure robust transactions.

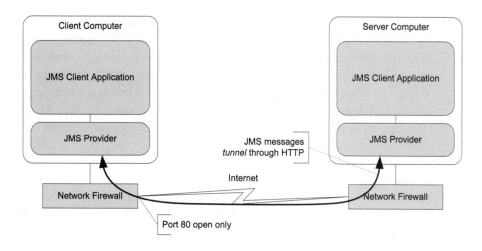

FIGURE 9.2 Most JMS providers support HTTP as a message transport system.

Option 1 will be explored later in this chapter with the implementation of the stock quotes data Web Service. We explored option 2 in Chapter 3, Chapter 4, and Chapter 5 while discussing JMS application programming concepts. Option 3 was discussed in the previous section. Of all the options listed, the fourth is very intriguing because it combines the reliability of JMS communications with the language and platform independence of SOAP messaging. Using software adapters, JMS can even interface to other messaging systems on various platforms, maintaining platform independence to some degree. However, in most implementations of this option, an adapter will be used at either end of the Web Service to translate from SOAP to JMS and back to SOAP (see Figure 9.3).

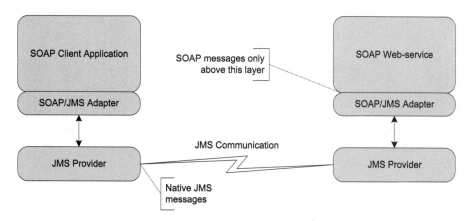

FIGURE 9.3 SOAP messaging over JMS helps ensure the delivery of messages to and from a Web Service.

It is conceivable to combine option 4 with option 3, resulting in a Web Service that communicates with its clients using SOAP only but that uses an adapter to translate to and from JMS messages for reliability. Further, to ensure reliable and secure Internet connectivity in this configuration, the JMS providers can be configured to tunnel over HTTP (see Figure 9.4). The result is *not* equivalent to SOAP over HTTP messaging; by tunneling JMS over HTTP you can still take advantage of message acknowledgments and transactions, which deliver a higher level of reliability than plain SOAP over HTTP.

Additionally, with the proper adapter software, JMS over HTTP messaging can be utilized even by Web Services (and client applications) written to handle SOAP messages only. The adapter can, in a sense, intercept the SOAP messages and translate them to JMS messages for further propagation. The use of Java API for XML Messaging (JAXM) or JAX-RPC in this case is ideal in that these APIs hide the message transport from the SOAP-based application. Simply choose a JAXM or JAX-RPC provider that handles the translation and reliable Web Service messaging will be achievable—without any application code changes.

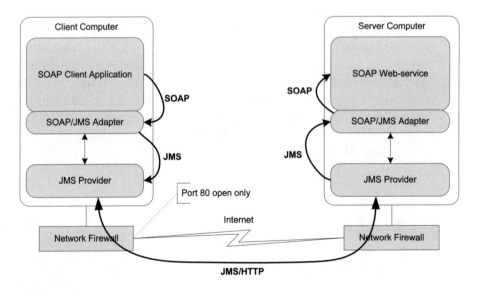

FIGURE 9.4 SOAP messaging with JMS, tunneled over HTTP, offers secure and reliable Web Service communication over the Internet.

The remainder of this chapter will take the options and techniques discussed so far and apply them to the distributed trading system application. Read along as these patterns are applied to the implementation of each component of the system.

The JMSSOAPConnection Class

Let's examine SOAP messaging over JMS in more detail with a utility class that transparently transports SOAPMessage objects as JMS ObjectMessage objects. Packages are available that perform this task, such as Apache Axis (*http://ws.apache. org/axis*), but they are sometimes restricted in terms of which JMS providers they work with. The JMSSOAPConnection class we will examine now should work with any JMS provider, and it serves as a good exercise.

ON THE CD

The JMSSOAPConnection class is located on the book's CD-ROM in the folder named /Chapter9/toolkit/messaging. A very simple Web Service application that uses this class is located in the folder named /Chapter9/SOAPReceiver. To invoke this Web Service, a sample client is located in the folder named /Chapter9/SOAPSender. Both application folders contain scripts to run them.

A Java application uses SOAP messaging by first creating an object of the SOAPConnection class, which is retrieved through the SOAPConnectionFactory class, illustrated here:

```
import javax.xml.soap.*;
    ...
SOAPConnectionFactory scf =
    SOAPConnectionFactory.newInstance();
SOAPConnection con = scf.createConnection();
```

Therefore, to build the utility class, we implement a class name that extends SOAPConnectionFactory, called JMSSOAPConnectionFactory (see Listing 9.1). This class does nothing more than return a new instance of itself when newInstance is called and return a new instance of the JMSSOAPConnection class when createConnection is called. It's in this connection class that the SOAP-over-JMS work is done.

LISTING 9.1   The JMSSOAPConnectionFactory Class

```
package com.toolkit.messaging;

import javax.xml.soap.*;

public class JMSSOAPConnectionFactory extends SOAPConnectionFactory
{
    public static SOAPConnectionFactory newInstance()
        throws SOAPException, UnsupportedOperationException
    {
        return new JMSSOAPConnectionFactory();
    }
```

```
public SOAPConnection createConnection() throws SOAPException
{
    return new JMSSOAPConnection();
}
}
```

The JMSSOAPConnection class (see Listing 9.2) extends the javax.xml.soap. SOAPConnection class and provides an implementation of the base class's call and close methods. The constructor connects to the JMS provider using JNDI and creates two Destination objects for the destinations named "JMSSOAPConnectionReq" and "JMSSOAPConnectionResp" (these are text names, not object names). If this class is used by an object that sends SOAP messages to a service, it creates a JMS Producer for the "JMSSOAPConnectionReq" destination and a Consumer for the "JMSSOAPConnectionResp" destination (see Figure 9.5). If this class is used by an object that listens for (and responds to) SOAP messages, it creates a JMS Producer for the "JMSSOAPConnectionResp" destination and a Consumer for the "JMSSOAPConnectionReq" destination.

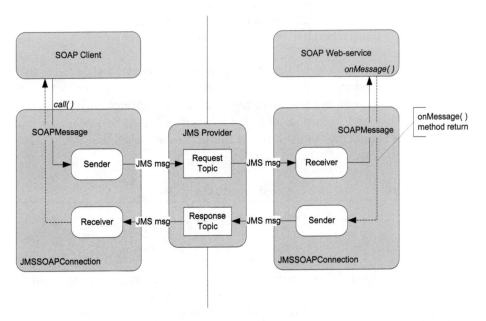

FIGURE 9.5 The flow of SOAP messages from the client, through JMS, and to the server.

LISTING 9.2 The `JMSSOAPConnection` Class

```
package com.toolkit.messaging;
import javax.xml.soap.*;
...


public class JMSSOAPConnection extends SOAPConnection
{
    ...

    // this class sends JMS messages
    class Sender {
        ...
    }

    // this class receives JMS messages
    class Listener extends Thread implements MessageListener {
        ...
    }

    public JMSSOAPConnection()
    {
        try {
            InitialContext jndi = new InitialContext();
            ...
            req = (Destination)jndi
                .lookup("JMSSOAPConnectionReq");
            resp = (Destination)jndi
                .lookup("JMSSOAPConnectionResp");
        }
        catch ( Exception e ) {
            e.printStackTrace();
        }
    }

    public SOAPMessage call(SOAPMessage request, Object to)
    {
        try {
            // Send requests, listen for responses
            sender = new Sender(req);
            listener = new Listener(resp);
```

```java
            // Send over JMS
            sender.send(to, request);

            // Wait for response
            SOAPMessage response = waitForResponse(to);
            return response;
        }
        catch ( Exception e ) {
            e.printStackTrace();
        }

        return null;
    }

    public void close()
    {
        try {
            // stop sender and listener
            ...
        }
        catch ( Exception e ) {
            e.printStackTrace();
        }
    }

    public void register(Object obj)
    {
        try {
            // Listen for requests, send responses
            sender = new Sender(resp);
            listener = new Listener(req);

            Class[] params = new Class[1];
            params[0] = SOAPMessage.class;
            this.receiver = obj;
            method = receiver.getClass().getMethod(
                                "onMessage", params);
        }
        catch ( Exception e ) {
            e.printStackTrace();
        }
    }
```

```
public void onSOAPRequest(Object url, SOAPMessage request)
{
    try {
        // Use reflection to invoke onMessage method
        Object[] params = new Object[1];
        params[0] = request;
        SOAPMessage response =
            (SOAPMessage)method.invoke(receiver, params);

        // Send the SOAP response back to the caller
        sender.send(url, response);
    }
    catch ( Exception e ) {
        e.printStackTrace();
    }
}
}
```

The producer and consumer objects are set up properly in the `call` method (used by SOAP clients) and in the `register` method (used by SOAP services). Components that are implemented to listen for SOAP messages are required to do the following:

1. Implement a method named `onMessage` that takes `SOAPMessage` as a parameter (the SOAP request) and returns a `SOAPMessage` (which is a SOAP response).
2. Call the `JMSSOAPConnection.register` method when ready to receive SOAP requests.

The implementation of the register method first sets up the JMS `Producer` and `Consumer` objects and then uses Java reflection to get a reference to the listener's `onMessage` method. The `onSOAPRequest` method is called when a JMS message arrives, which in turn calls the SOAP receiver's `onMessage` method using reflection. The returned SOAP response is sent back to the caller via JMS.

The code to send the JMS messages is encapsulated in a nested class named `Sender` (see Listing 9.3). When a `SOAPMessage` object is to be sent, it is streamed into a byte array through a combination of a `ByteArrayOutputStream` object, and the `SOAPMessage.writeTo` method. The resulting `byte` array and the object that represents the destination Web Service are wrapped in a `SOAPMsgData` object (included on the CD-ROM) and sent as a JMS `ObjectMessage` object.

ON THE CD

LISTING 9.3 The Nested Class `JMSSOAPConnection.Sender`

```java
class Sender {
    private MessageProducer producer;
    private Session session;

    public Sender(Destination dest) {
        ...
    }

    public void send(Object url, SOAPMessage soapMsg)
    {
        try {
            ByteArrayOutputStream bs = new ByteArrayOutputStream();
            BufferedOutputStream bos = new BufferedOutputStream(bs);
            soapMsg.writeTo(bs);
            bs.flush();

            SOAPMsgData data = new SOAPMsgData();
            data.msg = bs.toByteArray();
            data.url = url;

            ObjectMessage msg = session.createObjectMessage();
            msg.setObject(data);
            producer.send(msg);
        }
        catch ( Exception e ){
            e.printStackTrace();
        }
    }

    public void close() {
        ...
    }
}
```

The code to receive the JMS messages is encapsulated in a nested class named `Listener` (see Listing 9.4). By extending the `Thread` class, this class runs in its own thread, which is started in the constructor. It also implements the `MessageListener` interface and spends its time waiting for JMS messages to arrive. When a message does arrive, it is cast to an `ObjectMessage` class and the `SOAPMsgData` object is retrieved from it. The next step is to convert the `byte` array back into the original `SOAPMessage` object. The `MessageFactory` class is always used to create `SOAPMessages`, and it supports doing so from a `ByteArrayInputStream`. Therefore, the code performs the following steps:

1. Creates a `ByteArrayInputStream` object with the byte array.
2. Creates a `MimeHeaders` object.
3. Add a header named "Content-Type" with the value of `text/xml;charset=utf-8`.
4. Call `MesssageFactory.createMessage`, providing the above two objects.

LISTING 9.4   The Nested Class `JMSSOAPConnection.Listener`

```
class Listener extends Thread implements MessageListener {
    private Session session;
    private MessageConsumer consumer;
    private Destination dest;

    public Listener(Destination dest) {
        this.dest = dest;
        start();
    }

    public void run()
    {
        // Setup JMS
        ...
    }

    public void onMessage(Message message)
    {
        try {
            ObjectMessage msg = (ObjectMessage)message;
            SOAPMsgData data = (SOAPMsgData)msg.getObject();

            ByteArrayInputStream bas =
                new ByteArrayInputStream(data.msg);
            MessageFactory mf = MessageFactory.newInstance();
            MimeHeaders mh = new MimeHeaders();
            mh.addHeader("Content-Type", "text/xml;charset=utf-8");
            SOAPMessage soapMsg = mf.createMessage(mh, bas);

            if ( dest == req )
            {
                // A SOAP request was received
                onSOAPRequest(data.url, soapMsg);
            }
            else
            {
```

```
                        // A SOAP response was received
                        responses.put(data.url, soapMsg);
                }
            }
            catch ( Exception e ) {
                e.printStackTrace();
            }
        }

        public void close() {
            ...
        }
    }
```

Now that we have a valid SOAPMessage object, the code needs to determine what to do with it. Is it a request for a Web Service (which results in a call to onMessage) or is it a response to a request that needs to be returned from the call method that has been blocking this whole time? This turns out to be easy to determine with a simple rule. If the destination that the message was received from is the request destination (it is, in essence, listening for requests), then route the message via a call to the listener's onMessage method. Otherwise, if the listener is listening for responses, then route the response message to the sender as the return from the call method. This is implemented by placing the message in a HashMap object, where the key is the "to" parameter passed to the method call. The method, call, blocks on the original thread and waits for the message to appear within the HashMap. Once it's found in the HashMap, the method simply returns the data to the caller.

The relationships and interactions between the JMS sender and listener objects, and the SOAP sender and listener objects, may seem a little confusing at first. For the most part, you should be able to use this class without understanding exactly how it works. The best way to gain that understanding may be to step through the calls made from both the SOAPSender and SOAPReceiver sample applications.

Next Steps

The implementation of the JMSSOAPConnection class described here is a good start, but it is by no means complete. It should, at a minimum, be enhanced with the following features:

- Be able to make use of transactions
- Be able to use a queue or a topic
- Be able to report errors with a SOAP fault structure
- Be implemented as a true messaging provider for seamless usage from within a JAXM or JAX-RPC application

SOAP was originally designed to work on top of any protocol, although it has been mostly used with HTTP to perform synchronous remote procedure calls over the Internet. However, this can lead to new problems related to component dependencies. For instance, assume you're building an application that uses two SOAP Web Services provided by third-party vendors. It's likely that in the implementation of these Web Services, they themselves use *other* Web Services or are designed in some sort of a service-oriented architecture. Therefore, when your application makes a call to one of the external services, it results in additional calls to each service's child service(s) (see Figure 9.6).

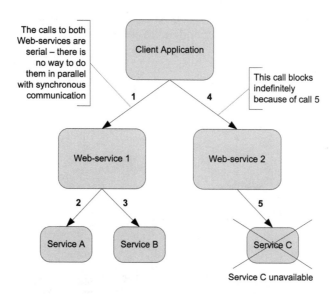

FIGURE 9.6   A tree of synchronous Web Service calls may result in unpredictable behavior at the client application.

Under normal operation, this design is sound and should present no problems. However, if all of the components (including your application) utilize synchronous messaging for their communication, the entire system will grind to a halt if only one of the services has an outage or a network problem. Because of this, there has been a growing trend toward *asynchronous* SOAP messaging [Chappell02]. This basically means that an application that sends a SOAP request will not need to wait for a response, as it does normally. If you recall from the example in the previous section, a call to SOAPConnection.call sends a SOAP request and then blocks until it receives a SOAP response message that is provided as the method's return value.

The entire application was effectively frozen until the response was received, unless some sophisticated threading scheme was used within the application. However, since JMS supports asynchronous messaging, why put this burden on every application that uses it?

The JMSSOAPConnection class should be modified to support both synchronous and asynchronous messaging for the client. This would require the added implementation of an onMessage method within the client application, since the response will no longer be returned when a request is made (see Figure 9.7). Instead, it will arrive some time later (though hopefully not too much later). The class will also require some record-keeping to track the potentially numerous asynchronous responses and route them to the original callers. This enhancement to support asynchronous SOAP messaging goes a long way toward limiting the issues that come with component dependencies and coupling.

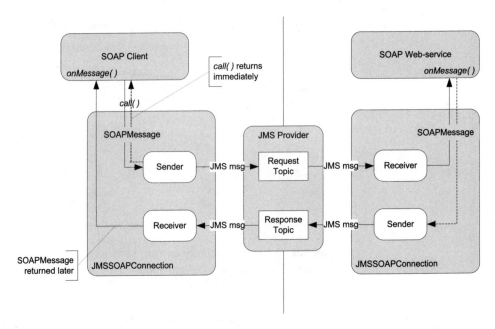

FIGURE 9.7   Asynchronous SOAP messaging can be achieved through the use of JMS.

LOOSELY COUPLED COMPONENTS (THE COMPANY DATA WEB SERVICE)

In Chapter 2, we discussed the perils of software dependencies. Dependencies at a component level within a piece of software, as well as dependencies between entire software systems, lead to complexities that can destroy an application's maintainability, performance, and thus its overall usability. A piece of software that has too many dependencies, or one that has dependencies on the *implementation* of another piece of software, is said to be *tightly coupled*. Tightly coupled software is generally regarded as a bad thing. The alternative is to either not use any other piece of software within your software (not a feasible solution) or to strive for loose coupling.

Loosely coupled software components are those that do not depend on each other's implementation details. Instead, the components are separated by an interface—logical and/or physical. By thoroughly describing the interfaces of software components to be used by other software components, the end result is a *well-integrated*, loosely couple software design. This means that the software was designed to embrace re-use through loose coupling. An example of a *poorly integrated* (not well-integrated) software design is a component that "scrapes" the HTML pages of a personal finance Web site to retrieve stock quote data. Although the components of this system are still loosely coupled, they are not well integrated, and hence the system is a hack. An example of a well-integrated, loosely coupled design is a piece of software that uses a stock quote Web Service to retrieve stock quote data.

The sample trading system application we've been exploring is based on a set of loosely coupled software components (deployed as Web Services) that integrate well to form one cohesive application. Let's explore this design further and illustrate with a component of this system: the company data Web Service.

The Service Tier

Web Services are often used to expose application functionality to paying customers or to integrate legacy systems to newer applications. However, Web Services can become part of an application's design to help achieve component isolation, gain greater scalability, and ease development. This section proposes adding a new tier to the traditional multitiered architecture: the *service tier*. An application built without a service tier can be considered to have a huge flaw: the lack of data hiding, or abstraction. This is because without a service tier, application code must have intimate knowledge of the data sources and associated details, such as database schemas, or low-level software APIs, as illustrated in Figure 9.8. Adding a service tier to your architecture—one that contains Web Services that abstract the data sources from the core business logic code—solves this problem. A service tier should be designed to achieve the following goals:

Abstraction: Hide the details of the data sources (i.e., schemas, APIs).

Simplicity: Generally simplify the process of accessing data. The purpose of adding a tier is to add simplicity to the design of the software as a whole. Introducing complexity here defeats the purpose of abstraction.

Loose coupling: As with all software layers, the service tier and the other tiers should be loosely coupled, with an interface that truly hides all implementation details.

Performance: Although nothing is free, the addition of the service tier should not introduce a significant amount of performance overhead.

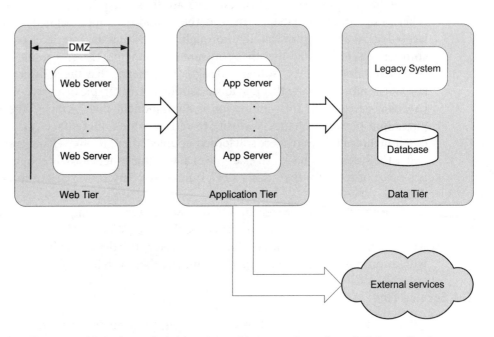

FIGURE 9.8 This is the typical three-tier architecture of Java-based Web applications.

In general, a service tier that achieves the goals outlined here can provide other benefits to the application developer. First, there is greater potential for software re-use as the service tier is accessed through a generic interface. Second, a more efficient development process is achieved as the application tier and the service tier can be developed independently. For example, a developer who is strong in JavaServerPages (JSP) development can concentrate on building the application front-end, while a database developer—or a developer familiar with an external API—can build portions of the service tier. This helps avoid maintenance problems that come from mixing database queries in application-tier code.

Third, system interdependencies, and associated complexity, are greatly re-duced. A well-designed service tier allows back-end data systems to change and evolve independently and transparently from the software components that use them. Finally, true implementation independence is achieved, as the service tier components can be written in a language or an environment different than that of the application. The Simple Object Access Protocol (SOAP) is perhaps the best choice when implementing components of a service tier. SOAP not only achieves the architectural goals and benefits outlined above, but it yields other, practical benefits as well. For example, a SOAP Web Service can be deployed across multiple servers and load-balanced using existing HTTP load-balancing technology.

The SOAP protocol itself defines a strict contract for communication between layers. In addition, SOAP—being based on XML—provides the right level of abstraction, allowing for implementation independence. Figure 9.9 shows a Web application architecture enhanced with a service tier. In this illustration, the Web tier and application tier have been combined for simplicity. The elegance of the design comes from the degree of separation and abstraction achieved across the tiers. The application code becomes simpler, as it no longer deals with the details of individual data sources. SOAP adds consistency to the way data is requested from and returned to the application code.

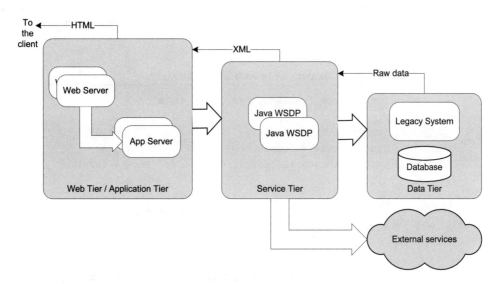

FIGURE 9.9 Adding a service tier to the typical Web-based architecture helps encapsulate data.

Building a service tier—an entire layer of Web Services within your application—adds value to an application's architecture by limiting the coupling between components and by creating the potential for future reuse. Conceivably, the service tier can be extended beyond the boundaries of one application. The service tier can become a company-wide deployment of Web Services available to all applications in your organization. Thus, the need for a meta-data service—a service that describes all available Web Services—may arise.

The Sample Company Data Web Service

The first sample Web Service from the trading system we will explore provides company data and financials when a symbol is provided. This service is implemented using SAAJ and extends the SAAJServlet class (see Listing 9.5), which hides some of the SAAJ/SOAP details from you. In particular, it creates a SOAP connection and retrieves an instance of the MessageFactory class. This is code that you would otherwise need to repeat in all of your Web Services.

When a SOAP request message arrives, the onMessage method is called with the SOAPMessage object. The important information, such as the company's stock ticker symbol, is pulled from request and used to retrieve data about the company from a third-party source. Included is basic data about the company (such as address, phone number, etc.) and the company's recent SEC financial filings. Since the data provider supplies this data as HTML, formatted in such a way that it's ready for presentation, the filings' HTML needs to be sent as an attachment to the SOAP response message.

LISTING 9.5 The Company Data Web Service Servlet

```
package com.TradingSystem.CompanyData;

import javax.servlet.*;
import javax.xml.soap.*;
import com.sun.xml.messaging.soap.server.SAAJServlet;
...

public class CompanyServlet extends SAAJServlet
{
    ...

    public SOAPMessage onMessage(SOAPMessage message)
    {
        try {
            SOAPEnvelope env =
                message.getSOAPPart().getEnvelope();
            SOAPBody bdy = env.getBody();
```

```
// Get stock symbol and CIK from the request
String symbol = "";
String CIK = "";
Iterator iter = bdy.getChildElements();
SOAPElement node = getNode("GetData", iter);
if ( node != null )
{
    iter = node.getChildElements();
    symbol = getNodeValue("symbol", iter);
    CIK = getNodeValue("CIK", iter);
}

// Get the company data from sec.gov
getCompanyData( CIK );

// Create reply SOAP message
SOAPMessage replyMsg = msgFactory.createMessage();
env = replyMsg.getSOAPPart().getEnvelope();
bdy = env.getBody();

// Add all company data to the SOAP body
//
bdy.addChildElement(
    env.createName("symbol")).addTextNode( symbol );
...

// Add the financials HTML as a SOAP Attachment
AttachmentPart ap =
    replyMsg.createAttachmentPart(
        financialHTML, "text/html");

ap.setContentId("financialHTML");
replyMsg.addAttachmentPart(ap);
return replyMsg;
}
catch(Exception e) {
    e.printStackTrace();
}

return null;
}

...
}
```

To do this, first create a response message with the `MessageFactory` object. Next, add the body to the SOAP message, which includes the basic company data. Next, create an `AttachmentPart` object from the response message via the `createAttachmentPart` method. You need to provide, as parameters, the HTML as a `String` object and the `String` "text/html" as the content type. Finally, supply a `String` as the attachment identifier and add it to the `SOAPMessage` object via the `addAttachmentPart` method. Return the `SOAPMessage` from the call, and it will be sent back to the original caller.

This provides an example of how a service-oriented architecture can be used to encapsulate and hide a data provider, thereby limiting the effects to the client if you switched data providers. The data provider may not even be a third-party offering; it may a legacy system within your own company. Fronting that system with a Web Service is an excellent way to bridge the gap between old technology and new. It also limits the coupling between applications, as XML is excellent at abstraction. Instead of importing and writing code to call an external API, you instead use XML to represent the external system requests and receive the responses. However, the resulting system is still cohesive and well integrated, as the SOAP messages (and the accompanying WSDL, if available) sufficiently describe the operations available and the data that is to be returned.

The full implementation of the company data Web Service can be found on the book's CD-ROM in the folder named `/Chapter9/com/TradingSystem/CompanyData`. The company data service is a servlet that needs to be deployed and run within a servlet engine such as Apache Tomcat or an application server that supports standard servlets. More information on how to deploy this servlet is provided later in this chapter.

BUILDING FOR SCALE (THE QUOTES WEB SERVICE)

Although the discussion so far has centered on how Web Services help reduce coupling and provide encapsulation and abstraction, there are some remaining problems that you still need to focus on. The most important of these are performance, scalability, and reliability. You must build into your distributed application the ability to load-balance and scale servers for high transaction rates and the ability to failover seamlessly to other servers when failures occur. This is not always as simple as deploying more hardware, installing the same software across each server, and then placing a load-balancer in front of it. Other issues, usually application-specific issues, first need to be addressed and then designed for. Let's explore an example of this in detail to highlight some problems and concerns that you may need to address.

The Quotes Web Service

The sample online trading Web application that we've been exploring throughout this book includes a system to serve stock quotes to the user. The quotes are integrated into the application's Web pages, but behind the scenes, it requires a separate infrastructure. Assuming we have identified a vendor to retrieve the delayed quotes from, we can embed calls to the vendor's servers directly in the application server code. However, as discussed, we can improve this design by adding to the application's service tier.

Quotes retrieval is abstracted from the application with the addition of a Quotes Web Service, built using the Java Web Service Developer Pack (JWSDP). In a nutshell, this provides us with a Java servlet that we can deploy across one or more servers. By deploying to more than one server, quote requests can be load-balanced between the servers. This provides for better scalability and ensures that we won't have a complete quotes "outage" if one of the servers fails.

In addition to a servlet handling quotes requests, we need a way to retrieve the stock quotes from the data vendor. This behavior is encapsulated in a separate component, called the *quotes requestor*. As requests are made to the quote servlet, similar requests are made by the quotes requestor component to the data vendor, as shown in Figure 9.10.

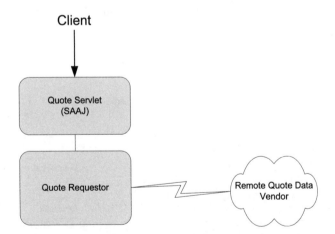

FIGURE 9.10 For each request made to the quote servlet, the quotes requestor retrieves the stock quote from the remote data vendor.

To further improve scalability, a cache component is added to the servlet. If multiple quote requests for the same stock arrive simultaneously—or within a reasonably short time—the data can be pulled from cache. Only the initial request for the stock quote will result in a call to the data vendor; subsequent requests will be satisfied using the cache until the cached value is deemed "old."

At first glance, the overall design seems sound; it takes into account load-balancing for scaling, redundancy for failover, and caching for performance. However, upon further inspection, the design falls apart once the quote servlet is deployed across more than one server. Consider the following scenario, illustrated in Figure 9.11:

1. A request for a stock quote arrives at server one.
2. The cache is checked and the value is not found.
3. A request is made to the data vendor.
4. The quote arrives.
5. The quote value is stored in cache.
6. The quote is returned to the client.
7. A split-second later, another request is made for the same stock, but this time it arrives at server two. Since most load-balancers send requests to different servers in a round-robin manner, or based upon some algorithm, this is a very real scenario.
8. The cache is checked and the value is not found.

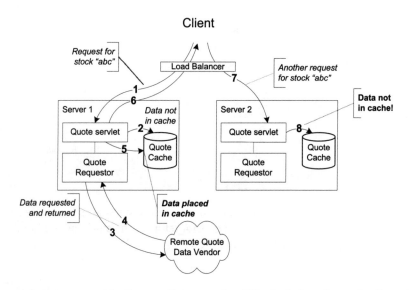

FIGURE 9.11 This diagram illustrates the difficulty in keeping a distributed cache up to date.

If both quote servers are observed as part of a single quote service, this is not acceptable behavior. As a rule, it's fair to state that when two requests are made to the servers in any order, within a reasonably short time, the second request should be served from cache. To satisfy the requirement, the cache for each quote servlet must be kept synchronized and hence identical. This is a distributed cache problem that can be solved with JMS publish/subscribe messaging, as shown in Figure 9.12. When quote data is retrieved from the data vendor, the data is published to each quote servlet, regardless of which servlet initiated the request.

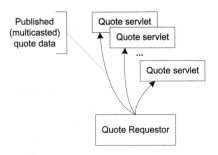

FIGURE 9.12 Quote data is published to all quote servlets, keeping each cache synchronized.

Each quote servlet maintains an equivalent quote cache by subscribing to the published quote messages. Additionally, this allows the quote requestor component to be deployed separately from the quote servlet, if desired. However, this raises a new question: how does the quote servlet make requests to the quotes requestor component? Looking in our bag of tricks, one obvious solution is to use a JMS topic, but in this case, publish/subscribe messaging will not work.

Consider the following scenario, illustrated in Figure 9.13:

1. A request for a stock quote arrives at server one.
2. The cache is checked and the value is not found.
3. A message, to request the quote from the remote data vendor, is published to a JMS topic.
4. Because all quote requestor components subscribe for the messages, they each make redundant remote requests for the quote data.

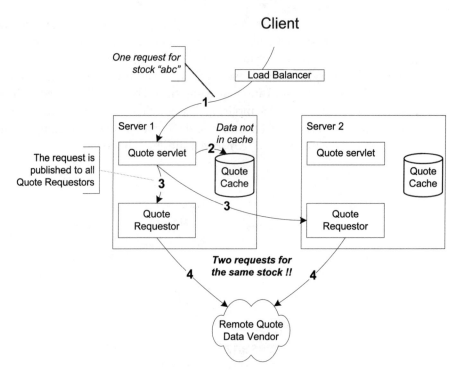

FIGURE 9.13 Pub/sub messaging doesn't solve every problem. In this case, multiple calls to the data vendor are made for each call to the quote servlet.

The redundant quote requests waste time, resources, and money, considering you will probably need to pay the data vendor per quote request. We need a solution that ensures that only one request per quote is made to the data vendor, regardless of the number of quote requestor components that are running. The solution should also ensure that no quote request gets lost, even if one (or more) of the quote requestors happens to fail.

To solve this problem, we will use a message queue with guaranteed, once-and-only-once message delivery, as shown is Figure 9.14. The queue ensures that no requests are lost, and that each message will be delivered only once, even when multiple components are listening to the queue. By deploying multiple listeners, the load will be shared and messages will continue to be processed if one fails. The use of a JMS topic for publishing the quote data ensures that all distributed quote caches are kept up to date, regardless of which server's quote requestor gets the quote data.

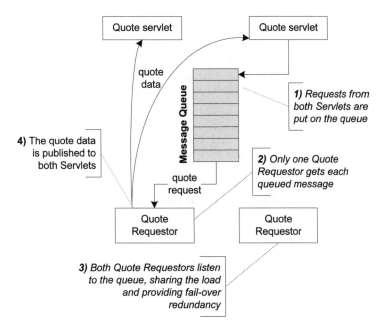

FIGURE 9.14   A message queue guarantees once-and-only-once delivery of quote request messages.

The Quote Service Final Architecture

The final architecture (see Figure 9.15) for the quotes service solves all of the issues we discussed in the previous section. Let's review some of the design goals for this Web Service, which should echo those of most in a service-oriented architecture:

Performance: A distributed cache algorithm shall be in place to make single-user response time as quick as possible. All access to remote systems and/or databases should be limited so as not to impede performance.

Scalability: A load-balance algorithm shall be in place to share the requests across multiple servers, hence increasing the ability of the service to maintain its single-user response time over larger numbers of concurrent users.

Reliability: Software and systems shall be put in place to ensure that all requests for data are satisfied 100% of the time.

Failover: Redundant hardware and software systems shall be deployed to eliminate downtime.

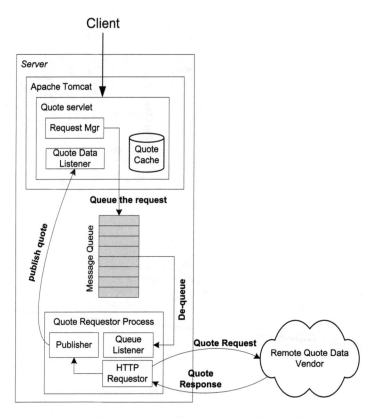

FIGURE 9.15 The complete quote service architecture.

The final architecture includes support for load-balancing by specifying the implementation as a Java Servlet. Off-the-shelf HTTP load-balancing hardware will be deployed to handle the distribution across any reasonable number of servers. If one server fails, the other servers will seamlessly pick up the load without losing any requests. Furthermore, the software making the requests, the quote requestor, is to be deployed on multiple servers as well. The use of a queue to distribute the work across the requestors ensures that each quote request is handled only once. If a quote requestor fails while processing a request, the unprocessed request it took off the queue will be rolled back and placed back on the queue. The remaining quote requestor processes will take over the load.

With the deployment of a transacted queue as well as multiple quote requestor processes, the result is that no quote request will *ever* be lost. JMS publish-and-subscribe messaging will be used to publish quote update data. These JMS messages will be consumed by listeners running within each quote servlet for the purpose of keeping its cache up to date. The result is that all instances of the quote servlet will always have an up-to-date cache.

Let's see how well this design works as we explore the quote service implementation in the following section.

The Quote Service Implementation

The quote service (see Listing 9.6) is implemented as a servlet using the SAAJServlet helper class. The implementation class, com.TradingSystem.StockTicker.QuoteServlet, implements its cache as a simple Java HashMap object, keyed by a stock ticker symbol (a String). For the sake of simplicity, the class removes the quote from cache almost immediately after it is returned to the caller. In the real-world implementation, the quote would be allowed to live in cache for a certain amount of time before removing it. It cannot be allowed to stay in cache too long, however, or the service runs the risk of returning embarrassingly stale data.

The servlet's init method handles the initialization of JMS, the creation of a JMS producer object that places quote requests on a queue, as well as the QueueDataListener nested class, which listens for quote data updates (as JMS messages) in its own thread. These steps are handled in the startQuoteRequestProducer and startQuoteUpdateConsumer methods.

When a SOAP request message arrives, SAAJ calls the onMessage method. The request's stock symbol is retrieved from the message, and a JMS TextMessage object containing the ticker is placed on the quote request queue. The servlet then waits on the cache until a response is sent back in the form of a quote data update JMS message. As soon as the cache is populated with the data, it is retrieved, wrapped in a SOAPMessage, and returned to the caller.

LISTING 9.6 The Quote Service Servlet Implementation

```
package com.TradingSystem.StockTicker;

import javax.xml.soap.*;
...
import com.sun.xml.messaging.soap.server.SAAJServlet;

public class QuoteServlet extends SAAJServlet
{
    ...

    // Quote data cache
    class QuoteData {
        public String symbol = "";
        public String last = "";
        public String date = "";
        public String time = "";
        public String change = "";
```

```java
        public String open = "";
        public String low = "";
        public String high = "";
        public String volume = "";
    }
    private HashMap quoteCache = new HashMap();

    // Listener for JMS Quote Updates
    class QuoteDataListener extends Thread
        implements MessageListener {
        ...
    }

    public void init(ServletConfig servletConfig)
        throws ServletException
    {
        super.init( servletConfig );
        servletContext = servletConfig.getServletContext();

        // Init JMS
        ...

        startQuoteRequestProducer();
        startQuoteUpdateConsumer();
    }

    private void startQuoteRequestProducer() {
        // Create JMS producer
        ...
    }

    private void startQuoteUpdateConsumer()
    {
        quoteListener = new QuoteDataListener();
    }

    public SOAPMessage onMessage(SOAPMessage message)
    {
        try {
            // Get symbol from message body
            SOAPEnvelope env =
                message.getSOAPPart().getEnvelope();
            SOAPBody bdy = env.getBody();
```

```
                Iterator iter = bdy.getChildElements();
                SOAPElement node = getNode("GetData", iter);
                iter = node.getChildElements();
                String symbol = getNodeValue("symbol", iter);

                // Queue a request for the quote data
                TextMessage msg = qSession.createTextMessage(symbol);
                producer.send(msg);

                // Wait for the quote data response
                QuoteData data = waitForQuoteData(symbol);

                // Create reply message with the quote data
                SOAPMessage replyMsg = msgFactory.createMessage();
                env = replyMsg.getSOAPPart().getEnvelope();
                bdy = env.getBody();
                bdy.addChildElement(
                        env.createName("last"))
                            .addTextNode( data.last );
                ...

                return replyMsg;
            }
            catch ( Exception e ) {
                e.printStackTrace();
            }

            return generateErrorMessage();
        }

        ...

    }
```

The process of listening for JMS messages to update the quote data cache is encapsulated in the nested class, QuoteDataListener (Listing 9.7). This class implements the JMS MessageListener interface and extends the Thread class to listen for messages on its own thread. Quote data updates arrive as JMS MapMessage objects, which contain each data element as a String by name. The data is retrieved, wrapped in a QuoteData object (another nested class), and put into the cache by the company ticker. If there was a previous entry in the cache for the same ticker, it will be replaced by the updated data.

LISTING 9.7 The QuoteDataListener Nested Class

```
class QuoteDataListener extends Thread
    implements MessageListener
{
    ...
    public QuoteDataListener() {
        start();
    }

    public void run() {
        // JMS init
        ...
    }

    public void onMessage(Message message) {
        try {
            MapMessage mapMsg = (MapMessage)message;

            QuoteData data = new QuoteData();
            data.symbol = mapMsg.getString("Symbol");
            data.change = mapMsg.getString("Change");
            data.date = mapMsg.getString("Date");
            data.high = mapMsg.getString("High");
            data.last = mapMsg.getString("Last");
            data.low = mapMsg.getString("Low");
            data.open = mapMsg.getString("Open");
            data.time = mapMsg.getString("Time");
            data.volume = mapMsg.getString("Volume");

            quoteCache.put(data.symbol, data);
        }
        catch ( Exception e ) {
            e.printStackTrace();
        }
    }
}
```

The quote requestor is implemented as a standalone Java process (see Listing 9.8). This class listens for quote requests placed on the request queue; hence it implements the MessageListener interface. A message consumer to retrieve queued requests, and a message producer to send the quote data update messages, are created in the class's constructor (not shown). When a request arrives via the onMessage method as a TextMessage, the symbol is retrieved and a request is made to an external data provider. The data is then wrapped in a JMS MapMessage and published to the quote update topic.

LISTING 9.8 The QuoteRequestor Class Implementation

```
package com.TradingSystem.StockTicker;

import java.io.*;
import java.net.*;
import javax.jms.*;
import javax.naming.*;

public class QuoteRequestor implements MessageListener
{
    ...

    private Destination requestQ;
    private MessageConsumer consumer;

    private Destination quotes;
    private MessageProducer producer;

    public QuoteRequestor() {
        ...
    }

    public void onMessage(Message msg)
    {
        try {
            TextMessage textMsg = (TextMessage)msg;
            symbol = textMsg.getText();

            // Get the quote data from vendor
            String data = getQuoteData( symbol );
            parseQuoteData( data );

            // Publish a MapMessage containing the quote data
            MapMessage mapMsg = pubSession.createMapMessage();
            mapMsg.setString("Symbol", symbol);
            mapMsg.setString("Last", last);
            ...
```

```
            producer.send(mapMsg);
        }
        catch ( Exception e ) {
            e.printStackTrace();
        }
    }

    ...

    public static void main( String[] args ) {
        QuoteRequestor req = new QuoteRequestor();
    }
}
```

The full implementation of the quote Web Service, as well as the order requestor, can be found on the book's CD-ROM in the folder named /Chapter9/ com/TradingSystem/StockTicker. The order requestor is a standalone Java application that can be launched with the startup file located in this folder. The quote service is a servlet that needs to be deployed and run within a servlet engine such as Apache Tomcat or an application server that supports standard servlets. More information on how to deploy this servlet is given later in this chapter.

RELIABILITY (THE ORDER PROCESSOR WEB SERVICE)

Although the previous section spoke about reliability in terms of load-balancing requests across multiple servers, coupled with the use of a JMS queue, this section will look at an implementation of the order processor service from Chapter 7, with the following minor changes:

■ When a market order is executed, a SOAP request is made to the quotes service (from the previous section) to get the latest trading price for the applicable stock.
■ Once the quote is retrieved, a SOAP request is made to a third-party stock broker back-office system to execute the order and handle the bank settlement and the procurement of the company stock.

Because of the sensitivity of the information that is transmitted, along with the mission-critical nature of the transaction, sending SOAP messages over the Internet is not acceptable. In this scenario, let's assume that the company that offers the online trading functionality to its users pays for a dedicated connection to the partner broker's system. To further ensure the reliability of the messaging between the two systems, the SOAP messages are transmitted using JMS.

The OrderProcessor class (see Listing 9.9) from Chapter 7 has been modified to use the JMSSOAPConnection class discussed earlier in this chapter. It has also been updated to make SOAP requests to the quote servlet, which effectively ties in all of the software components discussed in this book.

LISTING 9.9 The Updated Order Processor executeOrder Method

```
private double executeOrder(byte type, String ticker, int quantity)
{
    try {
        // Get the stock order information
        MessageFactory mf = MessageFactory.newInstance();
        SOAPMessage msg = mf.createMessage();
        ...

        // Get the latest quote from Quote Service
        URL urlEndpoint = new URL( reqBase + "/quotes" );
        SOAPMessage quoteReply = con.call( msg, urlEndpoint );
        SOAPEnvelope env = quoteReply.getSOAPPart().getEnvelope();
        bdy = env.getBody();
        Iterator iter = bdy.getChildElements();
        String last = getNodeValue("last", iter);

        // Send a SOAP/JMS request to the remote Order Broker
        Double price = new Double(last);
        SOAPMessage orderMsg = mf.createMessage();
        ...
        URL brokerUrl = new URL( reqBase + "/broker" );

        JMSSOAPConnection jmsSoapConnection = ...
        SOAPMessage orderReply =
            jmsSoapConnection.call(orderMsg, brokerUrl);
        ...

        return price.doubleValue();
    }
    catch ( Exception e ) {
        e.printStackTrace();
    }

    return 0;
}
```

The full implementation of the order processor Web Service can be found on the book's CD-ROM in the folder named /Chapter9/com/TradingSystem. This folder includes the file MyOrderProcessorService.war, which is a deployable Web application. This WAR file should deploy on any standard servlet engine or application server, although it was packaged and tested with the Sun Java System Application Server, which is a available as a free download with the latest J2EE SDK.

DEPLOYING AND RUNNING THE TRADING SYSTEM APPLICATION

This section provides an overview for the deployment of the portions of the sample trading system explored in this book. The order processing Web Service is a JAX-WS application that is deployed with the J2EE deploytool utility, as discussed in the section named "A Sample JAX-WS Web Service" of Chapter 8.

All of the artifacts for the order-processing service to be deployed are in the /Chapter9/deploy/OrderProcessor folder on the book's CD-ROM. The remaining Web Services for quotes and company data retrieval are deployed as SAAJ Java servlets in Tomcat. The files required to deploy these services (described below) are in the /Chapter9/deploy/TradingSystemWebApp folder.

In general, standard J2EE Web applications follow the directory structure shown in Figure 9.16. The source code files are in the directory WEB-INF/src where the complete path matches each component's package name. The same subdirectory structure is used for the compiled class files, in WEB-INF/classes.

FIGURE 9.16 Standard J2EE Web application directory structure for the trading system application.

The WEB-INF directory itself contains the deployment descriptor, web.xml, for the entire Web application containing the quotes service and the company data service (see Listing 9.10). The sample application, contained in the folder on the book's CD-ROM, contains an Ant script to build the project. Specifically, the Ant script contains the target, "war", which uses the Java archive (JAR) utility to package up the entire directory structure into a file named TradingSystem.war. This archive contains the class files, the application deployment descriptor, required libraries, and other miscellaneous files that make up the trading system application.

LISTING 9.10 The Trading System J2EE Deployment Descriptor

```
<?xml version="1.0" encoding="ISO-8859-1"?>

<!DOCTYPE web-app
    PUBLIC "-//Sun Microsystems, Inc.//DTD Web Application 2.2//EN"
    "http://java.sun.com/j2ee/dtds/web-app_2_2.dtd">

<web-app>

  <display-name>Trading System</display-name>
  <description>
    An online trading system application
  </description>

    <servlet>
        <servlet-name>
            quoteservlet
        </servlet-name>
        <servlet-class>
            com.TradingSystem.StockTicker.QuoteServlet
        </servlet-class>
    <load-on-startup>
        1
    </load-on-startup>
    </servlet>

    <servlet>
        <servlet-name>
            companyservlet
        </servlet-name>
        <servlet-class>
            com.TradingSystem.CompanyData.CompanyServlet
        </servlet-class>
    <load-on-startup>
```

```
          2
       </load-on-startup>
    </servlet>

    <servlet-mapping>
       <servlet-name>
          quoteservlet
       </servlet-name>
       <url-pattern>
          /quotes
       </url-pattern>
    </servlet-mapping>

    <servlet-mapping>
       <servlet-name>
          companyservlet
       </servlet-name>
       <url-pattern>
          /companydata
       </url-pattern>
    </servlet-mapping>

  </web-app>
```

The next step is to inform Apache Tomcat of the existence of the sample Web application. First, locate the path `tomcat-jwsdp-1.4/conf/Catalina/localhost` in the directory where you installed the Java WSDP/Tomcat bundle. In this location, add an application context file named `tradingsystem.xml`, which tells Tomcat where to find the application's WAR file. The contents of this file are simple and can be seen in Listing 9.11 and on the CD-ROM in the `/Chapter9/deploy/TradingSystemWebApp` folder.

LISTING 9.11 The Trading System Application Context XML for Apache Tomcat

```
<Context path="/tradingsystem"
  docBase=" /TradingSystemWebApp/TradingSystem/TradingSystem.war"
  debug="1">

  <Logger className="org.apache.catalina.logger.FileLogger"
    prefix="tradingsystem_log." suffix=".txt"
    timestamp="true"/>

</Context>
```

To see how the entire application works together, a very simple sample client application is included on the CD-ROM in the /Chapter9/com/TradingSystem folder in one source file named OrderClient.java.

SUMMARY

This chapter covered design patterns for building reliable, scalable, and robust distributed applications based on a service-oriented architecture. The concepts surrounding JMS application development, as well as the development and consumption of Web Services, were combined to form a design for reliable application communication. The book's messaging toolkit was expanded to include a helper class to be used by SAAJ-, JAXM-, and JAX-RPC-based applications to transport SOAP messages over JMS for reliability and a step toward asynchronous communication. Finally, the concepts were applied with the description and deployment of an application and a system of services: the sample trading system application. The next chapter discusses the formal standards for reliable Web Service communication, transactions, and business process coordination.

10 Grid Computing

In This Chapter

- What Is a Grid?
- Distributed Resources
- Jini™
- Sun Grid
- Oracle Grid
- IBM Grid
- Globus®

WHAT IS A GRID?

Grid computing is gaining interest in the world of distributed computing, especially as Web-based applications get more advanced and see growing numbers of users. But what exactly is it and how does it help? A grid is the unification of computing resources such as physical computers, CPUs, storage systems, and entire networks, for the development and deployment of large-scale user applications. The grid, although made up of large numbers of components, works as a single unit to perform intense, parallel computing tasks that would otherwise not perform or scale well. It is distributed computing to the extreme. An application deployed on a cluster, or one that uses a storage area network (SAN) for storage does not necessarily qualify as a grid. Application clusters and SANs are components of a grid. A grid is more of an architectural approach to designing and developing software than it is a single instance of a technology. It represents the next logical step after multitier software architecture (see Figure 10.1).

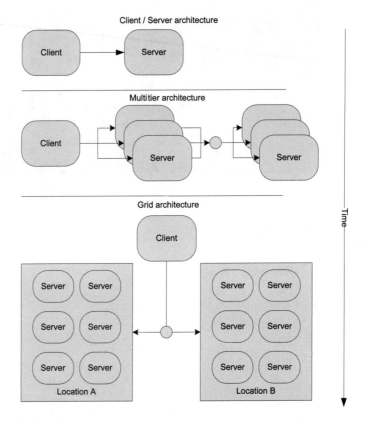

FIGURE 10.1 The architecture for distributed applications has progressed from client–server, to multitier, and now to the grid.

The resources in a grid can be located in the same data center, or they may be distributed in many geographic locations. Either way, with the proper grid hardware and software technology, all of the resources, regardless of quantity and location, can be combined to work as a single, virtual system. The benefits include the expanded capacity in terms of processing power, network bandwidth, memory, storage, and user response time based on these factors, including server proximity.

The description of a grid thus far has been constrained to the networks and data centers of *one* company. In reality, this is more of an intragrid, or one that belongs to one company (see Figure 10.2). In the future, grid technology is expected to allow grids from multiple companies to interconnect and grow into a computing grid that is similar to the nation's power grid (see Figure 10.3). Just as the power grid uses the resources of the distributed power companies to meet local demand within a region of the country, so might a global intercompany grid in the future [Jacob03].

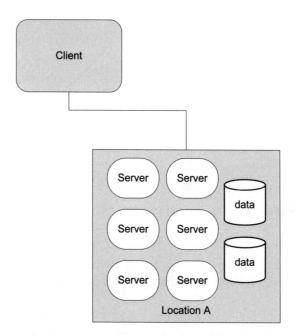

FIGURE 10.2 A single corporate grid.

This brings us to the reason for taking on such a large task: to meet customer requirements. The power grid was developed to ensure that the end user is never exposed to the fluctuation in power demands and generation. An analogous computing grid will help ensure that the resources needed to provide global computing services related to storage, bandwidth, and processing power required to run distributed applications will be available regardless of resource demand and Internet traffic.

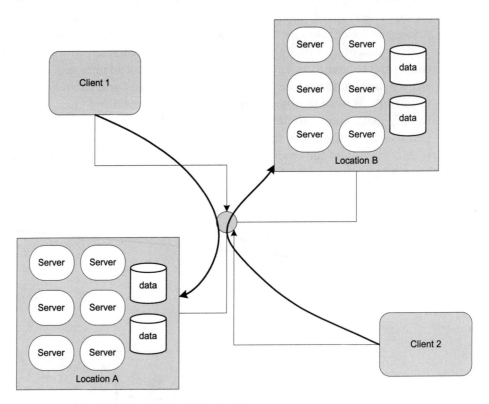

FIGURE 10.3   A global grid of individual grids.

There is enormous value to deploying an application in a grid environment. Let's go over the five key value elements of grid computing [Abbas04]:

1. Leveraging existing investments in hardware and infrastructure
2. Reducing operation expenses through self-automation, optimization, and administration
3. Creating scalability and flexibility
4. Improving time-to-market by utilizing an existing deployment of computing resources
5. Increasing productivity as a result of less down-time of critical computing resources

DISTRIBUTED RESOURCES

Take a moment and think of all of the computing power deployed on the desks of employees in companies around the world. The volume of computing power and storage that this represents is enormous, yet it goes unused most of the time. Taking advantage of unused distributed resources such as CPUs and storage is the goal in grid computing; but there are issues to consider. For instance, the type of processing that is to be done needs to be considered prior to assigning a job to a remote computer. If the job requires intense computations, where the overall work can be broken down into smaller pieces to be run in parallel, using the distributed resources of a grid is an advantage. However, if the job involves computations over a large amount of data, all of which needs to be transferred to remote nodes on the grid, or the processing requires interaction with the use, then using distributed grid resources may work against you.

The next issue to consider is security. Storing data and running software on potentially thousands of remote computers can be risky. You need to ensure that the computer is secure and that the data being processed on it does not get compromised. For some application types, the security requirements might be such that this is one of the most critical to guarantee. Still, having the ability to use computers that are otherwise mostly idle represents a potentially huge gain in processing power and return on investment.

Because of the potential offered by the concept of grid computing, companies such as Sun, Oracle, and IBM have product offerings in this area. Sun offers technologies such as Jini™ and JavaSpaces™ that allow developers to build grid-like functionality into their Java applications. Sun also offers an entire framework, the Sun Grid™, and hardware products, such as its StorEdge™ storage devices, specifically for grid computing. Oracle offers companion grid products for its database and application server offerings, and IBM has extensive grid support available for its software products, servers, and storage devices.

JINI™

Sun developed the Jini technology as a way to enable developers to make their Java software work seamlessly in a distributed application environment. Jini technology delivers access to services over any network for any platform, any operating system, and any application—regardless of the network complexity, distance, or host device. This means it provides an easy, simple, and fast way to interact with services simply by locating them on a network, with no further action required by the user [Sun01].

Jini technology offers application developers a set of components that can be used to build an infrastructure for a distributed application. The Jini programming model promotes the development, deployment, and operation of reliable distributed application components. These application components can then be shared in a standard, reliable way to build robust distributed application architectures. The goals of Jini are to enable the sharing of application resources, the discovery of application resources, and the constant growth of the applications that use these shared resources.

Jini Services

The concept of a *service* in Jini represents any shared resource in a distributed application, such as:

- A user
- A hardware component
- A software component
- A storage device
- A network communication link

Jini provides the tools needed to build, deploy, and locate services such as those listed. Some examples of services include a *storage area network* (SAN) device, a piece of software that formats and prints documents, a secure link to a database that contains sensitive data, or a database itself. The Jini *service protocol* is defined to allow services to communicate with one another and is defined as a set of Java interfaces based on Java remote method invocations (RMI).

Jini provides a *lookup service* that allows other applications to locate distributed Jini services. Applications develop their business logic to a service interface, which is then bound to the service implementation via the lookup service. Services can contain other services, resulting in a tree of related services that can be navigated. Access control lists, and the concept of leasing a service, control the access to and the use of services in a Jini-based software system. Finally, Jini services support distributed event registration and event notification, as well as distributed transactions that support two-phase commit (2PC).

Jini Components

Jini defines not only the concept of a service, but also that of a set of components that can be assembled to be used in a distributed application, called an infrastructure. The overall Jini programming model allows developers to not only build the services required, but also assemble them into meaningful applications, or subapplications, to perform some meaningful task(s). The infrastructure is based on the Java virtual machine, Java RMI, Java security, and Java Naming and Directory Interface (JNDI). The programming model allows for the leasing of services and transactions across services, as well as the events that are sent between them.

The end result is that Jini forms the foundation upon which small or large grids of application services built using Java can be deployed, dynamically moved (streamed), and discovered and can reliably communicate predictable results. Transactions are used not only to ensure data integrity within a database, but also to ensure reliable state transitions and event notifications across the services in a Jini application.

For more information on the details of using Jini to build large-scale distributed applications such as grid applications, visit the following links:

- *http://www.sun.com/software/jini/jini_technology.xml*
- *http://www.sun.com/software/jini/*
- *http://java.sun.com/developer/products/jini/index.jsp*
- *http://www.jini.org/*

JavaSpaces

Sun's JavaSpaces specification (*http://java.sun.com/products/jini/2.0/doc/specs/html/js-spec.html*) is part of Sun's Jini technology (see the previous section). JavaSpaces helps solve the problems related to the persistence and serialization of Java objects and data structures in a distributed application environment. It also helps in the design and implementation of business logic that uses these distributed data structures and persisted network objects. The end goal is to provide a toolkit that can be used to build distributed application protocols that model the flow of data (as Java objects) through the components of a large-scale distributed application. JavaSpaces offers a standard approach to defining and implementing the protocols, without requiring the developer to build customized server software to implement the protocol himself.

SUN GRID

Sun offers its Sun Grid technology, which provides the sharing of storage, computing, and network services to a corporation at the cost of $1.00 per CPU per hour (see *http://www.sun.com/service/sungrid/overview.jsp*). Not only does the Sun Grid technology help you to define and build a grid of your own, but it offers the use of Sun's large deployment of application servers and storage systems in an application service provider (ASP) model. The pay-as-you-use-it model offers as much or as little computing and storage capacity as your application requires at any single point in time. The advantage of this type of model is that you do not need to purchase, support, or maintain your own data centers full of servers to implement a grid-based application. Nor do you need to worry about capacity planning in terms of deploying new hardware or whole data centers themselves.

The Sun Grid model takes care of globally deploying and maintaining your application within their infrastructure, offering you access to the virtually limitless amount of computing, storage, and network capacity that Sun has deployed. Issues such as application availability and security may deter some companies from jumping into this application model. However, many companies like the fact that they don't need to concern themselves with the issues associated with running a grid-based application. Companies that require a grid to perform large-scale data analysis, number crunching, and research, can concentrate on the tasks the grid performs for them, not the grid itself.

ORACLE GRID

As further proof that grid/utility computing is gaining momentum in the industry, let's look at how Oracle has grid-enabled its products. Oracle has taken their database server and application server products and grid-enabled them with the Oracle $10g^{TM}$ family of grid computing software. Oracle, too, sees the need to deploy large-scale applications on even larger networks of computer and storage equipment running application and database servers. With this comes the added complexity and cost of maintaining these types of software systems in an ever-expanding data-center environment. To offer its clients a more cost-effective way to run applications built on their products, Oracle offers a grid/utility infrastructure upon which customers can deploy their distributed applications. The need for you to hire database and application server-aware administrative staff is thus reduced. Instead, you simply contract out to Oracle to maintain their own products within their own environment, but running your application.

IBM GRID

As yet further proof that grid/utility computing is building momentum, IBM also has extensive product offerings in this area, including toolkits for grid development, and its eBusiness On Demand™ (also called the On Demand Business™) initiative. IBM offers products and services, including IBM Redbooks™, software, hardware, consulting, and utility-based computing.

GLOBUS®

The Globus Alliance is a group of universities, organizations and individual developers that develop technologies and standards for grid application development (*http://www.globus.org/*). The Globus Toolkit™ (GT) is an open source toolkit and environment available for building grid-based applications. The toolkit integrates with the Sun Grid product offering and the IBM On Demand Business initiative and has become a widely used set of tools to enable the sharing of computing power, databases, and software securely over networks deployed around the globe.

The GT has been developed since the late 1990s to support the development of service-oriented distributed computing applications and infrastructures. Core GT components address basic issues relating to security, resource access and management, data movement and management, resource discovery, and so forth [Foster05]. The toolkit provides an infrastructure for building grid applications that support monitoring and discovery, security based on X.509, data access and integration, and what is called *choreography,* or the coordination of activities.

SUMMARY

This chapter served as a brief introduction to the world of grid computing, described as distributed application architecture to the extreme. The concept of a grid brings the concepts of distributed computing together in an environment where all computing resources are shared, regardless of physical and logical location.

A   UML Overview

The Unified Modeling Language (UML) is a standard specification for modeling application structure, behavior, business processes, and architecture. UML was designed by the "three amigos," Grady Booch, Ivar Jacobson, and James Rumbaugh, and is used as the foundation of the Rational Unified Software Development Process, which they also invented. This book utilizes UML for its diagramming models that convey a lot of information in standard ways. You can learn more about UML at *http://www.uml.org*, as well as the Rational Unified Process at *http://www-306.ibm.com/software/rational/*. The rest of this appendix offers a brief introduction to UML, specifically for the features used in this book.

CLASSES

UML can be used to describe one of the building blocks of object-oriented software: the class. A *class* is the encapsulation of business logic and data, exposed through a well-defined interface. UML represents a class as shown in Figure A.1.

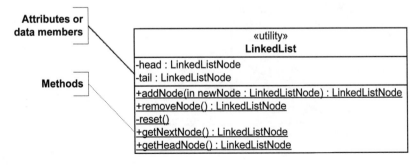

FIGURE A.1   A simple class in UML.

This simple diagram conveys a lot of information, such as the class's methods, whether each method is public or private, as well as each method's parameters and return values. Also shown are the class's data members, their types, and whether they, too, are public or private. Data members, or attributes, are displayed in the middle section, while methods are displayed in the bottom section of the class. Private methods and data members are displayed with a "-" in front of them, while public members are displayed with a "+" in front.

Notice the text "<<utility>>" on top of the class name. This is called a *stereotype,* which provides a way for the designer (you) to extend UML to represent concepts that are not precisely represented by what UML offers. For the most part, designers will use a stereotype to provide more detail about parts of their diagram. In this example, LinkedList is not just a class; it's defined as a *utility* class in the software being modeled. This book also uses stereotypes to provide more detail about the relationships between classes, such as *creates,* which shows that one class creates another.

If you look closely at the class, you will notice that the LinkedList class's members reference another class, LinkedListNode. Therefore, there exists a relationship between these two classes that belongs as part of the software model. Figure A.2 is a *class relationship diagram* because it shows both classes linked together, with a stereotype named *uses.* The stereotype, combined with the arrow at the end of the line for direction, tells us that the LinkedList class uses the LinkedListNode class (a *uses* relationship).

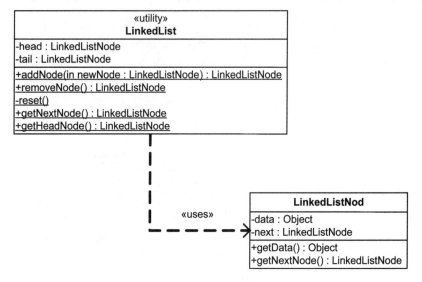

FIGURE A.2   A UML class relationship diagram.

Let's assume that the `LinkedList` class is part of a greater hierarchy of utility classes (as represented by the class stereotype). In this model, `LinkedList` is only part of a group of utility classes that provide data manipulation functionality. Assume further that all of the classes have a common base class, named `Collection`. In UML, inheritance is represented as *generalization*, illustrated in Figure A.3. The arrow always points to the base class, from the class that is inheriting from it. Also shown in this diagram is the class `Iterator`, which according to the stereotype, is created by the `Collection` class.

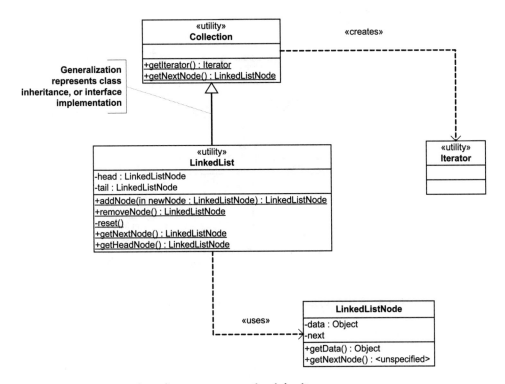

FIGURE A.3 A UML class diagram representing inheritance.

To be precise, the `LinkedList` class doesn't just use the `LinkedListNode` class; it contains instances of this class within it. The current relationship doesn't correctly represent this; the model in Figure A.4 is more precise. It tells us that `LinkedList` may contain zero or more instances of the `LinkedListNode` class. In UML, this relationship is called *aggregation*. The numbers at each end represent multiplicity, or the numbers of each class allowed in the aggregation. For instance, this diagram tells us that the LinkedList class may contain zero or more LinkedListNode classes. The LinkedListNode class, however, can only *belong* to zero or one LinkedList class. It is implied by the diagram that the implementation of these classes will be to enforce the multiplicity of this relationship.

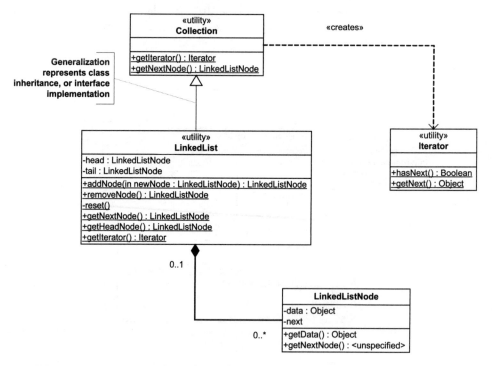

FIGURE A.4   A UML aggregation relationship is used to show that one class contains another.

INTERACTIONS

UML class diagrams convey much information about the relationships between classes in a software design. It does not, however, show the details of the interactions between these classes in the overall software system. For instance, we see that method calls exist within the classes of our model so far, but how are they called, and in what order? Which classes call into others in our model? This information is conveyed in a UML *sequence diagram* (see Figure A.5).

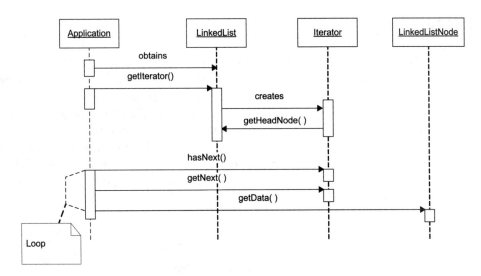

FIGURE A.5 A UML sequence diagram shows the messages (or method calls) that occur between objects.

Objects or classes are represented along the top of the diagram, and time is represented by the vertical lines extending downward from the boxes. Method calls are represented by horizontal lines with an arrow that points from the caller to the class being called. The overall intent is to show method calls (or messages) that occur between the objects over time. Although these diagrams are meant to show strictly method calls or messages, the sequence diagrams in this book show this, as well general actions. For instance, in this diagram the action "obtains" may translate into an entire, unrelated, sequence of calls that the designer chose not to show here. The fact that the application obtains a reference to the LinkedList class is all that is important in this sequence. As another example, there are cases within this book where "creates" will be shown as a substitute for the use of the Java new operator.

The vertical boxes on the object lines provide context (or show "focus") for each method call and are used to help the reader determine when a method has completed, or returned. For instance, the call to LinkedList.getIterator includes the creation of the Iterator object, and the call from that new object to LinkedList.getHeadNode. Afterwards, the stack unwinds as each call returns. Hence the vertical bar for the LinkedList object extends to include both operations.

STATE

Often, complex applications, such as those that are distributed across network nodes, will contain a state engine and involve state transitions to coordinate activities. A UML state transition diagram serves as an excellent vehicle to design such systems and convey the possible states, transitions, and their affects (see Figure A.6). In this example, it's important in a trading system that all distributed components be aware when the exchange-data download process is complete and the system is ready to perform stock trades. The initial and final states for the overall system are specifically labeled, and each transition contains a stimulus, or a reason for the transition.

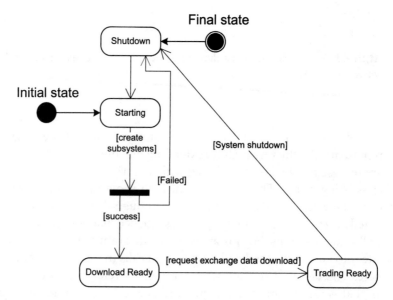

FIGURE A.6 This UML state diagram shows what happens when the trading system starts up.

PACKAGES

Groups of classes, such as Java packages, are represented in UML with a package diagram. The relationships between packages and package containment provide a meaningful system overview (see Figure A.7). In this diagram, the application, which contains its own packages, uses the external utility package.

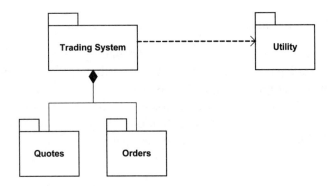

FIGURE A.7   UML package diagrams can provide an overview of software subsystems and their dependencies.

Deployment

Packages, and the components contained within them, can be used in a UML deployment diagram to show how the software will be physically deployed. If the designer's intent is to distribute particular objects across multiple servers, this information can be conveyed in a deployment diagram (see Figure A.8). This diagram shows the case where, regarding the book's sample trading system application, the order processor component is meant to run on its own server, while the quote server is meant to run both the quote service and quotes requestor components.

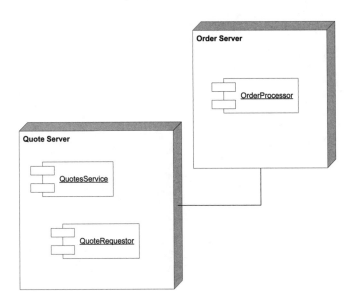

FIGURE A.8   A UML deployment diagram illustrates how components are intended to be physically deployed.

SUMMARY

This appendix serves as a quick summary of only the portions of UML used within this book. There is a lot more to UML, such as collaboration diagrams, activity diagrams, multiplicities, qualified associations, parameterized classes, and use-case diagrams. On top of that, the Rational Unified Process offers an entire methodology for software design, implementation, and maintenance that is iterative, visual, and ideal for today's rapid development pace.

Appendix

B

About the CD-ROM

The CD-ROM that comes with this book contains numerous tools and development APIs to help you start building Java messaging applications. The CD-ROM also contains the source code for all of the sample applications referenced in the book, along with scripts to build and run them. Most importantly, the book contains a toolkit of Java helper classes and modules to aid in the development and deployment of distributed Java messaging applications and SOAP Web Services. The following folders appear on the disc:

Chapter folders: These folders contain the sample applications referenced within each corresponding book chapter. Chapters 1, 7, and 10 do not contain any sample code.

Figures: This folder contains all of the figures from the book, arranged by chapter.

Java: This folder contains the open source tools used in the development of the book's sample applications and toolkit.

Toolkit: This folder contains the final, complete messaging toolkit that is explored throughout the book.

The tools in the Java folder include the following:

ActiveMQ: An open source JMS provider from Codehaus Protique, also available at *http://activemq.codehaus.org*

Apache Ant: an open source scripting tool used to build, package, and deploy Java applications

SYSTEM REQUIREMENTS

The software on the CD-ROM is capable of being used on any Windows or Linux-based computer that meets the following specifications:

Minimum RAM: 256 Megabytes

Recommended RAM: 512 Megabytes

Minimum Disk: 250 Megabytes free

Recommended Disk: 500 Megabytes free

Minimum JVM Version: J2SE 1.4.2_06

Recommended JVM Version: J2SE 1.5.0_02

You can download the latest versions of Standard Java (J2SE), Enterprise Java (J2EE), and the Java Web Service Developer Pack (JWSDP) at *http://java.sun.com*. To run the SOAP-based Web Services, you will need a Java Servlet container such as Apache Tomcat (*http://jakarta.apache.org/tomcat/index.html*), which is also available from Sun as a download bundle with the Java Web Service Developer Pack.

References

[Abbas04] Abbas, Ahmar, *Grid Computing: A Practical Guide to Technology and Applications*. Charles River Media, 2004.

[Armstrong04] Armstrong, Eric, et al., "J2EE 1.4 Tutorial." Available online at *http://java.sun.com/j2ee/1.4/docs/tutorial/doc/index.html*, December 16, 2004.

[Atkinson02] Atkinson, Bob, et al., "Web Services Security (WS-Security)." Available online at *http://www-128.ibm.com/developerworks/views/webservices/libraryview.jsp?type_by=Standards*, April 2002.

[Bilorusets04] Bilorusets, Ruslan, et al., "Web Services Reliable Messaging Protocol (WS-ReliableMessaging)." Available online at *http://www-128.ibm.com/developerworks/views/webservices/libraryview.jsp?type_by=Standards*, March 2004.

[Booch94] Booch, Grady, *Object-Oriented Analysis and Design with Applications,* 2nd ed. Benjamin/Cummings, 1994.

[Box04] Box, Don, et al., "Web Services Eventing (WS-Eventing)." Available online at *http://www-128.ibm.com/developerworks/views/webservices/libraryview.jsp?type_by=Standards*, August 2004.

[Byous98] Byous, Jon, "Java Technology: The Early Years." Available online at *http://java.sun.com/features/1998/05/birthday.html*, May 23, 1998.

[Cabrera04] Cabrera, Luis Felipe, et al., "Web Services Coordination (WS-Coordination)." Available online at *http://www-128.ibm.com/developerworks/views/webservices/libraryview.jsp?type_by=Standards*, November 2004.

[Chappell01] Chappell, David A., and Monson-Haefel, Richard, *Java Message Service*. O'Reilly & Associates, Inc., 2001.

[Chappell02] Chappell, David, "Asynchronous Web Services and the Enterprise Service Bus." Available online at *http://www.webservices.org/index.php/ws/content/view/full/1809*, May 6, 2002.

[Foster05] Foster, Ian, "A Globus Primer." Available online at *http://www.globus.org/toolkit/docs/4.0/key/GT4_Primer_0.6.pdf*, January 12, 2005.

[Gamma95] Gamma, Erich, et al., *Design Patterns: Elements of Reusable Object-Oriented Software*. Addison-Wesley, 1995.

[Gibson04] Gibson, Stan, "eBay: Sold on Grid." Available online at *http://www.eweek.com/article2/0,1759,1640234,00.asp*, August 30, 2004.

[Hapner02] Hapner, Mark, et al., *Java Message Service Specification*. Sun Microsystems, Inc., 2002.

[Jacob03] Jacob, Bart, "Grid Computing. What are the key components." Available online at *http://www-106.ibm.com/developerworks/library/gr-overview/*, June 2003.

[Monson-Haefel04] Monson-Haefel, Richard, *Enterprise JavaBeans,* 4th ed. O'Reilly & Associates, Inc., 2004.

[Shannon03] Shannon, Bill, "Java 2 Platform Enterprise Edition Specification, v1.4." Available online at *http://java.sun.com/j2ee/j2ee-1_4-fr-spec.pdf*, November 24, 2003.

[St. Laurent01] St. Laurent, Simon, Johnston, Joe and Dumbill, Edd, *Programming Web Services with XML-RPC*. O'Reilly & Associates, Inc., 2001.

[Sun01] Sun Microsystems, Inc., "Jini Network Technology: An Executive Overview." Available online at *http://java.sun.com/webservices/downloads/webservicespack.html*, 2001.

[Sun04] Sun Microsystems, Inc. "The Java Web Services Tutorial." Available online at *http://java.sun.com/webservices/downloads/webservicespack.html*, June 21, 2004.

[Titheridge04] Titheridge, Paul, "How Websphere Application Server Handles Poison Messages." Available online at *http://www.ibm.com/developerworks/websphere/library/techarticles/0405_titheridge/0405_titheridge.html*, May 26, 2004.

Index